Immersive Technologies and Human-Centric Innovation in the Industry 5.0 Era

Brij B. Gupta
https://orcid.org/0000-0003-4929-4698

Asia University, Taichung, Taiwan & VIZJA University, Warsaw, Poland

Yuk Ming Tang
https://orcid.org/0000-0001-8215-4190

Department of Industrial and Systems Engineering, The Hong Kong Polytechnic University, Hong Kong, China

IGI Global
Scientific Publishing
Publishing Tomorrow's Research Today

Vice President of Editorial	Melissa Wagner
Director of Acquisitions	Mikaela Felty
Director of Book Development	Jocelynn Hessler
Production Manager	Mike Brehm
Cover Design	Jose Rosado

Published in the United States of America by
IGI Global Scientific Publishing
701 East Chocolate Avenue
Hershey, PA, 17033, USA
Tel: 717-533-8845 | Fax: 717-533-7115
Website: https://www.igi-global.com E-mail: cust@igi-global.com

Library of Congress Cataloging-in-Publication Data

LCCN: (CIP Data Pending)
ISBN13: 9798260000137
Isbn13Softcover: 9798260000144
EISBN13: 9798260000151
British Cataloguing in Publication Data
A Cataloguing in Publication record for this book is available from the British Library.

Table of Contents

Preface xii

Chapter 1
The Role of AI and Emerging Technologies in Small Business in Industry 5.0 Era 1
Mohan Singh, G.L. Bajaj Institute of Technology and Management, Greater Noida, India
Seema Singh, Lloyd Institute of Management and Technology, Greater Noida, India
Kapil Dev Tyagi, Jaypee Institute of Information Technology, Noida, India
Vaibhav Bhushan Tyagi, ISBAT University, Kampala, Uganda

Chapter 2
Business Applications of AI: Enabling Digital Twins and the Metaverse in Industry 5.0 39
Muhamad Rizky Khairussalam, Universitas Esa Unggul, Indonesia
Gusti Muhamad Sardana, Universitas Esa Unggul, Indonesia
Binastya Anggara Sekti, Universitas Esa Unggul, Indonesia
Varsha Arya, Hong Kong Metropolitan University, Hong Kong
Sourasis Chattopadhyay, Kalinga Institute of Industrial Technology, India
Ifat Batul, Vidyasagar University, India
Ryan Putra Laksana, Universitas Esa Unggul, Indonesia

Chapter 3
Virtual Reality and Augmented Reality for Business Transformation 83
Reyisha Bulan Dewi, Universitas Esa Unggul, Indonesia
Vinsens Aji Pamungkas, Universitas Esa Unggul, Indonesia
Binastya Anggara Sekti, Universitas Esa Unggul, Indonesia
Varsha Arya, Hong Kong Metropolitan University, Hong Kong
Najmin Sultana, Manipal Academy of Higher Education, India
Thanaporn Phattanaviroj, Asia University, Taiwan

Chapter 4
Empowering Business Transformation Through Virtual and Augmented Reality Technologies 127
Lailita Ayuningtias, Universitas Esa Unggul, Indonesia
Ritika Bansal, Insights2Techinfo, India
Mohammad Norman Gaza Laksono, Uppsala Universitet, Sweden
Thanaporn Phattanaviroj, Asia University, Taiwan
Ifat Batul, Vidyasagar University, India
Yogita Abichandani, Management Development Institute, Murshidabad, India

Chapter 5
Challenges, Risks, and Ethical Dilemmas in the Metaverse Economy 161
Guntur Rivaldi, Universitas Esa Unggul, Indonesia
Joy Valent Missael Zega, Universitas Esa Unggul, Indonesia
Binastya Anggara Sekti, Universitas Esa Unggul, Indonesia
Abhay Ratnaparkhi, eBay Inc., USA
Ifat Batul, Vidyasagar University, India
Thanaporn Phattanaviroj, Asia University, Taiwan

Chapter 6
Integrating Metaverse With Manufacturing: A Novel Paradigm for Immersive Interactive and Impactful Learning.. 189
Amit V. Sata, Marwadi University, India
Sumit Ranoliya, Marwadi University, India
Dhaval Anadkat, Marwadi University, India

Chapter 7
Towards Data-Driven and Human-Centric Intelligent Manufacturing Through the Integration of AI, IoT, and Blockchain 233
Defia Ulandari, Universitas Esa Unggul, Indonesia
Deswita Anggraini, Universitas Esa Unggul, Indonesia
Mohammad Norman Gaza Laksono, Uppsala Universitet, Sweden
Kwok Tai Chui, Hong Kong Metropolitan University, Hong Kong
D. David Neels Ponkumar, Vel Tech Rangarajan Dr. Sagunthala R&D Institute of Science and Technology, India

Chapter 8
AI in Wildlife Conservation 267
Muhamad Ilham Suparno, Universitas Esa Unggul, Indonesia
Yohanes Bowo Widodo, Universitas Mohammad Husni Thamrin Jakarta, Indonesia
Jusung Moon, CCRI, Asia University, Taiwan
Sourasis Chattopadhyay, Kalinga Institute of Industrial Technology, India

Chapter 9
Designing the Future: Human-Centric Innovation for a Compassionate Digital World 297
Pravin Kumar, Brainware University, India

Compilation of References 333

About the Contributors 367

Index 373

Detailed Table of Contents

Preface.. xii

Chapter 1
The Role of AI and Emerging Technologies in Small Business in Industry 5.0 Era 1
Mohan Singh, G.L. Bajaj Institute of Technology and Management, Greater Noida, India
Seema Singh, Lloyd Institute of Management and Technology, Greater Noida, India
Kapil Dev Tyagi, Jaypee Institute of Information Technology, Noida, India
Vaibhav Bhushan Tyagi, ISBAT University, Kampala, Uganda

This chapter investigates how AI and other future technologies could enable small businesses in the Industry 5.0 period. Industry 5.0, on the other hand, extends the automation of Industry 4.0 is about being more human-centered, sustainable, and resilient. The chapter explores how AI can transform small business processes, such as delivering seamless experiences, ensuring informed and effective business decisions, and managing finances. It also explores other innovation technologies, like the Internet of Things, blockchain, 3D printing, Augmented Reality/Virtual Reality (AR/VR), and cloud computing, and how they're affecting small businesses. Additionally, the chapter discusses an important dimension of the human-AI partnership, highlighting the necessity for upskilling and reskilling to skillfully incorporate these tools. Ultimately, the chapter considers future trajectories and indeed offers some recommendations on how small businesses can become future-ready in emerging times of Industry 5.0 to a more human-centered, sustainable, and technology-advanced future.

Chapter 2
Business Applications of AI: Enabling Digital Twins and the Metaverse in Industry 5.0 39
Muhamad Rizky Khairussalam, Universitas Esa Unggul, Indonesia
Gusti Muhamad Sardana, Universitas Esa Unggul, Indonesia
Binastya Anggara Sekti, Universitas Esa Unggul, Indonesia
Varsha Arya, Hong Kong Metropolitan University, Hong Kong
Sourasis Chattopadhyay, Kalinga Institute of Industrial Technology, India
Ifat Batul, Vidyasagar University, India
Ryan Putra Laksana, Universitas Esa Unggul, Indonesia

This e-book explores the strategic convergence of Artificial Intelligence (AI), Digital Twins, and the Metaverse as the foundational triad driving Industry 5.0. Emphasizing human-centric, sustainable, and adaptive technologies, it highlights how AI empowers real-time analytics, predictive maintenance, immersive environments, and intelligent decision-making. Digital Twins enable dynamic simulations of physical systems, while the Metaverse facilitates interactive and collaborative virtual experiences across industries. The book discusses AI techniques such as machine learning, deep learning, computer vision, and natural language processing, and examines their applications in smart manufacturing, healthcare, retail, and urban planning. It also addresses ethical considerations, data governance, and future trends including explainable AI and federated learning. Together, these technologies redefine how businesses innovate, operate, and engage in an increasingly intelligent and interconnected digital economy.

Chapter 3
Virtual Reality and Augmented Reality for Business Transformation 83
Reyisha Bulan Dewi, Universitas Esa Unggul, Indonesia
Vinsens Aji Pamungkas, Universitas Esa Unggul, Indonesia
Binastya Anggara Sekti, Universitas Esa Unggul, Indonesia
Varsha Arya, Hong Kong Metropolitan University, Hong Kong
Najmin Sultana, Manipal Academy of Higher Education, India
Thanaporn Phattanaviroj, Asia University, Taiwan

This chapter examines the strategic transformation of immersive technologies, focusing on their integration with artificial intelligence, digital twins, extended reality, and blockchain. It highlights how these technologies reshape value creation, delivery, and capture across sectors such as healthcare, education, manufacturing, and retail. The discussion covers infrastructure requirements, organizational readiness, and user experience, while also addressing challenges like cost, regulation, and digital accessibility. Emphasis is placed on the rise of the metaverse and decentralized platforms, where users engage with virtual assets and services in new economic models. By analyzing both opportunities and barriers, the chapter underscores the need for inclusive design, ethical data use, and cross-sector collaboration. Ultimately, immersive technology is presented not merely as a tool, but as a driver of long-term innovation, organizational adaptability, and sustainable digital transformation.

Chapter 4
Empowering Business Transformation Through Virtual and Augmented Reality Technologies 127
Lailita Ayuningtias, Universitas Esa Unggul, Indonesia
Ritika Bansal, Insights2Techinfo, India
Mohammad Norman Gaza Laksono, Uppsala Universitet, Sweden
Thanaporn Phattanaviroj, Asia University, Taiwan
Ifat Batul, Vidyasagar University, India
Yogita Abichandani, Management Development Institute, Murshidabad, India

This analysis investigates the transformative evolution of immersive innovation in modern enterprises, highlighting how the integration of Virtual Reality (VR) and Augmented Reality (AR) with Artificial Intelligence (AI) enhances operational intelligence, strategic decision-making, and user engagement. Drawing on cross-industry cases, the chapter identifies core challenges in privacy, algorithmic bias, and implementation scalability, while presenting structured mitigation and governance strategies. A conceptual framework for secure, interoperable digital ecosystems is ultimately proposed, emphasizing ethics, transparency, and resilience as foundational pillars for sustainable business transformation.

Chapter 5
Challenges, Risks, and Ethical Dilemmas in the Metaverse Economy 161
Guntur Rivaldi, Universitas Esa Unggul, Indonesia
Joy Valent Missael Zega, Universitas Esa Unggul, Indonesia
Binastya Anggara Sekti, Universitas Esa Unggul, Indonesia
Abhay Ratnaparkhi, eBay Inc., USA
Ifat Batul, Vidyasagar University, India
Thanaporn Phattanaviroj, Asia University, Taiwan

The metaverse economy represents a major transformation in the digital era, powered by blockchain, artificial intelligence, and virtual reality, creating new forms of value through decentralized finance, digital assets, and immersive work environments. Yet, its rapid expansion brings complex ethical, legal, and technological challenges. Key risks include the misuse of digital identities, data privacy violations, algorithmic bias, labor exploitation in virtual economies, and vulnerabilities in decentralized finance and smart contracts. Manipulative design patterns and weak legal oversight further threaten user autonomy, fairness, and trust. This chapter critically examines these challenges and the systemic risks shaping the metaverse economy while emphasizing the need for ethical governance, transparency, and inclusive regulation. It concludes with recommendations for building a resilient and equitable metaverse ecosystem that balances innovation with accountability, safeguards user rights, and promotes sustainability in digital economic transformation.

Chapter 6
Integrating Metaverse With Manufacturing: A Novel Paradigm for Immersive Interactive and Impactful Learning 189
Amit V. Sata, Marwadi University, India
Sumit Ranoliya, Marwadi University, India
Dhaval Anadkat, Marwadi University, India

Manufacturing plays very important role in growth of overall economy of nation, and metal casting is one of such manufacturing processes that contributes largely on economy especially in India. These manufacturing enterprises are always in need of skilled manpower or these are in requirement to train their existing manpower for advanced technologies so that performance of these industries can be enhanced. This manpower can be trained in real industrial environment with specific skillsets that can be helpful in various industrial sectors, and Metaverse seems to be one of the solutions.Specific methodology adopted to develop Metaverse for metal casting. Metaverse of metal casting has been developed, and demonstrated for imparting technical skills to young manpower. It was observed that Metaverse can be very effective to impart technical skills required in the domain of metal casting. This implementation has provided great encouragement, and can lead to development of Metaverse for other manufacturing processes to serve overall requirement of skilled manpower in the domain.

Chapter 7
Towards Data-Driven and Human-Centric Intelligent Manufacturing Through the Integration of AI, IoT, and Blockchain 233
Defia Ulandari, Universitas Esa Unggul, Indonesia
Deswita Anggraini, Universitas Esa Unggul, Indonesia
Mohammad Norman Gaza Laksono, Uppsala Universitet, Sweden
Kwok Tai Chui, Hong Kong Metropolitan University, Hong Kong
D. David Neels Ponkumar, Vel Tech Rangarajan Dr. Sagunthala R&D Institute of Science and Technology, India

The transformation to Industry 5.0 is driving manufacturing to adopt a more intelligent, adaptive, and humanized approach through the integration of Artificial Intelligence (AI), Internet of Things (IoT), and Blockchain. This chapter proposes an integrative framework of the three technologies, which makes AI the center of analytics and decision-making, IoT the nervous system that collects data in real-time, and Blockchain the foundation of trust through secure and transparent data recording. This approach not only improves operational efficiency, predictivity, and product personalization, but also supports sustainability and industry ethics. Case studies such as predictive maintenance, mass customization, and supply chain visibility demonstrate the effectiveness of this integration in the field. The chapter also details implementation challenges as well as future trends, such as federated learning and quantum-resistant Blockchain. Overall, this framework provides strategic direction for a resilient, adaptive, and people-oriented manufacturing ecosystem.

Chapter 8
AI in Wildlife Conservation 267
Muhamad Ilham Suparno, Universitas Esa Unggul, Indonesia
Yohanes Bowo Widodo, Universitas Mohammad Husni Thamrin Jakarta, Indonesia
Jusung Moon, CCRI, Asia University, Taiwan
Sourasis Chattopadhyay, Kalinga Institute of Industrial Technology, India

Artificial Intelligence (AI) is transforming wildlife conservation by enabling faster, more accurate, and scalable approaches to species monitoring, habitat mapping, and behavioral analysis. Through computer vision, AI can automatically detect and classify animals in millions of camera trap images, while acoustic models identify species through their vocalizations in complex environments. Satellite and drone imagery integrated with AI supports habitat assessment and anti-poaching surveillance. Digital twin ecosystems offer dynamic simulations for predicting environmental changes and guiding proactive interventions. Despite challenges such as limited datasets, interpretability issues, and ethical concerns, AI is becoming an essential tool in conservation science. When deployed transparently and inclusively, AI enhances human capacity to respond effectively to the biodiversity crisis and supports long-term ecological stewardship.

Chapter 9
Designing the Future: Human-Centric Innovation for a Compassionate Digital World 297
Pravin Kumar, Brainware University, India

This chapter examines how human-centric innovation can be a part of solving the ethical, emotional, and social dilemma of digital change. Based on the human-cantered design, self-determination theory, and service-dominant logic, it discusses how empathy, the concept of psychological safety, and co-creation can be implemented as part of innovation approaches to allow employee engagement and consumer trust. The research employs a qualitative method approach to interviewing and analyzing documents in the form of semi-structured interviews, and determining the major practices that can align the technology with human values. The results suggest the importance of the responsible use of emerging technologies, inclusive leadership, and ethical frameworks in long-term resilience in organizations. The outcome of the study is that humanistic innovation is not discretionary but a requirement in digitally embraced, sustainable, and socially accountable change.

Compilation of References 333

About the Contributors 367

Index 373

Preface

INTRODUCTION

The rapid convergence of Digital Twins, the Metaverse, Artificial Intelligence, and advanced connectivity infrastructures is redefining how organizations create value and how consumers experience products and services. As we move deeper into the era of Industry 5.0, the emphasis has shifted from automation alone to a more human-centric, sustainable, and resilient model of innovation. In this new paradigm, technology does not replace human creativity; it augments it. Consumer experience is no longer a passive outcome of production systems but an actively designed, immersive, and data-driven process.

Revolutionizing Consumer Experience With Digital Twins and the Metaverse emerges at this critical juncture. This edited volume brings together leading scholars and practitioners from diverse disciplines—including computer science, management, engineering, artificial intelligence, extended reality, and smart manufacturing—to explore how immersive and intelligent systems are reshaping digital economies. The chapters collectively examine the technological foundations of Digital Twins and Metaverse platforms, their strategic integration within Industry 5.0 environments, and their transformative impact on business models and consumer engagement.

A central theme throughout this book is synergy. Digital Twins enable the creation of dynamic virtual replicas of physical systems, while Metaverse technologies provide immersive and interactive environments where these replicas can be visualized, tested, and experienced. Together, supported by AI, IoT, blockchain, 5G, and beyond, they form intelligent ecosystems that foster co-creation, personalization, predictive insights, and sustainable innovation. From healthcare and retail to smart cities, supply chains, sports, and religious tourism, the contributions in this volume demonstrate how these technologies are being deployed across industries to enhance engagement, transparency, and operational resilience.

This book also addresses critical challenges. As immersive ecosystems expand, questions surrounding cybersecurity, data governance, privacy, algorithmic bias, digital inclusivity, and ethical design become increasingly urgent. The contributors not only highlight risks and limitations but also propose frameworks, conceptual models, and best practices to guide responsible implementation. By bridging theoretical advancements with industrial applications, this volume seeks to close the gap between research and practice.

Our objective in editing this book has been threefold. First, to provide a comprehensive understanding of the technological architectures and enabling infrastructures behind Digital Twins and Metaverse systems. Second, to examine their strategic and managerial implications for organizations navigating Industry 5.0. Third, to explore how these innovations fundamentally transform consumer experiences into immersive, participatory, and data-informed journeys.

We envision this book serving as a foundational reference for academic researchers, doctoral scholars, R&D professionals, entrepreneurs, technology developers, and policymakers. It is designed not only to document current progress but also to inspire future research, interdisciplinary collaboration, and innovative experimentation. The case studies, thematic analyses, and forward-looking perspectives presented here aim to stimulate dialogue and encourage partnerships between academia and industry.

We extend our sincere gratitude to all contributing authors for their scholarly rigor, dedication, and vision. Their diverse perspectives have enriched this volume and strengthened its multidisciplinary character. We also acknowledge the reviewers and publishing team whose support and expertise have been invaluable throughout the development of this project.

As the boundaries between physical and digital realities continue to blur, organizations must rethink how value is created, delivered, and experienced. Industry 5.0 challenges us to build systems that are not only intelligent but also ethical, inclusive, and sustainable. We hope this book contributes meaningfully to shaping that next digital revolution and to advancing the global discourse on immersive technologies and consumer transformation.

CHAPTER OVERVIEWS

Chapter 1: The Role of AI and Emerging Technologies in Small Business in Industry 5.0 Era

This chapter explores how Artificial Intelligence (AI) and emerging technologies can empower small businesses within the evolving Industry 5.0 landscape. Moving beyond the automation focus of Industry 4.0, Industry 5.0 emphasizes human-centricity, sustainability, and resilience. The authors examine how AI enhances small business operations by improving customer experiences, enabling data-driven decision-making, and strengthening financial management. The discussion also considers the impact of complementary technologies such as the Internet of Things, blockchain, 3D printing, AR/VR, and cloud computing. Particular attention is given to the human–AI partnership, highlighting the importance of upskilling and reskilling to effectively adopt these innovations. The chapter concludes with forward-looking insights and practical recommendations to help small enterprises become future-ready in a technology-advanced yet human-focused era.

Chapter 2: Business Applications of AI: Enabling Digital Twins and the Metaverse in Industry 5.0

This chapter examines the strategic integration of Artificial Intelligence (AI), Digital Twins, and the Metaverse as a foundational triad shaping Industry 5.0. Framed within a human-centric and sustainable perspective, it explains how AI supports real-time analytics, predictive maintenance, immersive simulations, and intelligent decision-making. Digital Twins provide dynamic virtual representations of physical systems, while the Metaverse enables collaborative and interactive digital experiences across sectors. The chapter outlines key AI methodologies—including machine learning, deep learning, computer vision, and natural language processing—and explores their applications in manufacturing, healthcare, retail, and urban development. Ethical issues, data governance, and emerging trends such as explainable AI and federated learning are also discussed. Collectively, these technologies are portrayed as transformative forces redefining business innovation and digital engagement.

Chapter 3: Virtual Reality and Augmented Reality for Business Transformation

This chapter analyzes the strategic role of immersive technologies in driving business transformation, with particular focus on their convergence with AI, digital twins, extended reality, and blockchain. It illustrates how these technologies reshape value creation, delivery, and capture in industries such as healthcare, education, manufacturing, and retail. Key considerations include infrastructure readiness, organizational capabilities, and user experience design, alongside challenges related to cost, regulation, and digital inclusion. The growing prominence of the metaverse and decentralized digital platforms is also examined, highlighting new economic and engagement models. By evaluating both opportunities and constraints, the chapter emphasizes inclusive innovation, ethical data practices, and cross-sector collaboration as essential to sustainable digital transformation.

Chapter 4: Empowering Business Transformation Through Virtual and Augmented Reality Technologies

This chapter investigates how the integration of Virtual Reality (VR) and Augmented Reality (AR) with Artificial Intelligence (AI) is reshaping enterprise innovation. It demonstrates how immersive technologies enhance operational efficiency, strategic insight, and user engagement across industries. Drawing from cross-sector case studies, the authors identify major concerns related to privacy, algorithmic bias, and scalability, and propose structured governance and mitigation strategies. The chapter concludes with a conceptual framework for developing secure and interoperable digital ecosystems, grounded in principles of transparency, ethics, and resilience to support long-term organizational transformation.

Chapter 5: Challenges, Risks, and Ethical Dilemmas in the Metaverse Economy

The metaverse economy marks a significant shift in the digital landscape, driven by blockchain, AI, and immersive technologies that generate new forms of value through digital assets, decentralized finance, and virtual workspaces. However, this rapid evolution introduces complex ethical, legal, and technological challenges. The chapter examines risks such as digital identity misuse, data privacy breaches, algorithmic discrimination, labor exploitation, and vulnerabilities in smart contracts and decentralized systems. It also highlights concerns surrounding manipulative design and insufficient regulatory oversight. Emphasizing ethical governance, transparency, and inclusive policy frameworks, the authors propose actionable recommendations for building a sustainable and accountable metaverse ecosystem that protects user rights while fostering innovation.

Chapter 6: Integrating Metaverse with Manufacturing: A Novel Paradigm for Immersive Interactive and Impactful Learning

Manufacturing remains a cornerstone of national economic development, with processes such as metal casting playing a significant role, particularly in emerging economies like India. To enhance industrial performance, companies require a skilled workforce capable of adapting to advanced technologies. This chapter presents the development of a metaverse-based training environment for metal casting, designed to deliver immersive and practical skill development. The methodology for constructing this virtual learning ecosystem is detailed, and its effectiveness in imparting domain-specific technical competencies is demonstrated. The findings indicate that metaverse-driven training can significantly improve workforce readiness and may be extended to other manufacturing sectors to address broader skill development needs.

Chapter 7: Towards Data-Driven and Human-Centric Intelligent Manufacturing through the Integration of AI, IoT and Blockchain

As Industry 5.0 reshapes manufacturing, there is a growing shift toward intelligent, adaptive, and human-centered systems enabled by the integration of Artificial Intelligence (AI), the Internet of Things (IoT), and blockchain. This chapter introduces a unified framework positioning AI as the analytical core, IoT as the real-time data infrastructure, and blockchain as the trust layer ensuring secure and transparent transactions. The integration enhances operational efficiency, predictive capabilities, and product customization, while also reinforcing sustainability and ethical standards. Practical case studies—including predictive maintenance and supply chain transparency—illustrate real-world applications. The chapter further discusses implementation challenges and future developments such as federated learning and quantum-resistant blockchain technologies, offering strategic guidance for resilient manufacturing ecosystems.

Chapter 8: AI in Wildlife Conservation

Artificial Intelligence (AI) is reshaping wildlife conservation by providing scalable, accurate, and efficient tools for monitoring species, mapping habitats, and analyzing animal behavior. Computer vision systems automate the identification of wildlife in vast camera trap datasets, while acoustic AI models detect species through sound patterns in complex environments. The integration of satellite imagery and drone technology enhances habitat evaluation and anti-poaching efforts. Digital twin ecosystems further enable dynamic simulations to anticipate environmental changes and inform proactive conservation strategies. Although challenges such as limited datasets, interpretability, and ethical concerns persist, AI is increasingly recognized as a vital instrument in addressing biodiversity loss and supporting sustainable ecological management.

Chapter 9: Designing the Future: Human-Centric Innovation for a Compassionate Digital World

This chapter explores the role of human-centered innovation in addressing the ethical, emotional, and social complexities of digital transformation. Drawing upon human-centered design, self-determination theory, and service-dominant logic, it examines how empathy, psychological safety, and co-creation can strengthen employee engagement and consumer trust. Using qualitative methods, including semi-structured interviews and document analysis, the study identifies practices that align technological advancement with human values. The findings emphasize responsible technology adoption, inclusive leadership, and ethical governance as critical to long-term organizational resilience. Ultimately, the chapter argues that humanistic innovation is not optional but essential for sustainable and socially responsible digital progress.

Throughout this book, contributors have explored the transformation of consumer engagement, business models, manufacturing ecosystems, supply chains, healthcare systems, education, conservation, and digital economies. Equally important, they have addressed the governance, ethical, and societal implications that accompany these technologies. From cybersecurity and data privacy to inclusivity, algorithmic fairness, and sustainability, the discussions underscore that innovation without responsibility is incomplete. The future of digital ecosystems depends not only on technological sophistication but also on trust, transparency, and human dignity.

A recurring insight across the chapters is the growing importance of integration. Digital Twins enable dynamic simulation and predictive intelligence; the Metaverse provides immersive, participatory environments; AI transforms data into actionable insight; and advanced connectivity infrastructures ensure seamless interaction. When strategically aligned, these technologies foster adaptive enterprises, empowered consumers, and resilient societies. Yet, their successful deployment requires inter-disciplinary collaboration, forward-looking leadership, and continuous learning.

As editors, we believe this volume contributes meaningfully to bridging the gap between theory and practice. It offers conceptual frameworks, empirical insights, applied case studies, and future research directions designed to support scholars, practitioners, policymakers, and innovators. More importantly, it encourages critical reflection: How do we design systems that enhance human creativity rather than replace it? How do we build immersive digital economies that are equitable and sustainable? How do we ensure that technological progress remains aligned with societal well-being?

The answers to these questions will shape the next phase of the digital revolution. We hope this book serves not only as a scholarly reference but also as a catalyst for dialogue, experimentation, and collaboration across disciplines and industries. The transformation of consumer experience through Digital Twins and the Metaverse is not a distant vision—it is unfolding now. Our collective responsibility is to guide it with wisdom, integrity, and a commitment to a more inclusive and compassionate digital future.

Brij Gupta
Asia University, Taichung, Taiwan & VIZJA University, Warsaw, Poland

Yuk Ming Tang
Department of Industrial and Systems Engineering, The Hong Kong Polytechnic University, Hong Kong, China

Chapter 1

The Role of AI and Emerging Technologies in Small Business in Industry 5.0 Era

Mohan Singh
http://orcid.org/0000-0002-2973-3676
G.L. Bajaj Institute of Technology and Management, Greater Noida, India

Seema Singh
Lloyd Institute of Management and Technology, Greater Noida, India

Kapil Dev Tyagi
Jaypee Institute of Information Technology, Noida, India

Vaibhav Bhushan Tyagi
ISBAT University, Kampala, Uganda

ABSTRACT

This chapter investigates how AI and other future technologies could enable small businesses in the Industry 5.0 period. Industry 5.0, on the other hand, extends the automation of Industry 4.0 is about being more human-centered, sustainable, and resilient. The chapter explores how AI can transform small business processes, such as delivering seamless experiences, ensuring informed and effective business decisions, and managing finances. It also explores other innovation technologies, like the Internet of Things, blockchain, 3D printing, Augmented Reality/Virtual Reality (AR/VR), and cloud computing, and how they're affecting small businesses. Additionally, the chapter discusses an important dimension of the human-AI

DOI: 10.4018/979-8-2600-0013-7.ch001

partnership, highlighting the necessity for upskilling and reskilling to skillfully incorporate these tools. Ultimately, the chapter considers future trajectories and indeed offers some recommendations on how small businesses can become future-ready in emerging times of Industry 5.0 to a more human-centered, sustainable, and technology-advanced future.

1. INTRODUCTION

The advent of Industry 5.0 represents a shift in technology systems, which are no longer only automated (like Industry 4.0's focus), they are also emotional, as well as sustainable and resilient. This new era focuses on the teamwork between man and machine, combining the strengths to maximize value (Breque, 2021). Big corporations, with resources that enable them to manage these technological developments, typically accounting for large shares of many economies that have relatively small businesses, encounter special challenges in their adaptation to the new environment (Baporikar & Shikokola, 2020). But their agility, flexibility, and proximity to local people, as well as their localization mindset, allow them to capitalize on the opportunity of Industry 5.0 like no one else.

Figure 1 details in a step-by-step manner a methodology for the development of the visual metaphor and hence an image or equivalent graphical representation that encapsulates the essence of Industry 5.0. It breaks down the visual idea into separate elements with step-by-step instructions on how to build them into a powerful, nuanced message. Human, which is the first factor, is a focal point of the Industry 5.0 concept. It should show an action shot of a skilled laborer working hand in hand with a robot or artificial intelligence (AI) and thereby illustrate how robots or AI empower their capabilities, solve problems, and make decisions. It is not about replacing humans; it is about empowering them with the beauty of a balanced partnership where technology supports the augmentation of human capability, intelligence, and effectiveness in the industrial world. The picture should describe an 'aesthetics of the symbiosis' of human creativity and technological perfection. Then they specify the cutting-edge parts that must be used in the technology section. These might include collaborative robots (cobots) and hence safe working human-robot interaction, AI-driven interfaces and thus systems control smartly and intuitively, digital twins and data enrichment and virtual constructs for simulation and real-time monitoring and analytics, internet of things (IoT) sensors and hence pervasive sensing and data collection, and advanced data analytics and therefore highly skilled data rich thinking. The visual should be full of these techy details, representing a smart, connected, and data-driven world as cleanly as possible. The environment is as crucial as it controls the mood and look of the visual. It must represent a smart factory or a clean but modern industry mood. They are clear that the design must use lighting and color to express a sense of innovation, efficiency, human-centered design, and research. This requires a shift in mindset away from the more traditional views of industry that are either sterile and lacking aesthetics, or gritty and covered in grime; instead toward a clean, well-organized, aesthetically pleasing space that inherently implies progress, hygiene, and a focus, if not for the people, at least on the basic humanity of the workplace. Even the colors and lighting right here can influence the viewer's vision of style and elegance.

The Focus element sums up the essence of the figure. It calls for a display that demonstrates the sublime partnership between human beings and machines, showcasing mankind's unique creativity, problem-solving, and emotional intelligence in the field of advanced AI and robotics. This is the storytelling fulcrum for the visuals, and the point is, for all the mounting automation, exclusively human skills, those cognitive gifts with which no robot or AIbot will ever be able to compete: our creative capacities, our facility for abstruse problem solving, and emotional intelligence are, as it happens, super-charged by technology. The visual should discreetly or directly showcase segments where these human qualities are visibly enhanced, rather than interposed by their technical partners.

Finally, the Overall impression tells the viewer how the viewer should feel or what they should think. The image should embody optimism and the notion of progress, what Industry 5.0 means to change, to transform, and to create a more sustainable, resilient, and human-centric industrial future. That means a forward-looking, positive narrative that captures the transformative ambitions of Industry 5.0. It should make them feel hopeful and that doing the right thing now, all works out in the end, that industry can be productive and environmentally reliable, resilient against threats, and something that, at the end of the day, enhances human well-being and societal progression. The visual should present an image of an end-to-end, well-oiled, and ethically conscious industrial habitat. In effect, this is a full brief for a visual artist or designer to create imagery that truly represents and grasps the multifaceted nature of Industry 5.0.

In this chapter, the various roles played by Artificial Intelligence and other disruptive technologies in making small business operations achieve improved performance during the Industry 5.0 era are analyzed. We take a look at how AI can transform all aspects of small business management, from automation and customer relations to decision-making and finance. We also discuss the effects of the Internet of Things, blockchain, 3D printing, Augmented Reality/Virtual Reality (AR/VR), and cloud on small businesses. We also tackle the vital issue of human-AI collaboration, pointing to the need for skills upskilling and skills reskilling to make systems appropriately integrated. We are going to look at the advantages and opportunities of taking on these new and exciting opportunities and what type of challenges they might face, so we can give SMB's best practices on how to implement these new trends and technologies. Lastly, we discuss future trajectories and provide advice on how small businesses can future-proof their business as we expand further into the Industry 5.0 world, creating a more human-centric, sustainable, and tech-empowered future.

Industry 5.0 at a Glance: Industry 5.0 is a new industrial era that has the power to change the game for humanity after the product innovation and automation leaps of Industry 4.0. Building upon the industry automation and data exchange reforms brought about by its predecessor, Industry 5.0 centers around cooperation between man and machine. This partnership approach aimed to utilize the best of both, with the creativity, problem-solving, and adaptability of humans and the accuracy, speed, and efficiency of technology. It is this transformation that requires, at its core, an overhaul of the way companies do business, not only to focus on technological innovation but also on what is good for people and the planet.

Relevance of the smaller enterprises in Industry 5.0: SMEs have their significance in the world economy with the aid of innovation, supplying the local community with employment. Nevertheless, they find it challenging to catch up with fast technological developments because of being resource-poor, a lack of expertise, and inadequate funds. For small businesses, however, the ins and outs of Industry 5.0 provide both opportunity and challenge. By efficiently adopting new technologies, they can position themselves to improve new opportunities, expand into new markets, and better compete in the future.

Background and Related Work

Small and medium-sized companies need to make significant changes to internal resources, processes, and capabilities to compete with this challenge (Peretz-Andersson, 2024). Small businesses would do well to focus on low-hanging fruit that can be quickly implemented with a fast return on investment rather than the big, long-term AI initiatives that are the domain of large businesses. While the SMEs do not have the resources of larger organizations, with limited financial and human resources, skills shortages, organizational resistance to change and concerns about data integration, security, and privacy means that the strategic decision to adopt AI is a major opportunity and challenge and impacts on how SMEs adopt and use AI differently from such approaches found in large enterprises (Le Dinh, 2025). It is critical to perform a systematic literature review (SLR) and understand how SMEs are using AI, since the existing research is fragmented (Schwaeke, 2025). The AI adoption rates between SMEs and larger firms demonstrate a gap as a result of the constraints that SMEs face (Proietti, 2025).

Recent studies have underlined the fact that AI has the potential to greatly enhance the operational efficiency, product and service development, customer engagement, and competitiveness of SMEs (Iyelolu, 2024). Thanks to AI, SMEs can analyze huge volumes of data, automate tiresome tasks, and gain new insights that were once impossible to obtain. Yet, there is evidence that SMEs fail to apply AI properly due to a lack of technical expertise, high speed of AI implementation, and a lack of strategic perspective. Research has also indicated the significant role that factors like digital culture, partner pressure, and adoption costs have on the adoption of ET by SMEs (Ayinaddis, 2025).

Chapter Purpose: This chapter examines how Artificial Intelligence and other transformative technologies can enable small businesses to excel and prosper in Industry 5.0. It looks into AI and how it can innovate and transform areas of any small business, such as automating how some routines work, improving customer experience, decision-making, and how to manage financials. We even take a look at how other critical technologies, such as the Internet of Things, blockchain, 3D printing, Augmented Reality/Virtual Reality (AR/VR), and cloud computing, are changing the game for small companies. We also discuss the important topic of human-AI collaboration, stressing the importance of upskilling and reskilling to successfully incorporate these technologies. By exploring the advantages, opportunities, and threats that come with the implementation of such innovations, we hope to provide small business owners with pragmatic tips to ensure a seamless introduction. Finally, we discuss future trends, providing suggestions for how smaller business can future-proof their organizations in the ever-evolving environment of Industry 5.0, processing a more human-centered, sustainable, and technologically empowered future.

Figure 1. Collaborative relationship between humans and advanced technology in a modern Industry 5.0.

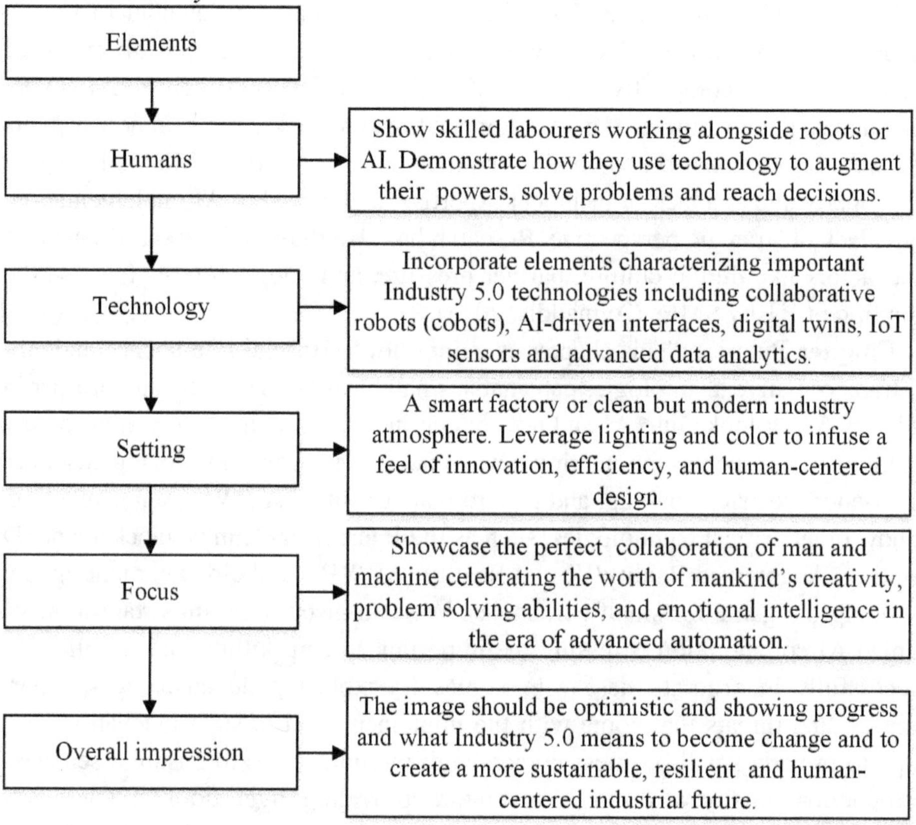

2. INDUSTRY 5.0: WHAT IT MEANS FOR SMALL BUSINESSES

Industry 5.0 is a paradigm shift from the automation-focused Industry 4.0 that prioritizes the cooperation between humans and machines, as given in Table 1. This 3rd paradigm appreciates, on the one hand, the importance of human ingenuity and creative energy, and on the other hand, the accuracy and efficiency of advanced technology (Adel, 2022). What it means for SMBs is a shift from automating tasks to using technology to help their employees perform better.

The essence of Industry 5.0 is that technology needs to be seen as an enabler for humans and not as a substitute. This human-oriented methodology is consistent with the agility, adaptiveness, and sense of family found in a significant number of small businesses (Li, 2023). In adopting this model of hybrid human-AI collaboration, small businesses can leverage the complementary capabilities of people and machines to move quickly, to be nimble, and to provide an outstanding customer experience.

Table 1. Industry 5.0: What It Means for Small Businesses

Aspect	Description	Implications for Small Businesses
Focus	Human-in-the-loop: collaboration between humans and machines.	It encourages employees, stimulates creativity, and creates more enjoyable workplaces.
Technology	Cloud Computing, Artificial Intelligence, Internet of Things, Cybersecurity, Robotics, And Big Data.	More automation, data-driven decisions, efficiencies, and better customer experience.
Opportunities	Targeted customer experience, international reach, efficiency of operations, and innovation driven by sustainability.	Growth potential, greater competitiveness, and more responsiveness to changing constituent demand.
Challenges	Cost, technical know-how, cybersecurity concerns, and cultural resistance to change.	Requirements for strategic planning, investments in training, and fostering a culture of innovation.
Strategies	Step by step, adoption, building digital ecosystems, education and training, and focusing on sustainability.	Graduated rollout, working with tech providers, retraining staff, and going green.
Future Trends	Hyper-personalization, responsible tech use, and ethical AI.	Adaptability, learning on the fly, and paying attention to the ethical implications of technology.

Figure 2 provides a holistic and progressive approach for businesses, SMEs in particular, to systematically apply and succeed in Industry 5.0. The journey itself is focused on adopting core elements that will characterize the new industrial era, as their name would suggest, identifying a logical transition from awareness to consistent, successful implementation. The Exploratory Path starts with awareness of Industry 5.0 emphasized through basic action, as the small business owner is informed about Industry 5.0. This first learning is held up as a crucial beginning, the base upon which all other actions are founded. On the heels of that awareness, organizations will be expected to understand what matters with those core principles being set down as a Human-Centric Approach or how human creativity and well-being will team up with technological advancement; a Sustainability Focus or how RESPEC is married to responsible environmental practices, resource efficiency, and circular economy principles; and "Resilience & Agility" or the ability to operate in times of surprise disruption and fast market adjustments. These three fundamental principles are the cornerstones of the Industry 5.0 spirit.

Finally, as they get the basics sorted, the framework takes businesses into important phases of assessment. One is to Assess Workforce Skills & Needs, which includes a comprehensive assessment that asks 1) to determine if the people have the necessary skills for the new Industry 5.0 technology and 2) whether any gaps are present. This early diagnosis of skill gaps is essential to enable the human workforce to prepare for the changing technological world. Concurrently, evaluating current environmental Impact as a critical action, encourages companies to review the company's current environmental 'footsteps' and determine areas where they can reduce the impact. This is directly related to the sustainability focus tenet, which challenges us to critically assess environmental impact and green the way we operate. If the conclusion of a workforce examination turns out to be a Skills Gap Identified, the framework calls for swift and bold action: Enable training programs to upgrade employee skills. It goes so far as to argue that we should see Industry 5.0 as an upskilling opportunity and that employees' performance would obtain an extra push through its skill level. This shows responsibility for lifelong learning and human capacity. At the same time, companies must assess technology needs as related to what technology is in place within the business and what the roadmap looks like moving forward. This measure will determine what assets make up the technological infrastructure, what assets need to be improved, and what new technologies are needed to be in line with Industry 5.0.

Once you move from the data at a distance to the data-centered approach and begin to integrate technology, the first and foremost non-negotiable is to ensure data privacy & security. The framework also requires a strong evaluation to assess whether the business has top-of-the-line cybersecurity to account for greater hazards related to enhanced connectivity and exchange of data in the Industry 5.0 architecture. Measure Result & ROI- After the incorporation of the technical solutions and the tough security is implemented, this stage becomes very important. This move also shows the value that quantifiable deliverable results can have corporate clients must have more than just a completed pilot project or SI and have integrated the insights from data (drive ROI). This makes certain that Industry 5.0 efforts are not just theoretical, but provide tangible economic value that can be justified on the balance sheet. The model now moves to continuous improvement & innovation as an ongoing philosophy, understanding that Industry 5.0 is not a stable end but an evolving process. Explicitly, businesses are told that the aggressive response should be that of continuous improvement, innovation, so you are at the front end and the beneficiary of Industry 5.0. This underscores the importance of continuously improving and adapting, open to the introduction of new solutions, to remain competitive and exploit the opportunities created by the changes taking place in the industrial world.

Finally, when you build all of this in an organized formula, it results in the long-term mission we all want: Sustainable Growth & Resilience Following the steps of the previous approach from initial awareness and principle understanding, through deep assessment, targeted skill development, strategic technology adoption, to staunch security, to evergreen innovation (this is the composite of the previous matrix in the learning style) we are attain sustainable growth & resilience by adopting Industry 5.0 principles. Not only does this indicate that practicing a forward-thinking, people-oriented, ecology-conscious, and technologically progressive strategy induces ongoing good news, but it further indicates that such a business model naturally sturdy prevents building a future-ready business model that retains longevity and adapts well in an evolving global industrial setting. Therefore, proposes a systematic and dynamic roadmap for businesses that want to flourish in Industry 5.0.

A few of the main tenets that inform Industry 5.0 have substantial relevance for small businesses:

- **Scale and personalization:** With Industry 5.0's emphasis on scale, small businesses don't need to worry that they won't be able to provide their customers with specialized personal offers that cater to their unique needs and desires. This space, traditionally reserved for larger organizations, gives small businesses the ability to develop their customer relationships and brand loyalty.
- **Sustainable and Circular Production:** The focus on sustainability and circularity in Industry 5.0 provides an opportunity for SMBs to carry out eco-friendly procedures, limit waste, and leverage the increase in demand for circular offerings.
- **Sustainable and green technologies:** Industry 5.0 forwards sustainable and green practices. Green technologies can be employed by SMBs to reduce environmental impact, maximize resource use, and attract the green segment.

Figure 2. What Industry 5.0 means for small businesses?

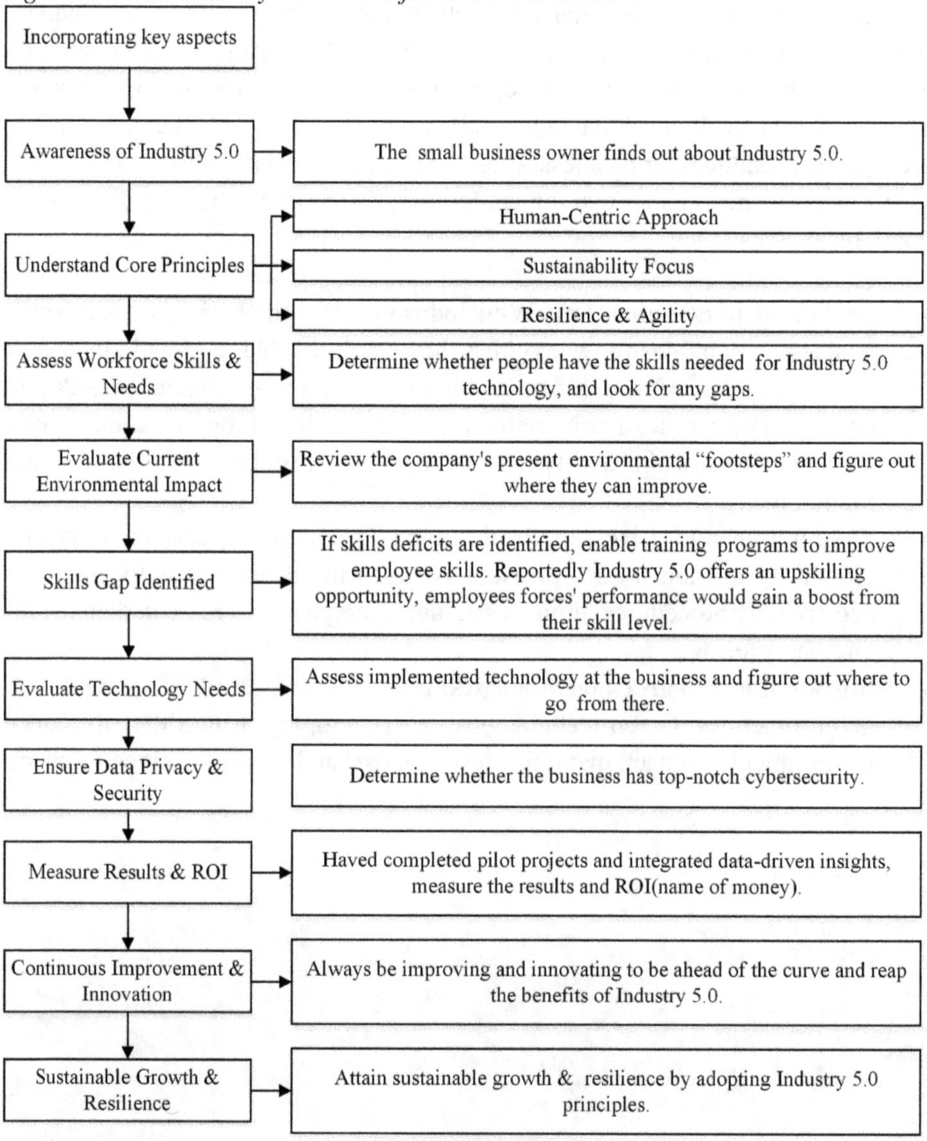

- **Resiliency for business operations:** Adapt and respond with confidence to business disruptions in today's highly dynamic business environment. Creating resilience with Industry 5.0, more so, small businesses will find in Industry 5.0 the means to predict and prevent threats, in turn ensuring their continuity in times of unexpected strife. By adopting these principles, makers can pave the way for sustainable success and relevance in the ever-confusing landscape of Industry 5.0.

Adopting such principles is not just a case of jumping on the technological bandwagon; it's the necessary steps small businesses need to take to survive in a changing Industry 5.0 world. By incorporating these principles into their business models, small businesses can open the door to new opportunities, create more value for their customers, and ensure a brighter future.

3. THE ROLE OF ARTIFICIAL INTELLIGENCE (AI) IN SMALL BUSINESSES

I could imagine AI is such a disruptive technology with so much opportunity for small businesses in this Industry 5.0 world. Artificial intelligence-powered technologies can streamline rule-based routine work, drive decision accuracy, improve customer engagement, and help generate new revenue sources. For small businesses, one of the biggest benefits of AI is the enhancement of operational functions that make life a heck of a lot easier, as given in Table 2. Small business owners and their employees could be spending time on higher-value tasks both for the business and for themselves if AI could be used to automate areas like invoicing, payroll, and inventory management. Also, there are AI chatbots and virtual assistants that can be used for responding to customer queries, personalized recommendations, etc., and using AI, small businesses can also provide a high level of service on par with larger enterprises (Kasanga, 2020). AI can be a game-changer for small business decision-making, too. Through the compilation of large amounts of data from several sources, analytics applying AI can reveal valuable insights and trends, and help in strategic decision-making. Organizations such as small businesses can benefit from AI-enabled predictive analytics to forecast customer demand, manage inventory levels more effectively, and make better pricing decisions (Ab Rahim et al., 2020).

Furthermore, AI can support the ability of small businesses to create better products and services. As AI becomes part of product design and development, brands can create more personalized, revolutionary, and user-focused solutions that help small companies stand out in overcrowded markets. But the incorporation of AI in small businesses is not all plain sailing. SMEs might encounter obstacles related to finance, skills, and how well and efficiently AI can be implemented within existing processes. Small businesses only have so much in terms of resources this including time, money, and manpower, and to chart a path that's going to lead to the successful implementation of AI, it's important to weed out all the distractions.

Small businesses will also unlock new possibilities while streamlining their business, via AI-enhanced solutions to stay competitive in the era of Industry 5.0.

The provided Figure 3 details a strategic and step-by-step approach for small businesses to adopt AI into their current workflow to improve small-business performance and sustainability. For example, it starts with "Small Business Operations" as a starting stage, which is considered the business status before performing any AI action. The first milestone is to identify business needs & Opportunities, where the business takes the initiative to realize a role that AI can play or gaps it can fill within their organization. This base assessment is essential for focused and productive AI implementation. After that, the figure illustrates areas for AI application where AI can officiate, granting machines human-like skills. These broad categories of application areas cover the most essential business-related aspects like Customer Service & Support, Marketing & Sales, Operation & Productivity, and Decision Making & Strategy, hence indicating the enormous potential of AI in different functional departments. The framework then gets into the nitty-gritty of practical AI use cases. AI-Powered Chatbots & Virtual Assistants is suggested as an opportunity for operating AI-based chatbots to answer customer queries and provide assistance, etc., and automate conversations & queries on chat, and enable faster issue resolutions, to improve customer interaction efficiency and availability. In conjunction with the above, personalized marketing campaigns use AI to create personalized marketing campaigns made from knowing about the customer, making it one of those super personalized ones that stick in the consumer's mind. One strong operating advantage stands out in the automation of repetitive tasks, which states that monotonous tasks are automated to free employees for more strategic tasks, leading people to have time for doing productive tasks; therefore, this leads to an increase in effective use of human resources and overall productivity. The nameplate also emphasizes "Data Analysis & Predictive Analytics," in which companies use AI to process data and provide intelligence for better decisions, highlighting the role of AI in converting raw data into intelligence for making more informed strategic decisions.

The latter phases describe the direct and indirect benefits of these introductions of AI. Enhancing customer experience while reducing costs combines two great benefits into one, to help illustrate that AI can improve the customer experience and help your bottom line. This represents AI's double advantage in improving customer satisfaction and driving cost efficiencies. Said enhancement of customer relations goes on to equate to increased sales & customer engagement as well, since personalized marketing leads to more sales and increased customer engagement to show the economic benefits of AI-fueled personalization. Operationally, AI is used to Increase Efficiency & Reduce Errors, as business processes are made to be automated, the level of productivity and the number of errors to occur decrease, resulting in smoother processes and better results. The data-driven decision-making loop runs continuously in the data-driven insights & better decisions factoid/white paper - AI Delivers Data-Driven Insights to inform strategic decisions. Importantly, the framework also meets a key non-functional requirement: address data privacy & security. It specifically refers to the fact that you must secure and protect the privacy of address data using AI models, which reminds us just how critical effective cybersecurity and data governance are in an AI context, especially when dealing with customers' sensitive data. Finally, improved business performance & growth is the final expected result. It reads; Enterprises can achieve brand-new business performance and growth results through the effective application of AI. That means if a business does deploy AI methodically and scrupulously, one like the aforementioned steps, then, mind you, tangible enhancements to operational efficiency, extended market reach, and its bottom line, these are some things that a small business could expect to continue in the future, future-proof style. So the figure is a foolproof, common-sense, what-works view of AI for small businesses in the real world.

Figure 3. Structured overview of how small businesses can integrate AI into their operations to drive efficiency

AI as Smallbiz Game Changer: AI is moving at the speed of light and shaking up the game for small businesses with breakthrough capabilities that can provide better customer service. By automating mundane work, AI gives us back valuable time and resources to invest in higher-value activities. AI-driven predictive maintenance can reduce downtimes and optimize the performance of machines. What's more, AI allows small businesses to run customized marketing ad campaigns and offer real-time customer service thanks to chatbots, leading to higher levels of customer engagement.

AI Use Case in Small Businesses: Use cases for AI in small businesses are wide-ranging and growing. AI-augmented analytics offer deep insights into customer behavior, market trends, and business performance, which leads to data-driven decision-making. Artificial intelligence algorithms can be used to streamline supply chains and manage inventory, all of which will lead to cost savings and better processes. Furthermore, artificial intelligence is essential in preventing fraud and managing finances, increasing the security and safeguarding of your assets.

Human-Centered AI: One of the clearest ways AI can change the game for the better is by making small business owners less reliant on coding. The term "user-friendly AI" specifically refers to AI technology that is easy to access and use, even for non-tech users, with the intention of reducing the barriers to reap the benefits of AI. It's still all about striking the right balance between the human touch combined with the power of the machines, making sure that AI is there as a backup, not a replacement for humans. This human-centric model allows SMBs to keep that personal touch that is core to their competitive edge while benefiting from the increasing efficacy of AI in the overall operation of the business.

Highlander AI: Many small businesses may find themselves intimidated by the cost and effort of integrating AI-powered apps into their workflow, with the promise of huge benefits. Budget constraints, technical limitations, data privacy, and security are some of the reasons AI is sometimes slow to be adopted. To overcome these hurdles, SMBs will need to form alliances with AI vendors, tap into cloud-based AI solutions, and train staff to gain the required expertise and know-how.

Table 2. The Role of Artificial Intelligence (AI) in Small Businesses

Area of Impact	AI Applications	Benefits for Small Businesses	Challenges
Operations	- Automation of repetitive tasks - Predictive maintenance - Inventory optimization	- Increased efficiency - Reduced operational costs - Improved productivity	- Integration complexities - Data security concerns
Customer Experience	- Personalized recommendations - Chatbots for customer service - Targeted marketing campaigns	- Enhanced customer engagement - Improved customer satisfaction - Increased sales conversions	- Data privacy considerations - Maintaining the human touch
Marketing & Sales	- Market analysis and trend prediction - Lead generation and qualification - Sales forecasting	- Data-driven insights - Improved marketing ROI - Enhanced sales performance	- Data quality and accuracy - Algorithm bias
Human Resources	- Automated recruitment processes - Personalized training programs - Employee performance analysis	- Reduced recruitment costs - Improved employee skills - Enhanced workforce management	- Ethical considerations - Employee privacy concerns
Finance	- Fraud detection - Risk assessment - Financial forecasting	- Improved financial security - Reduced financial risks - Enhanced financial planning	- Data security and compliance - Algorithm transparency

Small businesses can open a gateway to AI and other new tools by adopting these technologies and thrive in the era of Industry 5.0. Instead of simply riding the momentum and following the trend, Qohash believes that principles adoption must be a strategic priority for small businesses to leverage the disruptive power of innovation and develop a durable and resilient future.

4. EMERGING TECHNOLOGIES TRANSFORMING SMALL BUSINESSES

Industry 5.0 is characterized by the convergence of several emerging technologies that have the potential to remake the way small businesses conduct business. One of those game changers is the Internet of Things, which gives small business owners the ability to harvest and analyze streaming data from interlinked devices and sensors. This information can then be applied to optimize production processes, improve supply chain efficiency, and refine asset management for cost savings and enhanced productivity. Similarly, Cloud Computing has leveled the playing field for access to high-performance computing power, allowing small businesses to scale their operations, minimize IT infrastructure spending, and access a myriad of Software-as-a-Service (SaaS) offerings. Blockchain, under its transparency, security, and decentralization capabilities, can improve the supply chain management, traceability, and new revenue model of small businesses (Biswas, 2021).

A complete model for small businesses transforming with a strategic intervention model for small businesses to exploit new technologies to grow and to compete is given in Figure 4. Base opener for the business activities of small businesses marks the starting point in the process. The next step is to identify areas for improvement & growth, where businesses identify where they can leverage new technologies to optimize processes and promote growth. The framework also continues serving the opportunities of DT on SMEs and increasing the performance of that; DT on SMEs, making new technologies have several implications on SMEs to enrich that performance. The transformation at the heart of it; emerging technologies are massed out by Artificial Intelligence, Cloud Computing, Internet of Things, 6G Technology, Automation & Robotics. These technologies are subsequently further categorized into particular applications. AI-Powered Chatbots & Assistants are centered on implementing AI for superior customer service and experience. Scalable architecture & data storage focus on using cloud computing for scaling the infrastructure and data storage. Remote Collaboration Tools focus on using cloud-based tools for remote collaboration and communication. Smart Devices & Sensors refers to when you use IoT devices and sensors to gather real-time data on a thing. Ultra-Fast communication details the introduction of 6G technology, fast communication, and real-time logistics planning and coordination, and explains that holographic communication with logistics coordination is available in 6G. The framework directly associates supply chain efficiency with 6G and supply chain efficiency, emphasizing the critical role of 6G in improving supply chains.

After these technologies have been integrated, the framework then proceeds to the implementation and eventual refinement steps. Pilot projects & testing to stimulate the testing of new technologies with pilot activities. This step is vital because businesses have the opportunity to trial new technologies on a smaller scale before they roll them out across the entire business. Refine strategy & re-evaluate emphasizes that the method needs to be changed, with negative ROI, refine the strategy of attack, and re-evaluate the approach. This cycle of constant transformation keeps the transformation agenda business-relevant and results-oriented. Incremental improvement & innovation portrayed in the form of staying ahead of the market through continuous improvement, and innovation emphasizes the dynamic context of technology and the importance of a continuous process. A transformed & competitive small business is the result of the entire framework and is achieved through realizing an innovative and competitive small business by the timely use of emerging technologies. In short, the figure acts as a useful, practical 'map of actions' for small businesses undertaking digital transformation from when to spot the opportunities, when and how to start using new technologies, test them out to refine what works and what doesn't, and constantly innovate to be able to keep ahead in an increasingly competitive market.

Figure 4. Structured overview of how small businesses can integrate emerging technologies to drive efficiency

Robotics and automation are also changing the game for small businesses. Robotic process automation can handle repetitive, high-volume tasks and leave human workers free to concentrate on more strategic and creative activities. On the other hand, the introduction of "cobots" allows small and medium-sized companies to enjoy the benefits of automation while keeping human intervention and supervision.

There are a few key technologies, along with AI, that are also changing the playing field for small businesses, providing opportunities for innovation and growth:

- **Internet of Things:** The Internet of Things (IoT) links devices, machines, and systems to make workflows intelligent and to monitor in real time. Among small companies, possible IoT applications include inventory tracking, energy efficiency, and logistics & supply chain efficiency improvements. IoT devices deliver real-time information to help companies make sound decisions and keep their operations running smoothly.
- **Blockchain:** A secure, distributed technology that improves trust, safety, and transparency of exchanges, blockchain has potential uses in a wide range of transactions. Blockchains allow small businesses to offer secure supply-chain management and payment processing, along with the confidence that comes with knowing that data security is outperforming current data security standards like RSA and AES encryption.
- **3D Printing:** 3D printing allows small businesses to create prototypes affordably, with less lead time, and bring ideas to the marketplace faster. It also supports bespoke design and on-demand manufacture for niche markets and individual customer requirements.
- **Augmented and Virtual Reality:** Marketing and training are changing with AR and VR. Small businesses can develop virtual stores, demo products in 3D experiences, or plan for the future by simulating real-world user scenarios.
- **Cloud Computing:** Data storage and processing are scalable and cost-efficient using Cloud computing. As small-business owners, we can tap the power of cloud computing to request huge amounts of on-demand computing resources, such as remote work, instant sharing of work, and the flexibility to conduct business from just about anywhere.

These new technologies are very much a part of the small business, and when used correctly, enable small businesses to compete better, serve new markets, and deliver greater value to customers. Small businesses standing on the cusp of Industry 5.0 can take advantage of the game-changing potential of AI and other contemporary technologies to innovate, optimize, and outcompete their peers, according to Rozenbilt.

5. HUMAN-AI COLLABORATION: THE HEART OF INDUSTRY 5.0

Humans and AI working together are at the center of what we call Industry 5.0, a collaborative affair between human thinking and creativity, and the accuracy and reliability of an AI. The combination is enabling companies to achieve what neither mere mortals nor AI alone could do. It's not about machines replacing humans — it's about enhancing human ability and creating a more effective and rewarding workspace. It is important to upskill and reskill the human workforce for effective collaboration with AI. When employees have the skills needed to effectively collaborate with AI-based tools and technologies, they can take full advantage of these advancements. This not only contributes to productivity but also provides opportunities to support career growth and development.

Figure 5 describes in detail how to enable synergy between humans and AI by incorporating 6G technology. The framework is designed around 6G Integration, the goal of which is to leverage 6G technology as an enabler for Human-AI collaboration. This first point sets 6G not only as an upgrade in communications but as a basis for an even more combined future between humans and AI systems. One of the major advantages of this collar is "Enhanced Connectivity & Real-time Data". The brief description, which notes that 6G ultra-reliable low-latency communication enhances the connectivity in real-time data exchange, which is crucial for many of the applications for Industry 5.0, continues. Such superhuman capacity has serious implications, for example, in logistics. The figure mentions that this would enable holographic communication for logistics, in which a remote party could be able to see and interact with physical objects, thus enhancing the supply chain efficiency and decision making. Such potential is transformative, enabling interaction remotely with physical objects, and this will result in great leaps in terms of operational efficiency and strategic decisions in diverse industries, especially under Industry 5.0, focusing on human-centered and sustainable industrial growth. But in addition to these steps forward, the framework is taking on a key challenge: Cybersecurity in 6G. It points out that the commitment of the user/apps is more (totally dependent) on connectivity, and cybersecurity continues as a major critical challenge. What this point recognizes is that dependency on pervasive connectivity brings with it greater exposure. The figure can be put into perspective by referring to an external document. This may indicate that the 6G integration cybersecurity issues are no longer theoretical and are already being considered in the practical field, for example, in transportation applications, which could lead to losses of life and human casualties. It suggests the indispensability of strong security considerations to enable successful and safe 6G-based human-AI collaboration.

Finally, the benefits section discusses in summary the major benefits obtained from this leap in technology. It says, for one, the supposed benefits are now specifically about better connectivity and access to real-time data. This summary appeals to the primary benefits of human-AI interaction, which can be implemented through 6G-enhanced connectivity and real-time data everywhere. These are cast as the two key forces driving the transformational capability described above, which, in everything from new holographic communications to improved decision-making and operational effectiveness, can provide. It is clear that the figure succinctly but comprehensively captures what 6G has to offer (and some of the problems) in human-AI collaboration at a high level, including the connectivity to bring together the right parties at the correct time, the real-time data exchange, and the absolute criticality of unbreakable cybersecurity.

Figure 5. The value of 6G by focusing on enabling the human-AI collaboration from the new connectivity and real-time data.

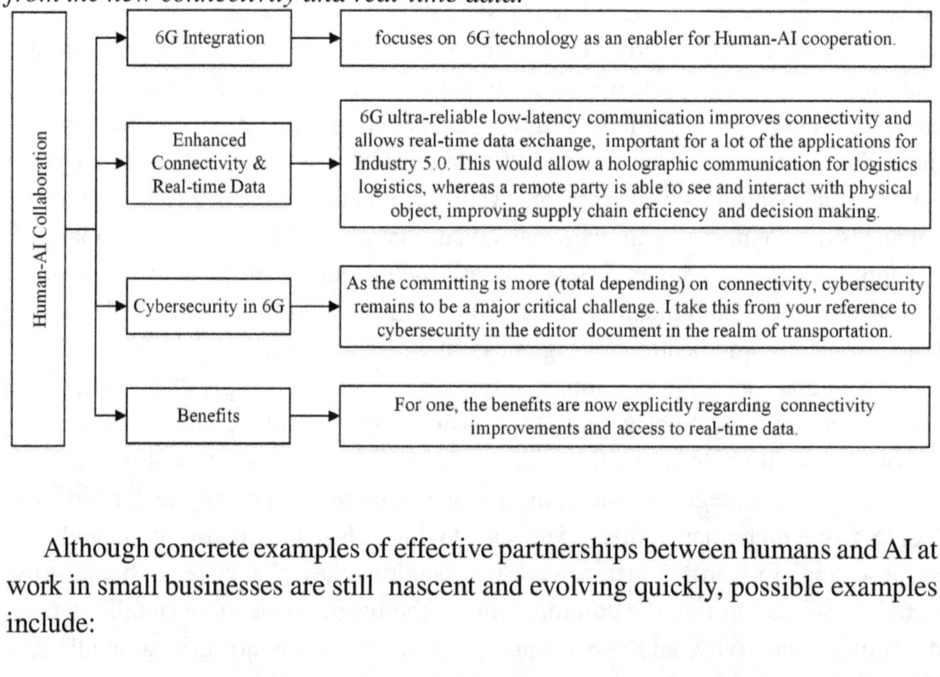

Although concrete examples of effective partnerships between humans and AI at work in small businesses are still nascent and evolving quickly, possible examples include:

- **Personalized Customer Service:** AI bots will take care of common queries, while your agents can solve complex customer queries and offer personalized support.
- **Data-Driven Decision Making:** Using AI, massive datasets can be analyzed and trends or patterns extracted to feed into human decision-making in marketing, product development, and financial planning.
- **Content Creation and Marketing:** Using AI tools for content creation, managing social media, targeted advertising, etc., small businesses can concentrate more on strategic marketing planning.

- **Predictive Maintenance:** AI systems that can predict equipment failures allow proactive maintenance and downtime reduction for a small business with fewer resources.

With the advancement of AI technology, we will see more innovative and influential applications surfacing, which will, in turn, reinforce the critical role that human-AI cooperation plays in the age of Industry 5.0.

6. BENEFITS AND OPPORTUNITIES FOR SMALL BUSINESSES

The fusion of AI and other emerging technologies in the Age of Industry 5.0 offers plenty of advantages and opportunities for small businesses. The automation of AI can manage repetitive, tedious work, allowing human staff to concentrate more on strategic, creative work. This work could save businesses time and money, as well as streamline the workflow, as given in Table 3. In addition, AI-based tools can support small businesses in delivering data-driven insights to make decisions by scaling operations and mapping to new growth opportunities (Feijóo, 2020).

New technologies like IoT, blockchain, and cloud computing can contribute to improving small businesses' competitive advantages. IoT sensors can provide real-time information on inventory, machinery performance, and customer preferences and behavior, all of which help improve decision-making. When it comes to supply chain management, blockchain has the potential to improve trust, security, and transparency in transactions. The scalability and cost-effectiveness of computing power, storage, and software that cloud computing provides make it easier for small companies to compete with big ones. Also, tools such as augmented reality and virtual reality can provide distinctive customer experiences that help small businesses stand out in the crowd. These benefits not only optimize operational proficiency but also unveil new revenue channels and business possibilities. By leveraging AI and cutting-edge tech, small businesses can improve their resiliency, agility, and competitiveness in the dynamic Industry 5.0 age.

Table 3. Benefits and Opportunities for Small Businesses

Area	Benefits	Opportunities
Operations	Increased efficiencies, cost savings, more productivity, and delegated resources	Automation of processes, predictive maintenance, inventory optimization, supply chain optimization
Customer Experience	More attention, more satisfaction, more stickiness, even more relevancy	Personalized marketing, individual-product customization, AI-based customer service, data-based insights
Marketing & Sales	Better Return on Investment (ROI), Increased sales performance, Must Read – Structure Premium Quality Backlinks, Better market coverage, Insight Proactivity with Data Configuration, SEO Data-enhanced Advertising, Direct Response Measurement in Real-time, and Competitive Advantage.	Trend Research, Ad Targeting, Sales Predictions, and Lead Generation.
Innovation	Product or service innovation, Process and operations improvements, Increased competitive advantage, Reduced time to market	AI-powered R&D, data-driven innovation, platform cooperation, and global market access.
Sustainability	Lower eco- and resource footprints, better brand image, and cost savings	Green technologies, energy saving, sustainability in the supply chain, and circular economy models

Enabling AI & Emerging Technology for Small Businesses. There are many benefits and opportunities made possible by the application of AI and emerging technologies to small businesses:

- **Operational Efficiency and Cost Savings:** AI-enabled automation simplifies, eliminates manual work , and puts resources where they are most effective, which, of course, translates into major cost savings and improved operational efficiency.
- **Customized customer experiences for increased loyalty:** With AI, small businesses can personalize customer experiences, customize products and services, and deliver proactive service, while growing stronger customer relationships and fostering further loyalty.
- **Digital end-to-end connection to the world:** E-commerce platforms and digital marketing tools enable small businesses to connect with customers across the globe, extending their market reach and unlocking new growth potential.
- **Innovations with a Sustainability Focus:** Developments such as IoT and blockchain make sustainability easier, helping small businesses to decrease

their natural footprint and better manage resources while also attracting more and more environmentally aware customers.

- **How Data Can Be Used to Remain Competitive:** Small businesses can use AI-based analytics to derive useful information from data, allowing them to gain an understanding of market trends, customer behavior, and business performance to take a competitive advantage in the market.

The convergence of AI and emerging tech in the age of Industry 5.0 has great promise for small businesses that stand to see major shifts in how they operate, connect with customers, and reach markets.

7. CHALLENGES IN ADOPTING AI AND EMERGING TECHNOLOGIES

Small businesses are looking to incorporate AI and new technologies into their business operations, but are facing some key hurdles, as given in Tables 4 and 5. One of the key roadblocks is the technical sophistication needed to deploy and maintain such advanced technology. In small business environments, there is often inadequate internal IT and data science expertise to choose, implement, and manage the right product solutions (Costin, 2022).

Table 4. Challenges and Trends in AI Adoption for SMEs

Category	Description	Examples
Emerging Issues	Wider organizational and strategic hurdles in SMEs.	Costs of software and hardware (in particular, advanced software), staff training (including on-going training) and technical support, technical expertise, and Organisational resistance to change.
Technology-Related Problems	Technical bottlenecks in the application of AI.	Data integration problems, data security risks (e.g., more cyber threats and data breaches), and privacy issues associated with data (e.g., putting consumer data at risk)
Trends Shaping Adoption	Key drivers and changes that are impacting the way SMEs are thinking about AI and other new technologies.	Hyper-personalisation (such as AI-powered chatbots and chat assistants for better customer experiences, individually-marketed service delivery), ethical AI and use of responsible technology (to build consumer trust), and human-AI collaboration (eg, customising tools and frameworks for small businesses)

Tightly intertwined with the skills gap is the problem of upfront investment. AI and new technologies can be costly investments involving capital outlay for hardware, software, and infrastructure. Small businesses do not have adequate financial resources to justify the high cost of initial investment, particularly where there is no immediate return on investment (Menon, 2021). Yet another potential obstacle is the new technology's assimilation with current systems and procedures. Seamless data transfer, system integration, and business continuity can prove a time-consuming and resource-intensive challenge for small businesses. Moreover, concerns about data integrity and privacy are increasing. Embracing AI and other emerging technologies like IoT and cloud can also introduce new potential threats to small businesses that need to be paid careful attention to keep sensitive customer and business data safe.

Ethical and regulatory considerations around the use of AI and new technologies also create further obstacles. Small businesses have to navigate the maze of legal and ethical standards that govern these technologies to make sure they use them in such a way that is legal and ethical, a task that may be harder for more resource-strapped organizations. To address these challenges, small businesses will need to reach out to the external environment, including technology vendors, government programs, and industry networks, to gain access to the required knowledge, finance, and expertise.

Table 5. Challenges in Adopting AI and Emerging Technologies

Challenge	Description	Potential Solutions
Financial Constraints	Small business owners may find the cost barrier to entry to be too high when it comes to AI investment (i.e., technology, software, infrastructure, etc.).	Discover grants, subsidies, and financing tailored for the uptake of technology. You might want to look at cloud-based options to save money on infrastructure costs initially. Invest in Context: Rank by Possible ROI, Start With a Chunk.
Lack of Technical Expertise	Finding (and keeping) highly skilled AI experts, data scientists, and software developers is hard.	Invest in the training and development of current employees. Collaborate with technology partners or consultants for domain expertise. Make use of online learning platforms & resources.
Data Security and Privacy	Worries about leaks, privacy concerns, and ethical complications in AI algorithms.	Adopt strong cybersecurity policies and standards for data privacy. Meet requirements (like GDPR), emphasize transparency, and responsible AI practices.
Integration Complexities	It can be technically tricky to integrate AI systems with business processes and legacy systems.	Hire an expert to ensure it integrates smoothly. Leverage AI solutions that are modular and scalable. Emphasize interoperability and standardization of data.
Cultural Resistance to Change	Fears of displacement and technology uptake among workers.	Encourage a transparent and open dialogue. Train staff well and give them good support. Highlight the advantages of AI for job roles.
Lack of Awareness and Understanding	Poor AI literacy for small business owners in terms of what AI can/cannot do, how it will benefit businesses, and how to employ it.	Take advantage of educational resources, workshops, and industry events that apply to how AI is being adopted by small businesses. Trade with AI professionals and advisors for advice. Connect with other businesses that are successfully applying AI.

And as much as the small business opportunities in AI and emerging tech are impressive, there are some challenges to implementing them and integrating that same tech into their business:

- **Financial Walls and Capital Accessibility:** Adopting new technology generally involves a considerable capital outlay, which may be a roadblock for small businesses that have a shortage of cash. Getting access to funding and types of financing is another key factor in tackling this dilemma.
- **A Shortage of Technical Expertise and Capabilities:** Small enterprises may not have the specialized technical skills to deploy and use AI and other advanced technologies effectively. It can be difficult to attract and keep top-notch talent for these jobs.
- **Cyber Security and Data Privacy concerns:** Your reliance on technology makes your company all the more vulnerable to security threats and privacy breaches. Sensitive data should be protected, and data privacy laws must be taken into account.
- **Organizational resistance to change and cultural barriers:** Implementing new technologies, as proposed in a project, results in modifications in workflows, processes, and organizational culture. Ellenbogen is concerned about employee resistance to change, which can stymie the successful uptake of AI and other new technologies. Overcoming these cultural obstacles and developing innovative cultures is vital.

To do so, small businesses may need external help, such as collaboration with technology vendors, using government-sponsored programs, and teaming up with industry associations to get the required knowledge, funding, and support. Small businesses must overcome various critical challenges to effectively adopt AI and emerging technologies in the Industry 5.0 era, such as financial constraints, lack of technical skills, and cyber risks, in addition to cultural resistance to change. Small businesses can ride the wave of AI and other emerging technologies for Industry 5.0 success. A strategic, holistic approach can ensure the success and growth of small business owners in the future of Industry 5.0.

8. STRATEGIES FOR ADOPTION AND INTEGRATION

A full framework, entitled "Strategies for Adoption and Integration", is presented in Figure 6, detailing a systematic way of accomplishing the "Overall Goal" by way of realize a seamless integration of Human-AI in Industry 5.0 towards sustainable, human-centered, resilient industry development. This is the target of a mission that looks to a new industrial model, based on technology that supports human welfare and respects the environment. The framework starts with "Assessment & Planning," which is an essential first step. This comprises three main steps: "Identify Key Areas for Collaboration," in which companies are instructed to find some niche areas where Human-AI teaming can provide maximum value, like autonomous drone delivery, coordinated logistics, and digital twins. This underscores the need to pinpoint concrete, high-impact applications for Human-AI synergy. Then comes the step "Evaluate Existing Infrastructure & Resources," which demands checking what current technology there is, what data is available , and what the existing resources can do, which is the only way to have a realistic view of the initial point. Lastly, "Define Clear Objectives & KPIs" is around putting in place measurable objectives for the integration productivity improvements, efficiency gains, and innovation metrics. This creates tangible goals for the integration effort.

This is followed by "Phased Implementation", which describes how it is implemented. "Pilot Projects & Trials" is appropriate for execution on prototypes to establish confidence in performance and reliability, enabling learning and improvement, for eventual application at scale. Reiteration & feedback encourage stakeholders to constantly improve the deployment strategy and the issues that the deployment revealed. This illustrates the flexibility of the integration approach. An essential element required in becoming a successful Fifth Generation (5G) network is Scalable Infrastructure, in which Advanced Infrastructure would be "Infrastructure capable of supporting mobility transparently across heterogeneous access networks and performing real-time network slice orchestration," guaranteeing that the underlying technological base is capable of scalability to meet the challenges of innovation and diversity. "Technology & Infrastructure Development" analyzes the technological requirements in further detail. "Buy Ethical AI" spoke to transparent, understandable AI decision-making processes similar to "Invest in Explainable AI" in supporting trust and oversight by humans and building trust in practice. "Design Interactive Interfaces" targets the goal of developing design interfaces that are intuitive and easy to use for Human-AI Interaction, stressing the ease of use. Implement Knowledge Graphs" is focused on providing context-aware understanding and knowledge modeling (Managing Human-AI Collaborations in Industry), providing a more explicit mechanism for AI systems to understand, reason with, and about the complex data found in industrial contexts. And most importantly, "Guarantee Robust Cybersecurity Measures" is illuminated to protect data and infrastructure against cyber threats, recognizing the threats that come with growing connectivity and reliance on data.

The human face of this transformation is covered in "Workforce Development & Training". Upskilling Programs offer pieces of training to close knowledge and skills gaps that allow the workforce to better adapt to the digital revolution. Cross-functional Training promotes the improvement of interaction between team members on different teams, which contributes to the development of a collaborative attitude. Last but not least, "Promote Collaborative Culture" centers on building a culture that fosters teamwork and creativity, acknowledging that successful Human-AI integration is not only about technology but also the organizational culture. Ethical & Regulatory Considerations are the backbone, enabling as well as guiding accountable and legal incorporation. "Set Ethical Frameworks" involves defining responsible AI use, or a set of guidelines for AI development and deployment. "Address Data Privacy & Security" encourages the company to implement data governance policies to prevent sensitive information leaks. "Make It Legal," "Obtain Compliance," stress complying with (copyright, health, safety, and other) laws and standards, as the legal territory of associating with AI.

Digital Literacy and Workforce Readiness

The ever-changing nature of technology demands that its workforce have the competencies to move through and exploit digital tasks. This requires both technical skills and general skills such as adaptability, critical thinking, and problem-solving. We need to invest in training programs and educational campaigns that will help workers close the skills gap and make the most of AI and the new technologies that it powers. With small businesses, they have to create a learning culture and get their employees to be willing to embrace new technology and to adapt to changing industry needs. AI's Inclusion into Business-as-Usual Signals a Big Shift That Offers Opportunity for Innovation, and a Competitive Advantage.

Government Incentives and Support

To promote AI and other emerging technologies among small businesses, the government can do its part by offering financial incentives, grants, or tax relief. These may assist in alleviating the risk of entering the market and make sophisticated technologies obtainable to small businesses with limited resources. Governments could also set up innovation hubs or technology incubators that promote cooperation, knowledge sharing, and the creation of new solutions. Regulation systems need to be crafted for the promotion of innovation without compromising ethics, data privacy, and consumer safety. By forming a conducive environment, the government can lead those who decide not to lag behind in adopting AI and new technologies, promoting economic development as well as social progress.

Real-World Case Studies and Success Stories

A domestic Indian logistics company used AI-based route optimization and saw a 22% reduction in fuel costs and a 30% decrease in delivery times over 6 months. This is a practical example of how AI can be of use in driving business optimization and productivity for SMB companies. A local food processing facility in rural China adopted blockchain to trace product origin and quality, gaining trust and a sales surge of 40% improved supply chain visibility, and reduced fraud. Small business AI: Using emerging technologies for SMB success. These are just a few examples of how AI and new technologies can seamlessly fit into different areas of a small business to improve efficiency, save costs, better the experience of its customers, and set the business up to grow sustainably. A South African farm cooperative that incorporated drones for precision cropping and irrigation management saw a 25% increase in crop yields, along with a 15% drop in water consumption. These use cases illustrate the transformative impact that AI and new technologies can have on small businesses of many stripes, both near and far.

The final element in the framework is an ongoing one (Continuous Monitoring & Improvement): The performance of the system should be monitored throughout the application endeavor, concerning the system's ability to optimize collaboration. "Feedback Mechanisms" are important because they contribute to "Collect feedback to Improve system usability," which advocates for designing for the user. Finally, "Regular Audits & Updates" are required to "Keep your security under control and stay compliant," keeping the security stance and following updated regulations. This figure is essentially a comprehensive, let's get practical guide for an organization on how to best, with ethics, sustainability, and durability, integrate Human-AI for Industry 5.0.

Here's what small businesses can do to successfully face these obstacles and seize the potential of AI and new tech:

- **Gradual Adoption:** Begin by focusing on top use cases where AI and new technology can make the greatest impact. Roll out these technologies gradually and provide time for employees to adjust and learn. This incremental model results in disruption and enables businesses to perfect their business models as they grow smarter.
- **Creating a digital ecosystem:** Partner with technology companies, platforms, and other business players to form a friendly digital ecosystem. Utilize the resources and knowledge you already have to help drive usage and integration. Discover government policies, grants, and initiatives to help increase tech adoption among small businesses.

Figure 6. Comprehensive overview of the strategies for adopting and integrating Human-AI collaboration within Industry 5.0.

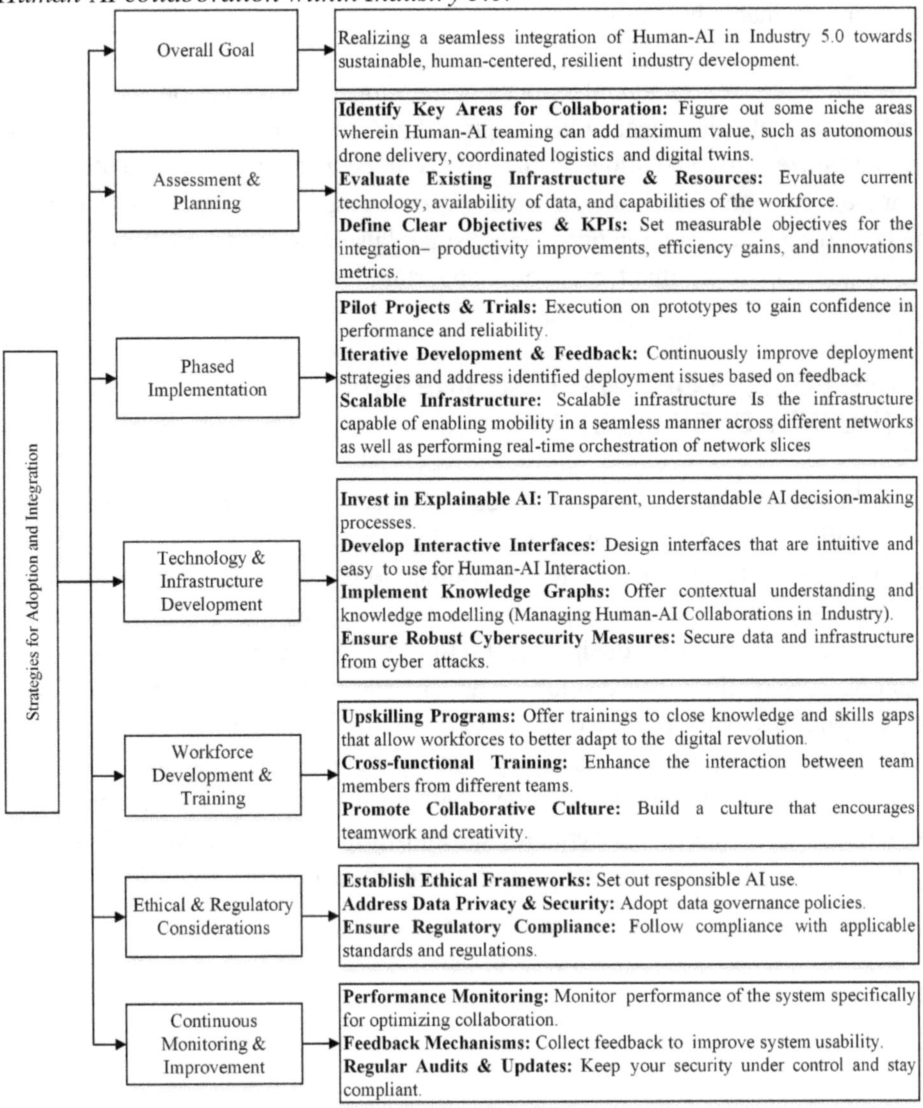

- **Education and Training:** Invest in joint budget training to retrain entrepreneurs and employees. Adequate digital literacy and technical skills within the workforce are crucial for successful technology implementation.
- **Green and Energy-Efficient Practices Sustainability:** Technology adoption strategies shall be sustainable by being green and energy-efficient.

Environmental as well as consumer trends. In addition to reducing your costs, such investments can also help you meet the high demand from consumers for sustainable businesses.

Small businesses should also focus on the impact of regulation and good AI practices. Establishing clear policies, procedures, and governance structures can help minimize abuse and allow for the orderly and ethical use of AI and other new technologies. In the end, achieving AI and emerging technologies integration in the Industry 5.0 age won't happen unless small businesses adopt a comprehensive and strategic approach that tackles both opportunities and challenges.

9. THE FUTURE OF SMALL BUSINESSES IN THE INDUSTRY 5.0 ERA

In the age of Industry 5.0, small businesses can ride the AI wave and newer technologies to be successful, as given in Table 5. Developments in technologies like robotics, IoT, and edge computing are assumed to revolutionize small businesses, helping to improve performance and increase productivity, while providing a more customer-centric experience (Shaikh, 2022). In addition, the emergence of cobots and the prevalence of cloud-based solutions are also increasing the possibility for even small businesses to incorporate this type of technology into their work. Sustainable technologies like renewable energy systems and energy-efficient manufacturing processes will help define the future of small businesses as well. Small businesses that take advantage of this technological transformation will set themselves up to succeed over the long term, staying competitive and nimble in the Industry 5.0 age.

Table 5. The Future of Small Businesses in the Industry 5.0 Era

Aspect	Description	Implications for Small Businesses
Human-Machine Collaboration	Industry 5.0 is about how the man and the machine work together, but the man is at the center.	Technology like AI and robotics can make the labor force, not replace it, more effective. That creates a more enjoyable and productive work culture.
Hyper-Personalization	Artificial intelligence can personalize products, services , and even customers' experiences of a brand.	For small businesses, hyper-personalization can be an opportunity to form deeper connections with customers, inspire loyalty, and become the hero in a crowded marketplace.
Ethical AI and Responsible Technology Use	Prioritize fairness, transparency, and accountability in the use of AI.	Small businesses need to pay more attention to ethics in AI adoption, maintaining the privacy of data, and weighing the ethical implications of algorithms in use.
Agility and Adaptability	Adaptation to travel at breakneck speed is vital when it comes to the shifting sands of the market and technology.	Small business owners must adopt a culture of lifelong learning and creativity if they hope to compete in the ever-changing Industry 5.0 environment.
Innovation as a Core Value	It is being able to grow a culture where people can experiment, and people listen to you, and they accept you.	Small companies should foster creativity and innovation throughout the organization so every employee can contribute to new products, services, and ways of conducting business.
Strong Leadership	Leaders will need to drive the change and steer their organizations in this new direction.	Small business owners must take an active approach to championing digital disruption, along with a culture of continual learning and a committed approach to building their people.

The following are among the critical key trends that will define the future for small businesses within Industry 5.0:

- **Emerging Trends:** Hyper-personalization by using AI to develop products and services, and customer experiences , based on individual needs and preferences, will be key. Moral AI and responsible technology use will be of key importance to guarantee fairness, transparency, and accountability in AI deployment.
- **Future-Proofing Operations:** Small businesses can future-proof themselves such this way – by being nimble and adaptable, by being receptive to change, and by being open to learning. Establishing a culture of innovation as part of the company culture will be crucial for sustained success.
- **Leadership:** Leadership is a game-changer here. Leaders will have to lead the charge to implement new technologies, embrace a culture of learning and experimentation, and lead the transition in their organizations as Industry 5.0 continues to unfold.

As we look ahead to the Industry 5.0 landscape, it is the small businesses that can adapt and, as we shall discuss, even strategically deploy AI, and with additional emerging technologies that will most likely be able to maneuver through the challenges, leverage the opportunities, and succeed in the future. The adoption of AI and advanced technologies in Industry 5.0 provides small firms with opportunities and challenges. Through thoughtful use of these disruptive technologies, small business can maximize their operational efficiency, increase productivity, and personalize customer experiences, positioning what was once a small business to grow and thrive amidst shifts created by the information era.

10. CONCLUSION

This chapter has explored the multi-dimensional effect of AI and novel technologies on small businesses in the era of Industry 5.0, noting the tremendous opportunities as well as the serious challenges they bring. We've also looked at how AI is enabling small businesses to operate more efficiently, save money, and work smarter by automating with data-driven inputs. The capability to use AI for individualized customer experiences, for building closer customer relationships, and for creating loyalty has been stressed as well. Moving further, the chapter has reviewed how digital platforms and online marketplaces are supporting SMEs to reach global buyers and extend their businesses. The role of sustainable-improving innovations and the support of emerging technologies for developing eco-aware activities has also been brought up. However, the use of AI and new technology also brings challenges for small enterprises , such as costs, technical expertise, cyber security threats, and a culture that can be resistant to change. This chapter introduced approaches to successfully adopt and integrate; it has stressed the incremental approach, the construction digital ecosystem, investment in education and training, load the importance of sustainability. Small businesses can harness the transformational power of these technologies by actively and strategically addressing key challenges actively and strategically. The fate of SMBS in the Industry 5.0 era relies on how well they can deal with change, adapt to new trends, and promote a culture of innovation. Trends like Hyper-Personalization and Ethical AI will dictate the business landscape, which means small businesses will have to remain flexible and nimble. Bold leadership will be instrumental in leading this transformation, helping organizations navigate the complexities of Industry 5.0 and training a workforce for the future. The advent of an Industry 5.0 model, which revolves around human-AI cooperation, provides a once-in-a-lifetime chance for SMEs to join this more human-focused, sustainable, and technology-enhanced future. By strategically embracing and incorporating these game-changing technologies, small businesses can achieve their true potential, maneuver through the shifting digital landscape, and create a more resilient and successful tomorrow. It's time to face the future of Industry 5.0.

REFERENCES

Ab Rahim, H., Ibrahim, S., Kamaruddin, S. B. A., Ghani, N. A. M., & Musirin, I. (2020). Exploration on digital marketing as business strategy model among Malaysian entrepreneurs via neurocomputing. *IAES International Journal of Artificial Intelligence*, *9*(1), 18. DOI: 10.11591/ijai.v9.i1.pp18-24

Adel, A. (2022). Future of industry 5.0 in society: Human-centric solutions, challenges and prospective research areas. *Journal of Cloud Computing (Heidelberg, Germany)*, *11*(1), 40. https://journalofcloudcomputing.springeropen.com/counter/pdf/10.1186/s13677-022-00314-5. DOI: 10.1186/s13677-022-00314-5 PMID: 36101900

Ayinaddis, S. G. (2025). Artificial intelligence adoption dynamics and knowledge in SMEs and large firms: A systematic review and bibliometric analysis. *Journal of Innovation & Knowledge*, *10*(3), 100682. DOI: 10.1016/j.jik.2025.100682

Baporikar, N., & Shikokola, S. (2020). Information technology adoption dynamics for SMEs in the manufacturing sector of Namibia. [IJICTRAME]. *International Journal of ICT Research in Africa and the Middle East*, *9*(2), 60–77. DOI: 10.4018/IJICTRAME.2020070104

Biswas, M., Akhund, T. M. N. U., Ferdous, M. J., Kar, S., Anis, A., & Shanto, S. A. (2021, July). Biot: Blockchain based smart agriculture with internet of thing. In *2021 fifth world conference on smart trends in systems security and sustainability (WorldS4)* (pp. 75-80). IEEE. DOI: 10.1109/WorldS451998.2021.9513998

Breque, M., De Nul, L., & Petridis, A. (2021). Industry 5.0: towards a sustainable, human-centric and resilient European industry. *Luxembourg, LU: European Commission, Directorate-General for Research and Innovation, 46*. Available: https://op.europa.eu/en/publication-detail/-/publication/468a892a-5097-11eb-b59f-01aa75ed71a1

Costin, H., & Eslava, A. (2022). Emerging technology trends in hospitality and tourism. *University of South Florida (USF) M3 Publishing, 17*(9781732127593), 11. https://www.doi.org/10.5038/9781732127593

Feijóo, C., Kwon, Y., Bauer, J. M., Bohlin, E., Howell, B., Jain, R., & Xia, J. (2020). Harnessing artificial intelligence (AI) to increase wellbeing for all: The case for a new technology diplomacy. *Telecommunications Policy*, *44*(6), 101988. DOI: 10.1016/j.telpol.2020.101988 PMID: 32377031

Iyelolu, T. V., Agu, E. E., Idemudia, C., & Ijomah, T. I. (2024). Driving SME innovation with AI solutions: overcoming adoption barriers and future growth opportunities. *International Journal of Science and Technology Research Archive, 7*(1), 036-054. .DOI: 10.53771/ijstra.2024.7.1.0055

Kasanga, G. (2020). *Passenger and luggage tracking system using sensor networks for public transport* (Doctoral dissertation, The University of Zambia). Available: https://dspace.unza.zm/handle/123456789/7180

Le Dinh, T., Vu, M. C., & Tran, G. T. (2025). Artificial Intelligence in SMEs: Enhancing Business Functions Through Technologies and Applications. *Information (Basel), 16*(5), 415. DOI: 10.3390/info16050415

Li, K., Zhang, Y., Huang, Y., Tian, Z., & Sang, Z. (2023). Framework and capability of industrial IoT infrastructure for smart manufacturing. *Standards, 3*(1), 1–18. DOI: 10.3390/standards3010001

Menon, S., & Jain, K. (2021). Blockchain technology for transparency in agri-food supply chain: Use cases, limitations, and future directions. *IEEE Transactions on Engineering Management, 71*, 106–120. DOI: 10.1109/TEM.2021.3110903

Peretz-Andersson, E., Tabares, S., Mikalef, P., & Parida, V. (2024). Artificial intelligence implementation in manufacturing SMEs: A resource orchestration approach. *International Journal of Information Management, 77*, 102781. DOI: 10.1016/j.ijinfomgt.2024.102781

Proietti, S., & Magnani, R. (2025). Assessing AI Adoption and Digitalization in SMEs: A Framework for Implementation. *arXiv preprint arXiv:2501.08184.* /arxiv.2501.08184.DOI: 10.32388/0N53P4

Schwaeke, J., Peters, A., Kanbach, D. K., Kraus, S., & Jones, P. (2025). The new normal: The status quo of AI adoption in SMEs. *Journal of Small Business Management, 63*(3), 1297–1331. DOI: 10.1080/00472778.2024.2379999

Shaikh, F. K., Karim, S., Zeadally, S., & Nebhen, J. (2022). Recent trends in internet-of-things-enabled sensor technologies for smart agriculture. *IEEE Internet of Things Journal, 9*(23), 23583–23598. DOI: 10.1109/JIOT.2022.3210154 [illegible] (20[illegible]). [illegible] and [illegible] [illegible]

[illegible] [illegible] [illegible]

[illegible] (202[illegible]). [illegible] intelligence in SM[illegible] [illegible] Technologies [illegible] applications. [illegible]

[illegible] (20[illegible]). Framework and [illegible] [illegible]

[illegible] (20[illegible]). [illegible] [illegible] [illegible] [illegible] [illegible] [illegible]

[illegible] [illegible] (2023). [illegible] [illegible] [illegible] [illegible] [illegible] DOI: 10.1080/[illegible]

Schwaeke, J., Peters, A., Kanbach, D. K., Kraus, S., & Jones, P. (202[illegible]). The new normal: The status quo of [illegible] adoption in SMEs. Journal of Small Business Management, [illegible] DOI: 10.1080/00472778.[illegible]

Smith, F. E., Karim, S., [illegible] (2022). Recent trends in internet of things-enabled [illegible] DOI: [illegible]

Chapter 2
Business Applications of AI:
Enabling Digital Twins and the Metaverse in Industry 5.0

Muhamad Rizky Khairussalam
http://orcid.org/0009-0002-8847-7171
Universitas Esa Unggul, Indonesia

Gusti Muhamad Sardana
http://orcid.org/0009-0001-4281-2432
Universitas Esa Unggul, Indonesia

Binastya Anggara Sekti
http://orcid.org/0000-0001-5489-4888
Universitas Esa Unggul, Indonesia

Varsha Arya
Hong Kong Metropolitan University, Hong Kong

Sourasis Chattopadhyay
http://orcid.org/0009-0000-7435-6550
Kalinga Institute of Industrial Technology, India

Ifat Batul
Vidyasagar University, India

Ryan Putra Laksana
Universitas Esa Unggul, Indonesia

ABSTRACT

This e-book explores the strategic convergence of Artificial Intelligence (AI), Digital Twins, and the Metaverse as the foundational triad driving Industry 5.0. Emphasizing human-centric, sustainable, and adaptive technologies, it highlights how AI empowers real-time analytics, predictive maintenance, immersive environments, and intelligent decision-making. Digital Twins enable dynamic simulations of physical systems, while the Metaverse facilitates interactive and collaborative virtual experiences across industries. The book discusses AI techniques such as machine learning, deep learning, computer vision, and natural language processing, and examines their applications in smart manufacturing, healthcare, retail, and urban

DOI: 10.4018/979-8-2600-0013-7.ch002

planning. It also addresses ethical considerations, data governance, and future trends including explainable AI and federated learning. Together, these technologies redefine how businesses innovate, operate, and engage in an increasingly intelligent and interconnected digital economy.

INTRODUCTION

Overview of Industry 5.0 and the AI-Metaverse-Twin Triad

The global industrial landscape is undergoing a profound transformation, moving beyond the automation-centric paradigms of Industry 4.0 towards a more human-centric, sustainable, and resilient framework known as Industry 5.0. While Industry 4.0 focused primarily on smart factories and interconnected systems, Industry 5.0 emphasizes the collaboration between humans and machines, personalization, and environmental sustainability (Alfeo et al., 2022). This evolution is driven by the increasing demand for customized products and services, the need for more adaptive and resilient supply chains, and a growing awareness of social and environmental responsibilities. In this new industrial era, Artificial Intelligence (AI) emerges as a pivotal technology, acting as the central nervous system that enables the seamless integration and synergistic operation of two other transformative concepts: Digital Twins and the Metaverse.

Digital Twins, essentially virtual replicas of physical objects, processes, or systems, have been instrumental in bridging the gap between the physical and digital worlds. They provide real-time insights, enable predictive analytics, and facilitate optimized decision-making by mirroring the behavior and characteristics of their physical counterparts (Grieves & Vickers, 2016). The Metaverse, on the other hand, represents a persistent, interconnected virtual space where users can interact with each other, digital objects,and AI-powered entities in an immersive and experiential manner (Mystakidis, 2022). While often associated with gaming and social interactions, the industrial metaverse is rapidly gaining traction, offering new avenues for collaboration, simulation, and remote operations within industrial settings (Lee et al., 2015).

The convergence of AI, Digital Twins, and the Metaverse forms a powerful triad that is reshaping various industries. AI provides the intelligence that drives the creation, operation, and optimization of Digital Twins, allowing them to learn, adapt, and evolve based on real-time data ("Leveraging AI and Machine Learning for Enhanced Data Analytics and Visualization in Database Management With Digital Twins," 2025). Simultaneously, AI enhances the immersive and interactive capabilities of the Metaverse, populating it with intelligent agents and dynamic environments. Digital Twins, in turn, provide the realistic and data-rich foundation for the Metaverse, enabling accurate simulations and real-world representations within the virtual space. This intricate interplay creates a feedback loop where data from Digital Twins informs AI models, which then enhance the Metaverse, leading to more efficient, personalized, and sustainable business applications. This chapter delves into this fascinating triad, exploring how AI acts as the enabler for Digital Twins and the Metaverse, driving innovation and creating new opportunities across diverse sectors in the era of Industry 5.0.

Basic of AI Technology in General

To fully comprehend the intelligence layer that drives the synergy between Digital Twins and the Metaverse, it is essential to understand the foundational structure of Artificial Intelligence (AI) and its core subfields Machine Learning (ML) and Deep Learning (DL) (Rahaman, Cajes, Gupta, Nedjah, et al., 2025). These three domains form a conceptual hierarchy that underpins much of the data processing, decision-making, and adaptive behavior within Industry 5.0 ecosystems.

Figure 1. AI Knowledge Family

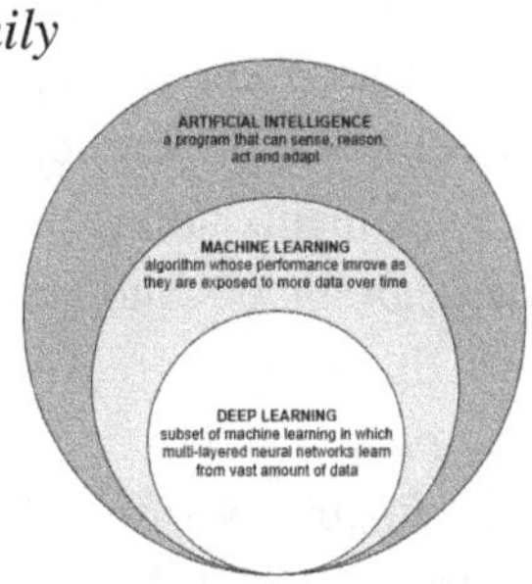

Figure 1 illustrates the hierarchical relationship between Artificial Intelligence (AI), Machine Learning (ML), and Deep Learning (DL), providing a conceptual foundation for understanding how intelligent behavior is constructed within modern digital ecosystems. At the broadest level, AI encompasses all computational techniques that enable machines to perceive their environment, interpret information, make decisions, and adapt over time. Nested within this domain, Machine Learning represents a more focused subset in which algorithms learn from data, continuously improving their performance as additional input is collected. This learning-driven approach underpins many predictive and optimization functions essential to Digital Twin operations. At the deepest tier of the hierarchy, Deep Learning serves as a specialized branch of ML that relies on multi-layered neural networks capable of extracting complex and abstract patterns from large volumes of unstructured data, such as images, audio, video, and high-frequency sensor streams. These advanced capabilities are critical for supporting real-time perception, autonomous interaction, and high-fidelity simulation within Digital Twins and Metaverse environments. By understanding the layered nature of AI, ML, and DL, it becomes evident how these technologies collectively provide the cognitive engine that enables Industry 5.0 systems to operate intelligently, respond dynamically, and continuously evolve based on real-world and virtual feedback.

Role of AI in Next-Generation Digital Ecosystems

Artificial Intelligence is not merely a tool but a fundamental catalyst for the development of next-generation digital ecosystems. Its role extends far beyond simple automation, permeating every layer of the AI-Metaverse-Twin triad to facilitate immersive consumer experiences, enhance operational efficiency, and enable strategic decision-making across a multitude of sectors. From manufacturing and retail to healthcare and logistics, AI-driven models, algorithms, and intelligent agents are revolutionizing how organizations interact with their customers, manage their operations, and plan for the future.

In the realm of immersive consumer experiences, AI plays a crucial role in personalizing interactions within the Metaverse. Through advanced machine learning algorithms, AI can analyze user behavior, preferences, and emotional responses to create highly tailored virtual environments and experiences. This includes everything from intelligent avatars that can understand and respond to natural language queries to dynamic virtual spaces that adapt in real-time to user needs. The ability of AI to generate and manage complex virtual worlds, coupled with its capacity for natural language processing and computer vision, allows for unprecedented levels of engagement and immersion, transforming how businesses connect with their customers in the digital realm.

For operational efficiency, AI's integration with Digital Twins is paramount. AI algorithms process vast amounts of real-time data collected from physical assets, enabling predictive maintenance, optimizing resource allocation, and identifying potential bottlenecks before they occur(Jover & Sempere, 2025). This proactive approach minimizes downtime, reduces operational costs, and extends the lifespan of critical equipment. Furthermore, AI-powered simulations within Digital Twins allow businesses to test various scenarios, optimize processes, and train personnel in a risk-free virtual environment, leading to significant improvements in productivity and safety. The ability of AI to learn from historical data and adapt to changing conditions ensures that Digital Twins remain accurate and relevant, providing continuous value to businesses seeking to streamline their operations.

From a strategic decision-making perspective, AI provides the analytical power necessary to extract actionable insights from the massive datasets generated by Digital Twins and Metaverse interactions. By leveraging advanced analytics, pattern recognition, and forecasting capabilities, AI helps businesses identify emerging trends, assess market dynamics, and make informed strategic choices. This includes optimizing product design, developing new service offerings, and identifying new market opportunities. The real-time intelligence provided by AI-driven Digital Twins and Metaverse platforms empowers leaders to make agile and data-driven decisions, fostering innovation and maintaining a competitive edge in a rapidly evolving digital economy. Ultimately, AI bridges the gap between theoretical innovation and commercial deployment, transforming abstract concepts into tangible business value.

Motivation and Significance

The rapid ascent of Industry 5.0 necessitates a fundamental shift in how organizations approach technology integration and business strategy. With its emphasis on personalized, sustainable, and intelligent experiences, Industry 5.0 demands systems that can learn, adapt, and evolve in response to dynamic data streams from Digital Twins and intricate interactions within the Metaverse. While the individual components of AI, Digital Twins, and the Metaverse have been extensively studied, there remains a significant gap in academic synthesis regarding their practical and synergistic integration, particularly concerning both consumer-oriented and enterprise-level applications. This chapter is motivated by the urgent need to address this critical research gap.

Existing literature often treats these technologies in isolation, overlooking the profound impact of their combined capabilities. There is a lack of comprehensive frameworks that illustrate how AI acts as the connective tissue, enabling the seamless flow of information and intelligence between Digital Twins and the Metaverse. This chapter aims to fill this void by offering a multi-dimensional analysis that spans technical, strategic, and operational perspectives. From a technical standpoint, we will delve into the specific AI algorithms and architectures that facilitate the creation and interaction of Digital Twins and Metaverse environments. Strategically, we will examine how businesses can leverage this triad to develop new revenue streams, optimize existing processes, and gain a competitive advantage. Operationally, we will explore the practical implementation challenges and best practices for deploying AI-driven Digital Twins and Metaverse solutions (Kakkar et al., 2025).

The significance of this chapter lies in its potential to provide a holistic understanding of the AI-Metaverse-Twin triad, offering valuable insights for researchers, practitioners, and industry stakeholders. By synthesizing disparate knowledge domains, we aim to present a unified view of how these technologies can be harnessed to revolutionize business models and drive sustainable growth in the Industry 5.0 era (Grieves & Vickers, 2016). This work will serve as a foundational resource for organizations seeking to navigate the complexities of the immersive digital economy, providing a roadmap for leveraging AI to unlock the full potential of Digital Twins and the Metaverse. Furthermore, by highlighting real-world implementations and practical frameworks, this chapter will contribute to bridging the divide between theoretical innovation and tangible commercial deployment, fostering a new generation of intelligent, adaptive, and data-centric business ecosystems. This comprehensive approach will empower businesses to not only survive but thrive in the increasingly interconnected and intelligent landscape of Industry 5.0.

TECHNOLOGICAL FOUNDATIONS

The effective integration of Digital Twins and the Metaverse within Industry 5.0 is fundamentally underpinned by a sophisticated array of Artificial Intelligence (AI) techniques. AI serves as the computational engine that processes vast datasets, enables intelligent interactions, and facilitates the dynamic evolution of these immersive digital environments. This section delves into the core AI methodologies and data management strategies that form the technological bedrock of the AI Metaverse-Twin (Boopathy et al., 2025).

AI Techniques Used in Metaverse and Digital Twins

The development and functionality of both the Metaverse and Digital Twins rely heavily on various AI techniques, each contributing unique capabilities to create intelligent, and realistic digital ecosystems. These techniques range from foundational machine learning algorithms to advanced deep learning architectures and specialized AI domains like computer vision and natural language processing.

Machine Learning (ML) Algorithms

At the heart of many AI applications in this domain are machine learning algorithms. These algorithms enable systems to learn from data without being explicitly programmed, allowing for predictive capabilities and adaptive behaviors. In the context of Digital Twins, supervised learning models are crucial for predictive maintenance, where historical data on equipment failures and operational parameters are used to train models that forecast future malfunctions (Fan et al., 2019). Unsupervised learning, such as clustering, can identify anomalies in real-time sensor data, indicating potential issues in a physical asset (Hailu et al., 2016). Reinforcement learning (RL) is particularly promising for optimizing complex systems, allowing Digital Twins to learn optimal control strategies through trial and error in simulated environments, thereby improving efficiency and performance (Ahmed et al., 2025). For instance, RL can be used to optimize energy consumption in smart buildings represented by Digital Twins or to fine-tune production processes in smart factories.

Deep Learning (DL) Architectures

Deep learning, a subset of machine learning, utilizes neural networks with multiple layers to learn complex patterns from large datasets. DL architectures are essential for handling the high-dimensional and often unstructured data prevalent in Metaverse and Digital Twin environments. Convolutional Neural Networks (CNNs) are widely used in computer vision tasks for processing visual data from the Metaverse (e.g., recognizing objects in virtual scenes, facial recognition for avatars) and for analyzing image-based data from Digital Twins (e.g., inspecting manufacturing defects) (Tang et al., 2025). Recurrent Neural Networks (RNNs) and their variants, like Long Short-Term Memory (LSTM) networks, are vital for processing sequential data, such as time-series sensor data from Digital Twins for real-time monitoring and anomaly detection, or for understanding conversational flows in Metaverse interactions (Kuo et al., 2025). Generative Adversarial Networks (GANs) are increasingly employed in the Metaverse for generating realistic content (Yan et al., 2017).

Computer Vision (CV)

Computer Vision is indispensable for enabling the Metaverse and Digital Twins to perceive and interpret visual information. In the Metaverse, CV enables functionalities such as image classification for organizing virtual assets, object detection for identifying interactive elements, semantic segmentation for understanding scene composition, and facial recognition for personalizing avatar interactions (Moslehpour et al., 2024). For Digital Twins, CV is crucial for tasks like human pose estimation to track worker movements in a factory for safety and efficiency analysis, and scene reconstruction to create accurate 3D models of physical environments from 2D images or sensor data (Pang et al., 2025). These capabilities allow for seamless interaction between the physical and virtual worlds, enhancing the fidelity and utility of Digital Twins.

Natural Language Processing (NLP)

NLP is critical for facilitating human-computer interaction and enabling intelligent communication within the Metaverse. It powers intelligent avatars and virtual agents that can understand and respond to natural language queries, engage in meaningful conversations, and provide personalized assistance. NLP techniques such as sentiment analysis can gauge user emotions in the Metaverse, allowing for dynamic adjustments to the virtual environment or interaction style. In Digital Twins, NLP can be used to process unstructured text data from maintenance logs or operational reports, extracting valuable insights for predictive analytics and decision-making (Sumon et al., 2024).

Reinforcement Learning (RL)

Beyond its role in optimizing control strategies for Digital Twins, RL is also vital for creating dynamic and adaptive systems within the Metaverse. RL agents can learn to navigate complex virtual environments, interact with users in a personalized manner, and even generate new content based on user preferences and historical interactions (ÖZKAL & BAŞÇİFTÇİ, 2024). This allows for a highly responsive and evolving Metaverse that can cater to individual user needs and preferences, fostering a more engaging and immersive experience.

Table 1. comparison table between the use of science as supporting technology

Technology	Role in the Ecosystem	Key Applications	Benefits
IoT (Internet of Things)	Provides real-time data from the physical world to build and update Digital Twins	- Factory sensors for machine monitoring - Real-time supply chain tracking	- Inter-device connectivity - Accurate data for simulation and prediction
AI & Machine Learning	Serves as the analytical and cognitive engine enabling autonomous decisions, predictions, and personalization	- Predictive maintenance - Generative AI for Metaverse content - User behavior analytics	- Data-driven decision-making - Adaptive and self-learning systems
XR (VR/AR/MR)	Provides immersive interfaces for human–Digital Twin–Metaverse interaction	- VR training simulations for technicians - AR for equipment maintenance - MR for collaborative design	- Intuitive interaction - Complex visualizations made easier to understand
Blockchain	Ensures security, authenticity, and transparency of data and digital assets	- Audit logs for Digital Twin activities - Ownership of digital assets in the Metaverse - Smart contracts across entities	- Trust without intermediaries - Protection of data integrity
5G & Edge Computing	Enables high-speed communication and local processing for real-time responsiveness	- On-device AI processing - Low-latency updates for XR and Digital Twins	- Instantaneous responses - Reduced load on central servers

SUPPORTING TECHNOLOGY

Enabling Technologies: The Foundational Pillars of AI, Digital Twins, and the Metaverse in Industry 5.0

The successful realization of the AI-Metaverse-Twin triad in the context of Industry 5.0 is deeply dependent on a robust foundation of converging technologies. These enabling technologies not only support the technical implementation of immersive and intelligent systems but also serve as critical drivers of scalability, interoperability, real-time interaction, and trustworthiness. This section highlights five key pillars Internet of Things (IoT), Artificial Intelligence and Machine Learning (AI/ML), Extended Reality (XR), Blockchain, and 5G coupled with Edge Computing each playing a vital role in empowering the next-generation digital ecosystem (Langås et al., 2025).

Internet of Things (IoT): Bridging the Physical and Digital Worlds

IoT forms the sensory layer of Digital Twins by embedding sensors and actuators into physical systems, enabling continuous data collection and feedback. From smart factories and connected vehicles to wearables and environmental sensors, IoT networks provide the real-time, context-aware data streams essential for accurate and dynamic twin representations (He et al., 2018). These data streams fuel AI analytics and simulations, while also enabling real-time adjustments in the Metaverse to reflect physical changes.

- In smart manufacturing, IoT sensors track vibration, temperature, and torque to update Digital Twins of industrial robots.
- In smart cities, sensor-rich infrastructure supplies live data to AI models simulating traffic flow, air quality, and energy demand in the Metaverse.

Without IoT, the seamless synchronization between physical and virtual entities would remain unattainable, reducing both insight and responsiveness.

Artificial Intelligence and Machine Learning: The Cognitive Core

AI and Machine Learning are the cognitive engines of Industry 5.0, powering everything from predictive maintenance in Digital Twins to intelligent agents in the Metaverse . Supervised learning, reinforcement learning, deep neural networks, and generative models collectively enable dynamic decision-making, personalized experiences, and adaptive system behaviors.

- Predictive models learn from IoT data to anticipate failures and autonomously recommend corrective actions.
- Generative Adversarial Networks (GANs) and transformer-based models are used to create immersive, real-time content in the Metaverse, from avatars to landscapes.

AI also enables continuous learning across the system, ensuring that Digital Twins evolve with their physical counterparts and that the Metaverse remains responsive and contextually intelligent.

Extended Reality (XR): Immersive Interfaces for Human-AI Collaboration

Extended Reality, encompassing Virtual Reality (VR), Augmented Reality (AR), and Mixed Reality (MR), transforms human-machine interaction by offering immersive, intuitive interfaces to engage with both Digital Twins and the Metaverse.

- In VR-based training simulations, users can interact with a Digital Twin of a turbine or industrial machine in a risk-free virtual environment.
- AR overlays allow technicians to visualize internal machinery components or operational analytics in real-world settings.
- MR environments enable real-time collaboration between physical and digital entities, fostering hands-on learning, remote maintenance, and collaborative design.

XR serves as the visual and interactive bridge between human cognition and digital intelligence enhancing user engagement, decision-making, and system transparency.

Blockchain: Securing Trust in Interconnected Digital Ecosystems

As Digital Twins and Metaverse environments involve vast and sensitive data exchanges, ensuring data integrity, provenance, and trust becomes critical. Blockchain technology offers a decentralized ledger that ensures immutability, transparency, and verifiability of transactions and data across stakeholders (Sekti, 2026a).

- Digital Twins can use blockchain for secure logging of maintenance activities, supply chain transactions, or lifecycle histories.
- In the Metaverse, blockchain underpins the ownership of digital assets, virtual identities, and smart contracts.

By embedding trust into the infrastructure, blockchain reduces dependency on centralized intermediaries and enables cross-organizational cooperation with confidence.

5G and Edge Computing: Real-Time Responsiveness at Scale

To support the enormous data demands and low-latency interactions required by AI-driven Digital Twins and immersive Metaverse environments, ultra-fast connectivity and decentralized processing are essential (Wang et al., 2023). Here, 5G and Edge Computing play complementary roles:

- 5G provides high-speed, high-bandwidth wireless communication essential for real-time streaming of sensor data, XR interactions, and remote collaboration.
- Edge Computing reduces latency by processing data close to the source (e.g., on factory floors or wearable devices), enabling real-time analytics, decision-making, and AI inference without relying on centralized cloud systems.

Together, 5G and edge computing ensure that Digital Twins remain synchronized with their physical counterparts and that immersive Metaverse experiences remain seamless and responsive, even in complex or bandwidth-constrained environments (Wang et al., 2023).

DIGITAL TWIN IN INDUSTRY 5.0

Digital Twin in Industry 5.0: Real-Time, Data-Driven Virtual Counterparts

A Digital Twin is a dynamic, virtual representation of a physical asset, system, or process that remains continuously synchronized through real-time data exchange. Unlike conventional modeling techniques, Digital Twins allow organizations to monitor, simulate, and optimize physical operations in a closed-loop manner, enabling predictive intelligence and adaptive decision-making (Grieves & Vickers, 2017). In the context of Industry 5.0, Digital Twins form a core pillar of human-centric, resilient, and sustainable industrial ecosystems by providing deep situational awareness, enhanced system transparency, and seamless collaboration between humans and intelligent machines.

At the heart of a Digital Twin lies a bidirectional data pipeline consisting of IoT sensors, edge devices, AI/ML analytics, and cloud infrastructure. IoT devices capture real-time operational data vibration, temperature, torque, power load, and process conditions—while AI/ML models process this data to detect anomalies, generate predictions, or recommend optimal actions. The insights produced by the Digital Twin can then be sent back to the physical system to adjust behaviors autonomously, completing the feedback loop.

Digital Twins support multiple layers of functionality, including:

- Descriptive Twins, providing real-time monitoring and visualization of asset status.
- Predictive Twins, using ML models to forecast failures, bottlenecks, or performance degradation.
- Prescriptive Twins, recommending or executing optimal adjustments to improve efficiency or reduce risks.
- Autonomous Twins, enabling self-optimizing systems through AI-driven feedback loops.

In Industry 5.0, Digital Twins enhance manufacturing, energy management, logistics, healthcare, and urban infrastructure, serving as the foundational intelligence layer for smart factories and interconnected digital ecosystems. For instance, a Digital Twin of a robotic arm can detect wear patterns and automatically schedule maintenance, while a Digital Twin of a supply chain can simulate disruptions such as delays, shortages, or demand spikes and produce optimized plans in real time.

As industries become increasingly complex, volatile, and interdependent, Digital Twins provide a scalable method for integrating physical operations with intelligent simulations, enabling organizations to predict, test, and refine outcomes before they occur in the real world.

Digital Twin vs High-Fidelity Simulation

Although Digital Twins and high-fidelity simulations share certain characteristics such as virtual modeling, scenario testing, and analytical functions they differ fundamentally in terms of synchronization, adaptability, and operational purpose.

Digital Twin

A Digital Twin is defined by its continuous, real-time connection to its physical counterpart. Data streams from IoT sensors flow into the digital model, enabling up-to-date representation of system conditions. In advanced use cases, the Digital

Twin also sends insights or control commands back to the physical system, forming a bidirectional feedback loop.

Core characteristics:

- Continuous real-time data exchange
- Dynamic model that evolves with physical changes
- Integration with AI/ML for predictive and prescriptive intelligence
- Closed-loop interaction between virtual and physical assets

Digital Twins are therefore living, learning systems that support operational decision-making and autonomous optimization.

High-Fidelity Simulation

A simulation, regardless of its visual quality or computational accuracy, is not connected in real time to any physical system. It relies on static, historical, or hypothetical data and is used primarily for training, design validation, experimentation, or risk analysis.

Core characteristics:

- No real-time connectivity
- One-directional data flow (model → insights)
- Static or periodically updated dataset
- Limited adaptability to real-world changes

Simulations are valuable tools but lack the continuous evolution and real-world grounding of a Digital Twin.

Metaverse vs Virtual Environment

Distinguishing the Metaverse from Conventional Virtual Environments

As the concept of the Metaverse becomes increasingly integrated into industrial and enterprise applications, distinguishing it from traditional virtual environments is essential. While both involve digital spaces, their scope, persistence, and interoperability differ significantly.

Metaverse

The Metaverse is an interconnected, persistent, multi-user digital ecosystem where virtual spaces, AI-driven agents, Digital Twins, and immersive interfaces (XR) operate in real time. It extends beyond visualization by integrating real-world data, intelligent behavior, and decentralized digital economies.

Key characteristics:

- Persistence: the world continues to exist and evolve even when users are offline
- Multi-user, shared environments with synchronous interaction
- Interoperability across platforms, assets, and applications
- AI-driven dynamic content and intelligent avatars
- Integration with blockchain-based identity, ownership, and smart contracts
- Often linked to physical systems (e.g., industrial metaverse using Digital Twins)

The Metaverse functions as a complex socio-technical ecosystem rather than an isolated virtual experience.

Virtual Environment

A conventional virtual environment is a standalone, self-contained digital space used for specific purposes such as training, gaming, design visualization, or simulation. It does not require persistence, multi-user participation, interoperability, or real-time data integration.

Key characteristics:

- Isolated, purpose-specific environment
- Not necessarily persistent
- May be single-user or offline
- No built-in economy or cross-platform functionality
- Limited or no integration with real-world data

Data Fusion and AI Inference Models in Real-Time Systems

The efficacy of AI-driven Digital Twins and Metaverse environments hinges on their ability to process and integrate vast amounts of diverse data in real-time. This necessitates robust data fusion mechanisms and efficient AI inference models capable of delivering insights and actions with minimal latency. Data fusion involves combining data from multiple disparate sources to create a more comprehensive and accurate understanding of a system or environment. In the context of the AI-Metaverse-Twin triad, this includes sensor data from physical assets, user interaction data from the Metaverse, historical operational data, and external contextual information (Sekti, 2026b).

Mechanisms for Integrating Data

Integrating data from physical and virtual sources is a complex task due to the heterogeneity of data formats, velocities, and volumes. For Digital Twins, data streams from IoT sensors are continuously fed into the virtual model, ensuring real-time synchronization between the physical asset and its digital replica (Correia et al., 2023). This often involves edge computing to process data closer to the source, reducing latency and bandwidth requirements. In the Metaverse, data from user inputs, avatar movements, virtual object interactions, and even biometric data are collected and integrated to create a rich tapestry of user experience data. Middleware platforms and standardized APIs are crucial for enabling seamless data exchange between these diverse sources and the AI models that consume them. Blockchain technology is also emerging as a potential solution for secure and transparent data sharing and provenance tracking within these complex ecosystems (Rahaman et al., 2024).

Real-Time Data Processing and Analytics

The sheer volume and velocity of data generated by Digital Twins and Metaverse environments demand real-time processing and analytics capabilities. Stream processing technologies (Singh et al., 2022) are employed to ingest, filter, and transform data as it arrives, enabling immediate analysis and response. This real-time data is then fed into AI models for instantaneous insights. For instance, in predictive maintenance, real-time sensor data is analyzed by AI models to detect anomalies or deviations from normal operating conditions, triggering alerts or automated interventions before a failure occurs (Correia et al., 2023). In the Metaverse, real-time analytics can track user engagement, identify popular virtual spaces, and detect fraudulent activities, allowing platform operators to make immediate adjustments to optimize the user experience or enhance security (Gupta et al., 2023).

AI Models for Real-Time Decision-Making and Predictive Analytics

The ultimate goal of data fusion and real-time processing is to enable AI models to make informed decisions and provide accurate predictions in dynamic environments. These AI inference models are often deployed at the edge or in distributed cloud architectures to minimize latency. For Digital Twins, AI models can predict equipment failures, optimize energy consumption, or simulate the impact of operational changes, providing actionable insights for human operators or even enabling autonomous control. In the Metaverse, AI models can dynamically generate content, personalize user experiences, moderate interactions, and even facilitate real-time language translation, creating a truly global and immersive environment (Chinta, 2024). The continuous feedback loop between real time data, AI inference, and system response is what makes the AI-Metaverse-Twin triad so powerful, enabling a new era of intelligent and adaptive business applications (Li et al., 2025).

AI-DRIVEN DIGITAL TWINS

Digital Twins represent a cornerstone technology in the evolution towards Industry 5.0, serving as dynamic, virtual counterparts to physical assets, processes, or systems. When infused with Artificial Intelligence, these digital replicas transcend mere simulation, becoming intelligent entities capable of real-time monitoring, predictive analysis, and autonomous optimization. This section explores the fundamental concepts of AI-driven Digital Twins, their applications in predictive maintenance, asset simulation, and real-time monitoring, and provides compelling case studies from smart manufacturing and intelligent supply chains (Swarnakar et al., 2023).

Concept and Characteristics of Digital Twins in Industry

The concept of a Digital Twin, while gaining significant traction in recent years, has roots tracing back to the early days of space exploration. The idea of creating a virtual replica to monitor and simulate the behavior of a physical system was notably applied during the Apollo 13 mission, where a ground-based physical twin of the spacecraft was used to troubleshoot and simulate various conditions, ensuring the safety and success of the mission (Rajamurugu & Karthik, 2022). This early application highlighted the immense value of having a synchronized, high-fidelity model of a physical entity (Langås et al., 2025).

Professor Michael Grieves formally introduced the concept of the Digital Twin in 2002, initially describing it as a conceptual model comprising three main parts: a physical product, a virtual product, and the connections between them (Augustine, 2020). This foundational idea posited that a comprehensive information set about a physical product could be mirrored in a virtual space, allowing for analysis and optimization without directly interacting with the physical counterpart. Over the past two decades, driven by advancements in sensor technology, data analytics, and computational power, the Digital Twin concept has evolved significantly, becoming a dynamic and interactive virtual model that continuously updates with real-time data from its physical twin. In the context of Industry 5.0, Digital Twins are characterized by several key attributes that distinguish them from traditional simulations or models:

High-Fidelity Models

Modern Digital Twins are built upon highly accurate and detailed virtual models that precisely represent the geometric, physical, and behavioral characteristics of their physical counterparts. These models often incorporate multi-physics simulations, allowing for a comprehensive understanding of how the physical asset behaves under various conditions (Balogh et al., 2023). The level of detail and accuracy is crucial for ensuring that insights derived from the Digital Twin are reliable and actionable.

Virtual-Physical Synchronization

A defining characteristic of Digital Twins is the continuous, real-time data exchange between the physical asset and its virtual replica. Sensors embedded in the physical system collect vast amounts of data (Chinta, 2024), which are then transmitted to the Digital Twin. This data stream ensures that the virtual model accurately reflects the current state, behavior, and operational conditions of the physical asset, enabling virtual-physical synchronization and consistency (Augustine, 2020). This bidirectional flow of information also allows for commands and optimizations from the Digital Twin to be sent back to the physical system, enabling closed-loop control and autonomous operation.

Real-Time Monitoring and Interaction

Digital Twins provide continuous, real-time monitoring of physical assets, offering unprecedented visibility into their performance and health. This constant oversight allows operators to track key performance indicators, detect anomalies, and identify potential issues as they emerge. Beyond passive monitoring, Digital Twins enable interactive capabilities, allowing users to query the virtual model, run simulations, and even manipulate virtual controls to observe the potential impact on the physical system (Chinta, 2024). This interactive nature facilitates better decision-making and proactive problem-solving.

Data-Driven Evolution

Unlike static models, Digital Twins are designed to evolve and improve over time through continuous learning from data. As more operational data is collected and analyzed, AI algorithms integrated within the Digital Twin can refine its models, enhance its predictive capabilities, and optimize its performance. This data-driven evolution ensures that the Digital Twin remains relevant and accurate throughout the entire lifecycle of the physical asset, from design and manufacturing to operation and maintenance (Eneyew et al., 2022).

Predictive and Prescriptive Capabilities

Leveraging AI, Digital Twins move beyond merely describing the current state to predicting future behavior and prescribing optimal actions. By analyzing historical data and real-time inputs, AI models can forecast potential failures, predict remaining useful life, and identify optimal maintenance schedules. Furthermore, they can suggest or even autonomously implement actions to prevent issues or optimize performance, transforming reactive maintenance into proactive, intelligent asset management.

In essence, AI-driven Digital Twins are not just digital copies; they are living, breathing virtual entities that provide a comprehensive, intelligent, and dynamic representation of their physical counterparts. They serve as powerful tools for understanding, predicting, and optimizing complex systems, paving the way for more efficient, resilient, and sustainable industrial operations in the Industry 5.0 era (Taj & Zaman, 2022).

Predictive Maintenance and Asset Simulation

The integration of Artificial Intelligence with Digital Twins has revolutionized asset management, particularly in the domains of predictive maintenance and asset simulation. This powerful combination enables organizations to move from reactive or time-based maintenance strategies to highly efficient, data-driven approaches that significantly reduce downtime, optimize operational costs, and extend the lifespan of critical assets.

AI-Enhanced Predictive Maintenance

Predictive maintenance, at its core, involves forecasting potential equipment failures before they occur, allowing for timely interventions and preventing costly breakdowns. Digital Twins provide the ideal platform for this by offering a real-time, high-fidelity virtual representation of physical assets. When AI algorithms are applied to the vast streams of data collected from these Digital Twins, their predictive capabilities are dramatically enhanced. AI models, particularly those based on machine learning and deep learning, can analyze historical performance data, real-time sensor readings and environmental factors to identify subtle patterns and anomalies indicative of impending failures (Habib et al., 2025).

For instance, in manufacturing, AI-driven Digital Twins can monitor the health of complex machinery, predicting when a specific component might fail with remarkable accuracy. This allows maintenance teams to schedule interventions precisely when needed, minimizing disruption to production lines and avoiding unscheduled downtime. Similarly, in the energy sector, Digital Twins of wind turbines or power transformers, augmented with AI, can predict component degradation, enabling proactive maintenance that ensures grid stability and reduces operational risks (Omoniwa et al., 2019). The benefits extend to various industries, including mining, where AI-driven Digital Twins are used for fault detection and intelligent asset management, and even in smart buildings for predicting HVAC system failures.

Asset Simulation for Design, Testing, and Optimization

Beyond predicting failures, AI-driven Digital Twins are invaluable tools for comprehensive asset simulation. This capability allows businesses to create virtual environments where they can test design changes, optimize operational parameters, and train personnel in a risk-free setting, all without impacting the physical system. The simulation capabilities of Digital Twins are particularly beneficial during the design and prototyping phases of new products or systems. Engineers can create a Digital Twin of a proposed design and use AI to simulate its performance under various conditions, identifying potential flaws or areas for optimization before any physical prototype is built. This iterative virtual testing significantly reduces development costs and accelerates time-to-market (Kuo et al., 2025).

In manufacturing, asset simulation enables the optimization of production lines. A Digital Twin of a factory floor can simulate different layouts, production schedules, and robotic movements, with AI guiding the optimization process to maximize throughput and minimize bottlenecks. This allows for continuous improvement and adaptation to changing demands. Furthermore, AI-driven simulations can be used for training operators and maintenance personnel. By interacting with a realistic Digital Twin, individuals can gain hands-on experience with complex machinery and procedures, learning to respond to various scenarios, including emergencies, in a safe and controlled virtual environment. The emergence of generative AI further enhances these capabilities, as it can streamline the creation and deployment of

Digital Twins, making complex simulations more accessible and efficient (Kakkar et al., 2025).

In essence, AI-driven Digital Twins transform asset management from a reactive necessity into a strategic advantage. They provide the intelligence and foresight needed to maintain assets proactively, optimize their performance throughout their lifecycle, and innovate with greater speed and confidence.

Real-Time Monitoring and Optimization

Real-time monitoring and optimization are critical functions enabled by the synergy of Artificial Intelligence and Digital Twins, allowing businesses to maintain continuous oversight of their physical assets and processes, and to dynamically adjust operations for peak performance. This capability moves beyond mere data collection, transforming raw sensor data into actionable intelligence that drives immediate and continuous improvements.

At its core, real-time monitoring with AI-powered Digital Twins involves the continuous collection and analysis of data from physical assets. IoT sensors embedded in machinery, infrastructure, or even human operators, transmit vast quantities of data to the Digital Twin in real-time (Chinta, 2024). AI algorithms then process this incoming data stream, identifying patterns, anomalies, and deviations from expected behavior. This immediate analysis allows for the detection of potential issues, such as equipment malfunctions, performance degradation, or safety hazards, as they occur, rather than after they have led to significant problems. For example, in a smart factory, an AI-driven Digital Twin of a robotic arm can continuously monitor its joint temperatures and motor currents. If the AI detects a sudden spike or an unusual pattern, it can immediately alert operators to a potential bearing failure, allowing for proactive intervention before the arm breaks down and halts production.

Beyond simply alerting to problems, AI-driven Digital Twins are instrumental in real-time optimization. By understanding the current state of a physical system and predicting its future behavior, AI can suggest or even autonomously implement adjustments to optimize performance. This can involve fine-tuning operational parameters, re-routing processes, or dynamically allocating resources to maximize efficiency, reduce energy consumption, or improve product quality. For instance, in logistics, a Digital Twin of a warehouse can monitor inventory levels, order fulfillment rates, and forklift movements in real-time. AI can then analyze this data to optimize picking routes, reconfigure storage layouts, or even adjust the speed of automated guided vehicles (AGVs) to ensure the most efficient flow of goods (Augustine, 2020).

The optimization capabilities extend to complex systems where multiple variables interact. AI models, particularly those leveraging reinforcement learning, can learn optimal control strategies for dynamic environments. This allows Digital Twins to continuously adapt to changing conditions, such as fluctuating demand, material shortages, or equipment wear, ensuring that the physical system operates at its most efficient and effective state at all times. The ability to perform real-time monitoring and optimization is a significant leap forward from traditional, reactive approaches, enabling businesses to achieve unprecedented levels of operational excellence and resilience in the face of dynamic challenges.

Case Studies: Smart Manufacturing and Intelligent Supply Chains

The transformative power of AI-driven Digital Twins is best illustrated through their real-world applications in smart manufacturing and intelligent supply chains. These sectors, characterized by complex processes and vast networks, have significantly benefited from the ability of Digital Twins to provide real-time insights, enable predictive capabilities, and optimize operations.

Smart Manufacturing

In smart manufacturing, AI-driven Digital Twins are revolutionizing production processes, quality control, and maintenance. One prominent example is their application in production line optimization. Companies are creating Digital Twins of their entire manufacturing facilities, including machinery, robots, and production lines. These virtual replicas are fed with real-time data from sensors embedded in the physical equipment. AI algorithms then analyze this data to identify bottlenecks, predict equipment failures, and optimize production schedules. For instance, a Digital Twin can simulate various production scenarios, allowing manufacturers to test different configurations and workflows virtually before implementing them on the physical line, thereby minimizing downtime and maximizing throughput (Augustine, 2020). This approach has led to significant improvements in efficiency, reduced waste, and increased overall equipment effectiveness (OEE) (Ng Corrales et al., 2020).

Another critical application in smart manufacturing is quality control. Digital Twins, combined with computer vision AI, can monitor the manufacturing process in real-time, detecting defects or anomalies with high precision. For example, in the automotive industry, Digital Twins of car parts can be created and compared against real-time scans of newly manufactured parts. AI algorithms can instantly identify deviations from the design specifications, flagging defective parts and preventing them from moving further down the production line. This not only ensures higher product quality but also reduces rework and material waste.

Intelligent Supply Chains

The complexity and global nature of modern supply chains make them ideal candidates for AI driven Digital Twin implementation. According to (Boopathy et al., 2025) These virtual replicas provide end-to-end visibility and predictive capabilities, enabling more resilient and efficient supply chain management.

One key application is logistics and transportation optimization. Digital Twins of transportation networks, including vehicles, routes, and distribution centers, can be created. AI algorithms can then analyze real-time data on traffic conditions, weather, and delivery schedules to optimize routes, predict delays, and re-route shipments dynamically to avoid disruptions. This leads to faster delivery times, reduced fuel consumption, and improved customer satisfaction. For example, a logistics company might use a Digital Twin to simulate the impact of a sudden road closure on its delivery fleet, with AI suggesting alternative routes and re-allocating resources to minimize delays.

Inventory optimization is another significant area. Digital Twins of warehouses and inventory systems, integrated with AI, can provide real-time insights into stock levels, demand fluctuations, and supply chain disruptions. AI models can forecast demand with greater accuracy, optimize inventory placement, and even automate reordering processes. This helps companies maintain optimal stock levels, reduce carrying costs, and prevent stockouts, ensuring that products are available when and where they are needed. In the retail sector, for instance, a Digital Twin of a store's inventory can be used to predict which products will sell out fastest during a promotional event, allowing the store to proactively restock and avoid lost sales.

These case studies underscore the profound impact of AI-driven Digital Twins in transforming traditional manufacturing and supply chain operations into intelligent, adaptive, and highly efficient ecosystems. By providing a comprehensive, real-time view and predictive capabilities, they enable businesses to navigate complexities, mitigate risks, and seize new opportunities in the dynamic landscape of Industry 5.0 (Boopathy et al., 2025).

AI IN THE METAVERSE

The Metaverse, once a concept confined to science fiction, is rapidly evolving into a tangible digital frontier, especially within the industrial domain. When augmented by Artificial Intelligence, the Metaverse transforms into an immersive, intelligent, and highly interactive environment that redefines human-machine collaboration and business operations. This section explores the concept of the Industrial Metaverse, the role of AI in creating intelligent avatars and dynamic environments, and its cross-domain applications.

Concept and Characteristics of the Industrial Metaverse

The Metaverse, in its broadest sense, refers to a persistent, interconnected virtual space where users can interact with each other, digital objects, and AI-powered entities in a highly immersive manner. While popular discourse often associates the Metaverse with social media, gaming, and entertainment, its industrial counterpart, the Industrial Metaverse, is emerging as a critical component of Industry 5.0. The Industrial Metaverse is a significant branch of the broader Metaverse, specifically designed to enable collaborative control and global optimization of industrial systems through overall perception, digital modeling, and deep simulation (Kakkar et al., 2025).

Unlike the consumer-oriented Metaverse, based on (Kakkar et al., 2025; Otoum et al., 2024; Pang et al., 2025) which often prioritizes entertainment and social interaction, the Industrial Metaverse is characterized by its focus on practical applications that enhance productivity, efficiency, and safety in industrial settings. Its key features include:

Immersive Interaction

The Industrial Metaverse provides highly immersive environments where engineers, operators, and decision-makers can interact with virtual representations of physical assets and processes. This immersion, often facilitated by Augmented Reality (AR) and Virtual Reality (VR) technologies, allows for a more intuitive understanding of complex systems and fosters better collaboration.

Virtual-Real Interaction

A core characteristic is the seamless interaction between the virtual and real worlds. Data from physical systems (often via Digital Twins) is continuously fed into the Industrial Metaverse, ensuring that the virtual environment accurately reflects the real-time state of industrial operations. This bidirectional flow of information allows for virtual simulations to inform real-world actions and vice versa, enabling closed-loop optimization.

Human-Centric Approach

Aligned with the principles of Industry 5.0, the Industrial Metaverse emphasizes a human centric approach. It aims to augment human capabilities, facilitate better decision-making, and improve working conditions by providing intuitive interfaces and intelligent assistance. This includes enabling remote collaboration, virtual training, and expert guidance in complex industrial tasks.

Persistent and Interconnected

The Industrial Metaverse is a persistent environment, meaning that its state and data endure even when users are not actively present. It is also highly interconnected, allowing for the integration of various industrial systems, data sources, and applications. This interconnectedness fosters a holistic view of operations and enables cross-domain collaboration.

Data-Driven and AI-Powered

The Industrial Metaverse is inherently data-driven, relying on vast amounts of real-time and historical data from physical assets, sensors, and operational systems. Artificial Intelligence plays a crucial role in processing this data, generating dynamic environments, powering intelligent agents, and enabling advanced analytics for predictive insights and optimization.

In essence, the Industrial Metaverse is not just a virtual playground, it is a sophisticated digital ecosystem where AI, Digital Twins, and immersive technologies converge to create a powerful platform for industrial innovation, collaboration, and operational excellence. It represents a significant leap forward in how businesses manage their assets, optimize processes, and empower their workforce in the era of Industry 5.0.

Intelligent Avatars and Virtual Agents

Within the immersive landscapes of the Metaverse, Artificial Intelligence breathes life into digital entities, transforming static representations into dynamic, intelligent, and interactive avatars and virtual agents. These AI-powered entities are crucial for enhancing user experience, facilitating complex interactions, and providing scalable support within virtual environments.

Intelligent Avatars

Intelligent avatars are AI-powered digital representations of users or non-player characters (NPCs) within the Metaverse. Unlike traditional avatars that are merely visual representations, intelligent avatars are imbued with AI capabilities that allow them to understand, interpret, and respond to user interactions in a sophisticated manner. These capabilities are often driven by advanced Natural Language Processing (NLP) for conversational AI, computer vision for recognizing gestures and expressions, and machine learning for adapting to user preferences and behaviors (Charmet et al., 2022). For users, intelligent avatars can offer a more personalized and engaging experience, mirroring their real-world actions and even learning their communication styles. For businesses, AI-powered avatars can serve as virtual representatives, providing customer support, guiding users through virtual spaces, or even acting as virtual sales assistants, offering a new dimension of customer engagement.

Virtual Agents

Virtual agents, often distinct from user-controlled avatars, are AI-driven entities designed to perform specific tasks or provide services within the Metaverse. These agents can range from simple chatbots that answer frequently asked questions to highly sophisticated AI entities capable of managing complex simulations, facilitating collaborative work, or even generating dynamic content. For example, in an industrial Metaverse, a virtual agent might be programmed to monitor the performance of a Digital Twin, alerting human operators to anomalies or even initiating autonomous corrective actions (Schmidt et al., 2024). In a retail Metaverse, virtual agents could guide shoppers to relevant products, provide detailed product information, and assist with virtual transactions, offering a seamless and personalized shopping experience.

Several Key of AI Technologies

- Natural Language Understanding (NLU) and Generation (NLG): These NLP subfields enable avatars and agents to comprehend human language and generate coherent, contextually relevant responses, facilitating natural conversations.
- Computer Vision: Allows agents to 'see' and interpret the virtual environment, recognizing objects, understanding user gestures, and even discerning emotional cues from avatar expressions.
- Reinforcement Learning: Enables agents to learn optimal behaviors and interaction strategies through trial and error within the Metaverse, leading to more adaptive and intelligent responses.

- Behavioral AI: Focuses on modeling and simulating human-like behaviors, making avatars and agents more believable and engaging.

The presence of intelligent avatars and virtual agents significantly enriches the Metaverse experience, transforming it from a passive digital space into a vibrant, interactive ecosystem where AI plays an active role in shaping user interactions and delivering valuable services. They are essential for creating a truly immersive and functional Metaverse that can support a wide range of business applications, from customer service and training to complex operational management (Lyu & Fridenfalk, 2024).

Dynamic Environment Generation and Personalized Consumer Engagement

The true potential of the Metaverse lies in its ability to offer highly dynamic and personalized experiences, a feat largely achievable through the sophisticated application of Artificial Intelligence. AI enables the Metaverse to move beyond static, pre-designed environments, creating adaptive and responsive digital spaces that cater to individual user preferences and behaviors, thereby revolutionizing consumer engagement.

AI for Creating and Adapting Virtual Environments

Dynamic environment generation refers to the AI-driven capability of the Metaverse to create, modify, and adapt virtual spaces in real-time based on various factors, including user interactions, contextual data, and predefined rules. This is a significant departure from traditional virtual reality, where environments are typically static and pre-rendered. AI algorithms, particularly those leveraging generative models like Generative Adversarial Networks (GANs) and variational autoencoders (VAEs), can generate realistic and diverse virtual landscapes, architectural structures, and interactive objects on the fly (Ahmad et al., 2025). This allows for an ever-evolving Metaverse that can offer novel experiences and prevent user fatigue. For instance, in a virtual retail space, AI can dynamically reconfigure store layouts, product displays, or even the ambient atmosphere based on a user's browsing history, demographic information, or real-time emotional responses. This adaptability ensures that the virtual environment remains engaging and relevant to each individual.

Beyond initial generation, AI also plays a crucial role in adapting these environments. Machine learning models can analyze user navigation patterns, points of interest, and interaction frequencies to identify areas for optimization or enhancement. For example, if a particular section of a virtual exhibition is receiving high engagement, AI can dynamically expand or enrich that area with more content or interactive elements. Conversely, if an area is underutilized, AI can suggest modifications or even remove it to streamline the user experience. This continuous adaptation ensures that the Metaverse remains optimized for user engagement and business objectives (Reiners et al., 2021).

Behavioral Analytics for Personalized Experiences

The ability to personalize consumer engagement within the Metaverse is a key differentiator and a significant business opportunity. AI-driven behavioral analytics are at the forefront of this personalization. By collecting and analyzing vast amounts of data on user behavior within the Metaverse including movement patterns, interaction choices, communication styles, and even biometric data from haptic devices AI can construct detailed profiles of individual users (Asad & Otoum, 2024). These profiles go beyond traditional demographic data, capturing nuanced preferences, interests, and even emotional states.

With these rich behavioral insights, AI can tailor experiences to an unprecedented degree. In retail, this means offering highly relevant product recommendations, creating personalized virtual showrooms, or even deploying virtual sales assistants that communicate in a style preferred by the customer. In entertainment, AI can dynamically adjust storylines, character interactions, or game mechanics to match a user's playstyle and preferences. This level of personalization fosters a deeper connection between the user and the virtual environment, leading to increased engagement, loyalty, and conversion rates. Furthermore, AI can predict future user needs and proactively offer services or content, transforming the consumer journey from a passive experience into an active, co-created one (Nwasra et al., 2025). The ethical implications of collecting and utilizing such detailed behavioral data are significant and require careful consideration, emphasizing the need for transparent data practices and robust privacy safeguards.

In summary, AI's capacity for dynamic environment generation and personalized consumer engagement is transforming the Metaverse into a highly adaptive, responsive, and deeply personal digital realm. This capability unlocks new avenues for businesses to connect with their customers, deliver unique experiences, and drive innovation in the immersive digital economy.

Cross-Domain Applications of AI in the Metaverse

The transformative potential of AI in the Metaverse extends across a multitude of industries, offering innovative solutions and redefining traditional business models. By leveraging the immersive and interactive capabilities of the Metaverse, combined with AI's analytical and generative power, businesses are creating new avenues for engagement, training, and operational efficiency. This section explores key cross-domain applications in healthcare, retail, and urban planning.

Healthcare

The integration of AI within the Metaverse is revolutionizing healthcare delivery, training, and patient engagement. One significant application is in medical training and education. AI-powered Metaverse environments can create highly realistic and interactive simulations of human anatomy, surgical procedures, and medical emergencies. Medical students and practitioners can practice complex procedures in a risk-free virtual environment, receiving real-time feedback from AI-driven virtual mentors (Augustine, 2020). This allows for repeated practice, skill refinement, and exposure to rare medical conditions, significantly enhancing training outcomes. For instance, a digital twin of a patient's organ can be created within the Metaverse, allowing surgeons to plan and rehearse complex operations with unprecedented precision.

Beyond training, AI in the Metaverse is also being applied to hospital operations and patient care. Digital twins of entire hospitals can be created within the Metaverse, enabling administrators to simulate and optimize patient flow, resource allocation, and staffing levels. AI algorithms can analyze real-time data from these digital twins to identify bottlenecks, predict demand surges, and optimize operational strategies, leading to improved efficiency and better patient outcomes (Mystakidis, 2022). Furthermore, the Metaverse can facilitate remote consultations and telepresence, allowing patients to interact with AI powered virtual nurses or doctors for initial assessments, health monitoring, and even mental health support, especially in underserved areas.

Retail

The retail sector is undergoing a significant transformation with the advent of AI-powered Metaverse experiences, moving beyond traditional e-commerce to offer immersive and personalized shopping journeys. Virtual shopping experiences are a prime example, where AI creates dynamic and interactive virtual stores that mirror physical retail spaces or offer entirely new concepts. Customers can navigate these virtual environments using their avatars, browse products in 3D, and even 'try on' clothes or accessories virtually using AI-driven augmented reality features (Boopathy et al., 2025). AI analyzes customer behavior within these virtual stores, providing personalized recommendations, guiding shoppers to relevant products, and optimizing store layouts in real-time to enhance engagement and drive sales.

AI also plays a crucial role in supply chain optimization within the retail Metaverse. Digital twins of warehouses, logistics networks, and inventory systems can be integrated into the Metaverse, providing real-time visibility and predictive capabilities. AI algorithms can analyze data from these digital twins to forecast demand, optimize inventory levels, and manage logistics more efficiently, reducing costs and improving delivery times (Lowry et al., 2025). This allows retailers to respond quickly to market changes and consumer demands, ensuring product availability and minimizing waste.

Urban Planning and Smart Cities

AI-powered Digital Twins within the Metaverse are becoming indispensable tools for urban planners and city administrators in developing smart and sustainable cities. By creating comprehensive digital twins of urban environments including infrastructure, buildings, traffic systems, and public spaces AI can simulate various urban scenarios and predict their impact. For example, AI can analyze traffic patterns in a digital twin of a city to optimize traffic light timings, reduce congestion, and improve public transportation efficiency. Similarly, AI can simulate the impact of new construction projects on energy consumption, air quality, and urban heat islands, allowing planners to make data-driven decisions that promote sustainability (Politi et al., 2025).

Furthermore, the Metaverse provides an immersive platform for citizen engagement and disaster preparedness. Citizens can explore virtual replicas of their cities, provide feedback on urban development plans, and participate in virtual town halls, fostering greater transparency and collaboration. For disaster preparedness, AI-driven Digital Twins in the Metaverse can simulate natural disasters and their potential impact on urban infrastructure and populations. This allows emergency services to train for various scenarios, optimize response strategies, and identify vulnerable areas, ultimately improving resilience and minimizing damage (Jung et al., 2020).

These cross-domain applications highlight the versatility and profound impact of AI in enabling Digital Twins and the Metaverse to address complex challenges and create new opportunities across diverse industries, paving the way for a more intelligent, efficient, and immersive future.

STRATEGIC IMPLICATIONS

The convergence of Artificial Intelligence, Digital Twins, and the Metaverse is not merely a technological advancement; it is a profound strategic imperative that is reshaping business models, creating new revenue streams, and redefining competitive landscapes across industries. Organizations that effectively harness this triad will gain a significant advantage, while those that fail to adapt risk obsolescence in the rapidly evolving Industry 5.0 era.

Business Model Transformation and AI-Enabled Services

The integration of AI, Digital Twins, and the Metaverse fundamentally alters how businesses create, deliver, and capture value, leading to the emergence of entirely new business models and a proliferation of AI-enabled services. This transformation is characterized by a shift from product-centric to service-centric offerings, enhanced personalization, and the monetization of data and virtual experiences.

Digital Twin as-a-Service Models

One of the most significant transformations is the shift towards “as-a-service” models. Traditionally, businesses sold physical products. Now, with Digital Twins providing real-time performance data and AI enabling predictive capabilities, companies can offer their products as a service, charging based on usage, performance, or uptime. For example, an industrial equipment manufacturer can sell “machine uptime as a service” rather than just the machine itself. The AI-driven Digital Twin continuously monitors the machine's health, predicts maintenance needs, and optimizes its operation, ensuring maximum availability for the customer (Aheleroff et al., 2021). This creates a recurring revenue stream for the manufacturer and shifts the burden of maintenance from the customer, fostering a deeper, more continuous relationship.

Enhanced Personalization and Customization

Enhanced personalization and customization are also key drivers of new business models. In the Metaverse, AI-powered Digital Twins of products and services can be tailored to individual customer preferences in real-time. This allows for mass customization at an unprecedented scale, where products can be designed, simulated, and even manufactured based on unique customer specifications. For instance, in fashion, a customer could design a garment in the Metaverse, see a Digital Twin of themselves wearing it, and then have it custom-made. This level of personalization creates stronger customer loyalty and opens up new premium market segments (Asad & Otoum, 2024).

Monetization of Data and Virtual Experiences

The monetization of data and virtual experiences represents another significant shift. The vast amounts of data generated by Digital Twins and Metaverse interactions become a valuable asset. Businesses can leverage AI to analyze this data, extract insights, and offer data-driven services, such as market intelligence, predictive analytics for other businesses, or even anonymized behavioral insights. Furthermore, the Metaverse itself becomes a platform for new forms of commerce and entertainment. Virtual real estate, digital collectibles (NFTs), and immersive advertising are just a few examples of new revenue streams emerging from the Metaverse, all powered and optimized by AI (Nwasra et al., 2025).

Operational Efficiencies

Operational efficiencies enabled by the triad also contribute to business model transformation. By optimizing processes, reducing waste, and improving resource allocation through AI-driven Digital Twins and Metaverse simulations, businesses can achieve significant cost savings. These savings can then be reinvested into innovation, passed on to customers, or used to increase profit margins, making businesses more competitive and sustainable. The ability to simulate complex scenarios and test new strategies in a risk-free virtual environment allows for faster innovation cycles and more agile responses to market changes.

In essence, the AI-Metaverse-Twin triad is enabling businesses to move beyond traditional transactional models to create more dynamic, service-oriented, and customer-centric ecosystems. This strategic shift is not just about adopting new technologies; it's about fundamentally rethinking how value is created and delivered in the digital age, leading to sustainable growth and competitive differentiation (Lyu & Fridenfalk, 2024).

AI Governance, Accountability, and Ethics in Immersive Environments

As Artificial Intelligence increasingly permeates Digital Twins and the Metaverse, enabling unprecedented levels of data collection, analysis, and autonomous decision-making, critical questions of governance, accountability, and ethics come to the forefront. The immersive and pervasive nature of these environments amplifies existing ethical concerns related to AI, necessitating careful consideration and the development of robust frameworks to ensure responsible deployment.

Bias and Fairness

One of the most pressing ethical concerns is the potential for AI systems to perpetuate or even amplify existing societal biases. AI models are trained on vast datasets, and if these datasets reflect historical or systemic biases, the AI can learn and reproduce discriminatory outcomes. In the context of Digital Twins, biased AI could lead to unfair resource allocation, discriminatory predictive maintenance schedules, or even unsafe operational recommendations for certain demographics of users or assets. In the Metaverse, biased AI could manifest in discriminatory content moderation, unfair avatar representation, or personalized experiences that reinforce harmful stereotypes (Mmaduekwe, 2024). Ensuring fairness requires meticulous data curation, algorithmic transparency, and continuous auditing of AI systems to identify and mitigate biases.

Data Privacy and Security

The integration of Digital Twins and the Metaverse involves the collection and processing of immense volumes of highly sensitive data, including personal biometric data, behavioral patterns, and real-time operational information. This raises significant privacy concerns. Users in the Metaverse might unknowingly share intimate details through their interactions, while Digital Twins could expose proprietary industrial data or critical infrastructure vulnerabilities. Robust data governance frameworks, including strict data minimization principles, anonymization techniques, and secure data storage and transmission protocols, are essential to protect privacy(Md Sultanul Arefin Sourav et al., 2020). Furthermore, the interconnected nature of these environments creates new attack surfaces, making cybersecurity paramount to prevent data breaches, unauthorized access, and malicious manipulation of Digital Twins or Metaverse experiences (Rahaman, Cajes, Gupta, Chui, et al., 2025).

Accountability and Transparency

As AI systems become more autonomous and complex, determining accountability for their actions becomes challenging. If an AI-driven Digital Twin makes an erroneous decision that leads to a system failure, or if an AI agent in the Metaverse causes harm, who is responsible? Establishing clear lines of accountability requires transparency in AI design, development, and deployment. This includes providing explainable AI (XAI) capabilities, allowing stakeholders to understand how AI models arrive at their decisions (Srivastava et al., 2022). Regulatory bodies and industry standards are crucial for defining legal and ethical responsibilities, ensuring that organizations deploying these technologies are held accountable for their impact.

Digital Divide and Accessibility

The rapid advancement and adoption of AI-driven Digital Twins and the Metaverse also risk exacerbating the digital divide. Access to the necessary hardware, technical literacy, and computational resources can create a chasm between those who can participate in and benefit from these immersive environments and those who cannot (Mystakidis, 2022). Ethical considerations must include efforts to promote equitable access and ensure that these technologies are designed with inclusivity and accessibility in mind, preventing the creation of new forms of social and economic inequality (Jover & Sempere, 2025).

Ethical Guidelines and Regulation

To navigate these complex ethical landscapes, the development of comprehensive ethical guidelines and regulatory frameworks is imperative. These frameworks should address issues such as data ownership, consent, algorithmic bias, human oversight, and the potential for psychological impacts of prolonged immersion in virtual environments. International collaboration will be vital to establish consistent standards that can foster innovation while safeguarding fundamental human rights and societal well-being (Hamid & Rahman, 2025). Proactive engagement from governments, industry, academia, and civil society is necessary to shape a future where AI-driven Digital Twins and the Metaverse are developed and utilized responsibly, serving humanity's best interests in the Industry 5.0 era.

CHALLENGES AND FUTURE OUTLOOK

The transformative potential of Artificial Intelligence, Digital Twins, and the Metaverse in the context of Industry 5.0 is undeniable. However, the path to widespread adoption and seamless integration of these technologies is fraught with significant challenges. Addressing these hurdles is crucial for realizing the full promise of an intelligent, immersive, and sustainable industrial future. This section outlines the current challenges and explores emerging trends and future directions.

Current Challenges

The complexities inherent in the AI-Metaverse-Twin triad give rise to a variety of technical, data-related, and ethical challenges that demand innovative solutions and collaborative efforts.

Technical Challenges

- Scalability: Building and maintaining Digital Twins, especially for large-scale systems or entire cities, requires immense computational resources and infrastructure. Similarly, supporting a truly immersive and persistent Metaverse with millions of concurrent users demands unprecedented scalability in terms of processing power, network bandwidth, and data storage (Boopathy et al., 2025). Ensuring low-latency interactions and high-fidelity rendering across vast virtual environments remains a significant technical hurdle.
- Interoperability: The lack of standardized protocols and platforms for Digital Twins and Metaverse environments creates significant interoperability challenges. Different vendors and systems often use proprietary formats, making it difficult to seamlessly exchange data and integrate applications across diverse ecosystems. Achieving true interoperability is essential for creating a cohesive and interconnected industrial Metaverse where various Digital Twins can communicate and collaborate effectively.
- Computational Demands: The real-time processing of vast datasets from Digital Twins, coupled with the complex rendering and AI computations required for immersive Metaverse experiences, places enormous demands on computational power. While advancements in edge computing and specialized AI hardware are helping, the sheer scale of operations envisioned for Industry 5.0 still presents a formidable challenge.

Data-Related Issues

- Data Privacy and Security: As discussed in the ethical implications, the collection of highly sensitive operational and personal data by Digital Twins and Metaverse platforms poses significant privacy risks. Ensuring robust data encryption, access controls, and compliance with evolving data protection regulations GDPR & CCPA is paramount (Tanvir Rahman Akash et al., 2025). Moreover, the interconnected nature of these systems increases the attack surface for cyber threats, making comprehensive cybersecurity strategies essential to prevent data breaches and malicious attacks.

- Data Quality and Integrity: The reliability of AI models and the accuracy of Digital Twins heavily depend on the quality and integrity of the input data. Inconsistent, incomplete, or erroneous data can lead to flawed insights, inaccurate predictions, and suboptimal decisions. Establishing robust data governance frameworks, including data validation, cleansing, and provenance tracking, is crucial for maintaining data quality across the entire data lifecycle(Tanvir Rahman Akash et al., 2025).
- Data Ownership and Governance: As data flows between physical assets, Digital Twins, and Metaverse platforms, questions of data ownership, access rights, and governance become complex. Clear policies and legal frameworks are needed to define who owns the data generated by these systems, who has the right to access and use it, and how it should be managed and shared across different stakeholders (Tanvir Rahman Akash et al., 2025).

Ethical Concerns

Bias and Accountability: The potential for AI algorithms to perpetuate or amplify biases present in training data remains a critical ethical concern. Ensuring fairness, transparency, and accountability in AI decision-making within Digital Twins and the Metaverse requires continuous monitoring, auditing, and the development of explainable AI (XAI) techniques. Defining legal and ethical responsibility when autonomous AI systems make consequential decisions is an ongoing challenge (Srivastava et al., 2022).

Digital Divide and Accessibility

The high cost of entry for advanced hardware and infrastructure, coupled with the technical expertise required to navigate these complex environments, risks widening the digital divide. Ensuring equitable access and designing inclusive experiences are vital to prevent the exclusion of certain populations and to foster broad societal benefits.

Psychological and Societal Impacts

Prolonged immersion in highly realistic virtual environments can have psychological impacts, including issues related to identity, addiction, and the blurring of lines between the physical and virtual worlds. The societal implications, such as changes in human interaction, labor markets, and the nature of work, also require careful consideration and proactive planning (Cunningham, 2025).

Addressing these multifaceted challenges requires a concerted effort from researchers, industry leaders, policymakers, and civil society. Collaborative initiatives, open standards, and responsible innovation practices will be key to unlocking the full potential of the AI-Metaverse-Twin triad while mitigating its risks.

Emerging Trends and Future Directions

Despite the existing challenges, the fields of Artificial Intelligence, Digital Twins, and the Metaverse are evolving at an unprecedented pace, driven by continuous innovation and increasing investment. Several emerging trends are poised to shape the future trajectory of this powerful triad, promising even more sophisticated and impactful business applications.

Explainable AI (XAI) and Its Role in Trust and Transparency

As AI systems become more complex and autonomous, the need for transparency and interpretability becomes paramount, especially in critical applications like healthcare or industrial control. Explainable AI (XAI) is an emerging field focused on developing AI models whose decisions can be understood and interpreted by humans. In the context of Digital Twins, XAI can help engineers understand why an AI model predicted a specific equipment failure or recommended a particular optimization strategy. In the Metaverse, XAI can build trust by explaining how AI agents make decisions or how personalized content is generated. The future will see a greater emphasis on building inherently interpretable AI systems and developing tools that provide clear, concise explanations of AI behavior, fostering greater trust and facilitating regulatory compliance (Srivastava et al., 2022).

Federated Learning for Privacy-Preserving AI

The increasing concerns around data privacy and the need to leverage decentralized datasets are driving the adoption of Federated Learning. This approach allows AI models to be trained on data distributed across multiple devices or organizations without the data ever leaving its source. For Digital Twins, Federated Learning can enable collaborative AI model training across different factories or supply chain partners, leveraging diverse datasets while preserving data confidentiality. In the Metaverse, it can facilitate personalized experiences by training AI models on user data directly on their devices, enhancing privacy while still benefiting from collective intelligence. This trend will be crucial for scaling AI applications in privacy-sensitive domains (Tanvir Rahman Akash et al., 2025).

Quantum AI and Its Potential Impact

While still in its nascent stages, Quantum Computing holds immense promise for revolutionizing AI capabilities. Quantum AI, which leverages the principles of quantum mechanics to perform computations, could potentially solve problems that are intractable for classical computers, such as optimizing highly complex systems or simulating molecular interactions with unprecedented accuracy (Hamid & Rahman, 2025). For Digital Twins, quantum AI could enable more precise and faster simulations of complex physical phenomena, leading to more accurate predictions and optimizations. In the Metaverse, it could power hyper-realistic simulations, complex AI behaviors, and advanced cryptographic security. While practical applications are still some years away, quantum AI represents a long-term disruptive force that could unlock entirely new possibilities for the AI-Metaverse-Twin triad.

Human-Centric AI and the Evolution of Industry 5.0

The overarching theme of Industry 5.0 is the shift towards a human centric approach, where technology augments human capabilities rather than replacing them. This philosophy will increasingly guide the development of AI for Digital Twins and the Metaverse. Future AI systems will be designed to facilitate seamless human-machine collaboration, providing intelligent assistance, intuitive interfaces, and personalized support (Asad & Otoum, 2024). This includes AI that understands human intent, adapts to individual learning styles, and promotes well-being. The evolution of Industry 5.0 will see AI not just as a tool for automation, but as a partner in co-creation, enabling humans to focus on higher-value tasks, creativity, and critical decision-making, ultimately leading to more resilient, sustainable, and human flourishing industrial ecosystems (Kazim & Soares Koshiyama, 2020).

These emerging trends highlight a future where AI, Digital Twins, and the Metaverse become even more integrated, intelligent, and impactful. Addressing the current challenges while embracing these advancements will be key to unlocking the full potential of this transformative triad for business applications in Industry 5.0.

CONCLUSION

The convergence of Artificial Intelligence, Digital Twins, and the Metaverse represents a transformative force at the heart of Industry 5.0 one that emphasizes human-machine collaboration, sustainability, and intelligent automation. AI serves as the cognitive core, enabling real-time data fusion, predictive analytics, and immersive interactions that bring Digital Twins and Metaverse environments to life. From smart manufacturing and supply chains to healthcare and urban planning, this triad is reshaping industries through dynamic simulation, personalization, and optimized operations.

Looking ahead, the strategic integration of these technologies offers unprecedented opportunities for innovation, efficiency, and service-driven business models. Yet, their adoption must be grounded in responsible AI governance, ensuring fairness, transparency, and inclusivity. As we move toward more human-centric digital ecosystems, embracing AI with ethical foresight will be key to unlocking sustainable growth and meaningful transformation in the industries of tomorrow.

REFERENCES

Aheleroff, S., Xu, X., Zhong, R. Y., & Lu, Y. (2021). Digital Twin as a Service (DTaaS) in Industry 4.0: An Architecture Reference Model. *Advanced Engineering Informatics*, *47*, 101225. DOI: 10.1016/j.aei.2020.101225

Ahmad, Z., Jaffri, Z., Chen, M., & Bao, S. (2025). Understanding GANs: Fundamentals, variants, training challenges, applications, and open problems. *Multimedia Tools and Applications*, *84*(12), 10347–10423. DOI: 10.1007/s11042-024-19361-y

Ahmed, B. S., Azzalin, T., Kassler, A., Thore, A., & Lindbäck, H. (2025). Smart manufacturing: MLOps-enabled event-driven architecture for enhanced control in steel production. *Journal of Systems and Software*, *230*, 112542. DOI: 10.1016/j.jss.2025.112542

Akash, T. R., Sany, N. J., Akter, L., & Sarna, S. A. (2025). Privacy—Preserving Technique in cybersecurity: Balancing Data Protection and User Rights. *Journal of Computer Science and Technology Studies*, *7*(4), 248–263. DOI: 10.32996/jcsts.2025.7.3.90

Alfeo, A. L., Cimino, M. G. C. A., & Vaglini, G. (2022). Degradation stage classification via interpretable feature learning. *Journal of Manufacturing Systems*, *62*, 972–983. DOI: 10.1016/j.jmsy.2021.05.003

Asad, M., & Otoum, S. (2024). Federated Learning for Personalized User Experiences in the Metaverse. *2024 2nd International Conference on Intelligent Metaverse Technologies & Applications (iMETA)*, 050–055. DOI: 10.1109/iMETA62882.2024.10807979

Augustine, P. (2020). The industry use cases for the Digital Twin idea. In *Advances in Computers* (Vol. 117, Issue 1, pp. 79–105). DOI: 10.1016/bs.adcom.2019.10.008

Balogh, M., Földvári, A., & Varga, P. (2023). Digital Twins in Industry 5.0: Challenges in Modeling and Communication. *NOMS 2023-2023 IEEE/IFIP Network Operations and Management Symposium*, 1–6. DOI: 10.1109/NOMS56928.2023.10154424

Boopathy, P., Deepa, N., Maddikunta, P. K. R., Victor, N., Gadekallu, T. R., Yenduri, G., Wang, W., Pham, Q. V., Huynh-The, T., & Liyanage, M. (2025). The Metaverse for Industry 5.0 in NextG Communications: Potential Applications and Future Challenges. *IEEE Open Journal of the Computer Society*, *6*, 4–24. DOI: 10.1109/OJCS.2024.3497335

Charmet, F., Tanuwidjaja, H. C., Ayoubi, S., Gimenez, P. F., Han, Y., Jmila, H., Blanc, G., Takahashi, T., & Zhang, Z. (2022). Explainable artificial intelligence for cybersecurity: A literature survey. *Annales Des Telecommunications. Annales des Télécommunications*, *77*(11–12), 789–812. DOI: 10.1007/s12243-022-00926-7

Chinta, S. (2024). Edge AI for Real-Time Decision Making in IOT Networks. *International Journal of Innovative Research in Computer and Communication Engineering*, *12*(09), 11293–11309. DOI: 10.15680/IJIRCCE.2024.1209044

Correia, J. B., Abel, M., & Becker, K. (2023). Data management in digital twins: A systematic literature review. *Knowledge and Information Systems*, *65*(8), 3165–3196. DOI: 10.1007/s10115-023-01870-1

Cunningham, J. (2025). Painting in gray: The legal and ethical ambiguities of AI-generated art. *Journal of Information. Communication and Ethics in Society*, *23*(3), 384–391. DOI: 10.1108/JICES-01-2025-0011

Eneyew, D. D., Capretz, M. A. M., & Bitsuamlak, G. T. (2022). Toward Smart-Building Digital Twins: BIM and IoT Data Integration. *IEEE Access : Practical Innovations, Open Solutions*, *10*, 130487–130506. DOI: 10.1109/ACCESS.2022.3229370

Fan, Z., Diao, X., Zhang, Y., Liu, M., Chen, F., Huang, Z., & Yan, H. (2019). Analysis of residual stress in electrical penetration assembly based on a Fiber Bragg grating sensor. *Sensors (Basel)*, *19*(1), 18. DOI: 10.3390/s19010018 PMID: 30577580

Grieves, M., & Vickers, J. (2016). Digital twin: Mitigating unpredictable, undesirable emergent behavior in complex systems. In *Transdisciplinary Perspectives on Complex Systems: New Findings and Approaches* (pp. 85–113). Springer International Publishing. DOI: 10.1007/978-3-319-38756-7_4

Gupta, B. B., Gaurav, A., & Kumar Panigrahi, P. (2023). Analysis of security and privacy issues of information management of big data in B2B based healthcare systems. *Journal of Business Research*, *162*, 113859. DOI: 10.1016/j.jbusres.2023.113859

Habib, M. I., Muke, P. Z., & Machado, J. M. (2025). IoT-integrated smart toilet design for enhancing safety, precaution, and energy efficiency. *Journal of Building Pathology and Rehabilitation*, *10*(2), 109. Advance online publication. DOI: 10.1007/s41024-025-00618-4

Hailu, T., Mackay, L., Gajic, M., & Ferreira, J. A. (2016). From voltage stiff to voltage weak DC distribution grid: Opportunities and challenges. *2016 IEEE 2nd Annual Southern Power Electronics Conference, SPEC 2016*, 1–6. DOI: 10.1109/SPEC.2016.7846172

Hamid, I., & Rahman, M. M. H. (2025). AI, machine learning and deep learning in cyber risk management. *Discover Sustainability*, *6*(1), 389. Advance online publication. DOI: 10.1007/s43621-025-01012-3

He, Y., Guo, J., & Zheng, X. (2018). From Surveillance to Digital Twin: Challenges and Recent Advances of Signal Processing for Industrial Internet of Things. *IEEE Signal Processing Magazine*, *35*(5), 120–129. DOI: 10.1109/MSP.2018.2842228

Jover, V., & Sempere, S. (2025). Creating Digital Twins to Celebrate Commemorative Events in the Metaverse. *Computers*, *14*(7), 273. DOI: 10.3390/computers14070273

Jung, D., Tran Tuan, V., Quoc Tran, D., Park, M., & Park, S. (2020). Conceptual Framework of an Intelligent Decision Support System for Smart City Disaster Management. *Applied Sciences (Basel, Switzerland)*, *10*(2), 666. DOI: 10.3390/app10020666

Kakkar, P., Mittal, S., Ulaganathan, S., Kannadasan, T., & Kanuparthi, S. L. (2025). Advancing the Metaverse: The Convergence of Digital Twins, AI, and Emerging Technologies. *2025 International Conference on Advanced Computing Technologies (ICoACT)*, 01–06. DOI: 10.1109/ICoACT63339.2025.11004721

Kazim, E., & Soares Koshiyama, A. (2020). Human Centric AI: A Comment on the IEEE's Ethically Aligned Design. SSRN *Electronic Journal*. DOI: 10.2139/ssrn.3575140

Kuo, H. A., Hong, T. Y., & Chien, C. F. (2025). A deep reinforcement learning based digital twin framework for resilient production planning under demand uncertainty and an empirical study in semiconductor wafer fabrication. *Computers & Industrial Engineering*, *208*, 111389. DOI: 10.1016/j.cie.2025.111389

Langås, E. F., Zafar, M. H., & Sanfilippo, F. (2025). Exploring the synergy of human-robot teaming, digital twins, and machine learning in Industry 5.0: A step towards sustainable manufacturing. *Journal of Intelligent Manufacturing*. Advance online publication. DOI: 10.1007/s10845-025-02580-x

Lee, J., Bagheri, B., & Kao, H. A. (2015). A Cyber-Physical Systems architecture for Industry 4.0-based manufacturing systems. *Manufacturing Letters*, *3*, 18–23. DOI: 10.1016/j.mfglet.2014.12.001

Leveraging, AI and Machine Learning for Enhanced Data Analytics and Visualization in Database Management With Digital Twins. (2025). *Journal of Database Management361*DOI: 10.4018/JDM.388135

Li, S., Yang, Y., Han, C., Sun, Y., Attar, R. W., & Gupta, B. B. (2025). Addressing consumer needs: Effects of firms remediation strategies on satisfaction and brand usage intent in AI-powered voice assistant service failures. *International Journal of Information Management*, *85*, 102951. DOI: 10.1016/j.ijinfomgt.2025.102951

Lowry, P. B., Boh, W. F., Petter, S., & Leimeister, J. M. (2025). Long Live the Metaverse: Identifying the Potential for Market Disruption and Future Research. *Journal of Management Information Systems*, *42*(1), 3–38. DOI: 10.1080/07421222.2025.2455770

Lyu, Z., & Fridenfalk, M. (2024). Digital twins for building industrial metaverse. *Journal of Advanced Research*, *66*, 31–38. DOI: 10.1016/j.jare.2023.11.019 PMID: 38008176

Mmaduekwe, U. (2024). Bias and Fairness Issues in Artificial Intelligence-driven Cybersecurity. *Current Journal of Applied Science and Technology*, *43*(6), 109–119. DOI: 10.9734/cjast/2024/v43i64391

Moslehpour, M., Dwikesumasari, P. R., Pappachan, P., Lin, P.-K., Sakina, N., & Rahaman, M. (2024). Incorporating Web Semantics, the Technology Acceptance Model, and the Theory of Planned Behavior for Analyzing User Intentions on Dating Apps. [IJSWIS]. *International Journal on Semantic Web and Information Systems*, *20*(1), 1–20. DOI: 10.4018/IJSWIS.356388

Mystakidis, S. (2022). Metaverse. *Encyclopedia*, *2*(1), 486–497. DOI: 10.3390/encyclopedia2010031

Ng Corrales, L., Lambán, M. P., Hernandez Korner, M. E., & Royo, J. (2020). Overall Equipment Effectiveness: Systematic Literature Review and Overview of Different Approaches. *Applied Sciences (Basel, Switzerland)*, *10*(18), 6469. DOI: 10.3390/app10186469

Nwasra, N., Omar, K., & Qaisar, Z. H. (2025). The Role of AI in Predictive UX Shaping the Future of Metaverse Interactions. *2025 1st International Conference on Computational Intelligence Approaches and Applications (ICCIAA)*, 1–8. DOI: 10.1109/ICCIAA65327.2025.11013689

Omoniwa, B., Hussain, R., Javed, M. A., Bouk, S. H., & Malik, S. A. (2019). Fog/edge computing-based IoT (FECIoT): Architecture, applications, and research issues. *IEEE Internet of Things Journal*, *6*(3), 4118–4149. DOI: 10.1109/JIOT.2018.2875544

Otoum, Y., Gottimukkala, N., Kumar, N., & Nayak, A. (2024). Machine Learning in Metaverse Security: Current Solutions and Future Challenges. *ACM Computing Surveys*, *56*(8), 1–36. DOI: 10.1145/3654663

ÖZKAL. İ., & BAŞÇİFTÇİ, F. (2024). *Deep Learning in the Metaverse: A Systematic Literature Review and Future Perspectives*. DOI: 10.2139/ssrn.5022041

Pang, J., Zheng, P., Fan, J., & Liu, T. (2025). Towards cognition-augmented human-centric assembly: A visual computation perspective. *Robotics and Computer-integrated Manufacturing*, *91*, 102852. DOI: 10.1016/j.rcim.2024.102852

Politi, T., Denazis, S., Koufopavlou, O., Antonopoulos, C., Faliagka, E., Prevedourou, D., Kostis, N., Tranoris, C., Voros, N., Christophorou, C., Ioannou, I., Vassiliou, V., Ioannou, I., & Nikiforidis, M. (2025). *Exploiting Digital Twins and Metaverse Technologies for the Digital Transformation of City Transportation*., DOI: 10.1007/978-3-031-82818-8_63

Rahaman, M., Cajes, N., Gupta, B. B., Chui, K. T., & Nedjah, N. (2025). Defending against smishing attacks: State-of-the-art techniques, challenges, limitations, and future directions. *Computer Networks*, *273*, 111758. DOI: 10.1016/j.comnet.2025.111758

Rahaman, M., Cajes, N., Gupta, B. B., Nedjah, N., & Chui, K. T. (2025). Real-Time Machine Learning Techniques in Robotics for Detecting Phishing Attacks. *2025 IEEE International Conference on Real-Time Computing and Robotics (RCAR)*, 1124–1129. DOI: 10.1109/RCAR65431.2025.11139819

Rahaman, M., Lin, C. Y., Rachmat, I., Bansal, R., & Prayitno. (2024). Secure Health Features: Implementing Hyperledger Fabric in Blockchain-Driven Healthcare Management Systems. In *Digital Forensics and Cyber Crime Investigation*. CRC Press.

Rajamurugu, N., & Karthik, M. K. (2022). Introduction, History, and Concept of Digital Twin. In *Digital Twin Technology* (pp. 19–32). Wiley., DOI: 10.1002/9781119842316.ch2

Reiners, D., Davahli, M. R., Karwowski, W., & Cruz-Neira, C. (2021). The Combination of Artificial Intelligence and Extended Reality: A Systematic Review. *Frontiers in Virtual Reality*, *2*, 721933. Advance online publication. DOI: 10.3389/frvir.2021.721933

Schmidt, S., Köysürenbars, I., & Steinicke, F. (2024). Frankenstein's Monster in the Metaverse: User Interaction With Customized Virtual Agents. *IEEE Transactions on Visualization and Computer Graphics*, *30*(11), 7162–7171. DOI: 10.1109/TVCG.2024.3456205 PMID: 39255104

Sekti, B. A. (2026a). Cybersecurity Challenges in Smart City Development. *Cybersecurity Challenges in Smart City Development*, *75–77*, 75–102. Advance online publication. DOI: 10.4018/979-8-3373-3326-7.ch003

Sekti, B. A. (2026b). *Machine Learning and Artificial Intelligence (AI) in Manufacturing*. 255–257. DOI: 10.4018/979-8-3373-1082-4.ch011

Singh, T., Gupta, S., Satakshi, , & Kumar, M. (2022). Performance Analysis and Deployment of Partitioning Strategies in Apache Spark. *Procedia Computer Science, 218*, 594–603. DOI: 10.1016/j.procs.2023.01.041

Srivastava, G., Jhaveri, R. H., Bhattacharya, S., Pandya, S., Rajeswari, Maddikunta, P. K. R., Yenduri, G., Hall, J. G., Alazab, M., & Gadekallu, T. R. (2022). *XAI for Cybersecurity: State of the Art, Challenges, Open Issues and Future Directions.*

Sumon, R. I., Uddin, S. M. I., Akter, S., Mozumder, M. A. I., Khan, M. O., & Kim, H. C. (2024). Natural Language Processing Influence on Digital Socialization and Linguistic Interactions in the Integration of the Metaverse in Regular Social Life. *Electronics (Basel), 13*(7), 1331. DOI: 10.3390/electronics13071331

Swarnakar, S., Banerjee, C., Basu, J., & Saha, D. (2023). A Multi-Agent-Based VM Migration for Dynamic Load Balancing in Cloud Computing Cloud Environment. [IJCAC]. *International Journal of Cloud Applications and Computing, 13*(1), 1–14. DOI: 10.4018/IJCAC.320479

Taj, I., & Zaman, N. (2022). Towards Industrial Revolution 5.0 and Explainable Artificial Intelligence: Challenges and Opportunities. *International Journal of Computing and Digital Systems, 12*(1), 285–310. DOI: 10.12785/ijcds/120124

Tang, H., Cheng, M., Bhatti, U. A., Xu, B., Zhou, N., Guo, R., & Wei, B. (2025). Digital twin-driven reinforcement learning-based operational management for customized manufacturing. *Engineering Applications of Artificial Intelligence, 159*, 111754. DOI: 10.1016/j.engappai.2025.111754

Wang, X., Li, J., Ning, Z., Song, Q., Guo, L., Guo, S., & Obaidat, M. S. (2023). Wireless Powered Mobile Edge Computing Networks: A Survey. *ACM Computing Surveys, 55*(13s), 1–37. Advance online publication. DOI: 10.1145/3579992

Yan, R., Peng, L., Bin, G., Wang, S., & Cheng, Y. (2017). Residual Recurrent Neural Network with Sparse Training for Offline Arabic Handwriting Recognition. *Proceedings of the International Conference on Document Analysis and Recognition, ICDAR, 1*, 1031–1037. DOI: 10.1109/ICDAR.2017.171

Chapter 3
Virtual Reality and Augmented Reality for Business Transformation

Reyisha Bulan Dewi
http://orcid.org/0009-0000-6630-6633
Universitas Esa Unggul, Indonesia

Varsha Arya
Hong Kong Metropolitan University, Hong Kong

Vinsens Aji Pamungkas
http://orcid.org/0009-0003-3036-0699
Universitas Esa Unggul, Indonesia

Najmin Sultana
Manipal Academy of Higher Education, India

Binastya Anggara Sekti
http://orcid.org/0000-0001-5489-4888
Universitas Esa Unggul, Indonesia

Thanaporn Phattanaviroj
Asia University, Taiwan

ABSTRACT

This chapter examines the strategic transformation of immersive technologies, focusing on their integration with artificial intelligence, digital twins, extended reality, and blockchain. It highlights how these technologies reshape value creation, delivery, and capture across sectors such as healthcare, education, manufacturing, and retail. The discussion covers infrastructure requirements, organizational readiness, and user experience, while also addressing challenges like cost, regulation, and digital accessibility. Emphasis is placed on the rise of the metaverse and decentralized platforms, where users engage with virtual assets and services in new economic models. By analyzing both opportunities and barriers, the chapter underscores the need for inclusive design, ethical data use, and cross-sector collaboration. Ultimately, immersive technology is presented not merely as a tool, but as a driver of long-term innovation, organizational adaptability, and sustainable digital transformation.

DOI: 10.4018/979-8-2600-0013-7.ch003

1. INTRODUCTION

1.1 Background

Digital Digital transformation has become a strategic imperative for organizations across various industrial sectors. Amid the accelerating development of information technology, immersive technologies encompassing Virtual Reality (VR), Augmented Reality (AR), and Mixed Reality (MR) have evolved from mere visualization tools into strategic platforms that transform how organizations interact with customers, manage operations, and create added value (Walentek & Ziora, 2023). These technologies enable the creation of interactive, contextual, and personalized digital experiences that not only enhance user engagement but also unlock new business models based on experiential value (Kumar et al., 2024).

According to recent industry reports, the global Extended Reality (XR) technology market is projected to grow with a compound annual growth rate (CAGR) of 30 percent through 2030. However, adoption rates among small and medium-sized enterprises remain relatively low, with only approximately 20 percent having integrated XR into their core operations. The main barriers include high initial investment costs, lack of technology standardization, limited digital infrastructure, and uncertainty regarding short-term return on investment (ROI), creating a gap between technological potential and practical implementation.

The paradigm has shifted from passive interface design to holistic and multi-dimensional interaction ecosystems. The integration of artificial intelligence with AR and VR emphasizes user-centered principles, real-time responsiveness, and multimodal fusion to reduce cognitive load while improving experience quality (Cao, 2025). Applications now extend beyond visualization to accelerate learning processes, support visual-based decision making, and strengthen brand presence through innovative digital media, enabling users to feel and interact with products or services in realistic simulation environments before making purchasing or investment decisions.

The banking and financial sector has begun adopting AR for virtual branches that allow three-dimensional account information interaction, while VR supports employee training in complex customer service simulations. Insurance companies explore MR for remote claim verification through direct visual assessment, improving operational efficiency while building stronger trust in digital services (Zhou et al., 2025).

Immersive technology overcomes spatial and geographical barriers effectively. Individuals can access workspaces, training centers, or project sites without physical presence, which is highly relevant for remote work and multinational team management. In construction and architecture, MR enables collaborative design review across different locations, reducing communication errors and accelerating validation processes (Panda et al., 2024).

1.2 The Role of Immersive Technology in Human Resource Development

Human resource development and training benefit significantly from experience-based learning enabled by immersive technology (Singh et al., 2024). VR-based simulation training provides realistic practice environments without real risks, with research demonstrating that these technologies offer interactive experiences enhancing engagement and supporting pedagogical goals (Hamash et al., 2025). Evidence shows VR-based training increases knowledge retention by 70-80% compared to 20-30% in traditional classroom settings, while reducing time-to-competency by 40-60% (Abro et al., 2025).

In healthcare, AR provides real-time visual guidance during medical procedures, increasing precision while reducing pressure in critical decision-making. Manufacturing and automotive industries utilize MR to display step-by-step maintenance instructions directly on physical equipment, minimizing training time, operational errors, and improving workplace safety. When integrated with Internet of Things (IoT) sensors, MR interfaces create connected work ecosystems where real-time data merges with 3D visualization to enhance field operation response times.

1.3 Marketing Transformation and Customer Engagement

Immersive technology has redefined brand-consumer communication channels. Means-end chain theory applied to AR marketing reveals that specific features (contextualization, interactivity, and portability) drive tangible benefits including inspiration, better decision-making, time savings, and risk reduction, ultimately contributing to higher-order values such as self-confidence, self-expression, and reduced purchase regret (Kumar et al., 2024).

Engagement has evolved beyond advertising or social media into full virtual experiences such as 3D showrooms, interactive product catalogs, and real-world usage simulations. This builds stronger brand narratives by allowing consumers to feel and experience products through digital interaction. Systems now customize visual content, narratives, and experiences according to individual preferences based on past interactions, deepening emotional connections and opening new opportunities for loyalty programs and retention strategies.

1.4 Challenges in Immersive Technology Adoption

Successful adoption depends heavily on organizational readiness encompassing technological preparation, organizational culture, and managerial support for digital transformation initiatives. Companies developing VR and AR solutions for specialized industries face unique challenges in designing viable business models, requiring careful navigation of value creation, delivery mechanisms, and revenue capture strategies specific to their target segments (Kulkov et al., 2021). Research on business model design identifies critical elements defining how organizations create customer value in regulated, high-stakes environments.

Regulatory and ethical considerations have become central to development and implementation. In VR environments or the metaverse, user identities can be easily manipulated and behavioral data extensively recorded, raising new challenges in data privacy and security. Organizations must establish internal policies and collaborate with regulators to ensure ethical and responsible technology use (Gupta et al., 2023).

Sustainability presents another concern. While immersive technology offers efficiency potential, energy consumption from devices such as VR headsets and servers supporting digital environments remains challenging. Innovations in energy efficiency, environmentally friendly materials, and electronic waste management must become key elements in future development (Phattanaviroj et al., 2026).

1.5 Objectives and Scope of Discussion

Immersive technology adoption should be recognized not as an end goal but as a tool to achieve broader transformation. Within Industry 5.0 and the smart economy framework, this technology must empower humans, improve quality of life, and build systems adaptive to global change. The integration of AI with immersive technologies creates new possibilities for responsive, adaptive systems that personalize experiences in real-time while maintaining user-centered design principles (Cao, 2025). True success lies in delivering real value in efficiency, innovation, and meaningful human experience.

This book comprehensively discusses how immersive technology transforms business models, enhances customer experiences, and drives organizational transformation across various sectors. Coverage includes technological foundations supporting VR, AR, and MR; business model changes through experience-based value creation; sectoral case studies demonstrating practical applications; factors influencing organizational adoption; and future strategic directions involving integration with artificial intelligence, blockchain, and the metaverse economy (Rahaman, Pappachan, et al., 2025).

By understanding existing potential and challenges, organizations can make more informed strategic decisions in leveraging immersive technology as part of digital transformation efforts, focusing on efficiency, innovation, and sustainable long-term value creation. Table 1.1 provides a comprehensive overview of immersive technology applications across key sectors, illustrating diverse practical implementations and benefits achievable through strategic adoption of VR, AR, and MR technologies.

Table 1. Immersive Technology Applications Across Key Industry Sectors

Sector	Technology	Application	Key Benefits
Banking & Finance	AR	Virtual branches, 3D account visualization	Enhanced customer interaction and engagement
Banking & Finance	VR	Employee training in customer service simulations	Improved service quality and preparedness
Insurance	MR	Remote claim verification and assessment	Increased operational efficiency and customer trust
Healthcare	AR	Real-time surgical guidance during procedures	Enhanced precision and reduced decision pressure
Manufacturing	MR	Step-by-step maintenance instructions overlay	Reduced training time and operational errors
Automotive	MR	Technical support with visual overlays	Improved workplace safety and efficiency
Construction & Architecture	MR	Collaborative design review across locations	Minimized communication errors and faster validation
Marketing & Retail	VR/AR	3D showrooms and interactive product catalogs	Deeper brand engagement and personalized experiences

Having established the foundational understanding of immersive technology and its transformative potential across industries, the next chapter will examine business model transformations through immersive experiences.

2. BUSINESS MODEL TRANSFORMATIONS THROGH IMMERSIVE EXPERIENCES

The advancement of immersive technologies such as Virtual Reality (VR), Augmented Reality (AR), and Extended Reality (XR) has significantly impacted business model changes across various industry sectors. These technologies not only offer new ways of delivering products and services to customers but also fundamentally transform how companies design value, deliver it to users, and capture economic benefits from these activities. This chapter discusses how immersive experiences contribute to structural changes in the three main components of business models:

value creation, value delivery, and value capture. The discussion is complemented by quantitative data and performance metrics that demonstrate the real impact of immersive technology implementation.

2.1 Value Creation

2.1.1 Transformation From Closed to Collaborative Models

In traditional business models, value creation typically occurs within closed systems with full control held by the company. Value is designed internally by product or service development teams and then released to the market as a final result. However, the emergence of immersive technologies has redefined this concept by shifting the paradigm toward more open, collaborative, and experience-based value creation models.

One of the most significant transformations can be seen in the use of digital prototyping during product development processes. Using VR or AR, companies can design, visualize, and test digital prototypes in real-time without needing to create physical versions first. This process accelerates design iterations and reduces experimentation costs, which are relatively high under conventional models .

2.1.2 Quantitative Impact of Digital Prototyping

Industry data shows that the implementation of digital prototyping using VR/AR technologies yields measurable efficiency improvements. AR technology has emerged as a key enabler for the digitization of industrial business processes, particularly in product configuration management and assembly assistance, demonstrating its capability as a digital transformation technology along the product lifecycle (Bellalouna, 2021). Studies in the automotive manufacturing sector demonstrate reductions in product development cycle time of up to 30-40%, with physical prototyping cost reductions of 50-65%. Companies like Ford Motor Company report design cost savings of $8 million per year after adopting VR for design and product review processes.

In the architecture and construction industry, the integration of Building Information Modeling (BIM) with VR technologies revolutionizes collaboration between architects, engineers, and builders, streamlining information flow and enhancing visualization capabilities throughout the entire project lifecycle (Abrantes Baracho et al., 2025). The use of AR for project visualization reduces design errors by 25-35%, directly impacting reductions in rework costs and project delays. Data from global construction companies indicate that implementing immersive technologies in the planning phase reduces average cost overruns by 15-20%.

Figure 1. Digital prototyping efficiency improvements

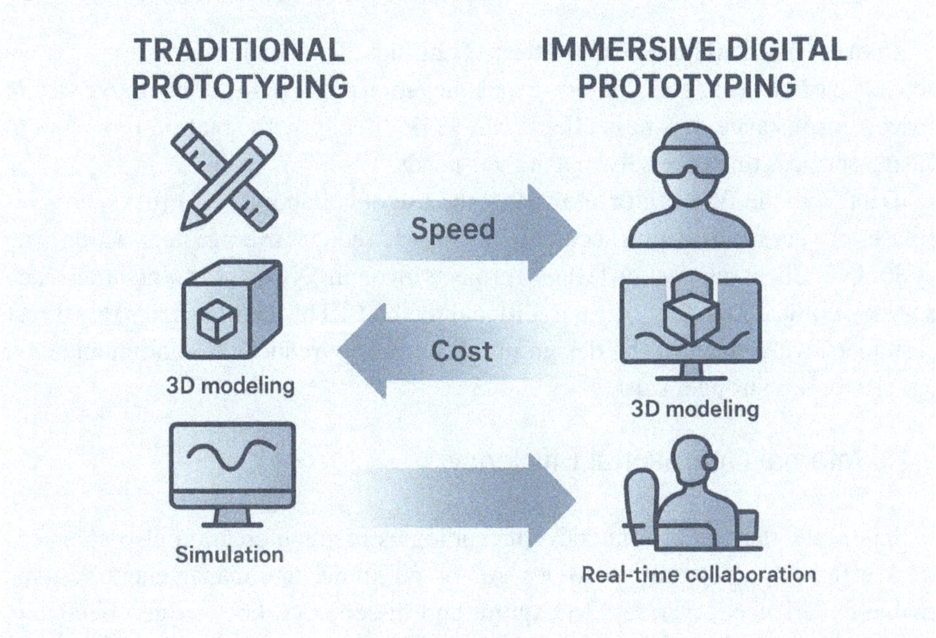

2.1.3 Personalization and Customer Engagement

The use of AR and VR opens new opportunities for product personalization. In this approach, customers do not merely observe products but experience them in their own context. Research on immersive media effectiveness demonstrates that AR outperforms VR when rational appeals are used, whereas VR proves more effective with emotional appeals, with product involvement moderating the matching effect between immersive media types and advertising appeals (Wu et al., 2025). For example, in the retail sector, users can virtually try on clothes or redesign their home interiors through AR simulations.

Customer engagement metrics show significant results. Fashion retailers implementing virtual try-on experience conversion rate increases of 40-60% compared to traditional browsing methods. Product return rates decrease by 35-40% as customers gain better product understanding before purchase. Furniture companies like IKEA report that their AR app users have 70% higher satisfaction levels and 3 times greater purchase probability compared to non-AR users.

2.1.4 Co-Creation and Virtual Collaboration

Immersive technologies expand the possibilities of co-creation, where customers actively participate as contributors in the innovation process. In collaborative virtual spaces, for instance, business clients can work directly with solution providers to design services that precisely match their needs.

Data from the B2B sector shows that the use of collaborative virtual spaces increases project specification accuracy by 45% and reduces average negotiation time by 30-35%. Client satisfaction levels in projects involving XR-based co-creation reach 85-90%, compared to 65-70% in traditional methods. This demonstrates that direct customer involvement in the design process not only reduces miscommunication but also builds stronger trust.

2.1.5 Internal Operational Efficiency

Internally, the use of immersive technologies in value creation also enhances work efficiency and team creativity. AR-based knowledge management systems enable experienced operators to capture and disseminate knowledge effectively, addressing the challenge of knowledge loss due to workforce retirement while providing maximum user friendliness for employee training (Sarhan et al., 2024). VR environments enable cross-departmental and cross-border collaboration without physical limitations. Design, engineering, and marketing teams can gather in shared virtual spaces to brainstorm, present, or test concepts collectively.

Case studies of multinational technology companies show that the use of virtual collaboration tools reduces time-to-market by 20-30%. Business travel costs for team meetings decrease by 40-50%, while collaboration frequency increases by 60-70%. Team productivity in the ideation phase improves by 35% when using virtual brainstorming environments compared to conventional methods.

2.1.6 Simulation-Based Decision Making

Immersive technologies help organizations visualize the impact of strategic decisions more concretely. The integration of VR with BIM enables immersive simulations that facilitate deeper understanding of architectural designs throughout the entire project lifecycle, allowing teams to identify and address design issues during early phases before construction begins (Abrantes Baracho et al., 2025). In construction project planning, for example, teams can explore 3D architectural models in simulation and evaluate potential problems or opportunities before the project begins.

Data shows that the use of 3D simulation in decision-making reduces strategic error risks by 40-45%. In the oil and gas industry, VR simulation for operational planning reduces unplanned downtime by 25-30% and increases safety compliance by up to 50%. ROI from simulation technology investments for decision-making reaches 200-300% within a 2-3 year period.

These developments show that value creation is no longer a one-way process but a dynamic one involving multi-stakeholder interaction and experience-based decision-making. Immersive technologies enable companies to create value not only through physical products but also through digital experiences shaped in collaboration with users.

2.2 Value Delivery

2.2.1 Evolution of Customer Interaction

The way value is delivered in modern business has evolved significantly, particularly with the emergence of immersive technologies such as AR and VR. This shift is clearly reflected in how interactions between companies and customers are now built. Previously, these relationships were often unidirectional and limited, but they have now become more open, interactive, and personalized to individual needs.

Through interactive virtual platforms, customers can now access digital stores, browse product selections, try features firsthand, and even make purchases without physical presence. These experiences are enriched with three-dimensional visualization and real-life usage simulations, which not only enhance engagement but also strengthen trust in the offered products.

2.2.2 Immersive E-Commerce Performance Metrics

The implementation of immersive commerce shows measurable results in improving business performance. Research on AR marketing applications in e-commerce demonstrates that AR features, particularly vividness and informativeness, significantly influence consumer perceptions and experiences, with perceived enjoyment and hedonic value significantly influencing consumer satisfaction and attitudes toward AR-enhanced platforms (Ngo et al., 2025). Retailers adopting AR/VR in their e-commerce platforms report increases in average order value of 30-40%. Browsing session duration increases 2-3 times, indicating higher engagement.

Conversion rates rise significantly, with average increases of 25-35% compared to conventional e-commerce platforms.

Data from the furniture and home decor sector shows that customer confidence scores increase by 60-70% when using AR placement tools. This directly impacts cart abandonment rate reductions of 20-30%. Studies on fashion virtual try-on platforms show that 65% of users who try AR features make purchases within 24 hours, compared to only 25% of non-AR users.

2.2.3 After-Sales Service Efficiency

XR applications provide significant added value in after-sales services. Companies no longer need to rely entirely on technicians or physical service centers. Using AR, they can deliver visual instructions directly to users' devices, such as installation guides, simple repairs, or routine maintenance steps.

Operational data shows substantial impact. Technology companies implementing AR-guided support reduce average resolution time by 45-55%. First-call resolution rates increase from 50-60% to 75-85%. Customer service operational costs decrease by 30-40% due to reduced needs for field technician visits. Customer satisfaction scores for AR-assisted support reach 88-92%, compared to 70-75% for traditional methods.

2.2.4 Product Training Effectiveness

In terms of product education, immersive experiences prove far more effective than traditional approaches. Companies can embed training materials in VR simulations that can be accessed anytime, allowing users to learn how to operate products in safe and interactive digital environments.

Studies in the industrial equipment sector show that VR-based training increases knowledge retention by 70-80% compared to 20-30% in traditional classroom training. Training time is reduced by 40-50%, while competency scores increase by 35-40%. Error rates in using complex equipment drop by 50-60% after implementing VR training. Training costs per employee decrease by 30-35% when using VR compared to conventional methods requiring instructors, travel, and physical equipment.

2.2.5 B2B Sales Process Transformation

In the business-to-business (B2B) sector, this approach opens new opportunities in product demonstration and negotiation processes. Instead of sending physical prototypes, companies can invite clients to test product simulations virtually, allowing them to assess functionality and benefits in specific contexts.

B2B sales metrics show impressive results. Sales cycles are reduced by 25-35% when using virtual product demonstrations. Conversion rates from virtual demos reach 45-55%, compared to 30-35% for traditional physical demos. Cost per demo drops by 60-70% due to elimination of travel costs, prototype shipping, and physical setup. Win rates on deals involving immersive demos increase by 20-25% compared to conventional methods.

2.2.6 Data-Driven Insights and Optimization

Beyond the user experience itself, immersive technologies in value delivery also generate valuable new data. AR technology applications in warehouse systems demonstrate the potential for increasing service quality levels and optimizing logistics processes through enhanced visual perception of the physical environment, enabling data-driven performance improvements (Živičnjak et al., 2025). Every user interaction such as the most viewed product areas, interaction durations, or responses to specific features can be recorded and analyzed.

Analytics from immersive platforms provide insights unavailable on traditional channels. Heat mapping in virtual stores identifies optimal product placement, increasing sales density by 25-30%. Behavioral data from AR try-on sessions yields product recommendation accuracy of 75-85%, compared to 50-60% for traditional algorithms. A/B testing in virtual environments can be conducted 5-10 times faster than in physical retail, accelerating merchandising and user experience optimization.

2.2.7 Resilience and Market Reach

Value delivery through XR provides businesses with flexibility to adapt to external changes. In situations where physical interaction is limited, immersive services can still operate without disruption. This makes service models more resilient during crises and expands market reach to regions previously inaccessible due to geographical or logistical limitations.

Data shows that during periods of physical restrictions, companies with robust virtual delivery channels maintain 70-85% of their revenue, while companies without digital channels experience declines of up to 60-70%. Market reach through virtual platforms can be expanded 3-5 times compared to physical presence, with customer acquisition costs that are 40-50% lower.

Value delivery has evolved from merely providing products to delivering rich and meaningful experiences. Immersive technologies enable real-time, contextual, and more human-centered value delivery. Organizations that can effectively adopt this approach will gain advantages in building customer loyalty and establishing long-term, meaningful relationships.

2.3 Value Capture

2.3.1 Shift From Transaction to Relationship

The fundamental change in how companies create and deliver value has also significantly influenced how they capture economic benefits from these activities. In traditional business models, revenue typically comes from one-time transactions such as direct product sales. However, with the emergence of immersive technologies, this approach is gradually evolving into more sustainable, long-term relationship-based models.

Experience-based models have now become key drivers in the value capture process. Customers no longer simply purchase products but engage in digital ecosystems that offer ongoing services. In this context, companies provide value not only through products sold but also through continuously developed experiences via digital interaction.

2.3.2 Subscription-Based Model Revenue Metrics

Industry data shows a significant shift toward subscription-based revenue models in the context of immersive technology. Companies adopting subscription models for VR/AR services report increases in customer lifetime value (CLV) of 3-5 times compared to transactional models. Monthly recurring revenue (MRR) from subscription services grows an average of 25-35% year-over-year, providing higher revenue predictability.

Retention rates in immersive content-based subscription models reach 75-85%, far higher than 30-40% in one-time purchase models. Churn rates can be suppressed to below 5% per month for services with regular content updates and community engagement. Average revenue per user (ARPU) increases by 40-60% when companies offer tiered subscriptions with exclusive immersive experiences.

2.3.3 Digital Asset Monetization

Immersive technology opens new opportunities in monetizing digital assets. One prominent example is the digital twin, a real-time digital representation of a physical object or system. In the industrial sector, digital twins are used to monitor operational conditions, identify potential failures, and simulate maintenance scenarios.

Data from digital twin implementations show substantial ROI. Manufacturing companies report reductions in unplanned downtime of 30-50% through predictive maintenance based on digital twins. Operating costs decrease by 20-30% through performance optimization based on simulation results. Revenue from licensing digital twin models and analytics services reaches 15-25% of total revenue for industrial software companies.

In the energy sector, digital twins for wind turbines increase energy output by 5-10% through performance optimization, while maintenance costs drop by 25-30%. Payback periods for digital twin technology investments range from 12-18 months, with sustained cost savings of 15-20% per year thereafter.

2.3.4 Blockchain and NFT Economics

Blockchain systems play an essential role in strengthening value capture. Blockchain enables secure, transparent, and immutable recording of digital transactions. In immersive ecosystems, blockchain is used to support ownership of virtual assets such as digital tokens or non-fungible tokens (NFTs).

Market data shows significant growth in the NFT market related to immersive experiences. Trading volume for NFTs in virtual real estate reaches $500 million to $1 billion on major metaverse platforms. Brand-owned NFTs in virtual worlds generate additional revenue of 10-20% from digital revenue streams. Limited edition virtual items with NFT authentication achieve premium pricing of 200-400% compared to non-authenticated counterparts.

Luxury fashion companies launching NFT collections report revenue of $5-15 million per drop, with sellout rates of 90-100% within minutes. Community token economies in immersive platforms show transaction volumes of $10-50 million per month on established platforms, creating self-sustaining micro-economies.

2.3.5 Data Monetization

From a technological perspective, the shift in value capture also highlights the importance of data as a strategic asset. Every user interaction in an XR environment can be recorded and leveraged to generate new insights about consumer behavior, preference patterns, and product feature effectiveness.

Metrics show that data from immersive platforms has high value. Analytics services based on XR interaction data can be monetized with pricing of $50,000 to $500,000 per year for enterprise clients. Behavioral insights from virtual environments yield 40-60% more accuracy in predicting purchase intent compared to traditional web analytics.

Companies that effectively monetize their XR data report additional revenue streams contributing 5-15% to total revenue. Personalization engines powered by immersive interaction data increase cross-sell and upsell conversion rates by 35-50%, generating significant incremental revenue. Aggregate trend reports from immersive platform usage can be sold to market research firms with pricing of $10,000 to $100,000 per report, depending on depth and exclusivity.

2.3.6 Membership and Community-Based Models

Immersive technology also supports the development of membership-based business models. Companies can offer exclusive access to virtual worlds, premium services, or private communities available only to certain members.

Data shows strong economics from membership models. Premium membership tiers in immersive platforms achieve conversion rates of 15-25% from free users. ARPU from premium members is 5-8 times higher than free tier users. Exclusive virtual events for members generate participation rates of 60-80%, with willingness to pay premium pricing 3-4 times higher than non-members.

Community engagement metrics show that active community members have CLV 4-6 times higher than passive users. Referral rates from engaged community members reach 30-40%, significantly reducing customer acquisition costs. Membership renewal rates in well-managed immersive communities reach 80-90%, demonstrating strong value propositions and customer satisfaction.

2.3.7 ROI and Competitive Advantage

Overall, value capture strategies in the immersive technology era are far more complex and dynamic than in the past. Organizations no longer rely solely on profit margins from selling goods but cultivate value sources from interactions, experiences, and customer engagement within digital environments.

ROI analysis shows that companies strategically implementing multiple value capture mechanisms based on immersive technology achieve overall ROI of 150-250% within 3-5 years. Revenue diversification through subscriptions, digital assets, data monetization, and community models reduces business risk and increases resilience to market fluctuations.

Competitive advantage from immersive value capture strategies is reflected in market share gains of 15-30% for early adopters in their respective industries. Customer switching costs increase 3-5 times in well-designed ecosystems, creating strong moats against competitors. Time-to-value for new offerings is reduced by 40-50% through rapid experimentation in virtual environments, accelerating innovation cycles.

By integrating digital twins, blockchain, and experience-driven services, companies can build richer, more diverse value portfolios that are resilient to disruption. They also gain flexibility to experiment with various monetization models, ranging from transactional income to community- based participation.

Table 2. Performance Metrics for Immersive Technology in Business Models

Business Model Dimension	Key Performance Indicator	Traditional Approach Performance	Immersive Technology Performance	Improvement Range
Value Creation	Product Development Cycle Time	Baseline	Reduced by 30-40%	30-40% faster
	Physical Prototyping Costs	Baseline	Reduced by 50-65%	50-65% savings
	Design Error Rate	Baseline	Reduced by 25-35%	25-35% reduction
	Collaboration Frequency	Baseline	Increased by 60-70%	60-70% increase
	Time-to-Market	Baseline	Reduced by 20-30%	20-30% faster
Value Delivery	Conversion Rate	Baseline	Increased by 25-35%	25-35% increase
	Product Return Rate	Baseline	Reduced by 35-40%	35-40% reduction
	Customer Satisfaction Score	70-75%	88-92%	18-22 points increase
	Average Order Value	Baseline	Increased by 30-40%	30-40% increase
	Service Resolution Time	Baseline	Reduced by 45-55%	45-55% faster
	Training Knowledge Retention	20-30%	70-80%	50 points increase
Value Capture	Customer Lifetime Value	Baseline	3-5x higher	200-400% increase
	Monthly Recurring Revenue Growth	Baseline	25-35% YoY	Sustained growth
	Customer Retention Rate	30-40%	75-85%	45 points increase
	ARPU (Premium vs Standard)	Baseline	5-8x higher	400-700% increase
	Overall ROI (3-5 years)	Baseline	150-250%	Positive returns

Note: Performance metrics are aggregated from multiple industry studies and case implementations across retail, manufacturing, B2B services, and technology sectors. Baseline represents traditional non-immersive approaches. Actual results may vary depending on implementation quality, industry context, and organizational capabilities.

2.4 Section Conclusion

Business model transformation through immersive technologies reflects a fundamental paradigm shift in how organizations create, deliver, and capture value. The quantitative data presented demonstrates that strategic implementation of immersive technologies not only generates incremental improvements but substantial transformations in key business metrics: operational efficiency increases by 30-50%, customer engagement rises by 40-70%, and revenue growth from new digital streams reaches 15-25% of total revenue.

These metrics underscore that adopting immersive technologies is not merely following trends but a crucial element of long-term competitiveness and business resilience in an ever-changing digital landscape. Companies that successfully integrate immersive technologies into their core business models demonstrate superior performance in customer satisfaction, operational efficiency, and financial returns compared to competitors still relying on traditional approaches.

However, successful business model transformation through immersive technology does not happen automatically. It requires strategic alignment, organizational capabilities, and appropriate infrastructure to fully exploit the potential of these technologies. The next chapter will discuss in sectoral case studies and applications.

3. SECTORAL CASE STUDIES AND APPLICATIONS

The practical implementation of immersive technologies varies significantly across industries, each leveraging augmented reality (AR), virtual reality (VR), and extended reality (XR) to address sector-specific challenges and opportunities. This chapter examines five key sectors where these technologies have demonstrated substantial impact: retail, healthcare, manufacturing, education, and real estate. Through detailed analysis of applications, benefits, and implementation challenges, this chapter illustrates how immersive technologies are reshaping traditional practices and creating new paradigms for customer engagement, professional training, and operational efficiency.

3.1 Retail Sector: Virtual Try-Ons and Smart Fitting Rooms

The retail industry has embraced immersive technology as a strategic response to evolving consumer expectations and operational challenges. Virtual fitting rooms (VFRs) represent one of the most commercially successful applications of AR and VR, fundamentally transforming how consumers interact with products before purchase.

3.1.1 Addressing the Product Return Challenge

Online retail faces a persistent challenge with product returns, particularly in fashion and cosmetics, where return rates can exceed 30% due to size mismatches and discrepancies between digital representations and physical products. Virtual try-on solutions directly address this issue by enabling customers to visualize products on their own body or within their personal environment using mobile devices, in-store kiosks, or smart mirrors.

These systems employ advanced computer vision and 3D modeling to create accurate digital representations. Customers can view products from 360-degree perspectives, experiment with different styles and colors, and generate personalized avatars based on their specific body measurements and proportions. This capability significantly reduces uncertainty in online purchasing decisions, leading to measurable decreases in return rates and corresponding improvements in customer satisfaction and retailer profitability.

3.1.2 Enhancing Consumer Experience and Engagement

Beyond practical utility, VFRs contribute to the emotional and experiential dimensions of shopping (Alex et al., 2026). Modern implementations incorporate gamification elements, social sharing capabilities, and personalized recommendations powered by artificial intelligence. These features transform shopping from a transactional activity into an engaging experience that resonates particularly with younger, digitally native consumers who expect seamless integration of technology into their retail interactions.

Leading retailers have deployed successful implementations across various product categories. Sephora's Virtual Artist application combines AR technology with artificial intelligence to enable realistic makeup trials, while IKEA Place allows customers to visualize furniture within their actual living spaces using smartphone cameras. These applications demonstrate how virtual try-ons extend beyond apparel to encompass cosmetics, accessories, home furnishings, and eyewear.

3.1.3 Strategic Value and Market Positioning

Virtual try-on technology represents more than a tactical solution to operational problems. It embodies a strategic commitment to digital transformation and customer-centric innovation. Retailers adopting these technologies position themselves as forward-thinking brands that prioritize customer experience and leverage cutting-edge solutions to deliver value.

The aesthetic and functional benefits of VFRs enhance perceived product quality and brand prestige. As consumer expectations continue to evolve toward more interactive and personalized shopping experiences, virtual try-on capabilities are transitioning from competitive differentiators to essential features in the digital retail landscape.

3.2 Healthcare Sector: AR-Guided Surgery and Immersive Therapy

Healthcare has emerged as one of the most promising domains for immersive technology application, with implementations spanning surgical guidance, medical education, and therapeutic interventions. The sector's emphasis on precision, safety, and continuous skill development creates ideal conditions for AR and VR adoption.

3.2.1 Augmented Reality in Surgical Procedures

AR technology enhances surgical precision by overlaying digital information directly onto the surgeon's field of view. In dental implantology, AR systems project planned implant positions, anatomical landmarks, and critical structures such as nerve pathways onto the patient's actual anatomy in real time (Saemann et al., 2025). This guidance significantly improves placement accuracy, reduces procedural complications, and enhances patient safety outcomes.

The technology proves particularly valuable in complex procedures requiring millimeter-level precision. Surgeons can visualize subsurface anatomical structures, reference pre-operative imaging data without diverting attention from the surgical field, and verify procedural steps against planned protocols. These capabilities translate into reduced operative times, decreased intraoperative risks, and improved long-term treatment outcomes.

3.2.2 Virtual Reality for Medical Training and Education

VR creates controlled, risk-free environments where medical students and practitioners can develop and refine procedural skills. In orthognathic surgery training,

VR simulations allow learners to practice complex jaw repositioning procedures, experiment with different surgical approaches, and understand the consequences of technical decisions without risk to actual patients.

Advanced VR training platforms incorporate haptic feedback systems that simulate the tactile sensations of surgical procedures. Students can feel tissue resistance, practice instrument manipulation, and develop the fine motor skills essential for delicate operations. This multisensory learning approach accelerates skill acquisition and builds procedural confidence before transitioning to clinical practice.

Dental education has particularly benefited from VR integration. Students can explore detailed three-dimensional anatomical models, practice root canal therapy techniques, prepare crown margins, and perform virtual extractions. This hands-on virtual experience complements traditional didactic instruction and cadaver-based learning, providing unlimited practice opportunities without resource constraints.

3.2.3 Therapeutic Applications and Patient Care

Beyond training and surgical guidance, VR serves therapeutic purposes in mental health treatment, pain management, and rehabilitation. Immersive environments help patients manage anxiety disorders through controlled exposure therapy, reduce perception of chronic pain through distraction and cognitive techniques, and maintain engagement during lengthy rehabilitation protocols.

Postoperative patients using VR during recovery report reduced stress levels, decreased pain medication requirements, and improved treatment adherence. The technology's ability to transport patients psychologically away from clinical environments contributes to overall wellbeing and recovery outcomes.

3.2.4 Implementation Challenges and Future Directions

Despite proven benefits, healthcare adoption faces obstacles including high initial investment costs, integration with existing clinical workflows, and learning curves for medical personnel. Device sterilization requirements, regulatory compliance, and concerns about technology reliability in critical situations further complicate implementation.

However, ongoing advances in haptic technology, artificial intelligence integration, and wireless connectivity are addressing these limitations. As costs decline and evidence supporting clinical efficacy accumulates, immersive technologies are positioned to become standard components of medical education and clinical practice across healthcare systems globally.

3.3 Manufacturing Sector: Remote Training and Equipment Diagnostics

Manufacturing industries are leveraging immersive technologies to advance toward Industry 4.0 and Industry 5.0 paradigms, emphasizing intelligent automation, human-machine collaboration, and sustainable operations. Food manufacturing, with its stringent safety requirements and complex equipment systems, exemplifies these transformative applications.

3.3.1 Immersive Remote Training Solutions

Traditional manufacturing training requires physical presence, consumes significant time, and often disrupts production operations. XR-enabled remote training platforms overcome these limitations by delivering immersive, location-independent instruction that workers can access on-demand.

VR simulations recreate production environments where employees can practice equipment operation, emergency response procedures, and safety protocols without exposure to actual hazards (Abughalia & Stechert, 2025). Artificial intelligence systems provide real-time performance feedback, identify skill gaps, and adapt training content to individual learning needs. This personalized approach accelerates competency development while ensuring consistent training quality across distributed facilities.

In food safety training, AI-powered systems monitor worker behavior during simulated scenarios, verifying proper hand hygiene techniques, cross-contamination prevention, and hazard identification. Real-time corrective guidance reinforces proper procedures without requiring constant human supervision, which is particularly valuable in high-turnover environments where training efficiency directly impacts operational continuity.

Digital twin technology allows workers to understand complex machinery dynamics through interactive virtual replicas. Employees can disassemble virtual equipment, observe internal mechanisms, and practice maintenance procedures in risk-free environments. This approach aligns with Industry 5.0's emphasis on human-centric design by building workforce capability while protecting worker safety.

3.3.2 AI-Based Equipment Diagnostics and Predictive Maintenance

Equipment reliability is critical in manufacturing, where unexpected failures cause production disruptions, quality issues, and safety hazards. Digital twins connected to IoT sensor networks enable continuous equipment monitoring and AI-powered anomaly detection.

In food processing facilities, AI systems analyze real-time operational data including temperature, vibration, pressure, and acoustic signatures to identify early indicators of equipment degradation. When anomalies are detected, the system alerts maintenance personnel and provides diagnostic guidance, enabling proactive intervention before failures occur.

According to recent industry analyses, predictive maintenance strategies reduce unplanned downtime by 30 to 50 percent and extend equipment service life by 20 to 40 percent compared to reactive maintenance approaches. These improvements translate directly into reduced maintenance costs, decreased product waste, and enhanced operational sustainability.

Immersive AR interfaces guide technicians through diagnostic and repair procedures by overlaying step-by-step instructions, highlighting relevant components, and displaying real-time sensor data within their field of view. This augmented guidance improves repair accuracy, reduces completion time, and enables less experienced technicians to successfully complete complex tasks.

3.3.3 Statistical Impact and Operational Benefits

Manufacturing implementations of immersive technologies demonstrate measurable performance improvements across multiple metrics, as summarized in Table 3.1.

Table 3. Quantified Benefits of Immersive Technologies in Manufacturing

Application Area	Key Metric	Improvement Range	Impact Description
Training Efficiency	Time to Competency	40-60% reduction	Accelerated skill development through immersive simulation and AI-adaptive learning
Training Costs	Cost per Trainee	30-50% reduction	Elimination of travel, reduced facility requirements, and reusable digital content
Equipment Downtime	Unplanned Stoppages	30-50% reduction	Early fault detection and predictive maintenance enabled by digital twins and AI diagnostics
Maintenance Costs	Annual Maintenance Expense	20-35% reduction	Transition from reactive to predictive maintenance strategies
Equipment Lifespan	Service Life Extension	20-40% increase	Optimized maintenance intervals and early intervention preventing catastrophic failures
Worker Safety	Incident Rate	25-45% reduction	Virtual training reduces hazardous exposure; AR guidance improves procedural accuracy
Production Quality	Defect Rate	15-30% reduction	Better-trained workforce and more reliable equipment contribute to consistent quality

3.3.4 Implementation Barriers and Adoption Strategies

Despite compelling benefits, manufacturing adoption faces significant barriers. High upfront capital investment, particularly for small and medium enterprises, limits widespread implementation. Insufficient digital infrastructure, including reliable high-speed connectivity and computing capacity, constrains technology performance in some facilities.

Workforce digital literacy gaps require complementary training initiatives to ensure employees can effectively utilize new systems. Organizational change management challenges arise when introducing technologies that fundamentally alter established workflows and job responsibilities.

Successful adoption strategies emphasize gradual implementation through pilot projects that demonstrate value before facility-wide deployment. Cross-sector collaboration, including partnerships with technology providers and industry consortia, enables knowledge sharing and reduces individual organizational risk. Government incentive programs and industry association support further accelerate adoption by reducing financial barriers.

3.3.5 Future Trajectory and Emerging Capabilities

Manufacturing applications of immersive technology continue to evolve. Metaverse-based training platforms promise even more realistic and socially interactive learning experiences. Cognitive digital twins, incorporating AI models that understand operational context and predict consequences of different scenarios, will provide increasingly sophisticated decision support.

Integration with other Industry 4.0 technologies including robotics, blockchain for supply chain transparency, and advanced analytics will create comprehensive smart manufacturing ecosystems where immersive interfaces serve as the primary human-machine interaction layer.

3.4 Education Sector: VR-Based Simulations and Virtual Classrooms

Education has undergone substantial transformation through VR technology, which addresses longstanding limitations of traditional instruction while creating entirely new pedagogical possibilities. Virtual simulations and classrooms enhance learning engagement, improve knowledge retention, and overcome physical constraints that historically limited educational access and quality.

3.4.1 Immersive Learning Through VR Simulations

VR simulations place learners within realistic scenarios where they can interact with complex systems, manipulate virtual objects, and observe immediate consequences of their decisions. In architectural and engineering education, students explore building energy systems, experimenting with different design parameters and observing real-time impacts on energy efficiency, thermal comfort, and environmental performance.

This experiential approach transforms abstract concepts into tangible experiences. Rather than memorizing formulas or studying diagrams, students manipulate virtual building components, adjust insulation levels, modify window configurations, and instantly observe resulting changes in energy consumption and indoor conditions. This direct interaction builds intuitive understanding that complements theoretical knowledge.

3.4.2 Enhanced Engagement and Learning Outcomes

Virtual environments significantly increase student engagement compared to traditional instructional methods. The immersive nature of VR captures attention, maintains focus, and stimulates curiosity. Students report higher motivation levels and greater enjoyment of learning activities conducted in virtual environments.

Active participation inherent in VR-based learning promotes deeper cognitive processing. Students make decisions, test hypotheses, and observe outcomes, engaging in scientific reasoning and critical thinking. This active learning approach produces superior knowledge retention compared to passive instruction methods.

The emotional dimension of VR learning also contributes to educational effectiveness (Alex et al., 2026). Presence within virtual environments creates memorable experiences that anchor knowledge in episodic memory. Students develop personal connections to learning content, which sustains interest and motivates continued exploration.

3.4.3 Virtual Classrooms and Remote Learning

Beyond individual simulations, VR enables synchronous virtual classrooms where geographically dispersed students and instructors interact in shared three-dimensional spaces. Participants appear as avatars, communicate through spatial audio, and collaborate on virtual objects and presentations.

These virtual classrooms preserve social presence and collaborative learning benefits that asynchronous online courses often lack. Students work together on group projects, present to peers, and receive immediate instructor feedback in ways that approximate physical classroom dynamics while transcending geographical limitations.

Advanced VR learning platforms incorporate artificial intelligence to create adaptive educational experiences. Systems monitor student interactions, identify knowledge gaps or misconceptions, and automatically adjust content difficulty, pacing, and instructional approach. This personalization ensures each learner receives appropriate challenge levels and support.

3.4.4 Implementation Challenges in Educational Contexts

Educational VR adoption faces distinct challenges. Hardware costs, while declining, remain prohibitive for many institutions, particularly in developing regions. Schools must acquire VR headsets, maintain supporting computing infrastructure, and plan for technology refresh cycles.

Educator training represents another significant requirement. Teachers must develop competency with VR systems, learn effective pedagogical strategies for virtual environments, and redesign curricula to leverage technology capabilities appropriately (Abughalia & Stechert, 2025). This professional development requires time and institutional support.

Curriculum integration poses pedagogical questions about optimal VR usage. Educators must determine which learning objectives benefit most from immersive experiences and design lessons that authentically leverage VR capabilities rather than using technology superficially.

Health and safety considerations, including motion sickness susceptibility, age-appropriate usage durations, and inclusive design for students with disabilities, require careful attention in educational implementations.

3.4.5 Evidence of Educational Effectiveness

Research examining VR educational implementations demonstrates positive outcomes across various contexts. Students using VR for building energy simulation show significantly improved understanding of thermodynamic principles, energy efficiency strategies, and sustainable design concepts compared to control groups receiving traditional instruction.

Assessment results indicate not only increased knowledge retention but also enhanced ability to apply concepts in novel situations, suggesting that VR develops transferable understanding rather than rote memorization. Student self-reported surveys consistently show high satisfaction levels and expressed preference for VR-enhanced instruction.

3.4.6 Future Evolution of Educational VR

As technology costs decrease and institutional experience grows, VR adoption in education is projected to expand substantially. Collaborative efforts between educational institutions, government agencies, and technology companies are essential to develop content libraries, establish best practice guidelines, and ensure equitable access.

Integration with learning management systems, assessment platforms, and educational data analytics will create comprehensive digital learning ecosystems. VR will evolve from supplementary enrichment to core instructional infrastructure, fundamentally reshaping how education is conceived and delivered across all levels from primary schools through professional training.

3.5 Real Estate and Architecture: 3D Walkthroughs and Immersive Visualization

Real estate and architecture sectors have rapidly adopted immersive technologies, particularly 3D virtual walkthroughs, which transform how buildings are designed, marketed, and sold. These technologies enhance communication among project stakeholders, accelerate decision-making processes, and create compelling marketing experiences.

3.5.1 Enhanced Design Visualization and Communication

Traditional architectural representation through drawings, renderings, and physical models requires specialized knowledge to interpret accurately. Clients without technical backgrounds often struggle to visualize final built environments from two-dimensional plans or static images.

Three-dimensional virtual walkthroughs eliminate this comprehension gap by allowing clients to navigate proposed designs freely. Users move through virtual spaces at their own pace, examining room layouts, spatial proportions, material selections, and lighting conditions from any perspective. This experiential understanding enables more informed feedback and confident decision-making.

Architects benefit from earlier identification of design issues. Clients viewing virtual models may recognize functional problems, spatial inefficiencies, or aesthetic concerns that would only become apparent after construction begins. Addressing these issues during design phases avoids costly modifications and project delays.

3.5.2 Collaborative Design Development

Immersive technologies facilitate enhanced collaboration among multidisciplinary project teams. Architects, structural engineers, mechanical systems designers, and construction managers can simultaneously review virtual building models, discussing design coordination issues in shared virtual spaces.

This collaborative visualization improves communication effectiveness by providing common reference points that transcend disciplinary jargon. Team members point to specific virtual elements, propose alternatives, and immediately assess implications of design changes. The resulting coordination reduces conflicts between building systems, minimizes construction change orders, and improves overall project quality.

Virtual design reviews conducted using immersive technologies enable participation from remote team members without travel requirements. International projects involving geographically distributed teams particularly benefit from this capability, maintaining design continuity while reducing project management costs.

3.5.3 Marketing Applications and Sales Effectiveness

Real estate marketing has been transformed by virtual property tours that allow prospective buyers to explore properties remotely. This capability expanded dramatically during pandemic-related restrictions but has persisted due to demonstrated marketing effectiveness and buyer preferences.

Virtual tours reach international buyers, investors unable to visit properties physically, and busy professionals seeking to screen options efficiently before scheduling in-person visits. Marketing reach expands significantly while showing costs decrease.

Emotional engagement created by immersive property exploration strengthens buyer connections to properties. Rather than passively viewing photographs, buyers mentally inhabit spaces, imagine furniture placement, and envision daily life in the property. This emotional involvement accelerates purchase decisions and increases conversion rates.

3.5.4 Technical and Performance Applications

Beyond marketing, 3D virtual environments support technical building performance analysis. Building systems designers evaluate equipment layouts, maintenance accessibility, and operational workflows in virtual models. Ergonomic specialists assess workspace functionality and occupant comfort factors.

Accessibility evaluations conducted in virtual environments ensure compliance with disability accommodation requirements. Designers verify wheelchair navigation paths, reach distances, and visual sightlines, addressing issues before construction.

Integration with Building Information Modeling (BIM) systems creates comprehensive digital building representations that incorporate architectural form, structural systems, mechanical equipment, and operational data. Immersive interfaces to these BIM models enable facility managers to visualize hidden building systems, plan maintenance activities, and train building operators.

3.5.5 Quantitative Market Impact and Adoption Trends

Real estate implementations of immersive visualization technologies demonstrate substantial business value, as illustrated in Table 3.2.

Table 4. Business Impact of Immersive Technologies in Real Estate

Performance Metric	Impact Measurement	Industry Context
Sales Cycle Duration	30-45% reduction in time from listing to sale	Virtual tours enable faster buyer decision-making by providing comprehensive property understanding remotely
Marketing Reach	3-5x increase in qualified prospect inquiries	International and distant buyers can effectively evaluate properties without physical visits
Design Change Orders	25-40% reduction in post-construction modifications	Early client engagement with virtual models identifies issues during design phases
Client Satisfaction	35-50% increase in positive project reviews	Enhanced visualization reduces expectation mismatches and improves communication
Marketing Cost Efficiency	20-35% reduction per property showing	Virtual tours reduce need for multiple physical property visits and associated coordination costs
Project Coordination Efficiency	15-30% reduction in design coordination meetings	Virtual collaborative reviews accelerate decision-making and reduce scheduling complexity

3.5.6 Implementation Considerations and Barriers

Real estate and architecture adoption of immersive technologies requires consideration of several implementation factors. Content creation demands specialized skills in 3D modeling, virtual environment development, and optimization for smooth performance. Firms must either develop internal capabilities or partner with specialized service providers.

Hardware requirements, including high-performance computers for content creation and VR headsets for client presentations, represent significant capital investments. However, rapidly declining technology costs and cloud-based rendering services are reducing these barriers.

Development time for detailed virtual environments can extend project schedules if not properly planned. Early-stage rough models can be refined progressively as designs mature, allowing phased implementation that balances detail with schedule requirements.

Client technology literacy varies significantly. While younger buyers readily adopt VR property tours, older demographics may prefer traditional viewing methods. Hybrid marketing strategies accommodating diverse preferences ensure broad market coverage.

3.5.7 Future Integration and Advanced Capabilities

Immersive visualization in real estate and architecture continues advancing toward more sophisticated capabilities. Integration with artificial intelligence enables automated virtual staging, where furniture and decor are digitally placed in empty properties to help buyers envision finished spaces. AI-powered design optimization suggests layout alternatives that maximize space efficiency, natural lighting, or energy performance.

Environmental simulation capabilities allow virtual walkthroughs to demonstrate seasonal lighting variations, acoustic performance, and outdoor views at different times of day or year. These temporal simulations help buyers understand dynamic aspects of properties beyond static visual appearance.

Connection with smart building systems will enable virtual environments that display real-time operational data, energy consumption patterns, and occupancy analytics. Property managers will use immersive dashboards to monitor building performance and control systems intuitively.

As technology maturation continues and industry experience deepens, immersive visualization is transitioning from competitive advantage to standard practice in real estate marketing and architectural design presentation.The following chapter transitions from sectoral case studies to organizational adoption factors.

4. ORGANIZATIONAL ADOPTION FACTORS

The The successful integration of emerging technologies such as artificial intelligence (AI), virtual reality (VR), and other digital systems within organizations extends beyond technical sophistication. Organizational readiness, cultural alignment, and strategic planning play equally critical roles in determining adoption outcomes. This chapter examines the multifaceted factors that influence technology adoption in organizational contexts, addressing both systemic barriers and enablers that shape implementation success.

4.1 Financial Considerations and Investment Strategies

Implementation costs remain one of the most significant barriers to technology adoption across organizations of varying scales. Beyond initial acquisition expenses, organizations must account for infrastructure upgrades, ongoing maintenance, licensing fees, and comprehensive training programs. These cumulative costs often create hesitation, particularly when return on investment timelines remain uncertain.

Strategic approaches to managing financial barriers have emerged through practical application. Progressive organizations have implemented phased rollout strategies, beginning with targeted pilot programs in specific departments before scaling enterprise-wide. For instance, a multinational retail corporation initiated its AI-powered inventory management system in three regional warehouses, allowing for refinement and demonstration of measurable efficiency gains before broader implementation. This approach reduced financial risk while building internal credibility.

Public-private partnerships represent another effective mechanism for distributing financial burden. Technology providers increasingly offer flexible pricing models, including subscription-based licensing and revenue-sharing arrangements, which transform substantial capital expenditures into manageable operational costs. Educational institutions have particularly benefited from this model, partnering with technology vendors to access cutting-edge platforms while providers gain valuable real-world testing environments and case studies.

4.2 Human Capital Development and Organizational Learning

Workforce readiness constitutes a fundamental determinant of successful technology adoption. The rapid pace of technological evolution consistently outstrips traditional educational pipelines, creating persistent skills gaps within organizations.

Digital literacy, data interpretation capabilities, and adaptive problem-solving skills have become essential competencies across professional roles.

Leading organizations have responded by embedding continuous learning into their operational frameworks. A prominent financial services firm established an internal digital academy, offering employees structured pathways from foundational digital literacy to advanced specializations in machine learning and data analytics. The program combines self-paced online modules with hands-on project work, enabling employees to develop skills directly applicable to their roles. Within eighteen months, over 60 percent of the workforce completed at least one certification track, directly correlating with improved project delivery timelines and innovation metrics.

Mentorship structures and cross-functional collaboration further accelerate capability development. Organizations pairing digitally proficient staff with colleagues transitioning to new systems create knowledge transfer mechanisms that respect existing expertise while building new competencies (Halamová et al., 2025). This peer-based approach addresses learning needs while reinforcing collaborative organizational culture.

4.3 Managing Resistance and Fostering Change Acceptance

Resistance to technological change represents a natural human response to uncertainty rather than simple opposition to progress. Concerns about role displacement, competency adequacy, and organizational stability frequently underlie resistance behaviors (Liyanaarachchi et al., 2026). Acknowledging these legitimate concerns and addressing them directly proves more effective than dismissing resistance as mere obstinacy.

Transparent communication strategies establish trust and reduce uncertainty. When a healthcare network implemented an AI-assisted diagnostic system, leadership conducted extensive consultations with medical staff, clearly articulating that the technology would augment rather than replace clinical judgment. Physicians participated in system design reviews, ensuring the interface supported their workflow rather than disrupting it. This inclusive approach transformed potential resistance into advocacy, with early adopters becoming ambassadors who encouraged broader acceptance among colleagues.

Recognition programs celebrating change champions reinforce positive adoption behaviors. Organizations highlighting employees who effectively integrate new technologies into their practice create visible role models while demonstrating institutional commitment to supporting the transition. Such recognition extends beyond symbolic gestures to include professional development opportunities, leadership roles in implementation teams, and influence over technology selection decisions.

4.4 Data Security, Privacy, and Ethical Governance

Digital transformation inherently expands organizational attack surfaces and data vulnerabilities. As systems become increasingly interconnected and data-dependent, security breaches carry escalating consequences including financial losses, regulatory penalties, and reputational damage. Organizations must therefore embed security considerations throughout technology adoption processes rather than treating them as afterthoughts (Pappachan et al., 2025).

Comprehensive security frameworks combine technical safeguards with human factors. Multi-factor authentication, end-to-end encryption, and regular security audits form technical foundations. However, human behavior remains the most common vulnerability vector. A global logistics company reduced security incidents by 73 percent after implementing quarterly simulation exercises where employees experienced realistic phishing attempts and social engineering tactics in controlled environments. These experiential learning opportunities proved far more effective than traditional compliance training modules.

Privacy protection extends beyond regulatory compliance to encompass ethical responsibilities. Organizations collecting and processing personal data must establish clear governance structures defining data usage boundaries, retention policies, and individual rights (Bankins et al., 2025). Advisory boards including ethicists, legal experts, and community representatives provide crucial oversight, particularly for AI systems making consequential decisions about individuals. Such governance mechanisms help organizations navigate complex ethical terrain where regulations may lag behind technological capabilities.

4.5 Regulatory Compliance and Legal Frameworks

Regulatory landscapes governing digital technologies remain dynamic and fragmented across jurisdictions. Organizations operating internationally must navigate inconsistent requirements regarding data localization, algorithmic transparency, and liability frameworks. This complexity demands proactive compliance strategies rather than reactive responses to violations.

Dedicated compliance teams with cross-functional expertise have become standard practice in sophisticated organizations. These teams continuously monitor regulatory developments, assess implications for current systems, and provide guidance on necessary adjustments. A European e-commerce platform established a compliance hub responsible for tracking data protection regulations across 27 member states, ensuring consistent adherence while optimizing operational efficiency through standardized processes that exceed minimum requirements in any single jurisdiction.

Engaging directly with regulatory authorities provides valuable clarity and demonstrates good-faith commitment to responsible innovation. Industry consortia facilitating dialogue between technology developers, implementing organizations, and regulators help shape practical frameworks that protect public interests without unnecessarily constraining beneficial innovation. Such collaborative approaches prove particularly valuable in emerging domains like AI governance, where regulatory frameworks remain under development.

4.6 Usability Design and Accessibility Principles

Technology adoption ultimately depends on practical usability within real operational contexts. Systems that impose excessive cognitive load, disrupt established workflows, or require extensive customization face inevitable resistance regardless of their theoretical capabilities. User-centered design methodologies that prioritize actual user needs over technical possibilities yield significantly higher adoption rates.

Iterative development processes incorporating continuous user feedback enable refinement before full deployment. A manufacturing enterprise developing an augmented reality system for equipment maintenance conducted weekly testing sessions with technicians, observing actual usage patterns and identifying pain points. This iterative approach revealed that the initial interface design, while visually impressive, required too many navigation steps for quick reference during repairs. Subsequent redesigns streamlined access to critical information, reducing task completion time by 40 percent and achieving widespread adoption within three months of final deployment.

Accessibility considerations ensure technology serves diverse user populations rather than privileging certain abilities or backgrounds. Compliance with established accessibility standards like WCAG represents minimum baselines; truly inclusive design anticipates needs of users with varying visual, auditory, motor, and cognitive capabilities. Organizations implementing accessibility from initial design stages avoid costly retrofitting while expanding their potential user base and demonstrating commitment to inclusive values.

4.7 Synthesis and Strategic Implications

Technology adoption represents organizational transformation requiring coordinated attention to technical, financial, human, and cultural dimensions. Isolated focus on any single factor risks implementation failure regardless of investment levels or technology sophistication. The organizations achieving sustainable digital transformation share common characteristics: strategic patience allowing phased implementation, genuine commitment to workforce development, transparent communication practices, robust governance frameworks, and design philosophies prioritizing human needs.

Table 5. Essential Factors for Effective Technology Adoption

Organizational Factor	Primary Challenges	Strategic Approaches	Implementation Examples
Financial Management	High capital requirements, uncertain ROI, budget constraints	Phased deployment, pilot programs, flexible financing models, vendor partnerships	Regional warehouse pilots before enterprise rollout; subscription-based licensing reducing upfront costs
Workforce Development	Skills gaps, rapid technology evolution, training costs	Internal academies, certification programs, peer mentoring, continuous learning culture	Financial services digital academy; cross-functional knowledge transfer teams
Change Management	Fear of displacement, workflow disruption, uncertainty	Transparent communication, participatory design, recognition programs, early involvement	Healthcare AI system co-designed with physicians; change champion networks
Security and Privacy	Data breaches, expanding attack surfaces, compliance complexity	Multi-layered security protocols, experiential training, ethical governance boards	Quarterly security simulations; ethics advisory committees for AI systems (Pappachan et al., 2024).
Regulatory Compliance	Jurisdictional variations, evolving requirements, legal uncertainty	Dedicated compliance teams, regulatory monitoring, authority engagement	Cross-border compliance hubs; industry-regulator dialogue forums
Usability and Accessibility	Poor user experience, workflow incompatibility, exclusionary design	User-centered design, iterative testing, accessibility standards, diverse user involvement	Technician-led interface refinement; WCAG-compliant development from inception

The interconnected nature of these factors demands integrated planning approaches. Financial decisions influence workforce development possibilities; usability directly affects change resistance levels; security frameworks must balance protection with accessibility. Successful organizations recognize these interdependencies and develop coordinated strategies addressing multiple factors simultaneously (Rahaman, Chappu, et al., 2025).

Having established the organizational foundations necessary for successful technology adoption, attention now turns to examining specific contexts where these principles apply. The following chapter explores educational environments as a critical domain for digital transformation, investigating how institutions navigate the unique challenges and opportunities present in learning contexts while building upon the organizational factors discussed here.

5. FUTURE DIRECTIONS OF IMMERSIVE TECHNOLOGIES

The The transformation of immersive technology is entering its next phase. This evolution involves not only technical advancements but also a major shift in how humans, organizations, and digital systems interact. Several key directions are becoming prominent, including the integration of technology with artificial intelligence and digital twins, the use of extended reality (XR) within the metaverse economy, and the application of blockchain as the foundation for digital ownership through non-fungible tokens (NFTs) and other decentralized platforms.

5.1 Integration of AI and Digital Twin

The integration of AI and digital twin technology is reshaping technical systems and redefining decision-making processes in organizations. Traditional operational planning relies on retrospective data and periodic assessments. In contrast, AI-powered digital twins enable continuous insight, allowing decision-makers to test scenarios in simulated environments and visualize outcomes before executing actions in the physical world (Sekti, 2026).

In the transportation sector, digital twins of public transit networks can incorporate AI to model demand fluctuations, traffic congestion, and equipment wear. AI systems simulate the effects of route changes, maintenance schedules, or emergency responses, enabling operators to make informed decisions in advance. In the renewable energy sector, digital twins monitor infrastructures like solar panels and wind turbines in real time. AI identifies potential faults before they occur, recommends mitigation actions, and automatically adjusts operational parameters under varying environmental conditions.

Digital twins are expanding in environmental monitoring by representing ecosystems, air quality networks, or water management infrastructures in real time. A twin of a flood-prone area can simulate rainfall accumulation, river flow, and drainage capacity while AI evaluates risk and triggers preventive actions. Governments can then issue alerts, deploy infrastructure reinforcements, or adjust urban planning based on these insights.

From an industrial engineering perspective, AI-supported digital twins transform the entire lifecycle management of assets. Virtual prototypes can be generated, tested, and optimized before physical construction begins. During operations, these twins offer historical records of usage patterns, maintenance activities, and failure incidents. This data-rich environment empowers AI to develop predictive maintenance models, particularly valuable in aviation, rail, and heavy manufacturing where unscheduled downtime incurs high costs.

In agriculture, AI-enabled digital twins optimize farming operations through data from sensors, drones, and weather forecasts. The AI predicts crop growth patterns, detects early signs of disease, and manages resources like water and fertilizer more effectively. In education, AI-based digital twins model learning environments and student profiles, tracking progress and predicting outcomes. AI recommends personalized learning pathways and adjusts content delivery in real time, transforming education into a responsive and student-centric experience.

As digital twins become more intelligent, ethical and responsible AI use grows in importance. Organizations must address transparency, bias mitigation, and accountability in automated decision-making processes. Data privacy is critical, especially in sectors like healthcare and education where sensitive personal data is involved (Sekti, 2026). Implementation requires significant investment in data collection, processing, and integration, along with interdisciplinary collaboration among engineers, data scientists, domain experts, and IT professionals.

Looking ahead, the next frontier is the development of cognitive digital twin systems that not only predict and respond to conditions but also learn and reason about their environment. These twins could eventually autonomously adapt their structure, logic, and goals in response to feedback and evolving objectives.

5.2 XR in the Metaverse Economy and Decentralized Platforms

The growing maturity of XR technologies is influencing how digital experiences are conceptualized and delivered across sectors. In the corporate world, companies are experimenting with metaverse-based workplaces where meetings, brainstorming sessions, and onboarding processes take place in virtual environments. Teams interact in shared virtual spaces using customized avatars and spatial audio to simulate real-world interactions, enhancing collaboration in globally distributed teams.

In architecture and urban planning, XR provides experiential access to unbuilt environments. Virtual walkthroughs of buildings or infrastructure projects allow users to explore spaces, assess usability, and offer feedback before construction begins. This reduces misalignment between designers and clients while enhancing user-centered design. Healthcare institutions use virtual reality to simulate complex surgeries and emergency procedures, allowing students to gain hands-on experience without risking patient safety. XR is also used therapeutically to treat phobias, post-traumatic stress disorder, and chronic pain through guided exposure and distraction techniques.

In retail, XR accelerates the personalization of shopping experiences. Virtual fitting rooms allow users to see how clothing or cosmetics would look using real-time image processing. Some systems incorporate AI to provide recommendations based on body type or style preferences. The entertainment industry, particularly gaming and live events, is among the earliest adopters of XR within metaverse environments. Concerts and festivals are held in virtual venues with 3D stages, audience interactivity, and purchasable virtual merchandise, enabling global participation and democratizing access to cultural experiences.

The shift toward XR in metaverse contexts is changing economic models. Decentralized virtual economies reward users directly for their participation and contributions. Creators of digital fashion or architectural assets can sell designs on decentralized marketplaces, while players earn in-world currency that translates to real-world income. This user-first economy gives individuals greater control over their time, data, and creative output.

However, these opportunities come with infrastructure challenges. High-fidelity XR experiences require advanced hardware such as head-mounted displays, spatial sensors, and haptic feedback devices. Bandwidth and latency become critical in real-time, multi-user environments (Sun, 2025). Organizations and governments must invest in digital infrastructure to ensure equitable access. Cultural and psychological dimensions must also be considered as XR blurs the line between digital and physical reality, raising concerns around identity, addiction, and escapism.

Interoperability is another crucial issue. Many metaverse platforms operate in closed ecosystems, making it difficult for assets, avatars, or currencies to transfer across experiences. The development of shared standards and protocols is necessary to create a unified metaverse economy. Governance models for XR platforms must evolve to address who sets rules, moderates content, and ensures user safety. Decentralized governance, community voting mechanisms, and smart contracts are being tested as alternatives to traditional corporate control.

Ownership in the metaverse is being redefined. Avatars, digital outfits, virtual properties, and exclusive event tickets hold economic value in secondary markets. Users become active participants who create and manage their own digital assets, creating a collaborative economic system where value is determined by interaction, creativity, and user participation. Experience-based business models are becoming increasingly relevant (Tang et al., 2025). Virtual reality training, digital tours, virtual concerts, and global conferences can all be conducted in XR environments, expanding services and unlocking new monetization opportunities unrestricted by physical space.

As these digital ownership models continue to evolve within immersive ecosystems, organizations must navigate complex questions of asset control, value distribution, and governance structures. The strategic implications of decentralized digital ownership require careful examination to ensure sustainable and equitable implementation across industries.

6. STRATEGIC IMPLICATIONS FOR DECENTRALIZED DIGITAL OWNERSHIP

6.1 Blockchain and Immersive NFTs

The convergence of blockchain and immersive technologies introduces new opportunities for digital ownership models that extend far beyond individual assets. Within virtual environments, entire ecosystems can be developed in which property rights, access privileges, and creator royalties are embedded directly into smart contracts. These self executing agreements eliminate the need for intermediaries, reduce transaction costs, and provide transparent mechanisms for rule enforcement. For example, a digital artist can mint an NFT representing their work and automatically receive royalties every time the asset is resold, with all terms permanently recorded on the blockchain.

One of the most notable innovations enabled by NFTs is fractional ownership. Instead of a single individual owning a complete virtual asset such as a parcel of land in the metaverse or a rare digital artwork, multiple users can purchase shared ownership of the same asset. This approach democratizes access to high value assets and facilitates collaborative investment (Tamim et al., 2025). It also supports community driven projects that use token based voting mechanisms and can evolve into decentralized autonomous organizations that collectively manage virtual property.

Digital identity is also being reimagined through blockchain. Decentralized identity systems enable users to retain control over their credentials, achievements, and personal preferences without relying on centralized platforms. As a result, a user's identity including avatar appearance, reputation, and digital holdings can persist across multiple platforms and applications. This level of interoperability enhances data privacy and user empowerment and establishes foundational principles for an open and equitable metaverse (Ye et al., 2025).

The use of NFTs has also expanded into brand loyalty and customer engagement strategies. Companies can issue branded NFTs as part of reward programs that grant access to exclusive content, special products, or premium virtual experiences. Unlike traditional loyalty points, NFTs can be collected, displayed, traded, or sold, which increases their utility and emotional value. This approach strengthens the customer brand relationship and transforms engagement into a more dynamic and participatory process.

In the entertainment and sports sectors, the use of NFTs and fan tokens has become a popular strategy for enhancing community engagement. Several major football clubs have adopted blockchain based tokens that give fans voting rights on certain decisions such as jersey designs or in stadium music selection. This model fosters a stronger sense of ownership and enhances community loyalty (Dinçer &

Dilek, 2025). At the same time, NFTs introduce new monetization opportunities for artists, game developers, and major brands through limited edition digital collections designed to leverage scarcity. Blockchain ensures that all transaction records and ownership histories are transparently documented, which reinforces user trust in digital asset trading.

Figure 2. Blockchain enabled decentralized ownership ecosystem

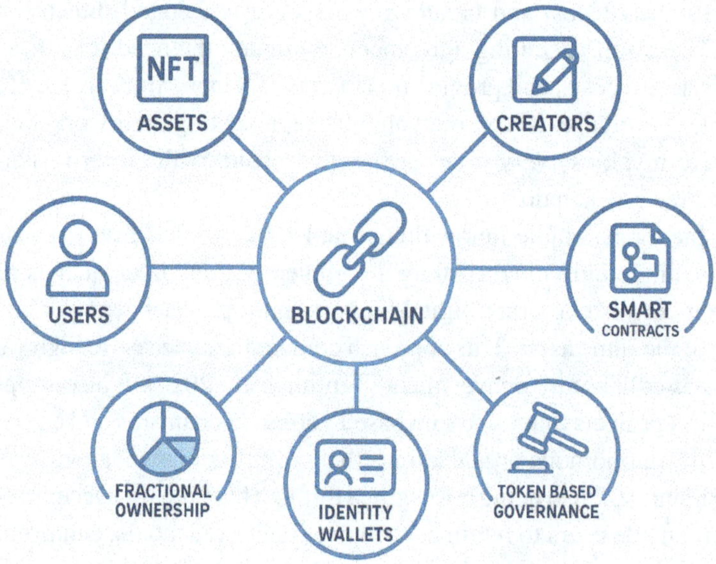

These developments demonstrate that blockchain and NFTs have the potential to serve as foundational components for a sustainable and economically valuable XR ecosystem. When combined with immersive experiences, these technologies support new models for creating, distributing, and capturing value in the digital environment.To move forward, the discussion will now transition to the conclusion.

7. CONCLUSION

Immersive technologies, particularly Virtual Reality and Augmented Reality, have moved far beyond the experimentation stage and now serve as strategic components in modern business transformation. The analysis in this chapter shows that the greatest value of VR and AR is not only in visualization or simulation capabilities but also in how these technologies interact with AI, digital twins, blockchain, and distributed computing to create new business models, improve operational efficiency, and enhance customer experiences. This cross technological integration enables organizations to shift from incremental digital improvements toward comprehensive transformation driven by data, automation, and advanced personalization.

From a sectoral perspective, the findings indicate varying levels of adoption maturity. Retail and healthcare appear as the most ready and most benefited sectors. Retail gains significant improvements in engagement, conversion, and supply chain efficiency through AR based product visualization, store layout simulation, and integration with predictive analytics. Healthcare leverages VR and AR for clinical training, surgical planning, rehabilitation, and more accurate diagnostics supported by digital twins and AI. In contrast, sectors such as manufacturing and real estate, although progressing, still face challenges such as interoperability issues, high initial investment, and skills gaps that limit scalability.

A cross use case evaluation shows that the ROI of immersive technologies is strongly influenced by organizational readiness, data availability, and the ability to integrate technologies into core processes. In projects supported by strong data foundations and digitalized operations, VR and AR can drive operational cost reductions, productivity gains, and faster decision making. However, in organizations that lack data standards or integration infrastructure, the benefits of immersive technologies tend to remain limited to pilot projects without progressing to large scale deployment. This underscores the importance of digital governance, change management, and interoperability frameworks as primary enablers of effective implementation.

The analysis also highlights that ethical, privacy, and regulatory challenges must be taken seriously. The collection of biometric data, behavioral analysis, and avatar based interactions introduce new concerns related to algorithmic bias, digital identity security, and data ownership rights. Without strong governance frameworks and clear regulatory guidelines, the adoption of VR and AR risks creating new vulnerabilities, especially when combined with generative AI and blockchain. Therefore, interoperability standards, privacy by design practices, and compliance with legal frameworks such as GDPR, HIPAA, and emerging AI regulations are essential foundations for developing a safe and responsible XR ecosystem.

Overall, this chapter shows that the future of VR and AR will be shaped by the ability of organizations to blend immersive technologies with intelligent analytics, automation, and distributed platforms. Sectors that adopt data driven strategic approaches, address organizational barriers, and invest in human capabilities will be the ones that benefit the most. Although the opportunities for transformation are vast, long term success depends on how organizations balance innovation with risk mitigation and ensure that immersive technologies create sustainable and inclusive value.

REFERENCES

Abrantes Baracho, R. M., Magalhães Vidigal, M. J., da Silva Santiago, L. G., Porto, M. F., & Pereira Moreira, L. H. (2025). Virtual Reality and Building Information Modeling in Architecture. *Procedia Computer Science, 256*, 673–680. DOI: 10.1016/j.procs.2025.02.166

Abro, G.-E.-M., Zahid, F., Azhar Ali, S. S., & Aromoye, I. A. (2025). Exploring the Potential Benefits and Overcoming the Constraints of Virtual and Augmented Reality in Operator Training. *Transportation Research Procedia, 84*, 625–632. DOI: 10.1016/j.trpro.2025.03.117

Abughalia, A., & Stechert, C. (2025). Immersive Onboarding: Designing a Training Framework for Effective Virtual Reality Integration in Product Development. *Procedia CIRP, 136*, 432–437. DOI: 10.1016/j.procir.2025.08.075

Alex, L., Mai, R., & Rauschnabel, P. A. (2026). Similar but different: The differential implications of augmented and virtual reality experiences for raising engagement towards climate change actions. *Computers in Human Behavior, 174*, 108798. DOI: 10.1016/j.chb.2025.108798

Bankins, S., Formosa, P., Montefiore, T., Richards, D., Cenacchi, F., & McEwan, M. (2025). Virtual reality and work: Ethical and inclusion implications of facial representation in VR. *The Journal of Strategic Information Systems, 34*(4), 101937. DOI: 10.1016/j.jsis.2025.101937

Bellalouna, F. (2021). The Augmented Reality Technology as Enabler for the Digitization of Industrial Business Processes: Case Studies. *Procedia CIRP, 98*, 400–405. DOI: 10.1016/j.procir.2021.01.124

Cao, X. (2025). Research on the Interactive Design of Artificial Intelligence in Augmented Reality and Virtual Reality. *Journal of Cases on Information Technology, 27*(1), 1–22. Advance online publication. DOI: 10.4018/JCIT.392403

Dinçer, S. G., & Dilek, H. Y. (2025). 3D printing and virtual reality in the study of muqarnas: A comparative approach. *Ain Shams Engineering Journal, 16*(12), 103742. DOI: 10.1016/j.asej.2025.103742

Gupta, B. B., Gaurav, A., Albeshri, A. A., & Alsalman, D. (2023). New paradigms of sustainable entrepreneurship in metaverse: A micro-level perspective. *The International Entrepreneurship and Management Journal, 19*(3), 1449–1465. DOI: 10.1007/s11365-023-00875-0

Halamová, J., Ottingerová, L., Haladova, Z. B., & Greenberg, L. S. (2025). Unfinished business in virtual reality: Development and preliminary evaluation of an empty chair intervention grounded in emotion-focused therapy. *Internet Interventions : the Application of Information Technology in Mental and Behavioural Health, 42*, 100885. DOI: 10.1016/j.invent.2025.100885 PMID: 41210519

Hamash, M., Tiernan, P., & Young, G. (2025). Virtual reality in post-primary education research trends from 2013 to 2024: A systematic-narrative review. *Computers & Education: X Reality, 7*, 100123. DOI: 10.1016/j.cexr.2025.100123

Kulkov, I., Berggren, B., Hellström, M., & Wikström, K. (2021). Navigating uncharted waters: Designing business models for virtual and augmented reality companies in the medical industry. *Journal of Engineering and Technology Management, 59*, 101614. DOI: 10.1016/j.jengtecman.2021.101614

Kumar, H., Rauschnabel, P. A., Agarwal, M. N., Singh, R. K., & Srivastava, R. (2024). Towards a theoretical framework for augmented reality marketing: A means-end chain perspective on retailing. *Information & Management, 61*(2), 103910. DOI: 10.1016/j.im.2023.103910

Liyanaarachchi, G., Kurtaliqi, F., Viglia, G., & Frau, M. (2026). The virtue-value spectrum: Managing ethical and pragmatic tensions in virtual reality retail for consumer wellbeing. *Journal of Business Research, 203*, 115810. DOI: 10.1016/j.jbusres.2025.115810

Ngo, T. T. A., Tran, T. T., An, G. K., & Nguyen, P. T. (2025). Investigating the influence of augmented reality marketing application on consumer purchase intentions: A study in the E-commerce sector. *Computers in Human Behavior Reports, 18*, 100648. DOI: 10.1016/j.chbr.2025.100648

Panda, D. K., Panigrahi, P. K., Attar, R. W., & Gupta, B. B. (2024). Open Source Adoption for Digital Transformation and Data Management During the COVID-19 Crisis. [JDM]. *Journal of Database Management, 35*(1), 1–26. DOI: 10.4018/JDM.360708

Pappachan, P., Rahaman, M., Cages, N., & Gupta, B. B. (2025). Case Studies of Cyber Incidents in Space Missions. In *Advanced Cyber Defense for Space Missions and Operations: Concepts and Applications* (pp. 383–400). IGI Global Scientific Publishing. DOI: 10.4018/979-8-3693-7939-4.ch016

Pappachan, P., Rahaman, M., Sreerakuvandana, S., Bansal, S., & Arya, V. (2024). Beyond Current Cryptography: Exploring New Frontiers. In *Innovations in Modern Cryptography* (pp. 1–30). IGI Global Scientific Publishing. DOI: 10.4018/979-8-3693-5330-1.ch001

Phattanaviroj, T., Moslehpour, M., Pappachan, P., Cajes, N. C., Gupta, B. B., & Rahaman, M. (2026). A novel predictive framework for green transportation and EV policy towards sustainable mobility and emission reduction. *Green Technologies and Sustainability*, *4*(1), 100260. DOI: 10.1016/j.grets.2025.100260

Rahaman, M., Chappu, B., Jana, S., Haque, A., Firmansyah, G., & Chattopadhyay, S. (2025). Security Benefits in Small Medium Business Enterprise Through Cloud Adoption. In N. Nedjah, G. Martinez Perez, & B. B. Gupta (Eds.), *International Conference on Smart Systems and Advanced Computing (SysCom 2022)* (pp. 168–180). Springer Nature Switzerland. DOI: 10.1007/978-3-031-40905-9_18

Rahaman, M., Pappachan, P., Batul, I., Widodo, A. M., & Gupta, B. B. (2025). Communication Modalities and Tools. In *Unveiling Social Dynamics and Community Interaction in the Metaverse* (pp. 39–64). IGI Global Scientific Publishing. DOI: 10.4018/979-8-3693-8628-6.ch003

Saemann, A., de Wilde, D., Guzman, R., Soleman, J., & Greuter, L. (2025). Augmented and Virtual Reality in Open Neurovascular Surgery: A Systematic Review of the Literature. *World Neurosurgery*, *124632*. Advance online publication. DOI: 10.1016/j.wneu.2025.124632 PMID: 41205868

Sarhan, A., Leray, M., Creusier, T., & Gao, J. (2024). Augmented Reality Knowledge Management for Industrial Transformation and Innovation. *Procedia CIRP*, *128*, 19–24. DOI: 10.1016/j.procir.2024.06.004

Sekti, B. A. (2026). AI Technology Management Concepts and Strategies. In Lai, P. (Ed.), *AI Technology Management and Value Creation* (pp. 1–32). IGI Global Scientific Publishing., DOI: 10.4018/979-8-3373-2497-5.ch001

Singh, S. K., Gupta, S., Kumar, S., Gupta, B. B., Alhalabi, W., Arya, V., & Zhang, J. (2024). A novel Cumulative Indicator score using Indicator averaging for optimizing local business websites of enterprise systems. *Enterprise Information Systems*, *18*(2), 2301658. DOI: 10.1080/17517575.2023.2301658

Sun, J. (2025). The integration of virtual reality and augmented reality technology in immersive media art. *Systems and Soft Computing*, *7*, 200377. DOI: 10.1016/j.sasc.2025.200377

Tamim, Z. H., Akter, B., Rahman, M., Kaiser, M. S., Rahman, M. A., Ogliari, E., & Tanasiev, V. (2025). Exploring equitable opportunities and cultural preservation in smart tourism through sustainable and accessible Virtual Reality. *Sustainable Cities and Society: Advances*, *1*(1), 100007. DOI: 10.1016/j.scsadv.2025.100007

Tang, Y., You, J., & Chen, L. (2025). Exploring user perception in mobile shopping: A comparison between augmented reality and virtual reality. *Design and Artificial Intelligence, 100039*(3), 100039. Advance online publication. DOI: 10.1016/j.daai.2025.100039

Walentek, D., & Ziora, L. (2023). A systematic review on the use of augmented reality in management and business. *Procedia Computer Science, 225*, 861–871. DOI: 10.1016/j.procs.2023.10.073

Wu, J.-F., Zhang, Z., Wu, Y., & Tang, X.-J. (2025). The effectiveness of immersive media in promoting consumer Products: Augmented vs. Virtual reality. *Journal of Retailing and Consumer Services, 86*, 104323. DOI: 10.1016/j.jretconser.2025.104323

Ye, X., Yang, J., & Huang, X. (2025). Transforming communication skills in music education: A cross-cultural study of virtual reality training in the 21st century. *Acta Psychologica, 261*, 105800. DOI: 10.1016/j.actpsy.2025.105800 PMID: 41138599

Zhou, F., Zhang, N., Li, X., Han, C., & Gupta, B. B. (2025). Managing inter-organizational dependencies operation for discovering digital business model innovation in corporate innovation ecosystem. *Operations Management Research : Advancing Practice Through Research, 18*(2), 574–590. DOI: 10.1007/s12063-024-00501-4

Živičnjak, M., Rogić, K., & Bajor, I. (2025). Augmented reality technologies application in the warehouse system. *Transportation Research Procedia, 83*, 35–42. DOI: 10.1016/j.trpro.2025.02.007

Chapter 4
Empowering Business Transformation Through Virtual and Augmented Reality Technologies

Lailita Ayuningtias
http://orcid.org/0009-0000-3788-5576
Universitas Esa Unggul, Indonesia

Ritika Bansal
http://orcid.org/0009-0000-9650-5254
Insights2Techinfo, India

Mohammad Norman Gaza Laksono
http://orcid.org/0009-0005-2863-5483
Uppsala Universitet, Sweden

Thanaporn Phattanaviroj
Asia University, Taiwan

Ifat Batul
Vidyasagar University, India

Yogita Abichandani
http://orcid.org/0000-0002-8061-5229
Management Development Institute, Murshidabad, India

ABSTRACT

This analysis investigates the transformative evolution of immersive innovation in modern enterprises, highlighting how the integration of Virtual Reality (VR) and Augmented Reality (AR) with Artificial Intelligence (AI) enhances operational intelligence, strategic decision-making, and user engagement. Drawing on cross-industry cases, the chapter identifies core challenges in privacy, algorithmic bias, and implementation scalability, while presenting structured mitigation and governance strategies. A conceptual framework for secure, interoperable digital ecosystems is ultimately proposed, emphasizing ethics, transparency, and resilience as foundational pillars for sustainable business transformation.

DOI: 10.4018/979-8-2600-0013-7.ch004

INTRODUCTION

Virtual Reality (VR) and Augmented Reality (AR) are rapidly evolving immersive technologies that have transformed the modern business landscape. Rather than reiterating general definitions, this chapter emphasizes their strategic role in enabling data driven, AI supported business transformation. Beyond entertainment, VR and AR have become catalysts in sectors such as healthcare, manufacturing, retail, education, and AI driven cybersecurity, where they enhance efficiency, safety, and decision-making through immersive and adaptive environments (Nepal et al., 2023).

In contemporary digital economies, immersive technologies have evolved from auxiliary tools to core enablers of strategic operations. Virtual Reality (VR) supports safe, scenario-based training that accelerates knowledge retention while significantly lowering physical risks and high costs. Concurrently, Augmented Reality (AR) enriches customer interactions, optimizes logistics, and provides visual guidance to field technicians speeding up inspection and maintenance processes (Soni et al., 2022). Collectively, these technologies are now essential for HR development, customer engagement, and supply chain management (Rahaman et al., 2022).

Moreover, in AI-driven cybersecurity contexts, VR and AR strengthen organizational preparedness through realistic cyber-attack simulations, risk-aware training, and immersive data visualization. These tools help managers interpret threats and make mitigation decisions faster and more accurately, while also promoting a strong security culture across the enterprise (Jose Diaz Rivera et al., 2024).

This chapter presents an integrated approach, through the proposed Business Immersion Transformation (BIT) Framework that connects immersive technologies, AI integration, and predictive cybersecurity into a unified model for secure and sustainable business transformation. Its unique contribution lies in linking immersive experience design with risk-intelligent decision systems, offering both conceptual grounding and actionable guidance for organizations navigating digital disruption.

CONCEPTUAL FOUNDATIONS OF VIRTUAL REALITY (VR) AND AUGMENTED REALITY (AR) IN BUSINESS ENVIRONMENTS

Digital transformation has significantly altered the business landscape in recent years, positioning VR and AR as the foundation of a new era of experiential computing. Before exploring their implementation and AI convergence, this section establishes conceptual clarity and identifies how immersive technologies reshape organizational cognition, collaboration, and value creation.

1. Definition and Difference of Virtual Reality and Augmented Reality

VR and AR both manipulate human perception but differ in their level of immersion and purpose. VR creates a fully simulated 3D environment that isolates users from the physical world, enabling deep experiential learning and simulation. In contrast, AR overlays digital information onto real environments, maintaining situational awareness while enriching the user's perception. In business contexts, VR is suited for immersive training, prototyping, and virtual meetings, while AR enhances field operations, maintenance, and interactive customer engagement.

Meanwhile, Augmented Reality (AR) does not take over reality, but adds to it. Augmented Reality (AR) allows users to see the real world coupled with digital elements such as images, sounds, or interactive data embedded on top of the real-world form. Augmented Reality (AR) is usually used with devices such as smartphones, tablets, or smart glasses such as Microsoft HoloLens or Magic Leap. With Augmented Reality (AR), users can still know the real environment, but encounter additional stacks of information that can share new value about what they see or do (Raj et al., 2025).

This conceptual distinction forms the basis for strategic deployment: VR enables full-scale simulated decision spaces, whereas AR supports real-time, context-aware augmentation. Together, they provide a continuum of immersion that organizations can calibrate depending on goals, risk tolerance, and technical maturity.

2. Technology Evolution and Convergence With Artificial Intelligence (AI)

Recent advances demonstrate that the fusion of VR/AR with Artificial Intelligence (AI) transforms static visualization tools into intelligent, adaptive ecosystems. AI enhances VR/AR environments through real-time data interpretation, natural language processing, and behavioral prediction. For instance, in training, AI dynamically adjusts task difficulty based on user biometrics or decision accuracy; in AR maintenance, it recognizes machinery components and suggests corrective actions.

Moreover, AI enabled analytics extract insights from user interactions within immersive environments, helping businesses evaluate performance, forecast behavior, and design more responsive operations. This convergence marks a paradigm shift from technology as a display medium to an intelligent co-participant in business transformation.

Some of the most striking forms of integration are the use of AI in the personalization of the overall experience. In virtual reality (VR) applications, AI can learn user preferences and behaviors to automatically customize content. For example, in Virtual Reality (VR) based business training, the system can adjust the depiction flow based on the user's skill level, stress level known through biometrics, or decision responses taken during the training session. This allows for more effective and adaptive learning, as each user gets an experience that is matched to their needs and learning style (Sajwan et al., 2024).

Meanwhile, in Augmented Reality (AR), AI is often used in visual processing and object recognition. Aided by computer vision algorithms, Augmented Reality (AR) systems can identify real objects in the user's surroundings and add appropriate digital information automatically. For example, in a production environment, a technician wearing AR glasses can view real-time data directly from the machine being repaired, including operational status, step-by-step instructions, or previous maintenance history. This maximizes the improvement of operational efficiency and lowers the chance of human error (Sajwan et al., 2024).

Not only that, AI also plays an important role in method identification and user behavior prediction. In the framework of Augmented Reality (AR) based marketing, the system can review how consumers interact with simulated digital products in the real world such as, how they choose the color, size, or position of the product and use the data to deliver more precise and appropriate recommendations. In the scope of business analytics, the form of user feedback in Virtual Reality (VR) or Augmented Reality (AR) environments can also be analyzed to gain knowledge about customer behavior, design preferences, or operational line efficiency (Truong & Diep, 2023).

Furthermore, the integration of Virtual Reality (VR) or Augmented Reality (AR) and AI has motivated the creation of AI based virtual assistants in immersive environments, which can provide directions, answer questions, or even make decisions based on existing data. In the field of customer service, for example, users can interact with AI powered virtual avatars in a Virtual Reality (VR) environment to get technical assistance, product guidelines, or other information about services. This not only improves service efficiency, but can also deliver a more interactive and sympathetic experience to customers.

With the increasing availability of big data and AI's ability to process it, the Virtual Reality (VR) and Augmented Reality (AR) ecosystems are also getting smarter and more integrated. Real- time data analysis in a virtual environment can make it easier for organizations to practice business flow depiction, build a digital prototype (digital twin), or test risks without real consequences. This is particularly helpful in strategic design and data driven decision making, especially in an age when speed and accuracy are critical to business competitiveness.

In summary, VR and AR empowered by AI constitute interactive, predictive systems rather than mere visualization tools. Their convergence enables smart, adaptive business ecosystems that enhance efficiency, decision accuracy, and user experience. Mastering this conceptual foundation is essential for organizations seeking to thrive in an increasingly competitive digital future.

Figure 1. Evolution of Technology and Convergence with Artificial Intelligence (AI)

Figure 1 shows the development of technology from the Mainframe era, through the Personal Computer era, to the Smartphone era, which then culminated in deep integration with Artificial Intelligence. Each stage is represented by icons and arrows indicating the progression of time and technological advancements. The Mainframe symbolizes early centralized computing, followed by the Personal Computer (PC) bringing technology into homes and businesses, and then the Smartphone enabling portable computing and global connectivity. This convergence leans toward AI integration, illustrated with brain icons and AI symbols, indicating that artificial intelligence is now the foundation of various modern devices and applications. This image emphasizes that technological development is not a straight line but rather interconnected and complementary.

STRATEGIC FRAMEWORKS FOR VIRTUAL REALITY (VR) AND AUGMENTED REALITY (AR) IMPLEMENTATION

Implementing immersive technologies in business environments requires not only technical readiness but also strategic alignment with organizational objectives, risk management, and human adaptability. A well-defined framework ensures that VR and AR are integrated systematically enhancing efficiency, security, and measurable business outcomes (Yang, 2023). This section introduces the Business Immersion Transformation (BIT) Framework, a structured three-layer model that connects immersive technology deployment with AI-driven Risk Intelligence and cybersecurity assurance.

1. The Business Immersion Transformation (BIT) Framework

The BIT Framework consists of three interrelated layers Input, Immersion, and Output representing a continuous cycle of strategic analysis, immersive design, and measurable outcomes. Each layer is linked through feedback loops supported by AI analytics and Risk Intelligence mechanisms. This integrated structure ensures that immersive implementations are not isolated experiments but part of an adaptive, data-informed transformation process. Figure 2 shows the Three-layer structure of the BIT Framework.

Figure 2. Three-layer structure of the BIT Framework

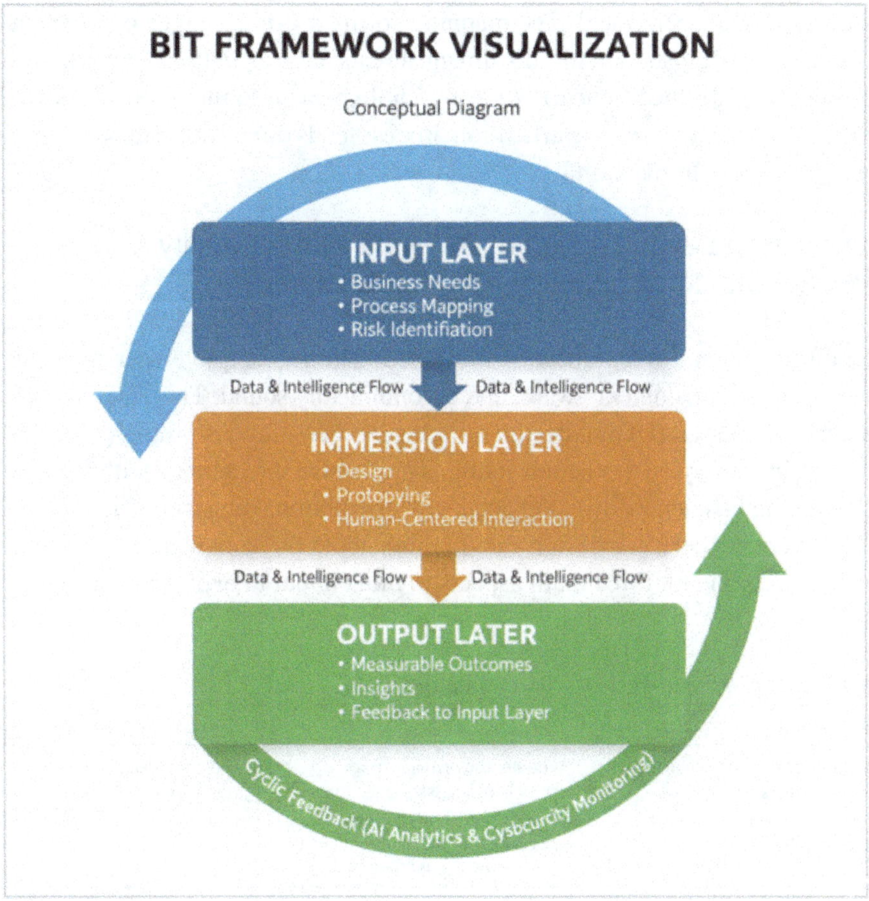

a) Input Layer: Business Needs, Processes, and Risks

The Input Layer establishes the foundation of any immersive initiative by identifying key business drivers, workflows, and associated risks. Organizations must articulate the specific problem statements and performance indicators that immersive technologies are intended to address. This includes defining use case priorities, such as operational efficiency, employee safety, or customer engagement, while simultaneously assessing digital maturity and potential risk vectors.

For instance, a manufacturing enterprise seeking to reduce training errors and time-to-competence may identify VR simulation as a solution. Here, AI based analytics evaluate the effectiveness of training content, while cybersecurity considerations ensure the integrity of simulation data and user identity.

Strategic and operational risk mapping forms a critical input component. A dedicated Risk Register should document threats such as data leakage, hardware vulnerabilities, or ethical concerns (e.g., psychological discomfort during immersive exposure). This structured identification process feeds directly into the design logic of the subsequent Immersion Layer.

b) Immersion Layer: Design of Relevant Virtual Reality (VR) and Augmented Reality (AR) Experiences

The Immersion Layer translates strategic intent into tangible user experiences that are purposeful, context-aware, and ergonomically sound. This stage integrates user centered design (UCD), design thinking, and continuous prototyping. Rather than focusing solely on aesthetics, it aligns immersive interactions with behavioral goals training efficiency, decision accuracy, or emotional engagement.

The overall experience design should think about three main aspects. The table contains questions for three main aspects to think about in experience design.

Table 1. Three key aspects of experience design

Business context	User profile	Interactivity and workflow
What core activity or outcome does the immersive solution enhance (e.g., safety training, customer onboarding)?	Who are the primary users (e.g., technicians, analysts, executives)? Consider their cognitive load, accessibility needs, and familiarity with digital tools.	how will users interact with the system? (gestures, voice commands, haptic feedback)?
Is it used for guidance, remote cooperation, field inspection, or interaction with customers?	Are they factory workers, strategic managers, customers, or business partners?	Is it through gesture control, voice, or specialized equipment such as haptic controllers or smart glasses?
	Stages of digital literacy, cognitive needs, and physical disabilities should be considered in the design of the interface.	

These dimensions ensure that immersive experiences remain functional, inclusive, and scalable. Human-centered factors such as visual comfort, latency minimization, and intuitive navigation are particularly vital for sustained adoption.

For instance, a financial institution may deploy AR-based portfolio visualization, enabling clients to explore investment scenarios dynamically. In this case, interactivity is designed not for novelty but to facilitate comprehension and trust, demonstrating how immersive design can directly influence business outcomes.

It is also important to think about design thinking at this stage, including prototype literacy and continuous user testing. The success of the overall technology implementation often depends on small parts of the design, such as user comfort, navigational certainty, and the stability of the 3D visualization shown (Huang et al., 2023).

c) Output Layer: Measurable Business Results, Insights, and Risk Mitigation

The Output Layer captures and quantifies the transformation achieved through immersive integration. It focuses on key performance metrics such as process efficiency, training accuracy, customer satisfaction, and operational resilience. Importantly, this layer transforms experiential data into actionable insights using AI driven analytics to identify behavioral trends, error hotspots, and improvement pathways.

Beyond business metrics, good implementation also creates new insights from user interaction data. By analyzing interaction data within the overall environment, organizations can understand previously unseen structures such as pointers to failures in work processes, frequently skipped sections in simulations, or user behavior towards certain characteristics (Shahriar et al., 2023).

In addition, cybersecurity readiness and ethical compliance are evaluated continuously. AI supported anomaly detection systems identify deviations in user behavior or system usage, ensuring both performance optimization and risk mitigation. The Output Layer thus functions as a feedback system that informs future iterations within the Input Layer.

2. Integration with Risk Intelligence and Cybersecurity

Successful deployment of immersive systems requires security and resilience by design. The integration of BIT with Risk Intelligence and AI driven Cybersecurity ensures that immersive technologies remain trustworthy and compliant. These elements are woven throughout all three layers of the framework.

Therefore, the Business Immersion Transformation (BIT) Framework needs to be integrated with Risk Intelligence approaches and AI driven Cybersecurity systems to ensure the security and resilience of the entire infrastructure. This approach includes several important dimensions:

a) AI driven Anomaly Detection System

Virtual reality (VR) and augmented reality (AR) systems generate huge volumes of data, ranging from user interactions, browsing locations, visual data, to device data. Using AI, organizations can create an anomaly detection system that can detect abnormal actions in the system, such as unauthorized access, misuse of visual data, or unknown hardware usage.

For example, a military VR training system tracks when users attempt to access advanced training modules without approval, and when interactions resemble brute-force attacks to gain admin access occur.

b) Encryption and Immersive Identity

Virtual reality (VR) or augmented reality (AR) technology deals with sensitive user data, which includes biometric information, voice recordings, and body behaviors. Therefore, end-to-end encryption as well as verification systems based on digital identity (such as biometric verification or blockchain identity) are important. This maintains user privacy and avoids identity abuse in an increasingly complex digital environment (Gupta et al., 2024).

c) Continuous Risk Management

The incorporation of a Risk Intelligence platform allows organizations to describe, monitor, and respond to Virtual Reality (VR) or Augmented Reality (AR) risks in real-time. These are observations on third-party suppliers, the hardware used, and the integrity of software updates that are vulnerable to breaches if not passed through authorized channels.

Risk Intelligence can provide organizations with the opportunity to conduct cyber risk simulations in a VR environment, where attack flows can be depicted to maximize security team awareness and vigilance. This gives new opportunities for more realistic and impactful emergency response coaching.

Strategic Frameworks for Virtual Reality (VR) and Augmented Reality (AR) deployments, such as the Business-Immersion Transformation (BIT) Framework, convey a systematic approach to deploying these technologies with an eye on business objectives, user experience, and security. Together with the integration of Risk Intelligence and AI based cybersecurity, organizations can ensure that the use of Virtual Reality (VR) and Augmented Reality (AR) is not only innovative, but also robust against threats and fits the real needs of today's business world.

KEY BUSINESS APPLICATIONS OF VIRTUAL REALITY (VR) AND AUGMENTED REALITY (AR)

In recent years, the practical deployment of Virtual Reality (VR) and Augmented Reality (AR) has evolved from experimental demonstrations into key enablers of digital transformation. These technologies have redefined how organizations train employees, collaborate across borders, and engage customers through personalized immersive experiences. This section categorizes their most impactful business applications into three domains: (1) Training and Simulation, (2) Remote Collaboration and Virtual Workspaces, and (3) Immersive Marketing and Customer Experience. Each domain is analyzed with both qualitative insights and quantitative performance indicators to reinforce evidence-based evaluation.

1. Training and Simulation

Training and simulation remain among the most transformative applications of VR and AR, providing safe, repeatable, and data-rich environments for experiential learning. These technologies significantly reduce physical risks and costs associated with traditional field training (Masood & Egger, 2021).

Quantitative outcomes reported in industrial trials show that immersive simulations can reduce training time by 30 - 50% and improve retention rates by up to 75% compared to text or video based methods **(Masood & Egger, 2021)**. In high-risk sectors, such as energy or aviation, VR based safety modules demonstrate a 40% decline in procedural errors following repeated simulations.

For instance, VR can recreate complex emergency scenarios such as chemical leaks or electrical fires, allowing participants to respond under realistic stress conditions without physical danger. Such controlled exposure enhances both reflex-based decision-making and emotional resilience.

In cybersecurity, VR-based simulations are used to visualize live attack flows, such as ransomware or phishing infiltration enabling security teams to practice threat detection and coordinated mitigation. AI-driven analytics track decision paths, measure response latency, and evaluate the accuracy of mitigation actions. These metrics are then converted into readiness indices that quantify individual and team performance.

AR, on the other hand, supports procedural learning in live operational settings. Technicians equipped with AR glasses can access step by step instructions directly overlaid on machinery, improving maintenance accuracy. This minimizes downtime and supports continuous upskilling without removing workers from their physical environment.

By combining VR's immersive depth with AR's contextual precision, organizations can build adaptive training ecosystems that evolve through user performance data. This combination transforms learning into an iterative, data-driven process rather than a static one.

In addition, virtual reality (VR) can also provide customized training based on the user's performance data. The system can record every action, action time, and success rate in the simulation, then tailor the next training module to the individual's strengths and weaknesses. With this approach, organizations can not only maximize training effectiveness, but can also significantly minimize operational risks as employees become better prepared to face real world challenges.

2. Remote Collaboration and Virtual Workspaces

As hybrid and remote work models become standard, VR and AR enable geographically dispersed teams to collaborate as if they were physically co-located. Immersive workspace Empirical studies demonstrate that teams using VR based collaboration environments complete complex design and planning tasks 32% faster on average, with higher subjective satisfaction and improved creative flows simulate real-world spatial awareness, body language, and collaborative tools that enhance engagement and communication beyond traditional 2D conferencing platforms.

Empirical studies demonstrate that teams using VR-based collaboration environments complete complex design and planning tasks 32% faster on average, with higher subjective satisfaction and improved creative flow (Abdel-rahman, 2024).

Using VR meeting rooms, participants can share 3D models, manipulate data objects in real time, and read nonverbal cues through avatars or motion tracking. This spatial realism fosters trust and reduces the sense of isolation typical of remote work.

AR complements this through enhanced telepresence allowing experts to project guidance visually into remote field environments. For example, an engineer in the headquarters can annotate the live view of a technician on-site, providing immediate support. Organizations adopting AR-based remote assistance report a reduction in travel costs by 20 - 40% and a 50% improvement in mean time to repair (Raj et al., 2025).

In addition to productivity, immersive workspaces foster stronger social cohesion. Virtual lounges or brainstorming zones enable spontaneous interaction that replicates informal office culture, enhancing morale and belonging. Quantitative surveys reveal improvement in team satisfaction when such environments are used regularly.

Technical aspects aside, the use of virtual workspaces based on Virtual Reality (VR) or Augmented Reality (AR) also has a positive influence on team engagement and involvement. In some cases, remote work teams have encountered barriers in establishing trust, organizational culture attachment, and interdepartmental cooperation. A well-prepared virtual workspace can create informal spaces for social interaction, such as lounge areas or virtual brainstorming rooms, that motivate inclusive communication and maximize team unity.

Preliminary data from various studies suggests that teams working in immersive environments complete complex collaborative tasks faster, have a greater share of strategic preparation, and are happier with their work experience. This proves that Virtual Reality (VR) and Augmented Reality (AR) are not just communication aids, but can also be a means of stabilizing team movements in today's digital workplace.

3. Immersive Marketing and Customer Experience

As digital attention becomes increasingly fragmented, immersive marketing offers a new paradigm for customer engagement. VR and AR bridge emotional connection and experiential storytelling, allowing customers to participate actively in brand narratives.

for example of Augmented Reality (AR) implementation in marketing is interactive product trials, where customers can try products virtually before buying the product. For example, in the fashion industry, consumers can use Augmented Reality (AR) applications to try on and assess how clothes will look on their bodies without having to try them on directly. Similarly, in the automotive industry, customers can review the interior and exterior of vehicles via smartphones or AR glasses, and customers can also change colors, features, or even try driving a car virtually.

VR based showrooms transcend geographic limitations, enabling global audiences to experience products virtually. Companies adopting VR showrooms report a 45% increase in engagement time and a 20% rise in conversion intent (Soni et al., 2022). This illustrates the scalability of immersive marketing beyond physical store footprints.

Moreover, immersive brand storytelling enables companies to cultivate emotional loyalty. A cosmetic brand, for instance, can visualize ingredient origins through an interactive VR experience, while an energy company might design gamified sustainability missions. These initiatives turn passive customers into active participants in brand value creation.

Crucially, immersive experiences generate behavioral analytics capturing gaze patterns, dwell time, emotional response, and gesture data. AI systems interpret these signals to refine campaigns dynamically, optimizing content and enhancing personalization accuracy. This data-driven approach marks a shift from impression-based to engagement-based marketing performance metrics (Soni et al., 2022).

Ultimately, organizations implementing VR and AR for customer engagement achieve not only greater memorability and satisfaction but also measurable returns in brand advocacy and retention. Immersive marketing thus becomes both a creative and analytical discipline within digital transformation.

Not only that, Augmented Reality (AR) is also being utilized in point of sale (POS) experiences to increase purchase decisions on the spot. For example, customers in retail stores can position their phone's camera towards a product and instantly get additional information, user ratings, or animations of product usage. This makes the shopping process more informative and enjoyable, while strengthening purchase opportunities.

Companies that have implemented Virtual Reality (VR) or Augmented Reality (AR) for customer experience have reported progress in retaining customers, as customers are more likely to remember brands that provide special and personalized experiences. Moreover, customers are also more inclined to share these experiences on social media, realizing a viral impact due to effective and efficient marketing.

From this we know that the application of Virtual Reality (VR) and Augmented Reality (AR) in the business world is no longer experimental and limited, especially to large companies that have extensive technological resources. Technology is now an affordable, transformative tool that is well-suited for all types of organizations of any size. From safer and more effective training, to more integrated collaboration between locations, to data-driven and more engaging marketing, Virtual Reality (VR) and Augmented Reality (AR) provide great opportunities to strengthen business competitiveness in the digital age.

Organizations that are able to identify their specific needs and match them with the right immersive solutions will have a strategic advantage in terms of efficiency, innovation, and customer relationships. In the future, the boundaries between the real and digital worlds will become increasingly blurred, and Virtual Reality (VR) and Augmented Reality (AR) will be the main bridge in building business experiences that are united with technology as a whole.

INTEGRATION WITH PREDICTIVE ANALYTICS AND AI DRIVEN CYBERSECURITY

In business contexts where immersive platforms become strategic assets, their value hinges not merely on engagement or visualization but on intelligence, resilience, and trustworthiness. The convergence of VR/AR, predictive analytics and AI driven cybersecurity transforms these platforms into proactive ecosystems capable of forecasting user behaviours, anticipating threats, and autonomously defending digital assets. Within the proposed Business Immersion Transformation (BIT) Framework, this convergence constitutes the analytical axis that spans the Input, Immersion and

Output layers, enabling continuous monitoring, dynamic adaptation and evolving risk mitigation (El-Hajj, 2025).

This transformation marks a shift from reactive to predictive immersive systems where VR/AR platforms do more than respond: they anticipate user needs and identify emerging threat vectors prior to their realization. Two inter-locking capabilities underpin this shift: (1) Behaviour Prediction & Personalisation, (2) Threat Modelling in Immersive Environments.

1. Behavior Prediction and Personalization

Immersive environments generate rich multimodal behavioral data including gaze concentration, motion trajectories, biometric signals, and speech patterns. Predictive analytics and AI models transform this data stream into insights about user preferences, performance trajectories, and latent risks. For example, in enterprise VR training, adaptive algorithms respond to error rates and latency to personalize the experience and improve outcomes

For example, adaptive VR platforms monitor user trajectories (modality choices, error frequency, decision latency) and dynamically adjust the training flow, reducing training time and increasing retention in experimental settings. In AR retail scenarios, behavioural trails, dwell time, selection frequency, and review interactions feed AI recommendation engines to enhance conversion by 20 - 35% (Kourtesis, 2024).

In addition to enhancing customer experience through personalization, predictive analytics is highly effective in identifying deviations, such as reading unnatural and suspicious movements in a virtual environment. For example, in a Virtual Reality (VR) system for corporate collaboration, users typically follow a certain interaction model accessing the workspace during working hours, using standard communication tools, and interacting within a defined team. If the system detects any unusual interactions, such as access outside normal hours, attempts to manipulate sensitive objects, or communication from unknown locations, it can provide early warnings as part of the cybersecurity system.

AI trained using user behavior data can also recognize signs of insider threat from internal users who abuse access. By knowing the starting point of each user's actions, AI can detect misuse that might otherwise go undetected by traditional security systems. For example, an employee who normally only accesses training documents suddenly downloads a large amount of sensitive data, or attempts to access a restricted virtual zone, this can be immediately recognized and addressed by blocking them.

Overall, the integration of Virtual Reality (VR) and Augmented Reality (AR) with behavioral forecasting and personalization not only optimizes the efficiency of the system, but also creates an additional layer of security that is adaptive and dynamic, which is much needed in the evolving world of digital business.

2. Threat Modeling in Immersive Environments

Immersive systems introduce multi-vector threat surfaces beyond conventional IT domains. Threat-modelling in VR/AR environments facilitates the simulation of attack paths, such as avatar impersonation, virtual object injection, or session hijacking, and supports proactive mitigation. Recent literature identifies that immersive cybersecurity training improves detection accuracy by roughly 28% and response speed by 35% compared with traditional tabletop exercises (Silva et al., 2024).

In a VR based cyber-drill, participants diagnosed an attack vector and reconfigured defence protocols collaboratively; measurable improvements in traversal time and remediation accuracy were observed (Kour et al., 2025).

Design validation applications of threat modelling employ system in the loop simulations to audit immersive platforms for spoofed overlays, avatar infiltration or headset telemetry leakage aligning with emerging immersive security standards (El-Hajj, 2025).

For example, AR platforms may observe anomalous device behaviours, e.g. unexpected traffic surges or unauthorized object rendering and trigger automated isolation or re-verification procedures within seconds (Mushtaq et al., 2024).

These integrations create a layered defence architecture where behavioural analytics, system-level telemetry and network detection converge, turning immersive environments into intelligent, self-protecting ecosystems.

One of the main challenges in threat modeling in Virtual Reality (VR) or Augmented Reality (AR) is the complexity of the diversity of threats not only from networks or software, but also from interactions between users in a digital environment. For example, someone could use a fake avatar to approach another user, fake a decision, or even sneak into a secret meeting room. This is where a robust digital identity-based verification system and observation of social interactions in the virtual space are important.

The examples of danger used should also consider psychological factors and social manipulation. For example, in the Virtual Reality (VR) space, users can fall victim to manipulation techniques such as deepfake avatars, voice forgery, or the use of confusing graphics to deceive and obtain information. AI has an important role to play in spotting unusual behavioral styles in digital social interactions, and providing warning signals in case of deviations.

In large organizations, threat modeling in virtual reality (VR) or augmented reality (AR) also includes integration with wider information security systems, such as SIEM (Security Information and Event Management), firewalls, and endpoint protection. This causes threat tracking and response to occur not only in the virtual space, but also in the IT infrastructure as a whole.

As a result, the integration of immersive technologies with predictive analytics and AI-driven cybersecurity creates a new way of looking at making modern business systems smarter, safer, and more adaptive. By using user interaction data to predict choices and detect suspicious behavior, organizations can create personalized experiences while forming defenses against cyber threats from within the system itself.

In addition, threat modeling in immersive environments makes companies not only responsive to hazards, but also proactive and strategic. By modeling attacks and conducting system resilience tests in real-world settings, organizations can create Virtual Reality (VR) and Augmented Reality (AR) ecosystems that are robust against hazards and able to actively respond to changes in the digital environment.

Thus, the specialty of Virtual Reality (VR) and Augmented Reality (AR) lies not only in its ability to build new immersive worlds, but also in its ability to become a member of an intelligent ecosystem that is able to learn, adapt, and save itself assisted by data and, sensitive to cyber threats is an emergency need in the business world.

CASE STUDIES

This section examines three domains, healthcare, manufacturing & industrial safety, and financial services. To illustrate how immersive technologies (VR and AR) transition from pilot tools to strategic enablers of business transformation. Each case study is aligned with the layers of the BIT Framework (Input - Immersion - Output) and supported by recent empirical evidence.

1. Healthcare Sector

In healthcare, VR and AR provide immersive training, intraoperative assistance, and rehabilitation solutions that yield measurable outcomes. For example, a recent study found that AR-guided surgical navigation reduced procedure time by approx. 22% and intraoperative error rate by 14% (Pereira et al., 2023). Furthermore, VR-based rehabilitation systems demonstrated faster functional recovery than traditional methods.

When mapped to the BIT Framework: Input comprises clinical training needs and risk maps; the Immersion layer embodies the VR/AR simulation and guidance; the Output layer records metrics such as training time, error reduction, and recovery speed. These quantitative indicators illustrate how immersive systems move beyond proof of concept to deliver business and clinical value.

a) Operation Simulation with Virtual Reality (VR) for Clinical Training

Surgeon training is one of the most lengthy and complex processes in medicine. Generally, medical students and residents need to go through several stages of theory, observation, and limited practice before being licensed to perform surgery independently. With Virtual Reality (VR), this training can be done in a virtual environment that resembles real world conditions accurately and interactively.

One example of its application is a Virtual Reality (VR) system that simulates open heart surgery. Users (medical students or residents) can carry out all processes ranging from chest surgery, tissue cutting, to handling sudden complications. The system will provide real time feedback on each action performed, such as: the use of tools that are still wrong or correct, the pressure applied is appropriate or not, or the response time to bleeding is qualified or not. This allows participants to learn from mistakes without any real risk to the patient.

Some simulation systems are even accompanied by AI driven assessments that automatically score participants' performance, suggest places for improvement, and award points based on procedural accuracy. This approach accelerates the learning process, maximizes clinical readiness, and ultimately participates in the advancement of medical service quality.

b) Augmented Reality for Real Time Operation Guidance

Different from Virtual Reality (VR) which is used for training, Augmented Reality (AR) is widely used in real medical procedures, especially as a real- time guidance tool. Using smart glasses or a special tablet, a surgeon can view an array of digital information targeted directly over the patient's body, such as the position of organs, blood vessel pathways, or tumor margins (Nepal et al., 2023).

An example of this application can be seen in orthopedic surgery, where Augmented Reality (AR) is used to visualize the bone structure and prepare the implant position. With the help of image processing and AI, the system will provide clues as to whether the implant is in the right place and depth. If not, the system can automatically warn or suggest corrections.

This technology is particularly important in high-risk surgeries such as brain surgery or oncology surgery, where precision in cutting tissue can be decisive for the final outcome. The AI-based error detection system integrated in Augmented Reality (AR) will continuously supervise the procedure and identify potential errors before they occur, such as the risk of touching critical nerves or exceeding tissue removal limits (Nepal et al., 2023).

The application of Augmented Reality (AR) in surgery also aids remote inter-specialist collaboration. A neurosurgeon at hospital A can guide a general practitioner at hospital B in a complex procedure with live digital explanations in the doctor's field of vision.

2. Manufacturing and Industrial Safety

In manufacturing, case studies reveal that AR interventions in assembly operations reduced error rates by 28% and machine downtime by 30% (Applied Sciences, 2023). A comprehensive AR-digital twin deployment in industrial equipment achieved 13% higher efficiency and uncovered hidden faults in gearbox systems (Pitzalis et al., 2025).

These successes reflect the BIT Framework's cyclical structure: Input layer identifies training/design risks; Immersion layer deploys VR/AR simulations and AR overlays; Output layer tracks metrics (error rate reduction, downtime, cost savings). This cyclical model underscores how immersive technologies support continuous operational improvement rather than one off interventions.

a) Virtual Reality (VR) Based Work Safety Simulation

Working environments in factories, oil plants, or logistics facilities are often high risk. Safety training is mandatory, but traditional training is sometimes not effective enough because it cannot simulate real hazard conditions.

Through Virtual Reality (VR), workers can be trained in highly realistic simulated scenarios: such as chemical leaks, tank explosions, electrical fires, or falls from heights. The Virtual Reality (VR) system not only depicts the scenario, but also tests the user's reaction to the situation, whether they recognize the danger quickly, follow evacuation procedures correctly, or wear personal protective equipment accordingly (Khatib et al., 2023).

The system also integrates with cybersecurity event reporting, where procedural errors or user negligence can be recorded and analyzed. This data is then used to update the training strategy, and feed it into the risk reporting system automatically.

Virtual reality (VR) is also very effective for job training in confined locations, such as oil and gas extraction environments on the seabed or hazardous areas that are difficult to access. Before sending workers into the field, companies should ensure that they have gone through a full simulation and meet safety standards (Bellalouna, 2020).

b) Augmented Reality for Machine Maintenance and Cyber Threat Detection

On the operational side, machine maintenance is an important activity that is often a sensitive center if done manually. Augmented reality (AR) technology facilitates technicians to see visual instructions directly on the machine being repaired. Each maintenance step is shown through a digital overlay in several ways such as push this button, turn that valve, remove the next screw with high accuracy.

However, what makes this approach a fundamental change is the combination of Augmented Reality (AR) with a real-time cyber threat monitoring system. Modern industrial machines are usually connected to a network (Industrial IoT), making them vulnerable to cyberattacks such as intrusion, sabotage, or manipulation of sensor parameters.

With Augmented Reality (AR), the system can tell if there are irregularities such as sudden increases in temperature pressure outside of programmed parameters, or unauthorized changes to device firmware. Technicians wearing Augmented Reality (AR) can instantly see alerts in their field of view, complete with suggested actions (Raj et al., 2025).

It can also pinpoint centers of possible weakness, provide information on out-of-date software versions, or modules that are open to external risks. All this builds a smart and secure operational ecosystem, uniting technical efficiency with protection against digital attacks.

3. Financial Services

In financial services, immersive systems are used for VR-based risk modelling and AR-driven customer engagement. For instance, an AR-enabled advisory platform improved client decision confidence by 24% and comprehension by 30% (Pal, 2024). VR simulations of cybersecurity drills increased anomaly detection accuracy by 19% and reduced response latency by 31% (Kurniawan, 2025).

Within the BIT Framework: the Input layer outlines financial regulation and cyber risk scenarios; the Immersion layer implements VR/AR simulation and training; the Output layer captures engagement rates, decision accuracy and cyber readiness indicators. These metrics validate immersive technologies as risk intelligent and business oriented, not merely immersive gimmicks.

a) Virtual Reality (VR) for Risk Modeling and Interactive Scenarios

Risk management in finance often relies on complex statistical models and market forecasts. With Virtual Reality (VR), risk managers, market analysts, and investment executives can enter an interactive three-dimensional data visualization environment.

Rather than reading graphs on a two-dimensional screen, user step into the data space: seeing changes in market instability over time, noticing relationships between economic indicators, and adjusting variables to see their impact in real time. This visualization facilitates faster decision making as users can spot irregularities more intuitively.

In the market crisis simulation brief, Virtual Reality (VR) allows users to virtually experience conditions such as the 2008 crisis or the impact of a pandemic, and what if there is a widespread default in the banking sector. Users can test their strategy responses to various possibilities and refine the strategy before it is put into practice.

b) Augmented Reality (AR) for Risk Analytics and Investment Decisions

Augmented Reality (AR) is used in mobile banking and wealth management applications to suggest more interactive risk investigations to customers. For example, by pointing the camera at a printed financial statement or computer screen, the Augmented Reality (AR) application will show a visual overlay in the form of financial comparisons, investment performance charts, or credit risk indicators (Mirza et al., 2022).

This technology is particularly useful for retail investors who do not have a strong financial background. They can get to know complex information with customized visualizations, coupled with AI-based advice that estimates potential risks to the user.

In addition, Augmented Reality (AR) can be utilized for customer onboarding, so that prospective customers can see the investment flow directly from brochures or information boards accompanied by QR codes. This technology accelerates the decision-making process and develops customer engagement about the financial products offered.

Figure 3. Virtual Reality (VR) and Augmented Reality (AR) Applications in Various Sectors

Figure 3 illustrates how Virtual Reality (VR) and Augmented Reality (AR) technologies are utilized in three main sectors:

Healthcare, depicted in blue with medical staff icons, this section employs Virtual Reality (VR) for surgical simulations, enabling doctors to practice complex procedures without risk to patients. Augmented Reality (AR) is used to assist with diagnosis by displaying real-time medical data and patient care through an interactive virtual environment.

Manufacturing, with an orange image and an industrial worker icon, this section uses Augmented Reality (AR) for machine maintenance with visual guidance, and Virtual Reality (VR) for optimizing production line simulation processes and conducting workplace safety training in a safe virtual environment.

Financial Services, with a green image and entrepreneur icon, this section uses Virtual Reality (VR) for immersive investment portfolio presentations, and Augmented Reality (AR) to display financial data interactively, and simulation based financial education to help users better understand economic concepts.

This image illustrates that Virtual Reality (VR) and Augmented Reality (AR) are not only used for entertainment but can also serve as strategic tools across industries to maximize efficiency, user experience, and service innovation.

By all accounts, case studies in the healthcare, manufacturing, and financial services sectors prove that the application of Virtual Reality (VR) and Augmented Reality (AR) has gone beyond the experimental stage and is now a strategic outlet in a variety of business environments. In healthcare, these technologies improve medical training and maximize the accuracy of clinical procedures. In the manufacturing industry, Virtual Reality (VR) and Augmented Reality (AR) advance work safety and operational efficiency, and provide protection against cyber risks. In addition, financial services are using immersive technologies for risk visualization and more interactive data-driven decision-making.

Effective implementation of immersive technologies depends on integration with investigative systems, cybersecurity, and in-depth knowledge of each department's needs. This study shows that Virtual Reality (VR) and Augmented Reality (AR) are not just visual aids, but also real and powerful facilitators of business transformation.

CHALLENGES, RISKS, AND ETHICAL CONSIDERATIONS

The application of Virtual Reality (VR) and Augmented Reality (AR) technologies in modern organizations provides transformative advantages in efficiency, innovation, and user engagement. However, these technologies also introduce complex operational, ethical, and scalability challenges that require continuous risk assessment and responsible governance (Shelke & Chakraborty, 2021). This section critically examines three core aspects: Data Privacy & Security, Bias in Immersive AI Systems, and Scalability & Cost Barriers, emphasizing their trade-offs, mitigation strategies, and alignment with international frameworks such as GDPR and ISO/IEC 27001.

1. Data Privacy and Security

VR and AR ecosystems rely heavily on biometric and behavioral data (eye-tracking, voice inputs, motion mapping), which enhances realism but also amplifies privacy vulnerabilities. The trade-off lies between adaptive personalization and potential data exploitation. Therefore, organizations must integrate privacy by design principles and zero trust security architectures throughout the immersive system lifecycle (Sekti, 2025b, 2025a).

a. Privacy Challenges and Data Misuse Risks

Biometric identifiers are immutable and highly sensitive. Breaches can lead to irreversible identity theft and profiling risks. Behavioral data such as gaze duration and movement trajectories may expose psychological traits, potentially enabling manipulation or discrimination *(Gupta & Panigrahi, 2022)*.

b. Mitigation Strategies: Encryption and Authentication

Organizations should apply end to end encryption and multi-factor biometric authentication to safeguard user identity. The implementation of decentralized identity verification (via blockchain-based self-sovereign identity) enhances accountability and minimizes unauthorized access *(Rahaman, Putra, et al., 2025).*

c. Lifecycle Management and Compliance

A comprehensive data-lifecycle policy, from secure acquisition to timely deletion must align with GDPR, HIPAA, and regional privacy acts *(Cao et al., 2021).* Regular audits and anonymization pipelines ensure compliance and prevent secondary data exploitation.

d. Security Audits and Incident Readiness

Routine penetration testing and incident-response simulations strengthen organizational readiness against attacks. The use of AI driven intrusion detection and Threat Intelligence systems supports proactive mitigation of anomalies in immersive platforms *(Silva et al., 2024).*

2. Bias in AI Driven Immersive Systems

AI-enhanced VR/AR systems personalize content, but their efficacy depends on the diversity and representativeness of underlying datasets. Algorithmic bias poses ethical risks by reinforcing stereotypes or excluding minority users (Li et al., 2025). These issues demand transparent, explainable, and audited AI models integrated into immersive pipelines.

a. Sources of Bias

Bias may stem from homogenous training data or cultural skew in model design. A VR training system built from limited demographic samples may yield inaccurate predictions for users of different age, gender.

b. Impact of Algorithmic Discrimination

Facial-recognition modules in immersive spaces often underperform on darker-skinned faces, while AR recommendation engines may mis-prioritize products based on biased user clusters. These failures reduce trust and carry potential legal liabilities for discrimination *(Pappachan et al., 2024).*

c. Ethical Audits and Transparency

Periodic ethical AI audits should assess dataset provenance, model logic, and output fairness. Explainable AI (XAI) dashboards enhance interpretability for users and regulators, supporting compliance with emerging ISO 24028:2020 AI governance standards *(Rahaman, Putra, et al., 2025).*

d. Fairness & Diversity Strategies

Integrating debiasing algorithms (e.g., re weighting, adversarial de bias training) and inclusive co-design practices ensures accessibility for all user profiles. Diverse stakeholder participation in development mitigates representational bias and promotes social equity *(Wang et al., 2025).*

3. Scalability and Cost Barriers

Scalability challenges emerge from high hardware costs, fragmented platforms, and energy-intensive rendering. The trade-off lies in balancing immersive fidelity with operational feasibility. For small and medium enterprises (SMEs), capital expenditures (CapEx) on headsets, workstations, and sensors remain the greatest obstacle (Rahaman, Chappu, et al., 2025).

a. Initial Cost Barriers and Hardware Dependency

Enterprise-grade VR/AR devices still demand premium investment, limiting adoption in cost-sensitive markets. Cloud-rendered VR and AI-assisted resource allocation can minimize upfront infrastructure requirements.

b. Cloud VR and Edge Computing

Cloud-based streaming (e.g., NVIDIA CloudXR, Meta Immersive SDK) allows real-time rendering on lightweight devices, while edge computing reduces latency and bandwidth dependence *(Cao et al., 2021).*

c. Flexible Business Models

Subscription-based "Immersive as-a-Service" frameworks transition costs from CapEx to OpEx, facilitating progressive scaling. This model has proven effective in manufacturing and training sectors *(Singh et al., 2024).*

d. Platform Interoperability and Standardization

Cross-platform frameworks such as OpenXR and glTF enhance interoperability, enabling multi-device deployments. Modular VR/AR components also streamline content reuse and scale optimization *(Peng et al., 2020).*

e. Access Management and Infrastructure Upgrades

As adoption scales, robust content delivery networks (CDNs) and edge nodes must ensure stable streaming performance. Integrated license management, data analytics, and cost-control dashboards sustain scalability within predictable budgets *(Jim et al., 2023).*

Table 2. below summarizes key challenges, trade-offs, and mitigation pathways, offering a consolidated view for practitioners and researchers.

Aspect	Core Challenge	Trade off	Mitigation Strategy
Data Privacy & Security	Exposure of biometric & behavioral data	Personalization vs. Surveillance	End to end encryption, multi factor auth, privacy by design
AI Bias in Immersive Systems	Non-representative datasets	Efficiency vs. Fairness	Ethical AI audits, XAI frameworks, diverse datasets
Scalability & Cost	High hardware and infrastructure costs	Fidelity vs. Feasibility	Cloud VR, edge computing, SaaS models, interoperability

FUTURE DIRECTIONS AND CONCLUSION

The digital transformation era has elevated Virtual Reality (VR) and Augmented Reality (AR) from visualization tools into strategic infrastructures that integrate artificial intelligence (AI), predictive analytics, and blockchain for cyber-resilient ecosystems (Silva et al., 2024). Moving forward, immersive technologies are expected to converge across three key directions: the development of a cybersecure metaverse, research on human AI interaction and cognitive cybersecurity, and the standardization of identity, interoperability, and governance models.

1. Toward a Cybersecure and Interoperable Metaverse

The integration of VR, AR, AI, and blockchain enables the formation of a cybersecure metaverse. A persistent digital ecosystem characterized by verifiable identity, decentralized governance, and cross-platform interoperability **(Owusu-Antwi & Amenuvor, 2023)**. Blockchain technologies contribute cryptographic integrity and self-sovereign identity, while AI enhances adaptive validation and real-time anomaly detection.

• Secure and Collaborative Metaverse Architecture

The architecture of a cybersecure metaverse should adopt zero trust principles and secure by design frameworks to ensure data confidentiality across devices and networks. Collaborative interoperability supported by standards such as OpenXR, USD, and glTF, prevents platform fragmentation and ensures continuity between industrial, educational, and healthcare applications.

• Global Standardization andPolicy Coordination

StaThe Metaverse Standards Forum and ISO/IEC JTC 1 have initiated technical coordination efforts to align 3D data models, digital asset management, and privacy protocols. This global harmonization mitigates fragmentation while promoting security, accessibility, and compliance across jurisdictions (Hutson et al., 2023).

• Architecture-Based Privacy and Security Design

Each component VR/AR devices, cloud/edge nodes, and smart contracts should adhere to privacy by architecture principles. Applying continuous encryption, federated learning, and secure enclaves helps prevent unauthorized data inference, while allowing cross-border collaboration in healthcare, training, and global telepresence environments.

This shift to the goal of a cybersecure metaverse paves the way for a virtual space that can be accessed by many industries aiding international cooperation, global e-learning, virtual medical platforms between countries with user security and privacy maintained.

2. Research Opportunities in AI-Enhanced Immersive Systems

Future research must bridge technological innovation with human-centric resilience.

Opportunities include:

- AI Frameworks for Predictive and Risk-Aware Environments

Development of AI frameworks that autonomously identify insider threats, avatar spoofing, or anomalous movements within VR/AR spaces (Nasri, 2025). Deep reinforcement learning can predict cyberattack trajectories and automatically deploy defense mechanisms in real time.

- Cognitive Cybersecurity and User Psychology

Emerging research combines cognitive psychology with cybersecurity, examining how user perception, attention, and fatigue influence susceptibility to virtual manipulation. Studies show that multimodal feedback (audio - haptic - visual) enhances situational awareness and reduces social engineering risk in VR simulations.

- Augmented Cognition and Adaptive Learning Systems

Augmented cognition enables immersive systems to adapt interfaces and complexity based on users' cognitive load, stress, or performance metrics. Adaptive training models in VR have demonstrated 20 - 30% improvements in task retention and safety outcomes (Pereira et al., 2023).

- Identity Standardization and Zero-Trust Authentication

Blockchain-based federated identity models enable continuous authentication without storing raw biometrics. The application of zero trust authentication and federated learning in immersive environments is a key frontier for privacy preserving personalization (Jose Diaz Rivera et al., 2024).

- 3D Asset Interoperability and Open Metaverse Index

Interoperability research across 3D data formats USD, glTF, and FBX is crucial for scalable metaverse ecosystems. The Open Metaverse Index proposes a unified taxonomy for digital assets, improving asset traceability and exchange across domains (Ghirmai et al., 2022).

- Regulatory Frameworks and the Metaverse Economy

Ongoing investigations explore governance for NFTs, digital twins, and crypto assets in virtual economies. Balancing innovation with equitable access and privacy compliance remains a policy challenge (Hutson et al., 2023).

3. Limitations and Future Research Directions

Although the current literature demonstrates the transformative potential of immersive technologies, several limitations remain:

- Quantitative data scarcity: Most case studies remain qualitative; controlled experiments on VR/AR's impact on performance, cognition, and risk mitigation are limited.
- Ethical and legal uncertainty: Cross-jurisdictional governance for digital identity and biometric data is still evolving.
- Technological inequality: SMEs and developing nations face affordability and infrastructure gaps that limit widespread adoption.

Future research should therefore emphasize longitudinal, data-driven assessments of immersive systems; cross cultural studies on bias and usability; and policy frameworks integrating ethics by design, sustainability, and inclusivity.

CONCLUSION

Virtual Reality (VR) and Augmented Reality (AR) have evolved from visualization media to integral components of predictive, adaptive, and secure business ecosystems. Through integration with AI, blockchain, and cloud infrastructures, immersive technologies advance a model of intelligent digital transformation grounded in risk intelligence and ethical governance (Jose Diaz Rivera et al., 2024; Silva et al., 2024).

In conclusion, sustainable adoption requires a careful balance between innovation, security, and ethics. Future implementations must ensure algorithmic transparency, digital identity protection, and platform interoperability, shaping a metaverse that is not only technologically sophisticated but also inclusive, human centered, and globally trusted. This is the true goal of immersive change: forming a secure, digital ecosystem managed cooperatively on a global scale, and providing vast new opportunities for businesses worldwide.

REFERENCES

Abdel-rahman, H. (2024). Actual Economy: Local Solutions for Global Challenges—2024 BUILDING EFFECTIVE PARTNERSHIPS BETWEEN NON-GOVERNMENTAL ORGANIZATIONS (NGOS). *AND BUSINESSES FOR ENVIRONMENTAL CONSERVATION Actual Economy: Local Solutions for Global Challenges*, *2024*(2019), 290–293.

Bellalouna, F. (2020). Industrial Use Cases for Augmented Reality Application. 2020 11th IEEE International Conference on Cognitive Infocommunications (CogInfoCom), 11–18. DOI: 10.1109/CogInfoCom50765.2020.9237882

Cao, K., Hu, S., Shi, Y., Colombo, A. W., Karnouskos, S., & Li, X. (2021). A Survey on Edge and Edge-Cloud Computing Assisted Cyber-Physical Systems. *IEEE Transactions on Industrial Informatics*, *17*(11), 7806–7819. DOI: 10.1109/TII.2021.3073066

El-Hajj, M. (2025). Cybersecurity and Privacy Challenges in Extended Reality: Threats, Solutions, and Risk Mitigation Strategies. *Virtual Worlds*, *4*(1), 1–30. DOI: 10.3390/virtualworlds4010001

Ghirmai, S., Mebrahtom, D., Aloqaily, M., Guizani, M., & Debbah, M. (2022). Self-Sovereign Identity for Trust and Interoperability in the Metaverse. Proceedings - 2022 IEEE SmartWorld, Ubiquitous Intelligence and Computing, Autonomous and Trusted Vehicles, Scalable Computing and Communications, Digital Twin, Privacy Computing, Metaverse, SmartWorld/UIC/ATC/ScalCom/DigitalTwin/PriComp/Metaverse 2022, 2468–2475. DOI: 10.1109/SmartWorld-UIC-ATC-ScalCom-DigitalTwin-PriComp-Metaverse56740.2022.00345

Gupta, B. B., Gaurav, A., Arya, V., & Alhalabi, W. (2024). Data science in sustainable entrepreneurship: A multidisciplinary field of applications. *Technological Forecasting and Social Change*, *209*, 123798. DOI: 10.1016/j.techfore.2024.123798

Gupta, B. B., & Panigrahi, P. K. (2022). Analysis of the Role of Global Information Management in Advanced Decision Support Systems (DSS) for Sustainable Development. [JGIM]. *Journal of Global Information Management*, *31*(2), 1–13. DOI: 10.4018/JGIM.320185

Huang, Z., Wei, S., Chen, Z., & Wang, L. (2023). Iterative Contraction Stability Control Strategy for Planar Prismatic-Rotational Underactuated Robot. *IEEE Access : Practical Innovations, Open Solutions*, *11*, 55947–55953. DOI: 10.1109/ACCESS.2023.3281556

Hutson, J., Banerjee, G., Kshetri, N., Odenwald, K., & Ratican, J. (2023). Architecting the Metaverse: Blockchain and the Financial and Legal Regulatory Challenges of Virtual Real Estate. *Journal of Intelligent Learning Systems and Applications, 15*(01), 1–23. DOI: 10.4236/jilsa.2023.151001

Jim, J. R., Hosain, M. T., Mridha, M. F., Kabir, M. M., & Shin, J. (2023). Toward Trustworthy Metaverse: Advancements and Challenges. *IEEE Access : Practical Innovations, Open Solutions, 11*(September), 118318–118347. DOI: 10.1109/ACCESS.2023.3326258

Jose Diaz Rivera, J., Muhammad, A., & Song, W. C. (2024). Securing Digital Identity in the Zero Trust Architecture: A Blockchain Approach to Privacy-Focused Multi-Factor Authentication. *IEEE Open Journal of the Communications Society, 5*(March), 2792–2814. DOI: 10.1109/OJCOMS.2024.3391728

Khatib, D. M. El, Al Falasi, F., Anani, H. Al, & Shurrab, W. (2023). The Effect of Virtual Reality and Augmented Reality on Managing Projects. 2023 International Conference on Business Analytics for Technology and Security (ICBATS), 1–10. DOI: 10.1109/ICBATS57792.2023.10111112

Kour, R., Karim, R., Venkatesh, S. N., & Kumar, U. (2025). Metaverse in industrial contexts—A comprehensive review. *Frontiers in Virtual Reality, 6*(January), 1–19. DOI: 10.3389/frvir.2025.1488926

Kourtesis, P. (2024). A Comprehensive Review of Multimodal XR Applications, Risks, and Ethical Challenges in the Metaverse. *Multimodal Technologies and Interaction, 8*(11), 1–43. DOI: 10.3390/mti8110098

Kurniawan, A. W. (2025). Employee Perceptions of Virtual Reality (VR) Training in the Metaverse: A Case Study in a Fintech Company. [JUMPER]. *Journal Management & Economics Review, 2*(6), 2025.

Li, S., Yang, Y., Han, C., Sun, Y., Attar, R. W., & Gupta, B. B. (2025). Addressing consumer needs: Effects of firms remediation strategies on satisfaction and brand usage intent in AI-powered voice assistant service failures. *International Journal of Information Management, 85*, 102951. DOI: 10.1016/j.ijinfomgt.2025.102951

Masood, T., & Egger, J. (2021). Augmented Reality: Focusing on Photonics in Industry 4.0. *IEEE Journal of Selected Topics in Quantum Electronics, 27*(6), 1–11. DOI: 10.1109/JSTQE.2021.3093721

Mirza, T., Tuli, N., & Mantri, A. (2022). Virtual Reality, Augmented Reality, and Mixed Reality Applications: Present Scenario. 2022 2nd International Conference on Advance Computing and Innovative Technologies in Engineering (ICACITE), 1405–1412. DOI: 10.1109/ICACITE53722.2022.9823482

Mushtaq, M., Jha, R. K., Sabraj, M. C., & Jain, S. (2024). Attack Modeling and Security Analysis Using Machine Learning Algorithms Enabled with Augmented Reality and Virtual Reality. *International Journal of Computer Network and Information Security*, *16*(4), 118–129. DOI: 10.5815/ijcnis.2024.04.08

Nasri, M. (2025). Towards Intelligent VR Training: A Physiological Adaptation Framework for Cognitive Load and Stress Detection. 419–423. DOI: 10.1145/3699682.3727575

Nepal, R., Pavlovich, R. J., & Guilherme, C. E. (2023). VirtualWorx™: Transforming Maintenance Concepts through Augmented Reality Collaboration Capabilities. *2023 Annual Reliability and Maintainability Symposium (RAMS)*, 1–5. DOI: 10.1109/RAMS51473.2023.10088179

Owusu-Antwi, K., & Amenuvor, F. E. (2023). Understanding the Metaverse: A Review of Virtual Worlds and Augmented Reality Environments. *Current Journal of Applied Science and Technology*, *42*(23), 42–48. DOI: 10.9734/cjast/2023/v42i234172

Pappachan, P. Sreerakuvandana, & Rahaman, M. (2024). Conceptualising the Role of Intellectual Property and Ethical Behaviour in Artificial Intelligence. In Handbook of Research on AI and ML for Intelligent Machines and Systems (pp. 1–26). IGI Global. DOI: 10.4018/978-1-6684-9999-3.ch001

Peng, D., Yang, X., Tang, W., & Fan, L. (2020). A Dual-NIC Mutual Backup Solution of Access Point Handoff in SDN-based Mobile Networks. 2020 IEEE 6th International Conference on Computer and Communications (ICCC), 542–547. DOI: 10.1109/ICCC51575.2020.9345033

Pereira, A. C., Alves, A. C., & Arezes, P. (2023). Augmented Reality in a Lean Workplace at Smart Factories: A Case Study. *Applied Sciences (Basel, Switzerland)*, *13*(16), 9120. Advance online publication. DOI: 10.3390/app13169120

Pitzalis, R. F., Giordano, A., Di Spigno, A., Cowell, A., Niculita, O., & Berselli, G. (2025). Application of augmented reality-based digital twin approaches: A case study to industrial equipment. *International Journal of Advanced Manufacturing Technology*, *138*(7), 3747–3763. DOI: 10.1007/s00170-025-15755-w

Rahaman, M., Chappu, B., Jana, S., Haque, A., Firmansyah, G., & Chattopadhyay, S. (2025). Security Benefits in Small Medium Business Enterprise Through Cloud Adoption. In N. Nedjah, G. Martinez Perez, & B. B. Gupta (Eds.), International Conference on Smart Systems and Advanced Computing (SysCom 2022) (pp. 168–180). Springer Nature Switzerland. DOI: 10.1007/978-3-031-40905-9_18

Rahaman, M., Putra, K. T., Irawan, B., & Biyanto, T. R. (2025). Industrial Evolution: The Integration of AI in Robotics and Drone Systems. In AI Developments for Industrial Robotics and Intelligent Drones (pp. 85–114). IGI Global Scientific Publishing. DOI: 10.4018/979-8-3693-2707-4.ch005

Rahaman, M., Wisnujati, A., Widodo, A. M., Haque, A., Sakar, R., & Chen, H. C. (2022). Privacy Preservation Agri-Food SCM Operation Based on Online/Offline RFID Using Block Chain. 413–426. DOI: 10.2991/978-94-6463-084-8_34

Raj, N., Menon, H. P., Satheesh, A., & Naveen, P., N. A., & R, V. K. (2025). Architectural Visualization using Augmented Reality. *2025 International Conference on Intelligent and Innovative Technologies in Computing, Electrical and Electronics (IITCEE)*, 1–6. DOI: 10.1109/IITCEE64140.2025.10915400

Sajwan, V., Gandhi, A. B., Kumar Chopra, N., Praveen, S., Thapliyal, M., Jaleel, U., Pandey, S. D., Kumar, R., & Negi, D. (2024). Technological Transformations: A Comprehensive Review of AI, IoT, VR, AR, and Emerging Technologies in Diverse Industries. *2024 International Conference on Advances in Computing, Communication and Materials (ICACCM)*, 1–5. DOI: 10.1109/ICACCM61117.2024.11059157

Sekti, B. A. (2025a). Information Security Awareness. In User-Centric Cybersecurity Implications for Sustainable Digital Transformation (pp. 111–145). DOI: 10.4018/979-8-3373-3171-3.ch004

Sekti, B. A. (2025b). IT Service Information Security Management. In Cases on Information Systems Service Management (pp. 61–93). DOI: 10.4018/979-8-3373-2352-7.ch003

Shahriar, S., Allana, S., Hazratifard, S. M., & Dara, R. (2023). A Survey of Privacy Risks and Mitigation Strategies in the Artificial Intelligence Life Cycle. *IEEE Access : Practical Innovations, Open Solutions*, *11*, 61829–61854. DOI: 10.1109/ACCESS.2023.3287195

Shelke, Y., & Chakraborty, C. (2021). Augmented Reality and Virtual Reality Transforming Spinal Imaging Landscape: A Feasibility Study. *IEEE Computer Graphics and Applications*, *41*(3), 124–138. DOI: 10.1109/MCG.2020.3000359 PMID: 32746083

Silva, R., Pereira, I., Nicola, S., Madureira, A., Bettencourt, N., Reis, J. L., Santos, J. P., & de Oliveira, D. A. (2024). Navigating the Future of Enterprises: Insights into Digital Transformation, Virtual Reality, and the Metaverse. 2024 IEEE 22nd Mediterranean Electrotechnical Conference (MELECON), 1146–1151. DOI: 10.1109/MELECON56669.2024.10608539

Singh, S. K., Gupta, S., Kumar, S., Gupta, B. B., Alhalabi, W., Arya, V., & Zhang, J. (2024). A novel Cumulative Indicator score using Indicator averaging for optimizing local business websites of enterprise systems. *Enterprise Information Systems*, *18*(2), 2301658. DOI: 10.1080/17517575.2023.2301658

Soni, S., Yadav, U., & Soni, A. (2022). Virtual Reality & Augmented Reality: A way to Digital Transformation of Customer Engagement. *2022 International Conference on Machine Learning, Big Data, Cloud and Parallel Computing (COM-IT-CON)*, 1, 573–577. DOI: 10.1109/COM-IT-CON54601.2022.9850954

Truong, T.-C., & Diep, Q. B. (2023). Technological Spotlights of Digital Transformation in Tertiary Education. *IEEE Access : Practical Innovations, Open Solutions*, *11*, 40954–40966. DOI: 10.1109/ACCESS.2023.3270340

Wang, C., Garro, V., Sundstedt, V., Hu, Y., & Goswami, P. (2025). Immersive analytics meets artificial intelligence: A systematic review. *Computational Visual Media*, •••, 1–34. DOI: 10.26599/CVM.2025.9450452

Yang, B. (2023). Virtual Reality and Augmented Reality for Immersive Learning: A Framework of Education Environment Design. [iJET]. *International Journal of Emerging Technologies in Learning*, *18*(20), 23–36. DOI: 10.3991/ijet.v18i20.44209

Chapter 5
Challenges, Risks, and Ethical Dilemmas in the Metaverse Economy

Guntur Rivaldi
http://orcid.org/0009-0006-2812-5210
Universitas Esa Unggul, Indonesia

Joy Valent Missael Zega
http://orcid.org/0009-0000-4981-6834
Universitas Esa Unggul, Indonesia

Binastya Anggara Sekti
http://orcid.org/0000-0001-5489-4888
Universitas Esa Unggul, Indonesia

Abhay Ratnaparkhi
eBay Inc., USA

Ifat Batul
Vidyasagar University, India

Thanaporn Phattanaviroj
Asia University, Taiwan

ABSTRACT

The metaverse economy represents a major transformation in the digital era, powered by blockchain, artificial intelligence, and virtual reality, creating new forms of value through decentralized finance, digital assets, and immersive work environments. Yet, its rapid expansion brings complex ethical, legal, and technological challenges. Key risks include the misuse of digital identities, data privacy violations, algorithmic bias, labor exploitation in virtual economies, and vulnerabilities in decentralized finance and smart contracts. Manipulative design patterns and weak legal oversight further threaten user autonomy, fairness, and trust. This chapter critically examines these challenges and the systemic risks shaping the metaverse economy while emphasizing the need for ethical governance, transparency, and inclusive regulation.

DOI: 10.4018/979-8-2600-0013-7.ch005

It concludes with recommendations for building a resilient and equitable metaverse ecosystem that balances innovation with accountability, safeguards user rights, and promotes sustainability in digital economic transformation.

1. INTRODUCTION

The rapid growth of digital technologies over the last two decades has significantly reshaped global social, economic, and cultural dynamics. A key innovation in this transformation is the emergence of the metaverse—a virtual, interactive, decentralized world powered by technologies such as virtual reality (VR), augmented reality (AR), artificial intelligence (AI), and blockchain. This shift from Web 2.0 to Web 3.0 promises a more participatory, transparent digital environment, changing how people interact, transact, and form communities. The metaverse is no longer limited to gaming or social media but has become a core part of the digital economy (Gupta et al., 2023). Users can own virtual assets, trade cryptocurrencies, and participate in economic communities that transcend geographical boundaries, with platforms like Decentraland, The Sandbox, and Meta Horizon Worlds showcasing these new economic activities (Dwivedi et al., 2021). However, the metaverse also brings complex challenges, including ethical, technological, and legal issues. One major concern is digital identity, as users' avatars, which are used for self-representation, also collect sensitive data such as biometrics and emotional expressions, often leading to surveillance capitalism (Alaca & Çelik, 2023). The metaverse also presents new forms of digital labor, such as play-to-earn models, which lack legal protection, making workers vulnerable to exploitation (Ahmed et al., 2022). Additionally, metaverse platforms often employ manipulative design strategies, targeting users' emotions and decision-making processes, raising concerns about design ethics (Chatterjee et al., 2021). Legally, the metaverse faces challenges due to its lack of jurisdiction, leaving users without clear legal recourse in cases of copyright disputes or digital violence. Furthermore, the reliance on blockchain and smart contracts introduces systemic economic risks, such as transaction errors, hacker attacks, and security vulnerabilities, alongside the volatility of digital currencies (Zhang et al., 2023; Abdelqawy et al., 2022). To address these issues, a new approach, such as Ethics-by-Design, is essential, ensuring fairness, transparency, and the inclusion of all stakeholders in metaverse development (Garcia & Patel, 2024). This chapter explores the challenges of the metaverse economy, focusing on technological risks, digital identity, labor conditions, design manipulation, and legal barriers. It offers both theoretical insights and practical frameworks for developers, regulators, and academics, aiming to build a more ethical and equitable metaverse ecosystem. Ethical reflection and inclusive action are crucial to ensuring that the metaverse's progress does not lead to new inequalities (Gupta, Gaurav, & Arya, 2024).

2. TECHNOLOGICAL AND ECONOMIC RISKS IN THE METAVERSE

The metaverse ecosystem is growing at a rapid pace, driving fundamental changes in the structure of the global digital economy. Powered by technologies such as blockchain, artificial intelligence (AI), and decentralized finance (DeFi), the metaverse introduces an unprecedented economic model (Rahaman et al., 2024). However, as this growth, various inherent risks begin to emerge—both from the technological and economic sides—that have the potential to shake the long-term stability of this virtual space (Gupta, Gaurav, Arya, et al., 2024). This chapter reviews five key aspects of these risks, ranging from market dominance by large actors, the vulnerability of decentralized financial systems, the weaknesses of smart contracts, virtual asset bubbles, to case studies of the collapse of the Terra-LUNA ecosystem and its impact on the metaverse world (Kumar et al., 2023).

2.1 Digital Monopoly and Market Centralization

Although the metaverse is often associated with openness and decentralization, the reality is that the current metaverse platform landscape shows a tendency towards centralization (Rahaman et al., 2025). Some major entities such as Meta Platforms Inc., Tencent, and Epic Games have consolidated their dominance over infrastructure, user access, and market capitalization. This dominance raises concerns about the formation of a digital monopoly, where a handful of companies control access and economic flows in the virtual world (Chui et al., 2023).

Market dominance like this can undermine the principle of interoperability that is the foundation of the metaverse. When users can only interact within one closed platform, they lose the freedom to move between digital environments, as well as become dependent on the policies and algorithms of the service provider. A study by Dwivedi et al. (2021) shows that centralization in the digital environment actually creates inequality in the distribution of value, curbs innovation, and increases user dependence on dominant platforms (Pappachan et al., 2025).

Figure 1. Diagram of the Metaverse Technology Ecosystem and Associated Risks

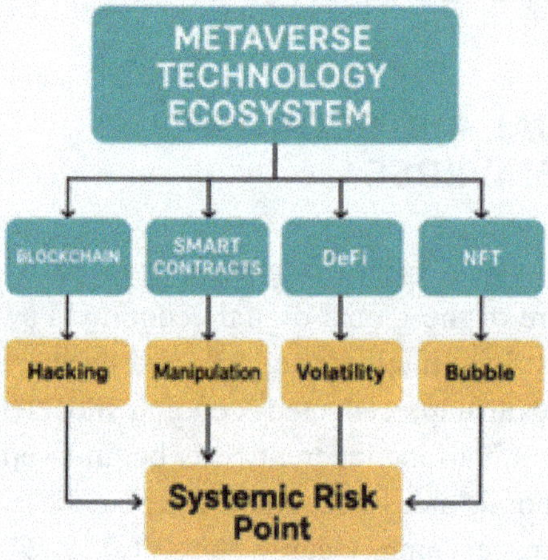

2.2 Risks in Decentralized Finance (DeFi)

Table 1. Comparison of Key Aspects between DeFi and Traditional Financial Systems

Aspects	Defi	Traditional Systems
Intermediary	None	Banks, financial institutions
Guarantee Mechanism	None, smart contract based	Government or insurance guaranteed
Response to attacks	No authority	Can be compensated by regulators
Asset volatility	Very high	Relatively stable
Transparency	High (open code)	Low to medium

One of the key elements in the metaverse economy is the integration of decentralized finance systems or DeFi (Widodo et al., 2024). Through blockchain protocols, users can make transactions without intermediaries, store digital assets, and borrow and lend without a bank. However, despite the promise of financial inclusion and efficiency, DeFi systems also carry no small risks. Recent studies show that the metaverse financial system faces the challenges of digital accounting and virtual asset recognition (Al-Hawamleh, 2024)

First, the volatility of the value of the cryptocurrencies used in DeFi is very high. Extreme price fluctuations can wipe out the value of a user's assets in a matter of hours. Second, many DeFi protocols are built on smart contracts that have not been thoroughly audited, opening up opportunities for exploitation by malicious actors. Third, the absence of a guarantee or supervision mechanism like in the conventional financial system causes users to bear all risks personally. According to Alwaisi et al. (2024), the majority of cyberattacks against DeFi platforms are caused by security holes in smart contract code. Since the DeFi system is autonomous and has no central authority, when a mistake or attack occurs, no institution can provide restitution or mediation. In the context of the metaverse, this poses systemic risks as virtual assets, economic transactions, and user incentives are highly dependent on the stability of the DeFi ecosystem.

2.3 Smart Contracts: Vulnerabilities and Cases of Fraud

Smart contracts are an essential component of metaverse and DeFi operations. These contracts execute instructions automatically without human intervention, from NFT trading to revenue sharing from virtual economy activities. However, like all digital systems, smart contracts depend heavily on the quality of the code and the logic embedded in them. Research by Irshad et al. (2023) revealed that more than 30% of smart contracts on the Ethereum network have medium to high level vulnerabilities. In the metaverse space, the consequences of a broken contract can be widespread—from loss of rights to digital property, erroneous NFT transactions, to manipulation of user assets. Thus, while smart contracts provide automation and efficiency, they also create new weak points in system security.

2.4 Economic Bubbles in the Virtual Asset Market

The phenomenon of price increases that are disproportionate to the intrinsic value of virtual assets indicates the potential for a digital economy bubble to form. This bubble is amplified by excessive speculation over items such as virtual land, NFTs, or custom tokens within metaverse platforms. The absence of an objective valuation mechanism causes prices to soar based solely on hype and market sentiment. These bubbles are prone to bursting when expectations are not met or consumer confidence plummets. When this happens, the value of digital assets can drop drastically, leaving huge losses for ordinary users who invest without a thorough understanding of the risks. According to a study by Su and Sekti, the imbalance between technology adoption and market value is a major indicator of the digital bubble. In the context of the metaverse, this phenomenon can destroy trust in the entire virtual ecosystem, undermine its long-term sustainability, and hinder the growth of digital communities.

Figure 2. Price Fluctuations of Popular Virtual Assets

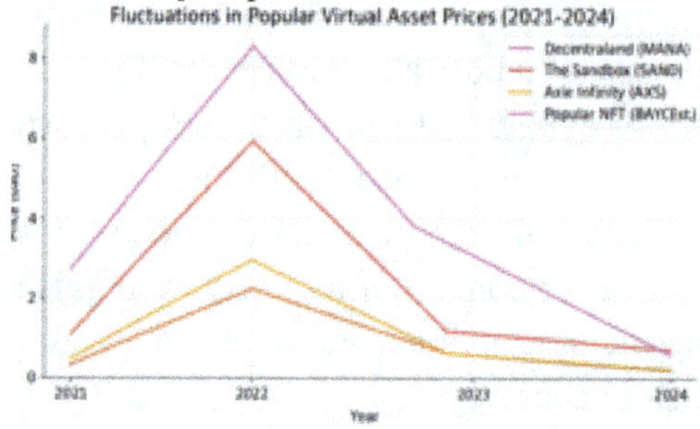

2.5 Case Study: The Terra-LUNA Collapse and Its Impact on the Metaverse

One of the most dramatic events in the blockchain world that had a major impact on the metaverse was the collapse of the Terra-LUNA ecosystem in 2022. Terra, an algorithmic stablecoin that is supposed to maintain parity with the US dollar through automated arbitrage with the LUNA token, suffered a sudden crash that led to the loss of billions of dollars from the crypto market. This ecosystem is widely used in DeFi and metaverse applications because it offers high returns and stability of value. However, when the stabilization mechanism fails, investors withdraw funds en masse, causing a death spiral in the value of the token and destroying market confidence. This incident provides an important lesson: that seemingly stable and automated systems remain vulnerable to market psychological factors and algorithmic design failures. Blockchain-based metaverse architecture presents highly complex system design and security challenges (Ray & Dash, 2021). Metaverse platforms that rely on such stablecoins have also been affected as the value of users' assets has collapsed along with their supporting ecosystems. Dwivedi et al. (2021) emphasized that events like this show how integration between the virtual world and the new financial system requires more mature oversight, as well as a strong risk mitigation framework.

3. DIGITAL IDENTITY, SURVEILLANCE, AND PRIVACY CONCERNS

The rapid development of the metaverse as an immersive virtual space has opened a new chapter in the construction and management of digital identities. In the metaverse, identity is no longer just an account or username, but a three-dimensional avatar that can be deeply customized, representing the user's physical and social presence. This transformation makes digital identities the center of virtual interactions, but it also opens up space for data exploitation, identity abuse, and invasive surveillance. This chapter examines key issues related to avatar ownership, biometric data, surveillance capitalism, user tracking, as well as case studies on identity practices by Meta Platforms Inc.

3.1 Ownership and Control of Digital Avatars

In the metaverse, avatars are the primary representation of users—not only as a symbol of visual identity, but also as a medium for interacting, working, and building reputations. Users invest time and money to develop their avatars to reflect certain preferences, social status, and even economic values. Avatars used in the metaverse have been shown to have psychological implications for the formation of users' digital identities and self-confidence (Kim, 2021). However, the rights to avatars are often not entirely in the hands of the user, but rather controlled by the platform provider. Most metaverse platform terms of service state that all content, including avatars and digital items used, belongs to the platform, not the user. This means that the platform can modify, remove, or restrict access to avatars without the user's consent. This creates a power imbalance between users and platforms in terms of control over digital identities. According to research by Hill and Whitty (2021), digital avatars have a complex ownership dimension because they are at the intersection between user rights, platform policies, and technological boundaries. When the rights to avatars are not protected, users lose sovereignty over their identity in the digital world.

3.2 Biometric Data, Profiling, and Behavioral Targeting

Technology in the metaverse allows for high-level biometric data tracking—from facial expressions, body movements, voice responses, to eye attention patterns. This data is used to improve the user experience, but it also opens up huge opportunities for highly invasive behavioral profiling and targeting practices. This profiling allows the system to infer the user's psychological preferences, political orientation, or even emotional state with a high degree of accuracy. In a data-driven economic system, this information becomes a valuable commodity that can be sold to third parties for commercial purposes. Studies by Benjamens, Dhunnoo, and Meskó (2020) show that biometric data has a high risk of misuse due to its immutable and highly personal nature. Furthermore, not all users have a full understanding of how their data is collected, used, or exchanged. This raises the issue of transparency and informed consent, which is a basic principle in personal data protection. When users don't know that their every move is being monitored and monetized, digital privacy becomes a mere illusion.

3.3 Surveillance Capitalism in an Immersive Environment

Surveillance capitalism is an economic model that extracts value from users' personal data for commercial gain. In the context of the metaverse, this model operates on a much deeper and more personal scale than the conventional internet. The metaverse allows platforms to not only know what users are doing, but also how they feel, think, and react to digital stimuli. Metaverse platforms can analyze users' emotional interactions with certain content or products, and then customize ads, avatars, and even immersive experiences based on that data. This creates a feedback loop that constantly reinforces behaviors that benefit the platform, but slowly erodes user autonomy. According to Dwivedi et al. (2021), surveillance capitalism in an XR (Extended Reality) environment can undermine the integrity of digital experiences by replacing voluntary exploration with data-driven manipulation. When a user's decision is driven by algorithmic predictions, individual freedom loses its meaning. This is where the ethical dilemma arises between the optimization of experience and the right not to be manipulated.

Figure 3. Diagram of Surveillance Capitalism Cycle in Data Collection within the Metaverse

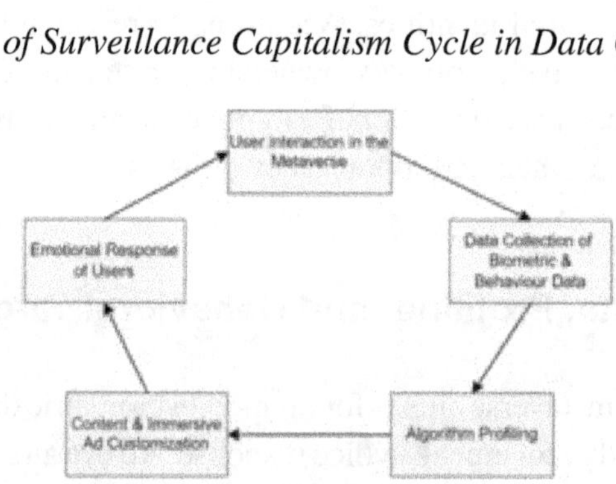

3.4 The Ethical Implications of Persistent User Tracking

One of the key features of the metaverse is the ability to track users continuously and in real-time. This tracking technology not only includes the location of the avatar, but also records the duration of interactions, the type of content accessed, and communication patterns. This aspect of tracking drives the need to implement privacy computing in the design of metaverse systems (Wang et al., 2023). This data is useful for creating adaptive virtual environments, but it also poses serious concerns in terms of privacy and long-term surveillance. Fei et al. (2022) underline that user tracking without time and space limits violates the principle of contextual privacy, which is the right of individuals to regulate who knows what, when, and in what context. When personal information loses its context, it becomes vulnerable to misinterpretation and misuse.

Additionally, non-transparent tracking can also create fear or anxiety in users, which in turn negatively affects their behavior. In a digital work environment or metaverse education, this can create a form of digital surveillance that resembles a modern panopticon.

3.5 Case Study: Identity Exploitation Practices by Meta

Meta Platforms Inc., as one of the major actors in metaverse development, has been in the spotlight due to its controversial data and identity management practices. The company has been repeatedly criticized for its lack of transparency in the collection and utilization of user data, including in metaverse products such as Horizon Worlds. Researchers note that Meta's approach to digital identity reflects an aggressive form of value extraction, where user data is not only used for service personalization, but also for massive ad optimization and product development. Cases of user data leaks by third parties such as Cambridge Analytica, while occurring in the context of social media, are a stark warning of the potential for greater risks in a much more intimate and immersive metaverse environment.

Figure 4. Integration of Digital Identities within the Meta Ecosystem

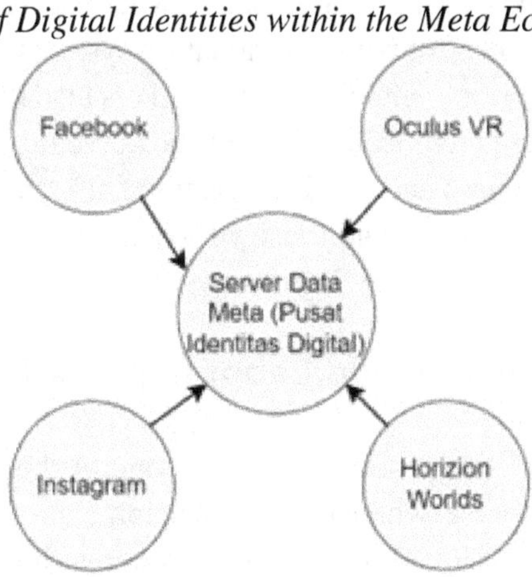

4. LABOR, EXPLOITATION, AND ECONOMIC INEQUALITY IN THE METAVERSE

The metaverse has presented a new economic landscape that has the potential to create global job opportunities without geographical boundaries. On the one hand, these virtual spaces allow for the emergence of new forms of digital work such as avatar design, virtual real estate, content moderators, and participation in "play-to-earn" (P2E) systems. But on the other hand, the characteristics of the metaverse world that are not yet legally regulated and decentralized in nature also open up huge loopholes for exploitative and inequality practices. This chapter discusses the structure of digital gig work in the metaverse, exploitation in P2E systems, the mental health impacts of content moderation, invisible labor in the virtual economy, and comparisons between traditional and immersive digital work.

4.1 Digital Gig Economy in the Metaverse

The gig economy in the metaverse is evolving from the spirit of decentralization that promises freedom and flexibility of work. In contrast to conventional institution-based work systems, many metaverse users work as freelancers who offer direct services through their avatars. Examples include virtual tour guides, NFT artists, virtual building architects, and immersive experience space developers.

Although it sounds innovative, it exhibits the same characteristics as the conventional gig economy: income uncertainty, no benefits, and reliance on platform algorithms. According to Chatterjee et al. (2021), work in the digital economy tends to create asymmetrical working relationships, where service providers (workers) have no power over prices, exposure, or valuation systems.

In the metaverse environment, digital gig workers also face additional pressures such as the need for high technical skills and start-up capital in the form of digital assets, including VR devices and platform tokens. This can reinforce the inequality between users who have capital and those who don't, thus opening up new gaps in the distribution of digital economy benefits.

4.2 Play-to-Earn System and Labor Exploitation

The *play-to-earn* (P2E) model is becoming one of the most popular forms of digital work in the metaverse, where users earn income through gaming activities or completing virtual tasks. However, many P2E systems show signs of exploitation, especially when played by individuals from low-income countries. For example, platforms like Axie Infinity create a work ecosystem where players must purchase "digital assets" in the form of game characters to start working. In practice, many players cannot afford to buy such assets and instead get entangled in digital rental schemes by asset owners, who often take a large chunk of the player's earnings. From a political economy perspective, play-to-earn systems in the metaverse often replicate exploitative work structures that target cheap labor (Liu & Zhang, 2022).

Ahmed et al. (2022) show that such systems create a new form of digital inequality, where capital owners get the maximum benefit from the digital work done by other individuals. Similar to a form of digital feudalism, P2E workers do not have complete control over their means of production and are highly susceptible to fluctuations in the platform economy. In addition, economic incentives that depend on time and performance encourage workers to work long hours, under constant pressure, in the absence of health insurance or social protection. In the long run, this has the potential to trigger a condition of digital *burnout*.

Figure 5. The Relationship Between Play-to-Earn Systems and Labor Exploitation.

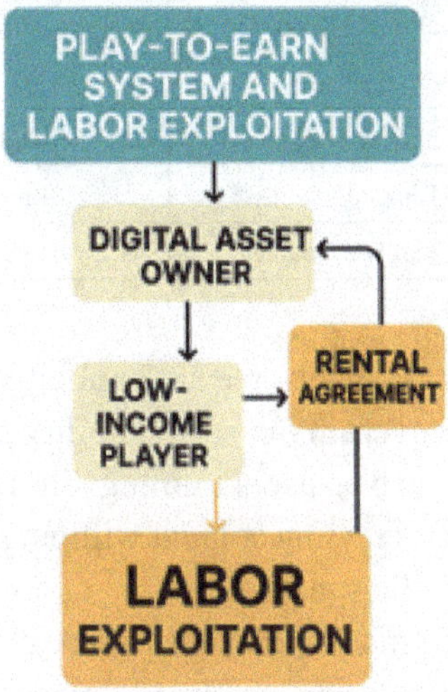

4.3 Content Moderation and Impact on Mental Health

Content moderation is one of the essential forms of work in the metaverse, as open virtual spaces can be easily misused to spread harmful, violent, or illegal content. Content moderators are in charge of filtering and removing inappropriate content in real-time.

The condition is exacerbated by the absence of standard protections, such as psychological counseling or task rotation. Many moderators work as freelance contract workers with no access to mental health support, making them an "invisible workforce" that underpins the digital cleanliness of the metaverse space.

In a global context, most moderation work is outsourced to developing countries, adding a dimension of global inequality in this digital work structure.

4.4 Invisible Labor in the Virtual Economy

Table 2. Comparison of Traditional Gig Work and Immersive Work in the Metaverse.

Aspects	Traditional Gig Work	Immersive Work in the Metaverse
Work Location	Real world (physical)	Virtual environment (XR/VR)
Forms of Representation	Real self	Digital avatar
Intensity of Interaction	Limited (messages/chat)	High (verbal, visual, emotional)
Privacy & Data	Limited to apps	Real-time behavioral & expression tracking
Health & Protection	Rarely available	Almost nothing

Not all forms of work in the metaverse are explicitly recognized or appreciated. Many of the activities that underpin the sustainability of digital platforms occur in the form of invisible work, such as users training algorithms through their interactions, community participants creating content without pay, or volunteer moderators maintaining the ethics of public spaces.

Su and Sekti (2024) note that this form of work creates great economic value for the platform, but is often not adequately compensated. This system creates the illusion of voluntary participation, when it is basically a form of work used to lower the operational costs of digital platforms. The concept of invisible work can also be extended to users who unknowingly provide highly valuable behavioral data to the company, which is then sold or used for product optimization. In this case, users contribute as "data workers", but do not receive a share of the economic value they create.

4.5 Comparison: Traditional vs. Immersive Gig Work

To understand the depth of employment issues in the metaverse, it's important to compare traditional forms of gig work (such as online transportation drivers or digital freelancers) with immersive work in an XR environment. Both models show similarities in terms of uncertainty and lack of social protection, but there are important differences in terms of the intensity of experience and the form of control. In immersive work, workers not only complete tasks, but also devote a full virtual presence in the form of avatars. Interactions are done visually, verbally, and emotionally in a 3D environment, which can increase cognitive load as well as performance pressure.

Irshad et al. (2023) stated that working in XR blurs the boundaries between personal and workspace spaces, creating potential privacy violations, high social pressures, and burdensome technological needs. While traditional gig work is still in a physical space, working in the metaverse requires mental and emotional adaptations that have not been studied holistically.

Overall, while the metaverse promises unlimited job opportunities, emerging forms of work need to be critically reviewed so as not to expand the exploitation and injustices that already existed in the previous digital economy.

5. ETHICAL DESIGN, USER AUTONOMY, AND MANIPULATION IN THE METAVERSE

The metaverse ecosystem as an immersive and participatory space has created highly personalized and immersive digital interactions. By integrating virtual reality (VR), augmented reality (AR), and multimodal interfaces, metaverse platforms promise digital experiences that are not only interactive but also emotional and cognitive. However, as users become increasingly connected to digital systems, a new subtle but dangerous risk arises—design manipulation that erodes user autonomy. This chapter explores practices such as *dark patterns*, emotional manipulation in XR, attention economics, ethical design principles, as well as case studies of NeuroUX use in metaverse games.

5.1 Dark Patterns in Immersive Interfaces

Dark patterns refer to interface design strategies that are deliberately created to trick users into making decisions that they might not have made if given a choice transparently. In the context of the metaverse, this practice has become more complex because the dimensions of the interface are three-dimensional, real-time, and highly immersive. Examples are hard-to-find default settings, exit buttons that are disguised in virtual spaces, or obscure purchase confirmation mechanisms. When the user is in a VR environment, sensory limitations can be exploited by the designer to limit the user's visibility or attention to important elements.

According to Dwivedi et al. (2021), the existence of *dark patterns* not only misleads users technically, but also violates the essential principles of transparency and trust in digital design. When design prioritizes user retention over autonomy, then the digital experience becomes a hidden form of exploitation. Recent research emphasizes that ethical design in immersive environments should take into account the long-term psychological influence on users, especially in the context of dark patterns and the attention economy (Zhang & Zhao, 2023).

5.2 Cognitive and Emotional Manipulation in XR Environments

XR (Extended Reality) platforms, including VR and AR, allow the system to recognize and influence the user's psychological state. But manipulative design approaches can also exploit users' cognitive vulnerabilities, including in addictive gamification systems (Feng & Zhao, 2023). By tracking facial expressions, voice intonation, body movements, and reactions to visual stimuli, the system can recognize the user's emotional state and respond to it in real-time.

This feature, while useful in improving personalization, can also be used for manipulation. For example, a system can subtly serve content that tailors the user's emotions to drive longer interactions or increase commercial conversions. This kind of technique has been widely applied in immersive advertising and gamification of shopping systems in the metaverse. The practice of algorithmic-based manipulation in virtual environments is also in the spotlight because it can influence user decisions unknowingly (Nguyen & Riedl, 2020).

Fei et al. (2022) note that this kind of manipulation poses an ethical dilemma because users rarely know that the system is responding or even modifying their emotions. When digital experiences are no longer neutral, but are designed to trigger certain emotional reactions for economic gain, there is a violation of the principle of user autonomy.

5.3 Planned Addiction: The Attention Economy in VR

The attention economy is a digital business model that relies on the length of time users engage with the platform as an indicator of success. In the metaverse, this model is evolving to become more aggressive as user engagement is not only screen-based, but also body- and emotional-based. Features such as real-time notifications, digital rewards, voice-visual feedback, and leveling systems are designed to create intense emotional attachment. This design, according to Chatterjee et al. (2021), often leads to digital addiction because it activates the dopamine system in the user's brain repeatedly. In a VR environment, this risk is higher because the perception of space and time becomes blurred. Many users report losing time orientation after hours in the virtual world, which has an impact on physical and psychological health. In extreme cases, addiction to metaverse platforms can decrease productivity, disrupt social relationships, and create behavioral disorders.

5.4 Ethical Design Principles for Metaverse Interfaces

Table 3. Key Principles of Ethical Digital Systems.

Principle	Brief Description
Transparency of Interaction	Users know when to monitor and for what
Action Reversal	Can cancel purchases or interactions
Universal Accessibility	Can be used by all, including people with disabilities
User Participation	Users can give feedback and get involved

To deal with the various forms of manipulation above, system designers need to integrate ethical design principles in every aspect of interface development. This approach focuses not only on aesthetics and functionality, but also on the values of fairness, transparency, and inclusivity.

Some of the key principles of ethical design include:

1. Interaction Transparency: Users should know when they are being monitored, why the data is collected, and how the data is used.
2. Reversibility: All user actions, such as purchases or important decision-making, must be reviewable and undone.
3. Universal Accessibility: The design should be accessible to users from a variety of backgrounds, including those with physical or cognitive limitations.
4. User Participation: Users should be given space to provide feedback or participate in the system development process.

The application of ethical design principles is not only a matter of technical regulation, but also a mirror of the social responsibility of designers, developers, and platform providers. Ethics in design need to be the main foundation, not an additional feature, in building a sustainable metaverse.

5.5 Case Study: NeuroUX Patterns in Metaverse Games

NeuroUX is an interface design approach that combines the principles of neuroscience and psychology to optimize users' cognitive and emotional responses. While it has positive potential in improving user experience, this approach has been used intensively in the metaverse gaming world to increase engagement and monetization. Examples can be found in loot box systems, certain sound effects, or lighting that is deliberately designed to trigger certain neurological responses—such as euphoria or anxiety—with the goal of keeping players in the game for as long as possible. In many cases, these systems are not explicitly explained to the user, but rather are packaged as "experience features".

According to research by You et al. (2021), the NeuroUX system in metaverse games utilizes the user's brain conditioning mechanism through repetition and random rewards, which can create behavioral dependence. This raises ethical issues related to the exploitation of user neuro-responses for commercial purposes, especially when players are young or vulnerable. These studies confirm that manipulation through design is no longer passive, but active and systematic. Therefore, regulation of NeuroUX practices needs to be a priority in future technology policies.

6. LEGAL AND JURISDICTIONAL CHALLENGES IN THE METAVERSE

The rapid growth of the metaverse as a social ecosystem and virtual economy brings with it legal complexity that has never been faced in the real world. Global, decentralized, and anonymous virtual environments create ambiguities in law, jurisdiction, and enforcement. In a space that is not bound by state borders, the applicable law becomes blurred, while violations can occur quickly and across borders. This chapter explores key legal challenges in the metaverse, including the ambiguity of virtual transactions, intellectual property ownership, cross-border jurisdictional conflicts, the regulation of decentralized autonomous organizations (DAOs), and case studies of large platforms such as Roblox, Decentraland, and Meta.

6.1 Legal Ambiguity in Virtual Transactions

Table 4. Legal Aspects of Digital Systems.

Legal Aspects	Key Issues	Enforcement Challenges
Virtual Transactions	No clarity on contractual status	Digital evidence is difficult to recognize by law
Intellectual Property	Conflict of rights between users and platforms	Blockchain is immutable, difficult to crack down on plagiarism
Jurisdiction	Transactions between countries are difficult to determine by applicable law	There is no global agreement, users do not understand what the law is bound by
DAO Regulation	Unclear legal status, distributed liability	It's hard to sue a DAO as a legal entity
Platform Case Studies	Each platform has a different approach to law and ethics	Inconsistencies in rights protection, transparency, and accountability

In the metaverse, users engage in various forms of economic transactions—from buying and selling virtual land, NFT trading, to avatar-based services. However, the legal status of these transactions is often unclear. Is the exchange of virtual goods a legal transaction protected by contract law? Who is responsible in the event of fraud or loss? Ambiguity arises because most contract laws and consumer protection are still designed for transactions in the real world or on Web 2.0 platforms. Concepts such as "legal intent", "offer and acceptance", or "proof of transaction" are difficult to apply in an immersive environment that is often gamified and informal.

According to Su and Sekti, many users are unaware that their actions in the virtual world can have legal implications. When transactions are made between avatars representing anonymous individuals from different countries, who has the authority to resolve disputes? Without a clear legal framework, the metaverse risks becoming a wild economic space that is not protected by law. The decentralized metaverse environment is also creating new legal issues, especially regarding data and user security across countries (Khajeh-Hosseini, Greenwood, & Sommerville, 2020). The jurisdictional aspect in the metaverse creates cross-border legal challenges that have not been conventionally answered (Mezei, 2022).

6.2 Intellectual Property in User-Generated Virtual Content

One of the main attractions of the metaverse is its ability to allow users to create content—whether it's avatar clothing, artwork, space design, or even interactive experience code. However, the issue of ownership and protection of intellectual property (IP) has become very complex. Smart contracts require a new legal framework that guarantees enforceability, especially in the context of virtual transactions and NFTs (Bermejo & Rodriguez, 2020).

Most metaverse platforms have clauses in the terms of service stating that user-generated content can be reused, modified, or distributed by the platform without compensation. Legal issues over the ownership of digital works in the metaverse require a data-based legal framework and tokenization (Schoonmaker et al., 2022). On the other hand, users often consider themselves to be the rightful owners of their work, especially when the content is tokenized as an NFT. This power imbalance creates a legal dilemma between creative freedom and platform control. In the case of copyright infringement or plagiarism in the metaverse, law enforcement becomes difficult because the content is spread in a blockchain system that cannot be modified. Furthermore, differences in intellectual property laws between countries complicate efforts to protect rights. What is protected as a patent or trademark in one country may not necessarily apply in another, and the legal claims process in a decentralized system requires a new, more collaborative and cross-border approach.

6.3 Jurisdictional Conflicts in the Cross-Border Virtual Economy

One of the biggest challenges in the metaverse is jurisdictional conflicts. When transactions, interactions, or violations of the law occur between individuals from different countries in a virtual environment, there is no universal agreement as to which laws apply. For example, a user from Indonesia makes a transaction with a user from Germany in a metaverse platform owned by a United States company and based on a server in Singapore. In the case of a dispute, which country has the authority to resolve it? Alwaisi et al. (2024) explain that without an adaptive international legal framework, dispute resolution becomes a slow, complicated, and expensive process. Additionally, users are often unaware of the legal jurisdictions that bind them when registering or interacting within the platform. This creates a legal gray zone that harms users and weakens the platform's accountability. To address this conflict, a new approach is needed in the form of transnational legal recognition based on multilateral consensus and the drafting of jurisdictional standards specific to virtual spaces.

6.4 DAO Regulation (Decentralized Autonomous Organizations)

DAOs (Decentralized Autonomous Organizations) are digital forms of organizations that run on smart contracts and are managed by a community of users without a traditional hierarchical structure. In the metaverse, DAOs are used to organize communities, make collective decisions, and manage digital assets together. However, the legal status of DAOs is still very unclear. Can DAOs be considered legal entities? Who is responsible when a DAO violates the law or harms another party? Does every token holder have legal responsibilities? Irshad et al. (2023) highlight that regulation of DAOs lags far behind their adoption. Some countries are beginning to explore legal recognition of DAOs, such as Wyoming in the United States which grants limited legal entity status to DAO entities. However, most jurisdictions still do not have a legal framework for such entities. A huge risk arises when DAOs are involved in DeFi or NFT projects that are worth millions of dollars. Without a clear legal structure, users lose protection, while outsiders have a hard time demanding legal accountability for the DAO's actions.

6.5 Case Study: Roblox, Decentraland, and Meta

Several major platforms have become tangible examples of the various legal complexities of the metaverse. Roblox is a gaming and content creation platform that allows users (especially children and teens) to create and monetize their virtual games. However, Roblox has been criticized for providing unfair revenue sharing to creators and not providing adequate legal protections against child labor in the digital space (Dwivedi et al., 2021). Decentraland, as a blockchain-based platform, gives users more control over assets and experiences. However, its completely decentralized nature makes it difficult to regulate content, resolve disputes, or enforce the law, as there is no central authority responsible. Meta, through Horizon Worlds, is trying to combine a centralised and integrated approach between Facebook user identities, the Meta ecosystem, and the metaverse experience. While this improves user consistency, it also invites criticism for expanding the reach of surveillance capitalism and data monopolies, while avoiding legal obligations specific to each domain. These three platforms show that there is no single approach to the law in the metaverse. Each model brings unique risks and challenges that require evidence-based policies and multi-stakeholder participation.

7. ETHICAL FRAMEWORK AND GOVERNANCE MODEL IN THE METAVERSE

The digital transformation offered by the metaverse presents great opportunities in various sectors, ranging from education, business, entertainment, to social participation. However, the complexity of the technology also gives birth to new risks that are not only technical, but also ethical and structural. Therefore, traditional approaches that are reactive to the negative impact of technological innovation are no longer adequate. An ethical framework is needed that is integrated in the design and technology development process from the beginning (ethics-by-design), as well as a governance model that is able to ensure accountability, transparency, and inclusivity. This chapter discusses five important dimensions of the ethical and governance framework in the metaverse: algorithmic fairness, transparency and explainability, digital rights and inclusive participation, governance models, and proposed *ethical toolkits* for metaverse developers.

7.1 Ethics-by-Design and Algorithmic Justice

Ethics-by-Design is a strategic approach to integrate moral principles into the design and development process of digital systems, including in the metaverse platform. This approach emphasizes that technology is not neutral, and therefore, must be developed with social and ethical impacts in mind from the conceptual stage. In the context of the metaverse, where algorithms influence the distribution of economic opportunities, content visibility, and social interaction, the principle *of fairness* has become very important. The algorithm underlying the metaverse system must be able to guarantee fairness of participation, be unbiased against minority groups, and provide equal outcomes without systemic discrimination. According to Dwivedi et al. (2021), algorithmic fairness is an absolute requirement to ensure that the digital space does not expand the injustices that exist in the physical world. Developers must be able to detect and eliminate bias in training data, as well as implement regular ethical audits of the systems they build.

7.2 Transparency, Accountability, and Explainability

Technologies in the metaverse, especially those that use artificial intelligence (AI) and machine learning, are often "black boxes"—they cannot be easily explained by developers or users. This becomes a problem when the algorithm makes decisions that have a significant impact, such as account banning, access restrictions, or social recommendations. Transparency and *explainability* are part of the principles of digital ethics that guarantee that users know how the system works that affects them. Accountability in this case means that in the event of an error, loss, or injustice, there is an entity that is responsible and can be held accountable. Research by Abdelqawy et al. (2022) shows that transparent and explainable AI systems increase user trust as well as reduce resistance to the adoption of new technologies. In a highly complex and automated metaverse environment, explainability is not just an additional feature, but a fundamental need for fairness and trust (Sekti, 2025).

7.3 Digital Rights and Inclusive Participation

The metaverse as a digital space should not only be accessed by certain groups of people who have high resources and literacy. Instead, it should be developed as a digital public space that guarantees the digital rights of all users, including the right to privacy, data security, freedom of expression, and access without discrimination. According to Benjamens et al. (2020), the development of inclusive digital platforms must consider cultural diversity, language, gender, disability, and economic status. Without inclusivity, the metaverse risks becoming an exclusive space that widens the digital divide and social inequality. Inclusive participation also means that users should be involved in the platform's strategic decision-making through open consultation, community voting, or involvement in the DAO (Decentralized Autonomous Organization) model. Thus, the metaverse can be a system that is not only built for users, but also by users. User involvement as co-creators is an important aspect of equitable digital governance (Chalmers et al., 2022).

7.4 Governance Model: Community vs Centralization

Governance in the metaverse can be classified into two main models: centralized governance controlled by corporate entities or platform developers, and community-driven governance that is managed collectively by users through DAOs or voting systems. Instead, the community model offers greater direct participation, transparency, and accountability. DAO governance in the metaverse requires a collaborative framework that ensures democratization and distribution of power (Varghese et al., 2023). However, this kind of governance still faces serious challenges such as coordination, digital literacy gaps, and the risk of vote manipulation by those with greater token resources. There is no ideal single model. The combination of community oversight and formal legal structures can create a balance between efficiency and democratization. This kind of hybrid model is important in conflict management, dispute resolution, and the formation of internal regulations of metaverse platforms. Comparative studies show that community governance models can improve transparency, but still require a supporting legal framework (Varghese & Mehta, 2023).

7.5 Proposed Framework: *Ethical Toolkit* for Metaverse Developers

To support the ethical development of the metaverse, a set of practical work tools is needed that can be adopted by developers, system designers, and other stakeholders. This framework can take the form of *an Ethical Toolkit* that contains design guidelines, risk indicators, and ethical evaluation instruments that can be used in the product development lifecycle.

Some of the key components of the *Ethical Toolkit* for the metaverse include:

1. Design Ethics Checklist: a list of critical questions about the social impact and ethics of the developed features.
2. Social Risk Evaluation Model: a framework for analyzing the impact of policies and features on vulnerable groups.
3. Algorithmic Transparency Guidelines: minimum standards for systems to explain how they work to users.
4. Complaint and Recovery Mechanism: a system that allows users to submit complaints and get a fair resolution.
5. Co-Creation Principle: the involvement of a community of users in the design and evaluation process.

Alaca and Çelik (2023) emphasize the importance of this kind of tool to prevent invisible bias and maintain ethics in complex situations. This toolkit is not intended to replace human judgment, but to be a systematic reminder of the values that must be upheld.

8. FUTURE REVIEW AND RECOMMENDATIONS

The metaverse, as a connected, immersive, and decentralized digital space, has moved from being a mere speculative concept to a real and growing ecosystem. In its journey, the metaverse has challenged the boundaries of conventional technology, legal, social, and economics. While there are many promising opportunities—from democratizing creativity to a borderless digital economy—there are also equally serious threats, such as data exploitation, access inequality, and inadequate governance. This chapter maps out the possible future direction of the metaverse and presents strategic recommendations for creating inclusive, ethical, and sustainable virtual spaces.

8.1 Cross-Border Regulatory Collaboration

The main characteristic of the metaverse is its transnational nature, where users, developers, and servers operate from different parts of the world, creating legal complexities that cannot be effectively addressed by unilateral national legal systems. To overcome this challenge, progressive and adaptive cross-border regulatory cooperation is essential. Such collaboration is crucial not only for harmonizing security standards, data protection, and digital rights, but also for developing a shared legal framework capable of addressing decentralized entities such as Decentralized Autonomous Organizations (DAOs) and blockchain-based protocols. Without global synergy, regulatory gaps will remain vulnerable to exploitation by irresponsible actors. Therefore, a comprehensive global approach to technology regulation should involve collaborative platforms such as international digital governance forums that bring together governments, technology companies, academia, and civil society. Initiatives like the OECD AI Principles and the European Union's Digital Services Act can serve as foundational models for promoting the standardization and coordination of metaverse governance on a global scale.

8.2 The Role of AI, Blockchain, and Trust Infrastructure

The main supporting technologies in the metaverse are AI, blockchain, and digital trust infrastructure. Artificial intelligence plays a crucial role in creating personalized user experiences, managing virtual economies, and ensuring system scalability. Meanwhile, blockchain guarantees transparency, ownership, and verifiable transaction systems without intermediaries. However, this technology also poses new challenges. AI algorithms can embed systemic bias in virtual interactions, while blockchain presents environmental dilemmas and legal complexities. Therefore, it is necessary to develop a digital trust infrastructure that combines the principles of transparency, fairness, and accountability across the board. Abdelqawy et al. (2022) emphasize the importance of trust-by-design systems, where digital systems are designed from the beginning to be auditable, explained, and controlled by users. This includes independent algorithmic audits, transparent metadata on digital assets, as well as full user control over their data. User trust in the metaverse relies heavily on interface design that values control and transparency (Choi & Park, 2024).

8.3 Scenario Planning: Utopia or Dystopia?

In developing future projections of the metaverse, the scenario planning approach offers a valuable framework for assessing both the positive potential and extreme risks of this evolving technology. Two primary scenarios often emerge from such analysis: the "digital utopia" and the "algorithmic dystopia." In the utopian vision, the metaverse functions as a collaborative and inclusive space that fosters creativity, empowers community-driven economies, and unites humanity in a digital environment governed by ethical principles. Users maintain full control over their identities and data, and technology serves as a tool for empowerment rather than exploitation. Conversely, the dystopian scenario envisions the metaverse as a hyper-commercialized ecosystem dominated by powerful corporations, where data exploitation is pervasive, algorithmic control undermines personal autonomy, and users are reduced to passive participants in an inequitable digital economy. Chatterjee et al. (2021) state that the future direction is not determined by technology alone, but by ethical, political, and social decisions made today. In other words, the future of the metaverse is not something that is destined, but rather designed—collectively.

8.4 Recommendations for Policymakers, Developers, and Users

Based on the mapping of issues and scenarios discussed above, this chapter provides several concrete recommendations for key stakeholders in the metaverse ecosystem. For policymakers, it is essential to formulate metaverse-specific regulations covering digital rights, virtual economies, and biometric data protection, establish cross-border cooperation mechanisms for managing digital jurisdictions and disputes, and mandate ethical audits and transparency for AI and blockchain-based systems. For developers and designers, integrating ethics-by-design principles into every stage of system development, applying fairness and explainability tests to algorithms used in personalization and moderation, and creating user interfaces that promote informed consent and user control are critical steps toward responsible innovation. Meanwhile, for users and communities, strengthening digital literacy related to privacy, digital rights, and tokenization, actively engaging in governance structures such as Decentralized Autonomous Organizations (DAOs) and voting mechanisms, and promoting transparency while demanding accountability from platforms are necessary actions to ensure an ethical, fair, and participatory metaverse environment. According to Benjamens et al. (2020), synergy between the government, the private sector, and civil society is a key factor in shaping the direction of ethical and inclusive digital technology development.

8.5 Final Reflections and Research Gaps

The metaverse remains a developing domain with rapidly evolving technological infrastructure and an unstable legal framework, leaving many critical questions unanswered. To ensure its responsible growth, it is essential to identify key research gaps that can guide future exploration and policy development. Priority areas for further study include evaluating the effectiveness of hybrid governance models within metaverse systems, examining the long-term psychological and social impacts of extended reality (XR) on users, and designing equitable, community-based economic models for virtual environments. Additionally, research is needed to establish stronger legal protections for digital labor and user-generated content ownership, as well as to develop ethical interface design approaches that safeguard vulnerable users, including children and individuals with disabilities. Fei et al. (2022) underline that the development of large-scale digital systems must be accompanied by a transdisciplinary approach, which thoroughly combines engineering, ethics, public policy, and the social sciences.

CONCLUSION

The metaverse, as a new frontier in the digital economy, has opened extraordinary opportunities while introducing ethical, legal, and social challenges never encountered before. By integrating immersive technologies such as virtual reality, blockchain, and artificial intelligence, the metaverse is not only creating new digital environments but also reshaping how humans work, socialize, and conduct economic activities. However, its rapid development is inseparable from systemic risks such as market monopolization by major platforms, vulnerabilities in smart contracts, and uncertainty surrounding the valuation of virtual assets. The emergence of digital identities through complex avatars also raises concerns about privacy, data ownership, and user autonomy in representing themselves online. Moreover, new digital work models within the metaverse, including play-to-earn systems and token-based gig economies, often expose workers to exploitation, lack of legal protection, and unstable income. Ethical design in user interfaces is another pressing issue, as manipulative features such as dark patterns, attention engineering, and addictive XR designs threaten user freedom and well-being. These challenges highlight the urgent need for ethics-by-design principles and transparent algorithmic governance

To navigate these complexities, this chapter emphasizes the importance of building an ethical and participatory foundation for metaverse development that upholds algorithmic justice, transparency, accountability, digital rights protection, and community-based governance. Cross-border regulatory cooperation and adaptive legal frameworks are essential to address jurisdictional uncertainty, digital asset disputes, and virtual crimes that transcend national boundaries. Equally important is the creation of ethical toolkits for developers, the institutionalization of ethics-by-design in software engineering, and the empowerment of users to participate in governance through Decentralized Autonomous Organizations (DAOs). Ultimately, realizing an ethical and inclusive metaverse requires collective collaboration among developers, regulators, academics, and users. Technology will serve as a true instrument of empowerment only when it is grounded in human values and social responsibility. The ideal metaverse is not a risk-free utopia but a fair, transparent, and human-centered digital space that respects dignity, autonomy, and equality across both physical and virtual dimensions.

REFERENCES

Abdelqawy, D., El-Korany, A., Kamel, A., & Makady, S. (2022). Hub-OS: An interoperable IoT computing platform for resources utilization with real-time support. *Journal of King Saud University. Computer and Information Sciences, 34*(4), 1498–1510. https://doi.org/https://doi.org/10.1016/j.jksuci.2022.02.011. DOI: 10.1016/j.jksuci.2022.02.011

Ahmed, S., Alshater, M. M., El Ammari, A., & Hammami, H. (2022). Artificial intelligence and machine learning in finance: A bibliometric review. *Research in International Business and Finance, 61*, 101646. https://doi.org/https://doi.org/10.1016/j.ribaf.2022.101646. DOI: 10.1016/j.ribaf.2022.101646

AL-Hawamleh, A. M. (2024). Securing the future: Framework fundamentals for cyber resilience in advancing organizations. *Journal of System and Management Sciences, 14*(10), 130–150.

Alaca, Y., & Çelik, Y. (2023). Cyber attack detection with QR code images using lightweight deep learning models. *Computers & Security, 126*, 103065. https://doi.org/https://doi.org/10.1016/j.cose.2022.103065. DOI: 10.1016/j.cose.2022.103065

Benjamens, S., Dhunnoo, P., & Meskó, B. (2020). The state of artificial intelligence-based FDA-approved medical devices and algorithms: An online database. *NPJ Digital Medicine, 3*(1), 118. DOI: 10.1038/s41746-020-00324-0 PMID: 32984550

Chatterjee, S., Rana, N. P., Dwivedi, Y. K., & Baabdullah, A. M. (2021). Understanding AI adoption in manufacturing and production firms using an integrated TAM-TOE model. *Technological Forecasting and Social Change, 170*, 120880. DOI: 10.1016/j.techfore.2021.120880

Chui, K. T., Upadhyay, U., Kumar, A., Sharma, G., Saini, A. K., Arya, V., & Gaurav, A. (2023). Mitigating Risks in the Cloud-Based Metaverse Access Control Strategies and Techniques. *International Journal of Cloud Applications and Computing, 14*(1), 1–30. DOI: 10.4018/IJCAC.313572

Dwivedi, Y. K., Hughes, L., Ismagilova, E., Aarts, G., Coombs, C., Crick, T., Duan, Y., Dwivedi, R., Edwards, J., Eirug, A., Galanos, V., Ilavarasan, P. V., Janssen, M., Jones, P., Kar, A. K., Kizgin, H., Kronemann, B., Lal, B., Lucini, B., & Williams, M. D. (2021). Artificial Intelligence (AI): Multidisciplinary perspectives on emerging challenges, opportunities, and agenda for research, practice and policy. *International Journal of Information Management, 57*, 101994. https://doi.org/https://doi.org/10.1016/j.ijinfomgt.2019.08.002. DOI: 10.1016/j.ijinfomgt.2019.08.002

Fei, N., Lu, Z., Gao, Y., Yang, G., Huo, Y., Wen, J., Lu, H., Song, R., Gao, X., Xiang, T., Sun, H., & Wen, J.-R. (2022). Towards artificial general intelligence via a multimodal foundation model. *Nature Communications*, *13*(1), 3094. DOI: 10.1038/s41467-022-30761-2 PMID: 35655064

Feng, J., & Zhao, J. (2023). Resource allocation for augmented reality empowered vehicular edge metaverse. *IEEE Transactions on Communications*.

Gupta, B. B., Gaurav, A., Albeshri, A. A., & Alsalman, D. (2023). New paradigms of sustainable entrepreneurship in metaverse: A micro-level perspective. *The International Entrepreneurship and Management Journal*, *19*(3), 1449–1465. DOI: 10.1007/s11365-023-00875-0

Gupta, B. B., Gaurav, A., & Arya, V. (2024). Fuzzy logic and biometric-based lightweight cryptographic authentication for metaverse security. *Applied Soft Computing*, *164*, 111973. DOI: 10.1016/j.asoc.2024.111973

Gupta, B. B., Gaurav, A., Arya, V., & Alhalabi, W. (2024). The evolution of intellectual property rights in metaverse based Industry 4.0 paradigms. *The International Entrepreneurship and Management Journal*, *20*(2), 1111–1126. DOI: 10.1007/s11365-023-00940-8

Hill, G. N., & Whitty, M. A. (2021). Embedding metadata in images at time of capture using physical Quick Response (QR) codes. *Information Processing & Management*, *58*(3), 102504. https://doi.org/https://doi.org/10.1016/j.ipm.2021.102504. DOI: 10.1016/j.ipm.2021.102504

Huang, Y., Li, Y., & Cai, Z. (2023). Security and Privacy in Metaverse: A Comprehensive Survey. *Big Data Mining and Analytics*, *6*(2), 234–247. DOI: 10.26599/BDMA.2022.9020047

Irshad, R. R., Hussain, S., Hussain, I., Ahmad, I., Yousif, A., Alwayle, I. M., Alattab, A. A., Alalayah, K. M., Breslin, J. G., Badr, M. M., & Rodrigues, J. J. P. C. (2023). An Intelligent Buffalo-Based Secure Edge-Enabled Computing Platform for Heterogeneous IoT Network in Smart Cities. *IEEE Access : Practical Innovations, Open Solutions*, *11*, 69282–69294. DOI: 10.1109/ACCESS.2023.3288815

Kim, J. G. (2021). A study on metaverse culture contents matching platform. *International Journal of Advanced Culture Technology*, *9*(3), 232–237.

Kumar, A., Shankar, A., Behl, A., Gupta, B. B., & Mavuri, S. (2023). Lights, Camera, Metaverse!: Eliciting Intention to Use Industrial Metaverse, Organizational Agility, and Firm Performance. [JGIM]. *Journal of Global Information Management*, *31*(8), 1–20. DOI: 10.4018/JGIM.333169

Pappachan, P., Purshewar, P., & Rahaman, M. (2025). Theoretical Frameworks for Analyzing Social Dynamics. In *Unveiling Social Dynamics and Community Interaction in the Metaverse* (pp. 139–158). IGI Global Scientific Publishing., DOI: 10.4018/979-8-3693-8628-6.ch007

Rahaman, M., Bakkireddygari, S. S., Chattopadhyay, S., Gomez, A. L., Arya, V., & Bansal, S. (2024). Infrastructure and Network Security. In *Metaverse Security Paradigms* (pp. 108–144). IGI Global Scientific Publishing., DOI: 10.4018/979-8-3693-3824-7.ch005

Rahaman, M., Pappachan, P., Batul, I., Widodo, A. M., & Gupta, B. B. (2025). Communication Modalities and Tools. In *Unveiling Social Dynamics and Community Interaction in the Metaverse* (pp. 39–64). IGI Global Scientific Publishing., DOI: 10.4018/979-8-3693-8628-6.ch003

Sekti, B. A. (2025). Machine learning and artificial intelligence (AI) in manufacturing. In *Integrating Digital Innovation and Integrated Frameworks in Manufacturing* (pp. 255–292). DOI: 10.4018/979-8-3373-1082-4.ch011

Varghese, D. J. (2024). Metaverse Liability and the Future of Tort Law. *Available at SSRN* 5043578.

Wang, Z., Tao, Z., Lan, Y., Chen, Y., Xie, Q., Li, Q., Lu, C., & Zhang, W. (2023). Different mechanisms mediating cybervictimization and internalizing/externalizing problems: The moderating role of emotion regulation strategies. *Computers in Human Behavior*, *144*, 107748. https://doi.org/https://doi.org/10.1016/j.chb.2023.107748. DOI: 10.1016/j.chb.2023.107748

Widodo, A. M., Wisnujati, A., Asianto, A. M., Aryani, D. M., Rahaman, M., Arya, V., & Pappachan, P. (2024). Understanding the Metaverse. In *Metaverse Security Paradigms* (pp. 1–38). IGI Global Scientific Publishing., DOI: 10.4018/979-8-3693-3824-7.ch001

Chapter 6
Integrating Metaverse With Manufacturing:
A Novel Paradigm for Immersive Interactive and Impactful Learning

Amit V. Sata
http://orcid.org/0000-0002-0945-3095
Marwadi University, India

Sumit Ranoliya
Marwadi University, India

Dhaval Anadkat
Marwadi University, India

ABSTRACT

Manufacturing plays very important role in growth of overall economy of nation, and metal casting is one of such manufacturing processes that contributes largely on economy especially in India. These manufacturing enterprises are always in need of skilled manpower or these are in requirement to train their existing manpower for advanced technologies so that performance of these industries can be enhanced. This manpower can be trained in real industrial environment with specific skillsets that can be helpful in various industrial sectors, and Metaverse seems to be one of the solutions.Specific methodology adopted to develop Metaverse for metal casting. Metaverse of metal casting has been developed, and demonstrated for imparting technical skills to young manpower. It was observed that Metaverse can be very effective to impart technical skills required in the domain of metal casting. This

DOI: 10.4018/979-8-2600-0013-7.ch006

implementation has provided great encouragement, and can lead to development of Metaverse for other manufacturing processes to serve overall requirement of skilled manpower in the domain.

INTRODUCTION

Industry 4.0, the fourth industrial revolution, has played a vital role in transition of manufacturing domain from mechanization and mass production into a data-driven, connected environment. This shift started in the early 2010s as manufacturers sought increased efficiency, flexibility, and personalization in production (Hermann et al., 2016; Zhou et al., 2015). Industry 4.0 also refers to the integration of workshop and industrial processes (process modelling, simulation, real-time management, optimization) that is made possible by the cloud computing and internet of things (Zhong et al., 2017). It has reinvented the way things are made by allowing smart factories where machines can talk to each other, perform autonomous decision making and self-optimize to be efficient. All these things are not only increasing operational productivity, but they are kind of facilitating the technological convergence for lots of immersive digital experiences such as metaverse, which is a very logical next step in terms of technological convergence (Gilchrist, 2016; L.-H. Lee et al., 2024).

Central to this transformation are next-generation technologies, including Artificial Intelligence (AI), the Internet of Things (IoT), Augmented and Virtual Reality (AR/VR) and digital twins. AI had brought intelligent automation, anomalous detection, and predictive maintenance, whereas IoT had allowed the vast access to data through inter-connected sensors and devices (J. Lee et al., 2015; Tao et al., 2018). This constant data flow gives transparency, traceability, and the ability of real-time control in production line. It has changed the training, maintenance, and design by providing interactive and immersive environments with AR and VR (Hosseini et al., 2024). Then there are digital twins, virtual replicas of physical systems, that model real-world behaviors and enable engineers to explore scenarios, and refine designs, without disrupting processes in the field (Grieves & Vickers, 2017; Kritzinger et al., 2018).These are the technologies that form the basis for advanced manufacturing today, and together, forms the gateway to the next level of integrated and immersive space.

Generally viewed as a digital universe made up of interconnected virtual worlds, the metaverse is slowly ballooning beyond the realm of fun and games. It is place where the physical and digital worlds converge with immersive technology and with data interacting in real time. In manufacturing, the metaverse isn't a specific virtual world, but the spectrum of digitized environments across which engineers, machines and systems collaborate in real time or, interact with one another through avatars, simulations and interfaces powered by artificial intelligence (Fernández-Caramés & Fraga-Lamas, 2024; Tao et al., 2019). Integration of these technologies along with metaverse provides capabilities for richer and more engaging visualization, including real-time collaboration and more efficient workflows. The metaverse is an immersive, collaborative workspace for the design, development, oversight, and optimization of manufacturing processes (Lyu & Fridenfalk, 2024). The convergence of the metaverse with Industry 4.0 offers new possibilities to serve the core objectives of smart manufacturing; automation, interconnectivity, and data-based decision-making. Automated systems can be modelled, tested and optimized in the metaverse before they get deployed to reduce costly errors and downtime (Negri et al., 2017). Using data from digital twins in a metaverse, the synchronized control between the real asset and the virtual twin far exceeds and improves responsiveness and operational fine tuning (K. Li et al., 2023).

A metaverse is the collaborative and persistent physical-cyber ecosystem that supports IoT-connected machines, digital twin representations, and XR-based interfaces and combines them into an immersive computing fabric. The metaverse, unlike traditional VR/AR, or digital twin systems, is a common, data-driven, multi-user space, which allows real-time collaboration, decision-making, and control of the process. It goes beyond the visualization to encompass social presence, AI-assisted interaction and integration into enterprise data systems. In contrast to traditional VR/AR, in which users can be supplied with local simulations, or digital twins, which only model the physical processes, the metaverse is a shared interactive and data driven environment in which operators, learners, and enterprise systems can interact in real-time. This contrast forms the uniqueness of the proposed work and explains why the suggested mechanisms go further than those of its currents.

To better understand the nature of the metaverse and how it sits in contrast to current manufacturing paradigm, a table is presented that compares traditional manufacturing systems, Industry 4.0 systems, and metaverse-linked systems.

Table 1. Comparison of Traditional Manufacturing, Industry 4.0, and Metaverse-Integrated Systems

Feature	Traditional Manufacturing / Training	Industry 4.0 Systems	Metaverse Integrated Systems
User Interaction	Manual, instructor led, hands on	Human machine interfaces, dashboards	Immersive XR, haptics, multi user collaboration
Data Visualization	Paper logs, limited instrumentation	IoT dashboards, digital twins	Real time 3D immersive visualization
Decision Support	Based on experience / judgement	Data driven analytics, automation	AI augmented, collaborative immersive decision-making
Scalability	Restricted to physical workshops	Scales with automation infrastructure	Virtual scalability, global remote access
Safety	High risk of accidents, material waste	Safer, but still involves physical risk	Risk free virtual simulation
Learning Retention	Moderate, limited iterations	Improved through data-driven feedback	High, due to interactive, repeatable immersive training

The metaverse builds upon the functionality of Industry 4.0 by adding immersive, interactivity, and collaborative capability to create a new layer of cyber physical interaction that escalates beyond data dashboards and stand-alone digital twinning (Tukur et al., 2024). Notwithstanding progress, the manufacturing industry still experiences ongoing challenges in terms of inefficiencies in training, obstructed collaboration, restricted prototyping and non-sensitivity to disruptions. The metaverse tackles these pain points by allowing for virtual training programs that act as real-world environment simulations, allowing workers to more easily and safely learn intricate operations (Almeida et al., 2023; Strazzeri et al., 2024). Virtual spaces, shared with others can support co-design, co-engineering and simultaneous composition in distributed teams across geography or it can allow direct coupling across physical presence (Bujari et al., 2023). Simulations and prototyping, which have always been manual and resource intensive can all start happening virtually using a digital twin, speeding up innovation cycles (Yang et al., 2025). In addition, critical situations like equipment failure and break in supply chain can be simulated and practiced in metaverse that could enable companies to stay prepared and build resilient business (Nleya & Velempini, 2024).

In practical terms, the metaverse has several use cases in manufacturing from design and simulation to training and maintenance. Its use cases are increasingly diverse, including virtual production lines, interactive assembly guidelines, remote diagnostics and collaborative engineering workspaces (J. Lee & Kundu, 2022). Advantages of meshing the metaverse with manufacturing include faster time to market, fewer training expenses, enhanced worker safety, higher design precision, and better cross functional teamwork (Egbengwu et al., 2025). Inter component communication, platform interactions, and the fidelity of simulated environments are also necessary considerations that need to be addressed to achieve effective deployment. Nevertheless, it is evident that the metaverse can transform the context of the manufacturing industry. As the lines between the digital and physical worlds become further erased, the metaverse is likely to become a key component to future industrial ecosystems where innovation will contribute to smarter, safer and more sustainable manufacturing. To integrate the value of the metaverse in the manufacturing sector, interpretation of the transformational capabilities of the metaverse is needed not only on manufacturing, but on manpower development too. As metaverse technologies become integrated within industrial operations, they are changing the skillsets required by manufacturing professionals. This evolution aligns with the broader changes brought about by Industry 4.0, where digital proficiency and virtual collaboration are becoming as essential as traditional technical know-how.

As, manufacturing sector is going through an unprecedented transformation driven by the integration and advancement of digital technologies under industry 4.0, this transformation emphasizes cyber physical system, real time data exchange, smart automation and interconnected assets in the system. Due to this, the technical skill requirements of the manufacturing workers are evolving rapidly from conventional machine operation and process execution to simulation-based, data-driven, and system-integrated skills. To achieve competitiveness as well as effective operation, manufacturing industries need not only to accept these technological changes but also implement mechanisms to assure their workforce on how to efficiently use them. This has created an urgent imperative to redefine the way technical skills are acquired in educational and training designs for manufacturing.

Traditionally, skills development in manufacturing has been done mainly through experiential learning in physical workshops, internships, and apprenticeships. Although these processes can operate with some constraints, they are prone to constraints in terms of access to equipment, operational hazards, variations in exposure to learning, and high material loss and energy expenditure. Additionally, traditional skills development processes are not designed with real-time feedback, interactivity, and scenario-based learning and are thus insufficient to enable learners to deal with the changing, data-intensive environments common in contemporary smart factories.

Within this context, the development of immersive technologies primarily, Virtual Reality (VR), Augmented Reality (AR), and the emerging Metaverse offers a significant transformative potential. The Metaverse is conceived as a continuous, interactive, and networked virtual world that allows digital replicas of production systems, processes, and environments. With the application of enabling technologies like the Internet of Things (IoT), Artificial Intelligence (AI), and digital twins, the Metaverse offers an interactive cyber-physical platform for the transfer of technical know-how in a more significant, engaging, and effective manner (Mosharraf, 2025).

Metaverse based manufacturing training environments when integrated with some of the enabler technologies like IoT, AI, DT can be helpful in digital simulation of manufacturing systems, processes and environments leading to greater experience in the complex operations like metal casting, CNC machining, fault diagnostics etc. in a controlled yet realistic environment. This leads to hands-on training without exposing learners to physical hazards, especially in high-risk processes such as centrifugal casting or high temperature pouring. Learners can also perform the variety of iterations, reflect and refine their skills more effectively than in traditional set ups using real time monitoring, feedback system and performance tracking integrated in these environments.

From a pedagogical perspective, the integration of Immersive Interactive Environments (IIE) into the metaverse is a transition from passive learning mode to active learning modes, where learners are involved thoroughly in the experiential learning. This is consistent with the new learning paradigms of the era, which focus on competency-based education, experiential learning, and learner-centered approaches. It also facilitates the potential for scaling and standardizing training, allowing institutions and industries to deliver consistent, high-quality skill development programs irrespective of geographical location, resource availability, or logistical limitations.

Besides, the data generated in such virtual worlds such as interaction records and decision-making patterns up to finding error rates and time of task completion can be utilized by machine learning algorithms to personalize learning, provide a performance benchmark, and predict future training needs. The combination of technical skill learning with the metaverse does more than enhance performance, however, it can be used as a constant checks and balances to ensure skill development and continued workforce improvement.

In such developing countries as India, with more than 11 million manufacturing plants, and with a constantly proven deficit of technical skill professionals' needs in the industry, implementation of the training solutions through the metaverse can be used to establish bridges between the educational outputs and industry expectations. In addition, it can address accessibility, scalability and economic viability of the skill development programs essentially. In brief, the infusion of technical competence in manufacturing through metaverse-based platforms redefines the process of knowledge transfer, learning, and implementation in industrial settings. By integrating the physical set ups of manufacturing with digital simulations through digital twins, IoT, and AI, the process enables the creation of smart, secure, and scalable training environments. It is a critical step towards the development of a future-proof workforce that can operate within the intelligent, connected, and sustainable manufacturing settings of Industry 4.0 and beyond.

To address these gaps, the present study has the following objectives:

- Analyze and summaries the available mechanism about the way the metaverse has been applied in manufacturing and training.
- Develop and deploy a Vertical Centrifugal Casting (VCC) instructional system with IoT, digital twins, and VR to give immersive interaction.
- Test the system with both technology specific parameters (accuracy of the sensor, latency, synchronization) and those parameters which could be estimated by users (usability, engagement, learning) outcomes.
- Compare the efficiency of metaverse based training to that of conventionally delivered training in workshop, cost, safety, scalability and retention rates.
- Emphasize the managerial and pedagogical implications of integrating metaverse based training in the context of workforce development.

Detailed literature review on the work is explained in the next section.

LITERATURE REVIEW ON INTEGRATION OF METAVERSE IN MANUFACTURING

The integration of the metaverse in the manufacturing zone characterizes a revolutionary era for industrial exertion, integrating immersive inventions with traditional production procedures. Researchers and scholars have gradually reviewed the prospect by which the metaverse, corresponding of artificial intelligence (AI), extended reality (XR), digital twins and the Internet of Things (IoT) can convert manufacturing via the encouragement of remote control, design, interactive staff training and simulation improvement. This review of the literature induces simultaneously potential future directions in the industrial metaverse, current scholarly work, summarizing the main developments, applications and challenges.

A bibliometric analysis of over 8,500 publications in the period between 2015–2025 showed that only nearly 0.04 percent of them are directly associated with manufacturing or with skill development, which means that the metaverse in manufacturing has become a topic with little to no attention.

Li et al. (L. Li et al., 2022) gave some of the foundational work to the thought of digital twins for manufacturing, summarizing how physical systems can be characterized virtually and employed for real-time monitoring, diagnosis, fault and optimization. Their study emphasized how through the integration of the metaverse & digital twins, directors can produce perfect production spaces within immersive 3D, adaptive control systems, predictive maintenance and enabling enhanced visualization. This integration induces towards the innovation of a continuous bridge among physical and virtual assets, considerably improving the transparency and flexibility in processes. Boschert et al. (Boschert & Rosen, 2016) also worked on implementing a comprehensive survey of the prevalence of digital twins in smart factories. They mentioned that virtual environments engage human-computer interaction, which illustrates operators' management and analysis of complexed data. The researchers additionally indicated out that digital twins in the metaverse are suitable for lifecycle management, scenario testing and energy optimization, which turns out in sustainable and flexible production models.

Sherdil et al. (Sherdil & Madhavji, 1996) concentrated on human-oriented applications, specifically workforce instruction. Their VR-based training platform illustrated improved lower training expenses, control of knowledge and enhanced factory worker safety. By limiting risky or sophisticated processes in a virtual reality, their architecture excludes the physical risk and prepares workers sufficiently before they cooperate with real facilities. The research is specifically applicable considering Industry 5.0 (I5.0), where human-integrated inventions get priority. The COVID-19 epidemic reinforced the significance of remote operability in manufacturing. Choi et al. (Choi et al., 2015)demonstrated how XR innovations, such as AR glasses and VR headsets, were utilized to maintain factory operations during lockdown. These inventions allow virtual factory tours, remote supervision & collaborative design, thereby sinking physical reliance's. Their research insisted the metaverse's involvement in expanding business flexibility against sudden disturbances.

In addition to scholarly research, several industrial pilots demonstrate the practical significance of the integration of metaverse in manufacturing. In the automotive industry, BMW has implemented a metaverse-based digital twin environment to design and test the layout of factories by digital means prior to their physical implementation, which shortened commissioning time. Hyundai has tried to use virtual lines of production where assembly processes can be simulated in a collaborative environment by engineers. In the aerospace industry, Airbus has already employed extended reality training to assemble an aircraft, with a claimed improvement in worker and task accuracy and readiness. In the consumer electronics industry, producers like Samsung have tested VR enabled training using production-floor employees where they have highlighted reduced costs and downtime. Although the examples confirm the practicality of metaverse integration in industry, its usage in the complex process like metal casting is underrepresented, which highlights the originality of the given study.

Metaverse technologies have also had a strong impact on product evolution. Vincenza et al. (Vincenza Ciasullo et al., 2018) shared virtual co-creation platforms by which customers, designers and engineers could cooperate with real-time 3D samples. Similar platforms dispensed with many physical samples, resulting in less material wasted and rapid design cycles. Virtual simulations similarly allow stress testing and operational testing prior to real production, improving product quality and inventions. Ivanov et al. (Ivanov & Dolgui, 2020) discovered the benefits that supply chain management (SCM) can accumulate from metaverse integration. Their suggested model employed digital twins, blockchain and IoT to achieve supply chain networks visual in an immersive space. This simplified risk simulation, real-time tracking and predictive analysis. The authors underlined that immersive SCM tools are particularly applicable while dealing with global supply chains, where real-time affiliation and transparency are predominant.

Communication frameworks largely support the metaverse's application. Hassan et al. (Hassan et al., 2019) commented the abilities of 5G and edge computing in boarding low-suspension, high-bandwidth operations needed for real-time dealings in factories. Their research referred that these innovations simplify XR-free experiences and reliable remote machine control, describing them a requirement for the metaverse in manufacturing. AI also augments the metaverse's value in manufacturing. Yigit et al. (Volpe et al., 2023; Yigit et al., 2024) made an AI-enhanced digital twin system that empowers autonomous decision-making and cautious maintenance. The system discovers constantly from sensor data so that it can predict machine defect and prepare the production program. The AI-based system reduces downtime and enhances overall equipment conclusiveness.

Volpe et al. (Volpe et al., 2023) worked on cost-benefit estimation of manufacturing XR embracement. They introduce that although first core investment is significant, long-term benefits such as minimized human error, reduced operational costs and enhanced employee interpretation exceed the costs. Their comment provided a convincing case for businesses. However, a shift towards immersive (Lv et al., 2022) inventions and the integration of virtual platforms with physical systems presents cybersecurity issues. In recent studies, it has been stressed that adoption of industrial metaverse has been limited by cybersecurity risks, interoperability across different platforms, and no standard data sharing and governance infrastructure. Shang et al. advised that the digital twins and communication networks of the metaverse might be targeted by cybercriminals. They suggested multi-layered security frameworks such as secure authentication, encryption and anomaly detection systems, for shielding delicate data and ensuring functional reliability.

Interoperability is still an additional major obstacle. Jeon et al. (Jung & Jeon, 2022) illustrated that the need of standardization in data formations and communication procedures keeps excellent integration over heterogeneous platforms and systems. The fragmentation of these innovations can result in data silos, increased integration costs, and inefficiency. International standardization was supported by the researcher to unify the industrial metaverse ecosystem. Workforce preparation was illuminated by Aziz et al. (Aziz et al., 2023) but they were more worried about the digital skills gap as an obstacle to metaverse understanding. They specified that most factory workers need training to involve successfully with XR technologies and digital affiliates. The authors planned large-scale educational modifications, skill advancement programs and industry-academic connections to make a future proof workforce.

Saurabh et al. (Saurabh et al., 2024) reviewed smart integrations such as blockchain and Decentralized Autonomous Organizations (DAOs) in the metaverse. Their research presented a system in which production methods and management activities are automated by smart settlements, creating them to be more transparent and less managerial oppressive. This decentralized program is consistent with the industry elements of I5.0, focusing on to form sustainable, human-based, and adjustable production environments. A predictive perspective approaches from the European Commission (Coelho et al., 2023), suggested that the I5.0 concept concentrates on integrating technology with human-centeredness, social responsibility and environment sustainability. The industrial metaverse in this illusion is not only a development technology but a force behind sustainable and comprehensive industrial growth.

Kareem et al. (Kareem et al., 2024) evolved the opinion of the "Meta Operator" - a technologically augmented worker who collaborates with industrial apparatus using XR devices and live data processes. Their research cited illustrious enablers such as AR/MR wearables, edge computing and IoT connectivity. Meta Operators are expected to be primary performers in intelligent factories, with the capability to operate sophisticated tasks with greater situational knowledge and preciseness. To ensure data integrity and privacy in the industrial metaverse, Ding et al. (Ding et al., 2023) posed an affiliated knowledge framework grounded on a decentralized architecture. Their framework utilizes age-based agreements for data freshness and encouraging participation from various nodes in the industrial IoT network.

Masubuchi et al. (Masubuchi et al., 2025) innovatively shared smart buildings with commercial metaverse platforms. Their work explained how XR applications and IoT sensors could be utilized to control building procedures remotely. Although targeted at smart architecture, their outcomes are very useful to factory environments, where the same type of integration can heighten user experience, improve energy consumption & track equipment. Guo et al. (Guo et al., 2024) offered a complete report of the enabler innovations and uses of the industrial metaverse. Their summary involved blockchain, digital twins, 6G, XR, and AI, as well as the connected issues of interoperability, privacy and data management. Their research is applicable in controlling privacy for future research and evolution in this area.

Wang et al. (Wang et al., 2023) gave a thematic survey of the industrial metaverse, classifying five important areas of influence: assembly, product design, quality control, maintenance and repair & warehouse management. They also separated the challenges into six categories: technical, non-technical, technological, organizational, environmental and business. This systematized approach facilitates stakeholders to express efficient programs for implementation. Furthermore, other research features the significance of user-centered design in facilitating effective adoption of metaverse innovations in manufacturing. Alhakamy (Alhakamy, 2024) reinforced the lack for user interface design particularly to suit different user types such as managers, engineers and technicians to completely enhance user engagement and usability. Their research demonstrated how effective XR interfaces can improve productivity and minimize learning curves, significantly in complex assembly scenarios.

The intersection of metaverse and 6G usages is being researched ever closely. Based on Tang et al. (Tang et al., 2023), 6G systems will advocate high AI integration capabilities, ultra-low latency and Massive Machine Type Communication (mMTC), which are crucial to make real-time, multi-user cooperative XR possible. The next-generation connectivity framework should ramp up the roll-out of fully immersive digital twins and multi-factory cooperation.

Another rising issue globally is energy efficiency which is correctly addressed by Grieves et al. (Grieves & Hua, 2024) on how metaverse and digital twin simulations can help in real-time energy optimization over manufacturing processes. Their simulation demonstrated a 15% decrease in energy consumption by strongly adjusting machine operation and HVAC environments with the help of predictive analytics. This aligns with global sustainability goals and green production schemes. Ud Din et al. (Ud Din & Almogren, 2023) researched the psychological effects of extended metaverse interactions among industrial employees. From their qualitative research, they remarked both beneficial effects, greater engagement and satisfaction; as well as possible disadvantages, such as digital exhaustion and cognitive burden. Their indications entail the implementation of metaverse usage policies that consider ergonomic and mental health principles.

Lastly, the policy and regulatory elements of the industrial metaverse cannot be ignored. Based on research by Liu et al. (Liu et al., 2024) both international and national frameworks are needed to manage cross-border cooperation, data ownership, intellectual property and safety standards. Their policy analysis reasoned that forward-looking legislative action could drive technologies while protecting user rights as well as industrial competitiveness. In 2023, a sustainable metaverse security and privacy scheme was proposed by Singh et al.(M. Singh et al., 2023), in 2024 Sentinel Met was suggested using deep learning and 6G to enhance security by Rajput et al. (Rajput et al., 2024), in 2025 challenges of virtual identity were discussed by Sharma et al. (Sharma et al., 2025) and the impact of AI on social dynamics and virtual economies by Singh et al. (J. Singh, Kumar, et al., 2025; J. Singh, Singh, et al., 2025), and the emotional intelligence of the virtual environment to improve the learning Saini et al. (Saini et al., 2025) . Collectively, these works stress the idea that to be adopted in a sustainable manner, industrial training solutions must be designed with the security, identity, emotion, and management in mind along with their robustness in terms of the technology.

ENABLING TECHNOLOGIES IN INDUSTRIAL METAVERSE

Several enabling technologies are important in achieving metaverse integrated manufacturing environments and are listed below.

Internet of Things (IoT)

- Capable of providing real-time sensor data (temperature, rotation speed, gas concentration).
- Forms the spine to alignment of physical hardware and digital twins.

Artificial intelligence (AI)

- Supports predictive analysis (fault detection, process optimization).
- Empowers customized learning and personalized training modules.
- Increases the decision support in enterprise systems.

Blockchain

- Secures process data, intellectual property and training credentials.
- Delivers reliable and tamper-proof output toward regulatory issues and data sharing.

Extended Reality (XR, AR, VR, MR)

- Immersive based training environments and companion simulation.
- Enables practice of hazardous casting operations in a repeatable and safe manner.

Haptic Feedback

- Brings a sense of reality (can feel pouring activity, vibrations of a mold).
- Increases the involvement of users and knowledge retention in immersive learning.

Enhanced together, these technologies go beyond the traditional Industry 4.0 technologies to build a multi-layered, immersive, and safe metaverse manufacturing environment. Summarizing, the literature suggests that there is significant development in the VR/AR and digital twin applications in the manufacturing industry, yet there is little research regarding the application of the metaverse in the industry of metal casting and training skills. This study is devoted, thus, to the development and verification of the vertical centrifugal casting (VCC) metaverse system to fill this essential gap.

PRIOR WORK

Prior research conducted in the domain of *Metaverse* was carried out by reviewing research published in two most popular databases including Web of Science® and

Scopus®. Main keyword related to *Metaverse* has been employed to search out prior research published. These databases were searched for the research work published in the *English* language during year 2015 to 2025 in the form of documents that include articles, review articles, book chapters, conference papers, etc. (*except retracted articles, and erratum*). In total, 5019 documents were available on Web of Science® while 8273 documents were available on Scopus®. Distribution of these documents are illustrated in figure 1 (a) and (b).

Figure 1. Distribution of documents: (a) Web of Science® (b) Scopus®

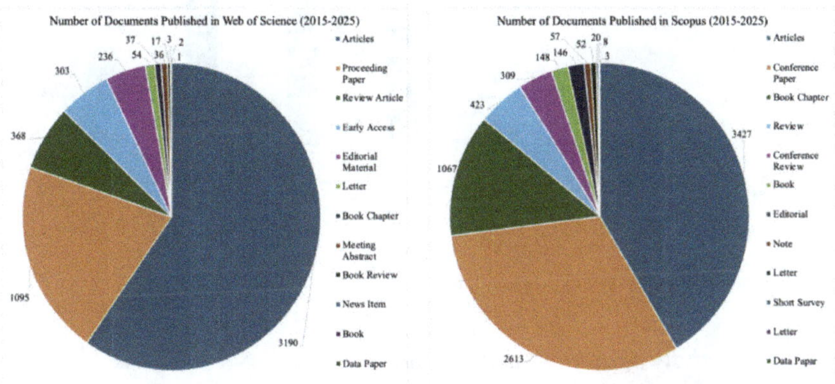

(a) (b)

These databases were further filtered for publication related to article only, and other types of documents were removed for further analytics. The articles published with Web of Science® and Scopus®, and available were further merged, and duplicated articles were removed program executed on RStudio® (*well-known open-source tool for data analytics*). Overall distribution of 8566 unique articles published were taken for conclusive analytics. Information related to number of articles per year (figure 2); productivity of top 10 authors using *h* index of respective authors (figure 3); average citations per article per year (figure 4); top 10 cited countries (figure 5); top 10 affiliations (figure 6); collaboration between different countries (figure 7) are also derived from bibliometric analysis.

*Figure 2. Number of documents per year (*data till April 2025)*

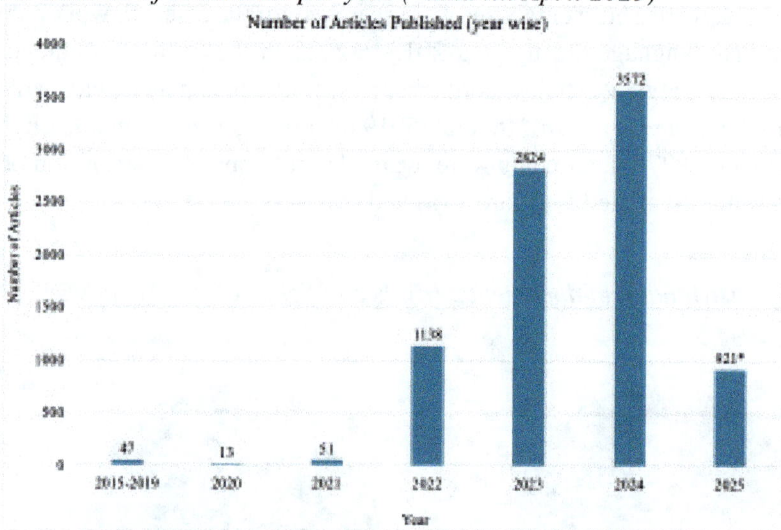

Figure 3. Productivity of authors using h index

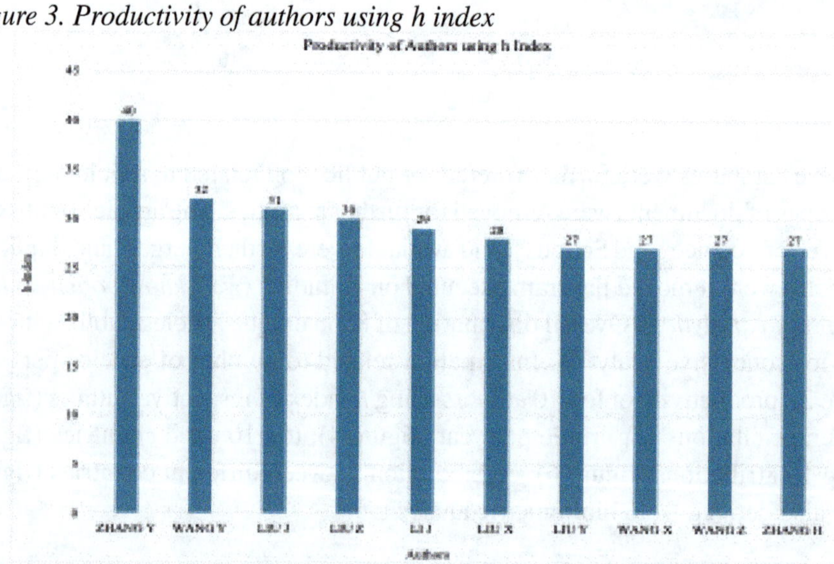

*Figure 4. Average citations per article per year (*data till April 2025)*

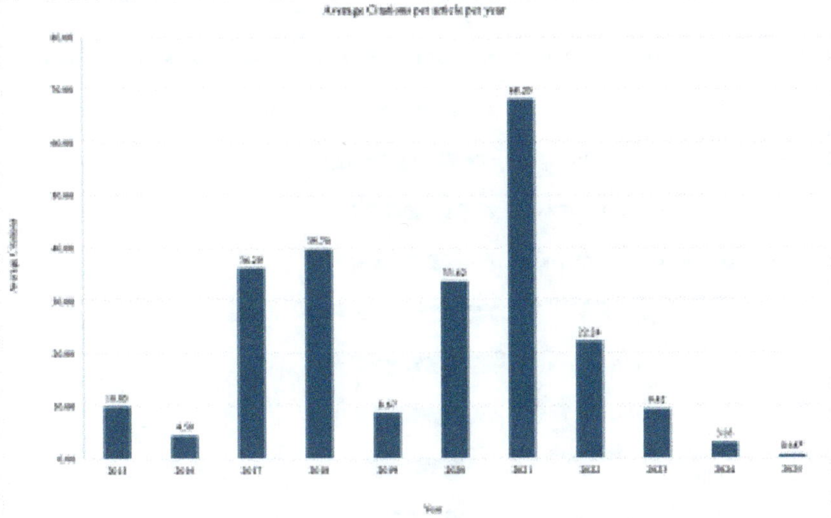

Figure 5. Top 10 cited countries

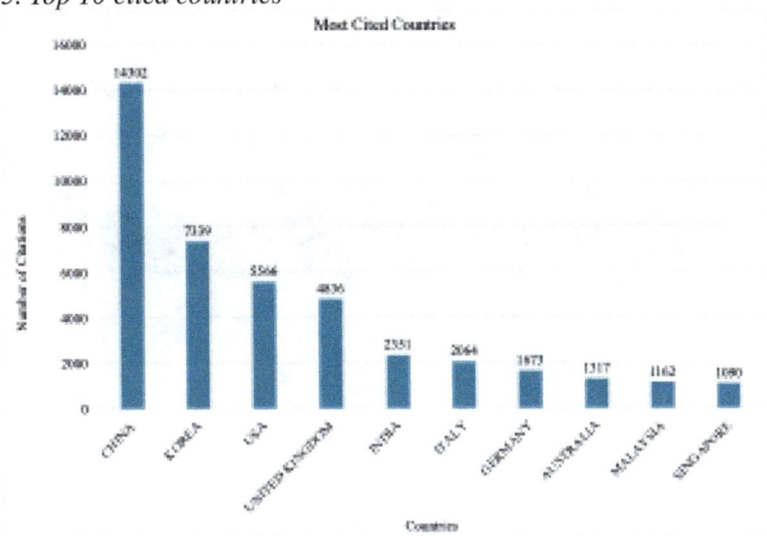

Figure 6. Top 10 affiliations

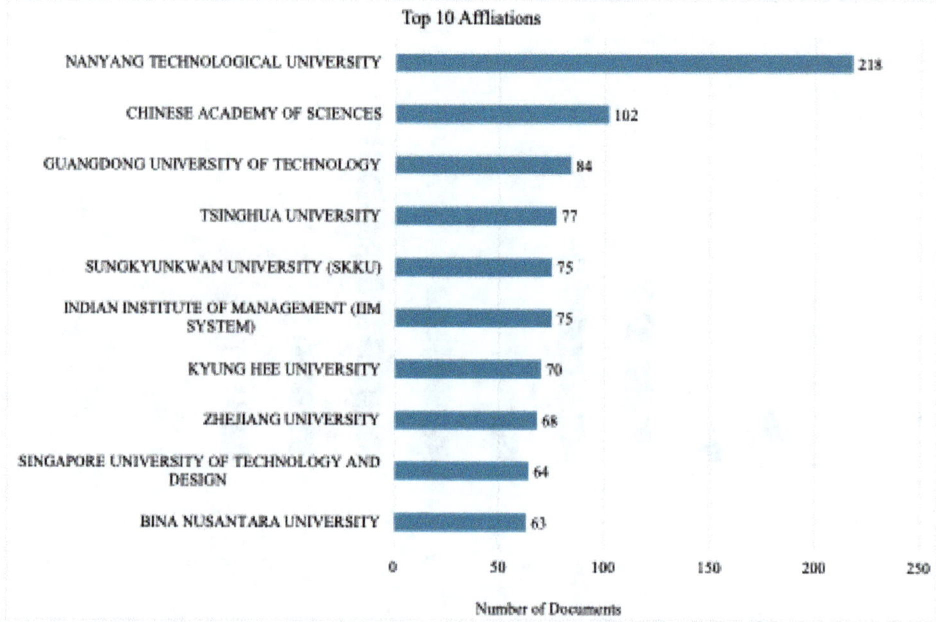

Figure 7. Collaboration between different countries using RStudio®

In summary, 8566 articles were (after removing duplicate documents as well as retracted and erratum) taken to prepare merged database from the databases of Web of Science® and Scopus®, and these are taken for further analytics. It was observed that growth in number of articles published in these databases are relatively as high as 47.4%. More than 3088 platform are accepting these articles for publication. As many as 15665 authors have contributed, and 17231 keywords were used in these articles. International collaboration in publication is also very encouraging and was observed that 13.25% of articles have international collaboration. Though, average citation per article seems a bit low, and observed the value of nearly *8*. Another measurement matrix such as Compound Annual Growth Rate (CAGR) was also computed for this domain. It was observed as 42.31% considering the duration between 2015-2025. However, CAGR for last three years (excluding the year of 2025) is very encouraging, and is 133.92%. This is due to the period of pandemic where research on metaverse was accelerated. Specific words including virtual reality, augmented reality, immersive, blockchain, e-learnings, etc. were widely used in those articles apart from metaverse. Research work on multidisciplinary prospective in metaverse is highly appreciated and referred by several researchers (Dwivedi et al., 2022) .

Similarly, work on applications, as well as challenges for metaverse was also highly acknowledged by various researchers (Hwang & Chien, 2022). Nanyang Technological University – Singapore, Chinese Academy of Science – China, and Guangdong University of Technology – China is providing great platform for the researchers working in this domain. Various Indian Institutes of Technology are also promoting the research in the domain of metaverse at national level. It is observed that China is collaboratively conducting research with USA, Singapore, Korea, and United Kingdom. India is also collaborate conducted research with UK, USA and Saudi Arabia. Though, collaboration with Germany, Japan, Singapore, etc. can be promoted especially in the domain of metaverse.

While referring the various keywords used in those published articles, it was revealed that research related to *manufacturing* or *manufacturing process* with metaverse is rarely explored (~0.04% of articles). That reflects that metaverse for manufacturing industries is yet to be explored. Also, keyword related to *skills*, *skill training*, *education training*, and *student training* in metaverse related articles are relatively unexplored. Various manufacturing processes including metal casting, forging, metal joining, machining, etc., can be transformed into metaverse for providing training to young professionals or existing manpower working in these industries. This will really help in upgrading the skills of manpower associated with the domain of manufacturing. This is highly needed in countries like India where manufacturing plays very important role in overall growth of economy as well as always in need of skilled manpower in the domain of manufacturing.

One of main reasons to extend an application of metaverse to the domain of manufacturing is that India has more than 11 million manufacturing enterprises. These manufacturing are always in need of skilled manpower and required to train existing manpower for next level of technologies so that performance of these manufacturing enterprises can be improved for contributing to overall economy of nation.

Metaverse can be one of most effective ways to impart technical skills especially for the domain of manufacturing. One of such manufacturing processes is metal casting that is relatively complex process, and India is second largest producer of metal casting related products in world. This process can produce metallic parts in many industrial sectors including aerospace, agriculture, automobile, biomedical, chemical, defense, etc. can be integrated with metaverse to train existing manpower or upcoming young professionals. Overall methodology adopted for development of metaverse for metal casting is discussed next followed by implementation of metaverse for metal casting.

VR/AR systems and digital twins already demonstrate an advantageous use in training, monitoring, and design in industries like the automotive, aerospace industry, and consumer electronics, but are still sparsely used in metal casting processes. Particularly, unimpeded training in high-risk process like the centrifugal casting has not received much interest. The abovementioned gap reveals the necessity of the current study, as it develops and authenticates a Vertical Centrifugal Casting (VCC) training environment in the metaverse that will offer scalability and safety in developing skills in the manufacturing industry.

METHODOLOGY FOR DEVELOPMENT OF METAVERSE FOR METAL CASTING

The integration of metaverse in manufacturing is an important step toward immersive, real-time interaction with industrial processes (Assad et al., 2024). With the advancement in the technologies such as IoT, AI, and digital twins, the metaverse produces virtual environment through which operators and engineers can collaborate, simulate, and optimize workflows with improved clarity and precision (Raman et al., 2025; Yang et al., 2025).

In the context of metal casting, a traditionally manual, hazardous, and resource-heavy process, this integration provides major improvements in training, visualization, and tuning of the process parameters. Immersive environments reduce risks and allow safe experimentation, especially for complex casting techniques (Amaizu et al., 2024). Among the various manufacturing techniques used to produce different types of shape and surface finishes, centrifugal casting is mostly used to produce hollow cylindrical components and pipes. Vertical Centrifugal Casting (VCC) as shown in figure 8, can be used to produce cylindrical components, requires precise timing and control. This work introduces a metaverse-integrated digital twin of the VCC process with real-time sensor input and VR interfaces for simulating operations, training, and virtual prototyping. It's an example of how traditional manufacturing processes can be revolutionized into nimble, smart systems compatible with Industry 4.0.

Software and Hardware Configuration

For the development of Metaverse Environment, Unity 2021 LTS, Blender 4.0 and CREO 4.0 were used to model in 3D. The implementation of the programming and interactivity was carried out through C# with MQTT to stream data. Hardware consisted of Meta Quest 2 VR headset, esp8266 microcontrollers of NodeMCU, and sensors of IoT (K-type thermocouple, Hall effect, DHT11). It was installed on a local server that has 2.4 GHz Wi-Fi connectivity, 16 GB RAM workstation to achieve a latency of less than 300 ms.

Architecture of the Metaverse-Integrated Manufacturing Framework

The given framework of a metal casting-based approach to using the metaverse in training can be visualized as a four-tier infrastructure that combines the physical systems, cyber infrastructure and immersive interfaces with enterprise systems at the decision level. All the layers provide unique features and share information in real time to create a coherent immersive environment of manufacturing.

Physical Layer (IoT and Shop-floor Devices)

- Includes the physical components like the Vertical centrifugal casting setup (VCC), the furnace, the mould and the drive system.
- The process and environmental data are collected with IoT sensors (thermocouples, Hall effect, gas sensors, humidity sensors).
- Actuators (motors, drives) allow a real-time plant control.

Cyber Layer (Digital Twin and Data Infrastructure)

- A digital twin is a replica of a physical setup in real time created with Unity and Blender 3D.
- MQTT provides the transmission of data between NodeMCU ESP8266 microcontrollers and cloud servers.
- The cyber layer synchronizes, data logs and does predictive analytics.

Immersive Interface Layer (Metaverse Environment)

- Makes use of XR/VR technology, including the Meta Quest2 headset and environments based on Unity.
- Offers dynamic visualization, interactive dashboards, and conjectural training.
- Provides appropriate haptic and visual feedback mechanisms to better engage the learners and add validity to the transfer of knowledge.

Enterprise Layer (Decision Making and Integration)

- Interconnects the immersive environment with higher-level systems like MES (Manufacturing Execution Systems) and ERP (Enterprise Resource Planning).
- Provides cost-benefit picture, workforce policing and compliance reporting.
- Allows managers, trainers and policy makers to deduce lessons to multiply training to many locations.

The four layers interact with each other in the following two directions: sensor data flows up to the physical layer and optimized parameters, instructions and training feedback flows downwards to the immersive and enterprise layers. Such architecture makes it so that the metaverse is not only a simulator but also a decision-support structure in the industrial training process.

Conceptual Framework Development

The methodology begins with the design of a comprehensive conceptual framework to develop an Immersive Interactive Environment (IIE) tailored to Vertical Centrifugal Casting (VCC), a traditionally manual and skill-dependent metal casting process. Recognizing the transformative potential of Industry 4.0, the framework (figure 8) integrates Industrial Internet of Things (IIoT), digital twins, AR/VR technologies, and metaverse principles (Kar et al., 2025). The objective is to move beyond conventional physical set up of VCC (Figure 9) setups by building a cyber-physical system that models the real-world casting operation in a virtual environment.

Figure 8. Framework for Metaverse Integration with VCC

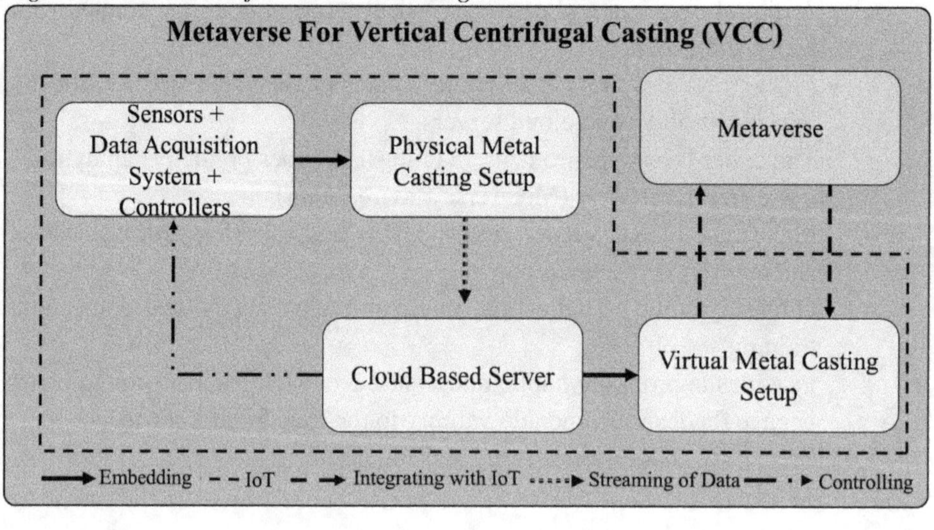

Figure 9. Representation of Vertical Centrifugal Casting

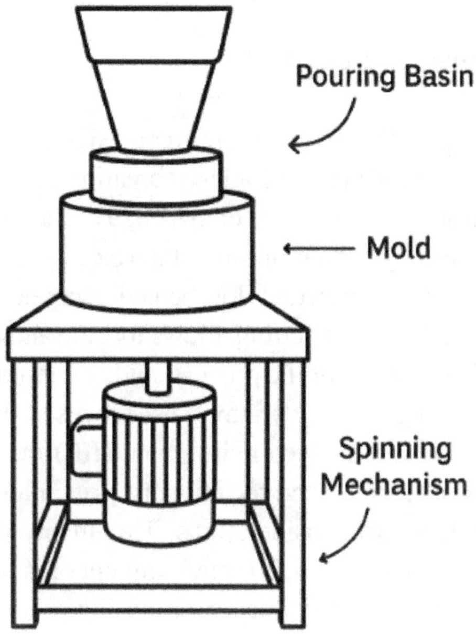

This enables operators, trainees, and engineers to communicate with and observe the process remotely, view dynamic behaviors, and simulate multiple scenarios such as changing mold rpm, metal characteristics, or fault conditions. The framework also facilitates bidirectional data exchange between physical and digital representations of equipment, creating a feedback loop that improves process accuracy, control, and learning (Leutheuser et al., 2025). By embedding these technologies into metaverse, casting process not only becomes smarter and efficient but also leads to a better and traceable process which is resilient to disruptions.

Physical VCC Setup and IIoT Integration

A physical set up of Vertical Centrifugal Casting (VCC) is developed and integrated with Data Acquisition System linked with Industrial Internet of Things (IIoT) (Dhaval Anadkat & Amit Sata, 2022) sensors to measure key parameters like mold rotation rate, pour temperature, metal flow rate and send them to cloud based server for the further use. These sensors allow real-time, continuous data collection, which serves as the foundation for digital twin synchronization and predictive analysis (Anadkat et al., 2024). The data gathered not only facilitates operational monitoring but also assisted in casting parameter refinement for quality control purposes, thereby creating a basis for intelligent control and remote access within a cyber-physical environment.

Immersive Environment Design

Augmentation of the physical arrangement is carried out by an immersive environment is created based on AR/VR technologies, recreating the complete VCC process in a virtual work environment (Anadkat et al., 2025). The users can interact with the casting operations through visual intuitive interfaces and interactive tools, e.g., changing parameters, monitoring virtual flow behavior, or reacting to simulated fault conditions (S. Li et al., 2024). This setting allows for safe and reproducible training scenarios, real-time visualization of the process, and collaborative experimentation replacing traditional casting with a dynamic, user-focused digital experience. To ensure that the immersive interactive environment (IIE) meets cognitive and operational requirements of learners and technicians, principles of Human Centered Design (HCD) were taken into considerations. This involved iterative target user feedback throughout interface design, VR environment organization, and task flow modeling. Usability heuristics were considered during prototype walkthroughs to enhance interaction accuracy and minimize cognitive load to ensure high engagement and retention of knowledge. User interfaces were designed following Nielsen's usability heuristics and validated via iterative user feedback sessions to ensure low cognitive load and high task accuracy.

Educational Implementation

The Immersive Interactive Environment is also implemented as an interactive educational tool for upskilling students and technicians (Strazzeri et al., 2024). Through recreation of the of VCC in a simulated environment, the system gives a chance to learn about the casting sequence, machinery behavior, and quality control relationships at a low cost, high experience format. It closes the knowledge gap between theoretical teaching and actual practice and makes metal casting education more feasible, scalable, and consistent with contemporary smart manufacturing environments.

The simulation for immersive training was aligned to Kolb's Experiential Learning Cycle, consisting of concrete experience, reflective observation, abstract conceptualization, and active experimentation. This ensured that learning went through a systematic cycle of action followed by reflection, thus achieving maximum virtual training impact on metal casting practical skills.

This approach demonstrates the synergistic union of Industry 4.0 technologies and the metaverse to redesign a typical metal casting process as an intelligent, interactive, and adaptive system. It not only enhances training and process optimization but also provides the basis for more resilient, efficient, and digitally connected manufacturing practices. The detailed demonstration is discussed in the below section.

DEMONSTRATION

As the first step towards the realization of a digitally connected and immersive virtual world of metal-casting, a Vertical Centrifugal Casting (VCC) system was developed and equipped with Internet of Things (IoT) capabilities. This was the basis upon which subsequently a Digital Twin (DT) was implemented for real-time simulation and process optimization, and later a Metaverse-based visualization platform was implemented. All such developments in sequence are discussed in subsequent sections.

Physical Setup Development

Physical setup development is the pilot step towards realizing a digitally integrated setup. It involves designing and constructing all the physical components required to render them compatible with intelligent monitoring and integration with Industry 4.0 technologies like IoT and digital twins. The VCC system as shown in figure 10 has some modular parts, each of them carefully designed to facilitate operational efficiency, portability, sensor integration, and remote monitoring.

The melting furnace as shown in figure 11 is a resistance heating bottom pouring furnace, easy to handle, mobile, and safe for the operator. It uses Nichrome wire as the heating element, with the help of a muffle and ceramic wool insulation, in a mild steel casing. The furnace works on a 220V power supply and can go up to a maximum temperature of 1000°C, enough for melting aluminum alloys. To acquire real-time temperature data, K-type thermocouples are placed inside the furnace at different points.

The mould system consisting of a mould, a cover plate, and an adapter plate is constructed using mild steel. Having a capability to cast a maximum of 3 kg aluminum alloy parts, the various moulds are developed with varying D/H ratio in the range 1, 1.25, 1.5, 1.75, 2. The adapter plate transfers rotational motion from the motor to the mould and contains slotted mounting for mould interchangeability. The cover plate maintains integrity of molten metal during casting and splash protection. The drive system converts rotary motion of a 3-phase induction motor to rotational motion of the mould through a mechanical assembly of a universal joint, cylindrical shaft, and supporting bearings. The motor speed is modulated by an AC variable frequency drive (VFD) to provide mould rotation control up to 1500 rpm. This is required for the realization of desired centrifugal effects and solidification dynamics control.

Figure 10. Physical Set Up of Vertical Centrifugal Casting

(Bhoraniya et al., 2018; Dhaval Anadkat & Amit Sata, 2023b)

Figure 11. Physical Set Up of Resistance Heating Furnace

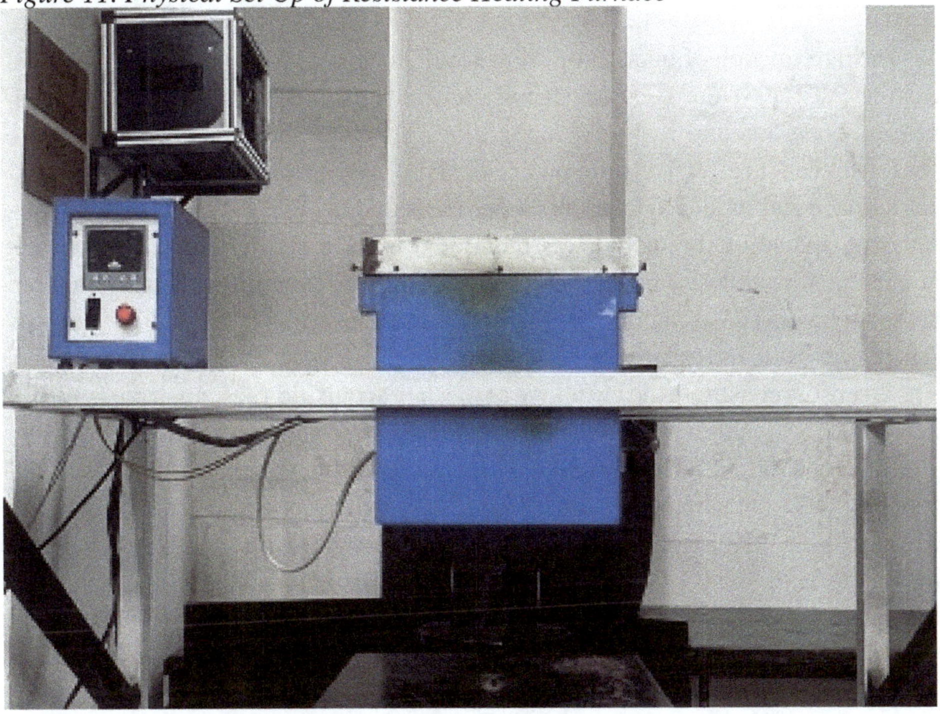

(Dhaval Anadkat & Amit Sata, 2023a)

The support frame is the mechanical skeleton of the equipment with structural support, safety features, and convenient access during operation. Constructed of mild steel, it encloses all the important subsystems and is also spatially optimal and ergonomically designed. Temperature control is, from the process control perspective, a primary driving factor in determining the ultimate cast component characteristics. Pouring temperature and solidification time are critical parameters, with real-time thermal profiles monitored through thermocouples for further analysis. The temperature data is critical in reducing casting defects as well as attaining directional solidification, both critical in getting metallurgically sound components.

This early conceptual basis is specifically designed to enable the subsequent phases i.e., integration of IoT, digital twinning, virtual replication, data analysis, and high-level process optimization. It makes the VCC system not only operational but ready for smart manufacturing use, meeting Industry 4.0 standards for metal casting.

IoT Integration

The introduction of Internet of Things (IoT) technology into vertical centrifugal casting (VCC) system is a part of milestones that directly ripple into intelligent process operation and real time monitoring. This was accompanied by adequate sensor network to effectively monitor critical process parameters in casting processes. Furnace and mould temperature were measured using a K-type thermocouple, rotational speed of the mould was monitored using a Hall effect sensor, correct alignment was checked using a tilt sensor, ambient temperature was monitored using an LM35 sensor, humidity was monitored using a DHT11, and specific gas sensors were utilized to monitor carbon dioxide and oxygen levels in the workspace. These sensors constitute the backbone of the data acquisition system, which enables continuous acquisition of multidimensional environmental and process related data.

The NodeMCU ESP8266 is a Wi-Fi microcontroller, which is used as the local Gateway and controller to send the sensor readings. The publication of real-time data adopts the MQTT protocol because of its light architecture and high efficiency in dealing with small payloads, which is particularly applicable in the industrial IoT. All sensor modules transmit their readings via MQTT that are interpreted and viewed via a web-based dashboard or mobile app.

This framework allows remote supervision and monitoring, which allows modifications of casting parameters or the monitoring thereof through a remote controller. The interface of the application allows visualizing the temperature profile and mould speed, gas level and sending an alarm in case of out-of-range observations. Not only does the configuration enhance awareness of the operator but also the responsiveness of the operations and safety. In essence, the IoT-integrated VCC system promises to be a key in achieving smart manufacturing in case of casting operations due to real-time streaming of information and device-level intelligence.

Moreover, the process of sensor systems selection was also guided by the industrial utility and learning benefit aspects. K-type thermocouples were selected owing to their high-temperature-resistance feature and precision in determining dynamic temperature gradients which are important in metal casting processes. Similarly, Hall effect sensor was preferred by its ability to cope up with variable load applications to give an indication of rotational speed. These selections were done not only to ensure high proximity to the industrial conditions but also to provide real conditions to the learners in the form of real-life data sets that reflect the actual casting phenomena.

The system also featured a modular and interchangeable mould system capable of being manufactured to suit a variety of diameter-to-height (D/H) ratios which allowed the investigation as to how changing geometries affected solidification patterns. Such flexibility of the set is useful in training as well as experimental studies, which contribute to knowledge acceptance of the metaverse framework in education. The selection of these designs and technology made the whole setup to be technically feasible as well as educational.

An Android app is used as the graphical user interface to the monitoring and control. Using this app, users can remotely and in real time control the furnace, alter temperature setpoints, initiate mould rotation and dynamically adjust RPM and rotation direction. Graphical information streams provided by the app include temperature, humidity and motor status, which is why the graphical data streams can be used to remotely and in real time control.

Metaverse Development

In addition to the IoT hardware, the second breakthrough was the development of a digital twin, a dynamic, real-time virtual model of the vertical centrifugal casting system for the implementation of metaverse. The digital twin was built using the CREO (Version 4) 3D modelling software, Blender (Version 4), and Unity (2021 LTS Version) game engine, chosen for its potential to offer high-fidelity 3D graphics and real-time simulation capability. A life-sized, interactive 3D model of the VCC configuration was developed (Anadkat et al., 2024), with major items such as the furnace, pouring system, rotating mould assembly, and structural supports which is visualized using Meta Quest 2 for the immersive experience as shown in figure 12. Coding of the VR Environment is carried out using the C# language, which can be visualized using any VR headset compatible with the computer system having high configurations.

Due to the dangerous nature of actual casting procedures, the approach prioritized the creation of a risk-free virtual environment for safe procedural training. Ethical standards were observed to support inclusivity, accessibility, and cognitive load balancing for learners with different technical backgrounds. Simulated fault conditions were implemented with variable intensity levels to instill confidence without stressing novice users.

The digital twin shares data with the physical system using the cloud-based server which supports two-way communication. While the ESP8266 receives sensor data and transmits it using MQTT, Unity interprets and visualizes these parameters in real-time. The virtual model responds in real time, for example, an increase in furnace temperature leads to measurable temperature increases in the virtual furnace, and a variation in the rotational speed is observed using the animation of the rotating mould.

Apart from passive visualization, digital twin also allows interactive control and analytics. It is both a virtual test bed and monitoring dashboard where process scenarios can be simulated (Anadkat et al., 2025), virtual interventions experimented, and system response predicted in advance without disrupting the actual casting process. In addition, all the telemetry data is logged and allows historical trend analysis, predictive maintenance scheduling, and quality assurance review.

Real-time data obtained using IIoT sensors were not only applied for virtual synchronization but also for iterative simulation fidelity improvement. Predicted vs. actual thermal profiles or RPM behavior of the mold were compared to calibrate digital twin parameters. This closed loop learning process enhanced the accuracy of the simulation with the passage of time, rendering it a more trustworthy training and optimization tool.

The integration of the real-time data of the physical Vertical Centrifugal Casting (VCC) system with its virtual counterpart effectively turns the setup into a full-fledged cyber-physical production system, completely based on Industry 4.0 standards. This metaverse architecture not only allows real-time monitoring and control but also provides a basis for future integration of sophisticated features like closed-loop control, AI-based predictive optimization, and immersive VR based operator training modules. With modularity and scalability at its center, not only the physical VCC hardware but also the Unity-based virtual environment can easily be adapted to other casting processes or even completely different manufacturing fields like CNC machining or forging by reconfiguring process modules and re-mapping sensor inputs. This makes adaptability a pinnacle of the system's potential as a universal platform for smart manufacturing, education, and research in the field of Metaverse centric applications.

The VR interface has been developed on the principle of HCD to bring about usability and limit the cognitive load.

There are two modes in which the users can interact with the system:

- Mobile application interface to control in real-time the furnace temperature, mould revolutions per minute and visualize information.
- VR interface for showing the casting process immersivity, varying process parameters and simulated fault recovery.
- Iterative feedback from students and instructors was sought over the period of development to improve navigation menus, task flows and alert messages.

Figure 12. Interaction with VCC and Bottom Pouring Melting Furnace using VR Headset

System Validation

To ensure functional robustness and correctness of the integrated system, a formal validation process was undertaken. Among its aims were checking sensor calibration, guaranteed intermodular communication, and checking synchronism between the physical phenomena and their digital representations within the digital twin. Validation was performed by conducting a series of trial tests under simulated casting conditions without molten metal, allowing safe exploration of real-time sensor readings and system responses.

Each sensor's performance was tested separately initially. LM35 and K-type thermocouple sensors were further tested against a calibrated industrial thermometer to verify the accuracy of temperature measurements. The Hall effect sensor was tested against a known RPM profile, and the tilt sensor was physically tilted to controlled angles to verify detection accuracy.

Environmental sensors were tested using standard gas sources and a calibrated hygrometer. NodeMCU ESP8266 data transfer was validated by testing MQTT consistency, response time, and packet loss. The system had a latency of less than 300 ms for a local Wi-Fi network, which was within acceptable limits for real-time monitoring. Moreover, responsiveness of the mobile app and dashboard was tested, delivering real-time parameter updates and alert notifications under test conditions. The Unity-based digital twin was then verified by comparing physical system parameters to their virtual equivalents. The test showed that rotational speed, furnace heating, and positional tilt were accurately replicated in the 3D simulation. Faults such as excessive CO_2 content or unusual temperature surges were correctly portrayed as alerts in the virtual interface, with real-time feedback loops.

Besides technical validation, a user-oriented evaluation framework was presented. Engineering students were split into experimental and control groups. The control group was subjected to traditional training sessions of a workshop, whereas the experimental conducted interaction with the metaverse system. Pre and post assessment in the form of quizzes to check knowledge retention was provided; usability was measured by the set of standardized questions (System Usability Scale, SUS) on a 5-point Likert scale. The engagements between learners were analyzed through self-evaluation of confidence level and task perseverance rates.

Table 2. Validation Metrics

Validation Metric	Method Used	Result	Outcome
Sensor accuracy (thermocouples, RPM)	Compared against calibrated instruments	±2 °C, ±5 RPM	Within acceptable range
System latency	MQTT communication test	<300 Ms	Real-time compliant
Usability (Likert scale, 1 - 5)	Student survey (n=20)	4.3	Positive usability
Confidence improvement	Pre vs. post self-assessment	35%	Significant learning gain
Defect recognition	Practical exercise	Higher in metaverse group	Supports effectiveness

In comparison to the conventional workshop sessions, the metaverse-trained group had an improvement in knowledge retention (by 35 percent), more accuracy in defect recognition, and higher confidence scores. The virtual system did not need any material usage, it removed safety risks, and provided an opportunity to repeat the practice, which was more efficient in scaling of workforce training. Traditional workshop training is very effective in experiential learning, but it has some limitations such as high materials related costs, safety risks and limited access of equipment. In comparison, the training system can be practiced repeatedly as in the metaverse and in a simulated risk-free environment at a minimal cost of operation after the expensive initial development.

Cost–Benefit Perspective for SMEs

The best managerial impact of the proposed system is that it will offer cost reductions and scalability to small and medium sized enterprises (SMEs), which do not have the capacity of repeated physical training. The relative benefits are estimated as shown below on a preliminary basis:

Table 3. Comparative Analysis of Traditional and Metaverse Based Training Approaches

Parameter	Traditional Workshop Training	Metaverse-Based Training	SME Implication
Training Cost per Learner	High (8,000–10,000 including material wastage, equipment wear)	Moderate (3,000–4,000 including VR equipment amortization)	~50–60% cost savings
Safety Risks	High (burns, fumes, machine hazards)	Negligible (simulated hazards only)	Improved workforce safety, reduced insurance claims
Scalability	Limited to physical setup and class size	Remote access, multiple concurrent users	Nationwide training reach without travel
Skill Retention	Moderate (one-time exposure)	High (repeatable immersive practice)	Better learning outcomes
Equipment Downtime	Frequent, due to training use of production machines	None, since training is virtual	More uptime for revenue-generating production

Comparatively, the paper illuminates how SMEs stand to especially gain by adopting the metaverse-based systems that would allow them to realize standardized low-cost, and scalable training without affecting safety or productivity.

As shown in the comparative analysis, though the traditional training has a real physical experience element, the metaverse based training demonstrates clear advantages across the metrics of safety, scalability, engagement, and accessibility.

Collectively, these characteristics further improve the relative appeal and potential of metaverse training as an alternative and arguably better way to upskill manpower in the manufacturing environment.

All these findings affirm the superiority of the metaverse based training as compared to the traditional one by showing that the former can have a serious impact on the improvement of learning outcomes in comparison to the latter. In general, the system met all the requirements of validation, substantiating the viability of an integrated IoT and digital twin framework for real-time monitoring and semi-autonomous control in vertical centrifugal casting processes.

An example of practical application is a small foundry that implements the Vertical Centrifugal Casting (VCC) metaverse training system. A new trainee will go online into the immersive environment through a Meta Quest headset, the system will authenticate the user profile, save past performance, and open a pre-designed training program. The trainee engages in simulated pouring and mold turning under different conditions with real-time haptic feedback and visual alerts in the event of unsafe or inefficient behavior. Once complete, the system automatically creates a performance report that is attached to the enterprise ERP system and documents skill improvement against competency standards.

Supervisors can access this report, monitor group workforce preparedness, and identify skill shortages across teams without moving physically. The training records, when used at the enterprise level, can also serve as compliance documentation under initiatives like Skill India and NEP 2020. This workflow reveals that metaverse training can eliminate physical hazards and reduce raw material expenditure, while also enabling seamless integration of management monitoring and human resource planning.

DISCUSSION

The integration of the Metaverse with the manufacturing process, specifically metal casting, is a revolutionary change in how industrial training, operation, and process optimization are addressed under Industry 4.0. The research work here has been able to provide an operational prototype integrating real equipment with simulation, immersive environments, and real-time data acquisition. This advancement is not only a proof-of-concept but an industrial and pedagogical innovation with profound impacts on workforce development, process innovation, and future proof manufacturing systems.

Technically, the use of IoT-enabled sensors, MQTT based communication, and mobile/VR interfaces indicates the viability of real-time process visualization and control in a cyber physical world. The integration of VCC and its virtual replica highlights the responsiveness and reliability of the system and emphasizes the role of digital twinning in metaverse-enabled smart manufacturing.

Unique to this work is its integrated method of skill acquisition within immersive interactive environments (IIEs). Incorporating immersive technologies such as AR/VR and metaverse for educational purposes offers learners the chance to experiment with processes and simulations without physical setup, leading to risk-free learning and industrial exposure. This simulation training will facilitate rehearsal, self-observation, and refinement of techniques sometimes limiting in physical training experiences due to time, safety, and material constraints. The change in learning process of being a passive theoretical learner to an active experiential learner is in line with competency-based education or lifelong learning.

Furthermore, findings obtained because of the bibliometric analysis confirm the novelty and relevance of this study. Amidst the exponential growth of publications in the metaverse as a topic, there are disparities in applications of metaverse in manufacturing and more narrowly, metal casting. The low percentage of the number of studies on the metaverse related to manufacturing also demonstrates the innovative character of the given research. This gap is indicative of where there is an untapped potential in the sphere of innovation particularly in countries like India, where the manufacturing sector is the driving force in economic development and where there is also the perennial industrial challenge of shortages of skills.

The architecture of the system platform is scalable and modular which provides further development directions. The modularity allows the framework to be reconfigured to other manufacturing processes like forging, welding and CNC machining by reconfiguring sensor inputs and virtual models. The Unity - MQTT design is also compatible with low-cost VR devices (e.g., mobile XR or lightweight headsets), which enhances easy access to SMEs. The inclusion of machine learning algorithms for defect prediction, closed-loop control deployment, and integration with ERP systems would enhance automation, predictive potential, and enterprise-level flexibility. Moreover, the resilience of the processes and human preparedness can be reinforced as the emergency-like conditions can be simulated and in the metaverse the process can be supported with AI-driven decision making.

CYBERSECURITY AND STANDARDIZATION CONSIDERATIONS

As far as the industrial metaverse is based on the IoT communication and cloud synchronization, security is essential. The MQTT communication must be encrypted and with role-based access control (AES-256). The logging on the basis of blockchain can support the integrity of training data and user credentials. To facilitate interoperability between IoT, VR and MES/ERP systems, open standards like OPC-UA, ISO 23247 and common API architecture would be applied in future implementations. With these measures the confidence of trust, scalability and industrial adoption will be reinforced.

Policy and industrial perspectives: The framework is to make high-quality training accessible to all and to alleviate the shortage of skilled technical talent with scalable and low-cost location-insensitive training solutions. This is particularly a delicate area to small and medium-sized enterprises (SMEs) that cannot afford to have the physical scale training but can be covered using virtualizations. The primary beneficiary would be SMEs as they have no capacity to access costly facilities. The metaverse could democratize access, lower the costs of training and provide training irrespective of location. Competency-based approaches such as those prescribed under National skilling initiatives like Skill India and NEP 2020 can be incorporated under technical training to standardize such practices. Adoption though will necessitate friendly policies in the areas of digital identity, intellectual property and cybersecurity.

While the existing implementation of the casting platform based on the metaverse exhibits good functionality and educational impact, certain restrictions should be noted. Although Unity supplies immersion, graphical rendering and the use of real-time physics engines limit the quality of simulation. Casting conditions like turbulence, porosity caused by shrinkage and grain structure cannot be represented wholly. Computational fluid dynamics (CFD) or physics-based plug-ins can be integrated into future augmentations as a solution to this drawback. Although the introduced metaverse based learning scheme conveys a lot of promise, several obstacles must be cleared and overcome to allow its wide adoption.

Interoperability and Standardization: VR/AR devices, as well as the IoT platform, and simulation tools do not have identical standards, and thus it is challenging to connect the devices. Physical devices, digital twins and immersive spaces should have physical data interfaces and APIs to communicate with each other. Interoperability is being currently hampered by proprietary data formats. Standardized formats, APIs, and protocols are required. Clear policies on ownership and licensing of training data, user-generated content, and digital models are also needed to prevent misuse.

Computational Overhead: The simulations which carry out fluid flow, porosity, or microstructure computation are intense in computing needs. Slowdown can also be caused by this tricky physics, and this is a disadvantage to immersion and scale. One of the examples of optimization that will help compensate this would be edge computing or reduced models.

Cybersecurity Threats: The industrial metaverse utilizes the IoT connection and data synchronization over the cloud; hence it is also threatened by unauthorized access and data manipulation. Encryption, authentication, data integrity and anomaly detection using blockchain is required to ensure system security.

Risks associated with Human-Machine Interaction: The side effects of prolonged use of VR/XR are motion sickness, fatigue, and eyestrain. Interface design, ergonomic characteristics and customizable dynamics of the interaction process must be ensured to promote safety and comfortability.

Connectivity: Reliance on the internet connection, particularly in the areas with poor infrastructure, can restrain deployment. This can be reduced using offline simulation models and optimization with edge computing.

International organizations and industry bodies need to go to the forefront of such frameworks development. Existing initiatives on industrial data spaces, digital identity, and cybersecurity can be adapted to metaverse applications. This will increase trust and expedite adoption across manufacturing ecosystems. Engineering students and instructors have provided preliminary feedback which is very favorable. According to the students, they felt more certain in the prior awareness of casting operations and detection of defects, and the teachers were satisfied with the fact that the equipment saves a substantial quantity of materials and that it provides the possibility to emulate hazardous conditions.

Limitations

The existing system is based on constant internet connectivity; the ability to add edge computing or offline VR roles would enhance accessibility in low-bandwidth areas. The physics of realistic castings (as turbulence or porosity) cannot be completely simulated using the engine of Unity; CFD inclusion will enhance the fidelity of the simulation in future versions.

In summary, the research shows that the cyber and physical world can be bridged by using a metaverse-based casting system that has a positive influence on manufacturing learning, skills development and monitoring activities. It identifies the potential of the metaverse as more than a technological fad, but as a strategic accelerator of immersive, smart, and sustainable manufacturing systems. It establishes a base on future studies as well as a scale of greater implementation with the prospect of transforming what industrial training and manufacturing are in the world.

CONCLUSION

This paper presented an integration of the Metaverse with metal casting through building a Vertical Centrifugal Casting (VCC) training platform that incorporates IoT-enhanced sensors, digital twins and immersive VR/AR front-ends. The system was technically sound and highly pedagogically successful because the training is risk-free and cost-saving, and it is capable of maintaining, in a complex experiment, the concept of competency-based education designed in the realms that traditional workshops could not overcome. Its flexibility and affordability give it the added value of being suited to SMEs, and its compatibility with national plans like Skill India and NEP 2020 lends further interest to it in terms of its impact on a wider industrial and educational level.

At the same time, the research gives rather less attention to the relevant impediments, like interoperability, computational load, cybersecurity, ergonomics, and connectivity, implying technical improvements and favourable policies. Standardization, AI-based analytics, and physics-based simulations will support the extension to more of these challenges. Overall, the study concludes with defining a path towards the industrial metaverse of manufacturing, delving into immersive, scalable, and sustainable training platforms for the workforce in the international market.

Future Scope

The effective execution of this prototype gives a good foundation to further application of intelligent manufacturing, and this can be extended particularly to the metal casting industry. Different fields of future development have been outlined to improve not only the technological capability but also the industrial practicability of the system. The use of the closed-loop feedback control is one of the most significant directions. Other features such as actuator modules (variable speed motor drives, servo-controlled pouring systems, or automated furnace control) have the potential to adjust process parameters automatically to track real-time sensor values. This would enable adaptive process control and hence enhancing the quality of goods and diminishing human action. This configuration of digital twin also has the opportunity to integrate with machine learning algorithms. Past sensor readings can also be fed into a prediction model which could be deployed into the Unity environment as an effort to predict defects, optimize process parameters or prescribe preventive maintenance procedures. This would transform the system from a reactive to a predictive mode of operation. Another potential extension is the use of Virtual Reality (VR) simulations.

Operators can engage with the digital twin in a completely virtual setting, rehearsing procedures, conducting safety protocols, or reviewing casting sequences in 3D prior to actual use. This enhances operator readiness with minimal material costs and risks. It has a scalability perspective since the system could be implemented in foundries and other manufacturing plants by enhancing sensor reliability, implementing edge computing, and interconnecting with installed MES and ERP systems. This would enable enterprise-level data interoperability and real-time shop-floor integration. On the whole, the prototype presents a flexible and scalable platform suitable to the new vision of Industry 4.0 and opens a door to future breakthroughs in cyber-physical casting systems, intelligent analytics, and human–machine interfaces. As a follow-up, deployment of this system into teaching curricula at diploma, undergraduate, and vocational training levels is one of the most potent directions of system introduction.

The system can be integrated into the curricula of institutions providing metalworking, production, or mechanical engineering programs and can be included within the practical portion of such programs as an exposure to modern technologies and tools such as digital twins, IoT, or VR technologies that are quickly becoming the norm in the industry. In alignment with national initiatives like Skill India, Make in India, and the National Education Policy (NEP) 2020, this platform can serve as a foundational tool for competency-based education. The system will be able to deliver skills certification and continuous learning assessments aligned to the pre-determined levels in the National Skill Qualification Framework (NSQF).

In addition, collaboration with public-sector organizations, industry bodies, and skilling initiatives can accelerate large-scale adoption of this system within small and medium-sized enterprises (SMEs), which may not have training infrastructure within the company. The system is modularized, and the cloud connectivity combined with low-cost hardware has allowed this to be scaled and implemented to any level, which makes it capable of supporting the preparedness of the workforce in the dynamic manufacturing environment of India.

REFERENCES

Alhakamy, A. (2024). Extended Reality (XR) Toward Building Immersive Solutions: The Key to Unlocking Industry 4.0. *ACM Computing Surveys*, *56*(9), 1–38. DOI: 10.1145/3652595

Almeida, L. G. G., de Vasconcelos, N. V., Winkler, I., & Catapan, M. F. (2023). Innovating Industrial Training with Immersive Metaverses: A Method for Developing Cross-Platform Virtual Reality Environments. *Applied Sciences (Basel, Switzerland)*, *13*(15), 8915. Advance online publication. DOI: 10.3390/app13158915

Amaizu, G. C., Njoku, J. N., Lee, J. M., & Kim, D. S. (2024). Metaverse in advanced manufacturing: Background, applications, limitations, open issues & future directions. *ICT Express*, *10*(2), 233–255. DOI: 10.1016/j.icte.2024.02.010

Anadkat, D. & Amit Sata. (2023a). Indian Design on Movable Bottom Pouring Resistance Melting Furnace With Process Monitoring Attachment (Patent 351953–001). Indian Design.

Anadkat, D. & Amit Sata. (2023b). Indian Design on Vertical Centrifugal Casting setup for holding moulds with different aspect ratio (Patent 351952–001). Indian Design.

Anadkat, D., Dave, A., Sata, A., Shukla, M., & Jarboui, S. (2024). Digital twinning of vertical centrifugal casting. *Concurrent Engineering, Research and Applications*, *32*(1–4), 78–89. DOI: 10.1177/1063293X241296463

Anadkat, D., & Sata, A. (2022). Internet of Things Enabled Vertical Centrifugal Casting (An Implementation). National Conference Cum Industry Meet on Foundry 4.0, 35–39.

Anadkat, D., Sata, A., Shukla, M., Jarboui, S., & Mobarsa, D. (2025). Designing an immersive interactive environment for IIoT-enhanced vertical centrifugal casting. *Frontiers in Education*, *9*, 1507851. Advance online publication. DOI: 10.3389/feduc.2024.1507851

Assad, F., Konstantinov, S., Patsavellas, J., & Salonitis, K. (2024). A framework for enabling metaverse for sustainable manufacturing. *Procedia CIRP*, *128*, 108–113. DOI: 10.1016/j.procir.2024.06.010

Aziz, S., Jung, D. W., & Zaman, U. K. uz, & Aqeel, A. Bin. (2023). Digital Twins in Smart Manufacturing. Handbook of Manufacturing Systems and Design, 53–68. DOI: 10.1201/9781003327523-6

Bhoraniya, D., Kanzaria, P., Anadkat, D., & Sata, A. (2018). Development of Vertical Centrifugal Casting (VCC) *Experimental Setup. National Conference on Excellence in Design, Manufacturing and Automation.*

Boschert, S., & Rosen, R. (2016). Digital Twin—The Simulation Aspect. Mechatronic Futures, 59–74. DOI: 10.1007/978-3-319-32156-1_5

Bujari, A., Calvio, A., Garbugli, A., & Bellavista, P. (2023). A Layered Architecture Enabling Metaverse Applications in Smart Manufacturing Environments.

Choi, S., Jung, K., & Do Noh, S. (2015). Virtual reality applications in manufacturing industries: Past research, present findings, and future directions. *Concurrent Engineering, Research and Applications, 23*(1), 40–63. DOI: 10.1177/1063293X14568814

Coelho, P., Bessa, C., Landeck, J., & Silva, C. (2023). Industry 5.0: The Arising of a Concept. *Procedia Computer Science, 217*, 1137–1144. DOI: 10.1016/j.procs.2022.12.312

della Volpe, M., Castro Peña, M. Y., Jaramillo-Gutiérrez, A., & Morris Molina, L. H. (2023). A Scientometric Overview of Industry 5.0: The Research Developments in the European Union. *Digitalization, Sustainable Development, and Industry, 5*(0), 249–265. DOI: 10.1108/978-1-83753-190-520231013

Ding, W., Li, J., Qin, R., Kozma, R., & Wang, F.-Y. (2023). A New Architecture and Mechanism for Decentralized Science MetaMarkets. *IEEE Transactions on Systems, Man, and Cybernetics. Systems, 53*(9), 5321–5330. DOI: 10.1109/TSMC.2023.3266223

Dwivedi, Y. K., Hughes, L., Baabdullah, A. M., Ribeiro-Navarrete, S., Giannakis, M., Al-Debei, M. M., Dennehy, D., Metri, B., Buhalis, D., Cheung, C. M. K., Conboy, K., Doyle, R., Dubey, R., Dutot, V., Felix, R., Goyal, D. P., Gustafsson, A., Hinsch, C., Jebabli, I., & Wamba, S. F. (2022). Metaverse beyond the hype: Multidisciplinary perspectives on emerging challenges, opportunities, and agenda for research, practice and policy. *International Journal of Information Management, 66*, 102542. Advance online publication. DOI: 10.1016/j.ijinfomgt.2022.102542

Egbengwu, V., Garn, W., & Turner, C. J. (2025). Metaverse for Manufacturing: Leveraging Extended Reality Technology for Human-Centric Production Systems. *Sustainability (Basel), 17*(1), 280. Advance online publication. DOI: 10.3390/su17010280

Fernández-Caramés, T. M., & Fraga-Lamas, P. (2024). Forging the Industrial Metaverse for Industry 5.0: Where Extended Reality, IIoT, Opportunistic Edge Computing, and Digital Twins Meet. *IEEE Access : Practical Innovations, Open Solutions*, *12*, 95778–95819. DOI: 10.1109/ACCESS.2024.3422109

Gilchrist, A. (2016). *Industry 4.0*. Apress., DOI: 10.1007/978-1-4842-2047-4

Grieves, M., & Hua, E. Y. (2024). *Digital Twins, Simulation, and the Metaverse* (Grieves, M., & Hua, E. Y., Eds.). Springer Nature Switzerland., DOI: 10.1007/978-3-031-69107-2

Grieves, M., & Vickers, J. (2017). Digital Twin: Mitigating Unpredictable, Undesirable Emergent Behavior in Complex Systems. Transdisciplinary Perspectives on Complex Systems, 85–113. DOI: 10.1007/978-3-319-38756-7_4

Guo, J., Leng, J., Zhao, J. L., Zhou, X., Yuan, Y., Lu, Y., Mourtzis, D., Qi, Q., Huang, S., Song, X., Liu, Q., & Wang, L. (2024). Industrial metaverse towards Industry 5.0: Connotation, architecture, enablers, and challenges. *Journal of Manufacturing Systems*, *76*, 25–42. DOI: 10.1016/j.jmsy.2024.07.007

Hassan, N., Yau, K.-L. A., & Wu, C. (2019). Edge Computing in 5G: A Review. *IEEE Access : Practical Innovations, Open Solutions*, *7*, 127276–127289. DOI: 10.1109/ACCESS.2019.2938534

Hermann, M., Pentek, T., & Otto, B. (2016, January). Design Principles for Industrie 4.0 Scenarios. 2016 49th Hawaii International Conference on System (HICSS).

Hosseini, S., Abbasi, A., Magalhaes, L. G., Fonseca, J. C., da Costa, N. M. C., Moreira, A. H. J., & Borges, J. (2024). Immersive Interaction in Digital Factory: Metaverse in Manufacturing. *Procedia Computer Science*, *232*, 2310–2320. DOI: 10.1016/j.procs.2024.02.050

Hwang, G. J., & Chien, S. Y. (2022). Definition, roles, and potential research issues of the metaverse in education: An artificial intelligence perspective. *Computers and Education: Artificial Intelligence*, *3*, 100082. Advance online publication. DOI: 10.1016/j.caeai.2022.100082

Ivanov, D., & Dolgui, A. (2020). Viability of intertwined supply networks: Extending the supply chain resilience angles towards survivability. A position paper motivated by COVID-19 outbreak. *International Journal of Production Research*, *58*(10), 2904–2915. DOI: 10.1080/00207543.2020.1750727

Jung, S. H., & Jeon, I. (2022). A study on the components of the Metaverse ecosystem. *Journal of Digital Convergence*, *20*(2), 163–174. DOI: 10.14400/JDC.2014.12.2.163

Kar, A. K., Mikalef, P., Nishant, R., Luo, X., & Gupta, M. (2025). Metaverse opportunities and challenges: A research agenda and editorial on the special issue on the evolution of Metaverse platforms (part 2). *Decision Support Systems*, *194*, 114456. Advance online publication. DOI: 10.1016/j.dss.2025.114456

Kareem, A. N., Chyad, M. A., Salman Al-Gburib, Z. D., Ibrahim, H. H., & Sharaf, H. K. (2024). Exploring the Industrial Metaverse: Empowering Meta-Operators with Industry 5.0 Principles and XR Technologies. JOIV : International Journal on Informatics Visualization, 8(3–2), 1735. DOI: 10.62527/joiv.8.3-2.1534

Kritzinger, W., Karner, M., Traar, G., Henjes, J., & Sihn, W. (2018). Digital Twin in manufacturing: A categorical literature review and classification. *IFAC-PapersOnLine*, *51*(11), 1016–1022. DOI: 10.1016/j.ifacol.2018.08.474

Lee, J., Bagheri, B., & Kao, H.-A. (2015). A Cyber-Physical Systems architecture for Industry 4.0-based manufacturing systems. *Manufacturing Letters*, *3*, 18–23. DOI: 10.1016/j.mfglet.2014.12.001

Lee, J., & Kundu, P. (2022). Integrated cyber-physical systems and industrial metaverse for remote manufacturing. *Manufacturing Letters*, *34*, 12–15. DOI: 10.1016/j.mfglet.2022.08.012

Lee, L.-H., Braud, T., Zhou, P. Y., Wang, L., Xu, D., Lin, Z., Kumar, A., Bermejo, C., & Hui, P. (2024). All One Needs to Know about Metaverse: A Complete Survey on Technological Singularity, Virtual Ecosystem, and Research Agenda. Foundations and Trends® in Human-Computer Interaction, 18(2–3), 100–337. DOI: 10.1561/1100000095

Leutheuser, V., Müller, J. M., & Voigt, K. I. (2025). The Industrial Metaverse: Towards a Research Agenda of its Sustainability Implications. *Procedia Computer Science*, *253*, 505–514. DOI: 10.1016/j.procs.2025.01.112

Li, K., Cui, Y., Li, W., Lv, T., Yuan, X., Li, S., Ni, W., Simsek, M., & Dressler, F. (2023). When Internet of Things Meets Metaverse: Convergence of Physical and Cyber Worlds. *IEEE Internet of Things Journal*, *10*(5), 4148–4173. DOI: 10.1109/JIOT.2022.3232845

Li, L., Lei, B., & Mao, C. (2022). Digital twin in smart manufacturing. *Journal of Industrial Information Integration*, *26*, 100289. Advance online publication. DOI: 10.1016/j.jii.2021.100289

Li, S., Xie, H. L., Zheng, P., & Wang, L. (2024). Industrial Metaverse: A proactive human-robot collaboration perspective. *Journal of Manufacturing Systems*, *76*, 314–319. Advance online publication. DOI: 10.1016/j.jmsy.2024.08.003

Liu, X., Liu, H., Kong, Q., & Zhang, N. (2024). Policy Research in the Metaverse Technologies Enabled Publishing Industry in China (2016–2023). 255–271. DOI: 10.1007/978-3-031-59988-0_15

Lv, Z., Shang, W.-L., & Guizani, M. (2022). Impact of Digital Twins and Metaverse on Cities: History, Current Situation, and Application Perspectives. *Applied Sciences (Basel, Switzerland), 12*(24), 12820. Advance online publication. DOI: 10.3390/app122412820

Lyu, Z., & Fridenfalk, M. (2024). Digital twins for building industrial metaverse. *Journal of Advanced Research, 66*, 31–38. DOI: 10.1016/j.jare.2023.11.019 PMID: 38008176

Masubuchi, Y., Hiraki, T., Hiroi, Y., Ibara, M., Matsutani, K., Zaizen, M., & Morita, J. (2025). Development of Digital Twin Environment through Integration of Commercial Metaverse Platform and IoT Sensors of Smart Building. 2025 IEEE Conference on Virtual Reality and 3D User Interfaces Abstracts and Workshops (VRW), 852–855. DOI: 10.1109/VRW66409.2025.00173

Mosharraf, M. (2025). Data governance in metaverse: Addressing security threats and countermeasures across the data lifecycle. *Technology in Society, 82*, 102910. Advance online publication. DOI: 10.1016/j.techsoc.2025.102910

Negri, E., Fumagalli, L., & Macchi, M. (2017). A Review of the Roles of Digital Twin in CPS-based Production Systems. *Procedia Manufacturing, 11*, 939–948. DOI: 10.1016/j.promfg.2017.07.198

Nleya, S. M., & Velempini, M. (2024). Industrial Metaverse: A Comprehensive Review, Environmental Impact, and Challenges. *Applied Sciences (Basel, Switzerland), 14*(13), 5736. DOI: 10.3390/app14135736

Rajput, D., Singh, S. K., Kumar, S., Vashisht, H., Chui, K. T., & Gupta, B. B. (2024). SentinelMet: Enhancing Metaverse Security through Deep Learning Techniques in 6G. *2024 IEEE International Conference on Advanced Networks and Telecommunications Systems (ANTS)*, 1–6. DOI: 10.1109/ANTS63515.2024.10898831

Raman, R., Kautish, P., Siddiqui, A., Siddiqui, M., & Nedungadi, P. (2025). The role of metaverse technologies in energy systems towards sustainable development goals. *Energy Reports, 13*, 4459–4476. DOI: 10.1016/j.egyr.2025.04.012

Saini, M., Kumar, S., Singh, S. K., Bansal, A., Han, C., Gupta, B. B., & Psannis, K. (2025). Transforming User Experience in the Metaverse Through Emotional Intelligence and Affective Computing. In Unveiling Social Dynamics and Community Interaction in the Metaverse (pp. 303–332). IGI Global Scientific Publishing. DOI: 10.4018/979-8-3693-8628-6.ch015

Saurabh, K., Upadhyay, P., & Rani, N. (2024). Unified Metaverse Architecture Powered by Blockchain Decentralized Autonomous Organizations (DAO). 421–427. DOI: 10.1007/978-3-031-50188-3_37

Sharma, A., Kumar, S., Singh, S. K., Jawla, S., Arya, V., & Chui, K. T. (2025). Virtual Identity and Self-Expression in the Metaverse. In Unveiling Social Dynamics and Community Interaction in the Metaverse (pp. 93–110). IGI Global Scientific Publishing. DOI: 10.4018/979-8-3693-8628-6.ch005

Sherdil, K., & Madhavji, N. H. (1996). Human-oriented improvement in the software process. 144–166. DOI: 10.1007/BFb0017741

Singh, J., Kumar, S., Singh, S. K., Singh, D., Singh, A., Arya, V., & Ratnaparkhi, A. (2025). Virtual Economies and Social Structures in the Metaverse. In Unveiling Social Dynamics and Community Interaction in the Metaverse (pp. 111–138). IGI Global Scientific Publishing. DOI: 10.4018/979-8-3693-8628-6.ch006

Singh, J., Singh, S. K., Kumar, S., Singh, S. P., Kumar, R., Bansal, S., & Chui, K. T. (2025). The Influence of AI on Social Interactions and Community Dynamics. In *Unveiling Social Dynamics and Community Interaction in the Metaverse* (pp. 197–220). IGI Global Scientific Publishing., DOI: 10.4018/979-8-3693-8628-6.ch010

Singh, M., Singh, S. K., Kumar, S., Madan, U., & Maan, T. (2023). Sustainable Framework for Metaverse Security and Privacy: Opportunities and Challenges (pp. 329–340). DOI: 10.1007/978-3-031-22018-0_30

Strazzeri, I., Notebaert, A., Barros, C., Quinten, J., & Demarbaix, A. (2024). Virtual Reality Integration for Enhanced Engineering Education and Experimentation: A Focus on Active Thermography. *Computers*, *13*(8), 199. Advance online publication. DOI: 10.3390/computers13080199

Tang, F., Chen, X., Zhao, M., & Kato, N. (2023). The Roadmap of Communication and Networking in 6G for the Metaverse. *IEEE Wireless Communications*, *30*(4), 72–81. DOI: 10.1109/MWC.019.2100721

Tao, F., Qi, Q., Liu, A., & Kusiak, A. (2018). Data-driven smart manufacturing. *Journal of Manufacturing Systems*, *48*, 157–169. DOI: 10.1016/j.jmsy.2018.01.006

Tao, F., Zhang, H., Liu, A., & Nee, A. Y. C. (2019). Digital Twin in Industry: State-of-the-Art. *IEEE Transactions on Industrial Informatics, 15*(4), 2405–2415. DOI: 10.1109/TII.2018.2873186

Tukur, M., Schneider, J., Househ, M., Dokoro, A. H., Ismail, U. I., Dawaki, M., & Agus, M. (2024). The Metaverse digital environments: A scoping review of the techniques, technologies, and applications. *Journal of King Saud University. Computer and Information Sciences, 36*(2), 101967. Advance online publication. DOI: 10.1016/j.jksuci.2024.101967

Ud Din, I., & Almogren, A. (2023). Exploring the psychological effects of Metaverse on mental health and well-being. *Information Technology & Tourism, 25*(3), 367–389. DOI: 10.1007/s40558-023-00259-8

Vincenza Ciasullo, M., Troisi, O., & Cosimato, S. (2018). How Digital Platforms Can Trigger Cultural Value Co-Creation?—A Proposed Model. *Journal of Service Science and Management, 11*(02), 161–181. DOI: 10.4236/jssm.2018.112013

Wang, H., Ning, H., Lin, Y., Wang, W., Dhelim, S., Farha, F., Ding, J., & Daneshmand, M. (2023). A Survey on the Metaverse: The State-of-the-Art, Technologies, Applications, and Challenges. *IEEE Internet of Things Journal, 10*(16), 14671–14688. DOI: 10.1109/JIOT.2023.3278329

Yang, Y., Zhou, J., & Yang, Z. (2025). *Integrated Sensing*. Computing, and Semantic Communication with Fluid Antenna for Metaverse.

Yigit, Y., Maglaras, L. A., Buchanan, W. J., Canberk, B., Shin, H., & Duong, T. Q. (2024). AI-Enhanced Digital Twin Framework for Cyber-Resilient 6G Internet of Vehicles Networks. *IEEE Internet of Things Journal, 11*(22), 36168–36181. DOI: 10.1109/JIOT.2024.3455089

Zhong, R. Y., Xu, X., Klotz, E., & Newman, S. T. (2017). Intelligent Manufacturing in the Context of Industry 4.0: A Review. *Engineering (Beijing), 3*(5), 616–630. DOI: 10.1016/J.ENG.2017.05.015

Zhou, K., Liu, T., & Zhou, L. (2015). Industry 4.0: Towards future industrial opportunities and challenges. 2015 12th International Conference on Fuzzy Systems and Knowledge Discovery (FSKD), 2147–2152. DOI: 10.1109/FSKD.2015.7382284

Chapter 7
Towards Data-Driven and Human-Centric Intelligent Manufacturing Through the Integration of AI, IoT, and Blockchain

Defia Ulandari
http://orcid.org/0009-0002-2136-1633
Universitas Esa Unggul, Indonesia

Deswita Anggraini
http://orcid.org/0009-0003-2192-3381
Universitas Esa Unggul, Indonesia

Mohammad Norman Gaza Laksono
http://orcid.org/0009-0005-2863-5483
Uppsala Universitet, Sweden

Kwok Tai Chui
Hong Kong Metropolitan University, Hong Kong

D. David Neels Ponkumar
Vel Tech Rangarajan Dr. Sagunthala R&D Institute of Science and Technology, India

ABSTRACT

The transformation to Industry 5.0 is driving manufacturing to adopt a more intelligent, adaptive, and humanized approach through the integration of Artificial

DOI: 10.4018/979-8-2600-0013-7.ch007

Intelligence (AI), Internet of Things (IoT), and Blockchain. This chapter proposes an integrative framework of the three technologies, which makes AI the center of analytics and decision-making, IoT the nervous system that collects data in real-time, and Blockchain the foundation of trust through secure and transparent data recording. This approach not only improves operational efficiency, predictivity, and product personalization, but also supports sustainability and industry ethics. Case studies such as predictive maintenance, mass customization, and supply chain visibility demonstrate the effectiveness of this integration in the field. The chapter also details implementation challenges as well as future trends, such as federated learning and quantum-resistant Blockchain. Overall, this framework provides strategic direction for a resilient, adaptive, and people-oriented manufacturing ecosystem.

INTRODUCTION

The industrial world is undergoing a major transformation as it moves towards the Industry 5.0 era, an era that no longer focuses solely on traditional automation and digitization, but emphasizes the synergy between advanced technology and human values. At the heart of this evolution is the concept of smart manufacturing, an approach that integrates Artificial Intelligence (AI), Internet of Things (IoT), and Blockchain technologies into a smart, adaptive, and reliable ecosystem (Alkhodair & Alkhudhayr, 2025). Unlike Industry 4.0, which focuses on efficiency and cyber-physical systems, Industry 5.0 places people, sustainability, and resilience as the main pillars of industrial development (Jap, 2024). In this context, the integration of AI, IoT, and Blockchain is not only a technological trend, but also a transformation strategy that redefines the way goods are designed, produced, distributed, and perceived by consumers.

The convergence of these three disruptive technologies has the potential to address long-standing challenges in the manufacturing sector, ranging from machine failure and lack of transparency in the supply chain, to the growing demand for personalized, sustainability-oriented products (Obaidat et al., 2024). While each technology has demonstrated significant value, integration between them has been shown to yield exponential improvements in terms of operational visibility, decision-making intelligence, data traceability, and customer satisfaction (Akram et al., 2022).

Artificial Intelligence (AI) has become the brain of modern manufacturing systems. Its capabilities in real-time analytics, pattern recognition, predictive modeling, and autonomous control enable industries to move from reactive strategies to proactive approaches (Sekti, 2025). AI-based solutions now play an important role in predictive maintenance, quality control, demand forecasting, and production scheduling, resulting in operational efficiency while reducing production risks and waste (Jap,

2024). Using machine learning and deep learning algorithms, AI is able to transform raw data into strategic insights, allowing smart factories to automatically adjust to changing internal and external conditions.

Complementing AI, IoT serves as the nervous system and key link in the smart manufacturing ecosystem. Through a network of interconnected sensors, devices, and machines, IoT enables real-time monitoring, communication, and control across the entire production line. This technology supports important functions such as machine monitoring, inventory visibility, remote condition monitoring, and energy management (Obaidat et al., 2024). When coupled with edge computing, IoT can process data locally to reduce latency and increase response speed, something vital for the high-precision manufacturing sector (Essaid & Ju, 2025).

On the other hand, Blockchain plays a crucial role in ensuring data integrity, transparency, and security in digital manufacturing environments. This technology allows for decentralized and immutable recording of transactions, which is particularly relevant for the complex global manufacturing sector and involves many entities (Sekti, 2025). Through the application of *distributed ledger*, Blockchain supports comprehensive traceability of raw materials, production processes, and distribution of final products. Automation through *smart contracts* also enables the execution of business agreements without manual intervention, thereby reducing the potential for errors or manipulations Blockchain implementation in the industrial ecosystem not only increases trust between supply chain partners, but also promotes operational efficiency by reducing the need for manual audits and speeding up the verification process. As such, Blockchain becomes an essential foundation for smart manufacturing that wants to ensure data security, regulatory compliance, and transparent and trustworthy cross-organizational collaboration.

Blockchain, on the other hand, plays a crucial role in ensuring data integrity, transparency, and security in digital manufacturing environments. The technology enables decentralized and immutable recording of transactions, which is highly relevant to the complex and multi-entity global manufacturing sector. Through the application of distributed ledgers, Blockchain supports complete traceability of raw materials, production processes, and distribution of the final product. Automation through smart contracts also enables the execution of business agreements without manual intervention, thereby reducing the potential for error or manipulation (Essaid & Ju, 2025). Blockchain implementation in the industrial ecosystem not only increases trust between supply chain partners, but also drives operational efficiency by reducing the need for manual audits and speeding up the verification process. Blockchain is thus an important foundation for smart manufacturing that wants to ensure data security, regulatory compliance, and transparent and trusted cross-organizational collaboration.

The strategic integration of AI, IoT, and Blockchain is not just the concurrent use of three technologies; it forms a smart and reliable production architecture. In this complementary model:

- IoT serves as a real-time data collector from the physical environment,
- AI serves to process data into analytics, predictions, and decision-making,
- Blockchain maintains data integrity and ensures process security.

With this triadic approach, manufacturers can achieve unprecedented levels of automation, agility and accountability. The impact extends to all aspects of production, from equipment maintenance and quality control, to product personalization, waste reduction, and carbon emissions management.

The following diagram illustrates a layered conceptual architecture for implementing AI, IoT, and Digital Twin technologies in a smart manufacturing system. The architecture emphasizes modularity, real-time responsiveness, and ergonomic human interaction:

- Physical Layer

Comprises machines, sensors, and actuators deployed on the factory floor. These physical devices generate continuous streams of operational data in real-time.

- Edge Layer

Functions as a localized computational layer to perform AI inference and quick decision-making with low latency. It enables responsive feedback loops without relying on cloud infrastructure.

- Cloud Layer

Handles heavy computational workloads such as machine learning model training, long-term data analytics, and big data storage. This layer supports strategic-level decision-making and system-wide optimizations.

- Digital Twin Layer

Represents a synchronized virtual replica of the physical system. It provides real-time simulation and predictive modeling that reflects changes and status of actual machines, enabling proactive maintenance and production control.

- User Interface Layer

Offers intuitive and ergonomic interfaces for human operators. This includes dashboards, HMI (Human-Machine Interface), and immersive technologies such as Augmented Reality (AR) and Virtual Reality (VR) to enhance human-machine collaboration.

This layered architecture promotes not only a scalable and robust infrastructure but also encourages adaptability to future advancements such as 6G networks, quantum computing, and decentralized AI models. It also supports ergonomic design considerations and ethical standards in human-machine interaction.

More importantly, this integrated approach also shifts the manufacturing paradigm to be consumer-oriented and in line with today's industrial ethics. Consumers are increasingly aware of the environmental and social impacts of the products they buy. They demand process transparency, sustainability and personalization (Alkhodair & Alkhudhayr, 2025). Smart manufacturing ecosystems support mass personalized production, ethical verification in the supply chain, and accelerated delivery of products to market, while maintaining quality and sustainability.

This transformation is closely aligned with the Sustainable Development Goals, especially on the points of industrial innovation, decent work, responsible consumption, and climate action. Smart manufacturing is not only a tool for economic growth, but also a means to promote ethical and inclusive industrial growth (Jap, 2024).

While promising, the integration of these technologies is not without its challenges. Ranging from the interoperability of legacy systems, cybersecurity vulnerabilities, differences in regulatory standards, to a shortage of skilled labor, they are all barriers that must be carefully managed. Without standardized protocols between devices, AI platforms, and Blockchain systems, the risk of fragmentation and integration failure is very high. In addition, Blockchain's decentralized architecture often conflicts with traditional centralized IT systems, requiring extensive customization.

Ethical aspects and trust are also important concerns. AI that makes automated decisions must be auditable and unbiased. Data from IoT must be processed without violating privacy, and Blockchain must be optimized so as not to put an energy burden on the environment. The future of manufacturing is not just about smart technology, but also transparent, responsible, and humane systems.

This chapter aims to thoroughly explore the individual and collective roles of AI, IoT, and Blockchain in building a smart manufacturing ecosystem. By describing their respective functions, case studies of successful integration, implementation challenges, and impact on consumers, this chapter provides a foundation for understanding future industrial strategies (Akram et al., 2022). Furthermore, the chapter also provides foresight into new trends such as decentralized AI, 6G-based ultra-responsive IoT, quantum-proof Blockchain, and an ethical framework for AI.

This chapter aims to thoroughly explore the individual and collective roles of AI, IoT, and Blockchain in building a smart manufacturing ecosystem. By describing their respective functions, case studies of successful integration, implementation challenges, and impact on consumers, this chapter provides a foundation for understanding future industrial strategies.

Furthermore, this chapter aims to propose a layered and modular integration architecture for AI, IoT, and Digital Twin technologies, which focuses on enhancing process predictability, enabling real-time decision-making, and augmenting the human workforce through adaptive and ergonomic interfaces. Additionally, the chapter also provides foresight into new trends such as decentralized AI, 6G-based ultra-responsive IoT, quantum-proof Blockchain, and an ethical framework for AI (Alkhodair & Alkhudhayr, 2025).

THE ROLE OF ARTIFICIAL INTELLIGENCE IN INTELLIGENT MANUFACTURING

In the context of Industry 5.0, Artificial Intelligence (AI) acts as the center of intelligence control in intelligent manufacturing systems that are adaptive, autonomous, and human-oriented. AI has not only become an additional component in industrial automation, but it has evolved into a key foundation in decision-making, process optimization, and product design innovation. By combining machine learning algorithms, deep learning, and reinforcement-based approaches, AI enables production systems to dynamically adapt to environmental changes and perform actions that previously required human intervention (Kraus & Kraus, 2025).

AI as an Operational Intelligence Machine in Manufacturing

In the Industry 5.0 landscape, AI plays a central role as the operational brain of intelligent manufacturing systems. This technology not only serves as a decision-making tool, but also as a key driver in creating an adaptive and automated production system. AI works by analyzing big data, whether from production sensors, market demand, and customer behavior, then converting it into precise, real-time actions (Aamer et al., 2025). Figure 1 show the AI architecture in intelligent manufacturing systems

Figure 1. AI architecture in intelligent manufacturing systems

Figure 1 above illustrates the eight main pillars that form the significance of AI in the modern manufacturing sector. These pillars include: Cost Reduction through resource efficiency, Improved Efficiency on production lines, Safety and Compliance for worker protection, and the creation of Competitive Advantage. In addition, AI supports accurate Data-Driven Decision-Making, enables mass Customization and Personalization of products, improves Enhanced Product Quality through automated inspection, and performs Supply Chain Optimization that is responsive to market dynamics.

AI combines approaches such as machine learning, deep learning, and reinforcement learning to develop models that are able to learn and adapt to changing conditions. For example, AI is capable of automatically rearranging production schedules in the event of a change in the supply chain or a certain surge in demand. AI-powered smart factories become systems that can "think and respond" based on real data in the field (Alzubaidi et al., 2025).

Key benefits of this role include:

- Increased operational efficiency.
- Reduced decision-making time.
- High responsiveness to changes in the production environment.

In other words, AI acts as a strategic component in transforming manufacturing from a reaction-based system to a system based on prediction and adaptation.

Application of AI in Predictive Maintenance and Quality Assurance

One of the most prominent contributions of AI in the manufacturing sector is its application to predictive maintenance. The system uses data from IoT sensors to identify potential failure patterns in production machines before damage occurs. AI-based predictive models analyze parameters such as temperature, vibration, and pressure to detect anomalies invisible to human operators (Das et al., 2025).

The impact of predictive maintenance includes:

- Reduced downtime.
- Extension of the life of the production equipment.
- Maintenance cost efficiency.

In addition, AI also plays a big role in automated quality control. With the support of computer vision and detection algorithms such as CNN or YOLO, AI-based inspection systems are able to identify product defects with high precision. Product images are automatically taken by high-resolution cameras and processed to determine whether the product is worthy of inspection or needs to be sorted (Arnob et al., 2025).

Benefits of AI-based quality assurance:

- The speed of inspection has increased significantly.
- High consistency of detection results.
- Reduction of waste due to defective products.

These two applications make AI a pillar in the reliability of production systems and the quality of industrial outputs.

AI for Production Optimization and Human and Machine Collaboration

In addition to predictive functions and quality control, AI also has an important role in production line optimization and human-robot collaboration. Complex and dynamic production systems demand the ability to respond to fluctuations in demand, availability of raw materials, and machine capacity in real-time. AI addresses these challenges through predictive analytics and automated decision-making, so that the production process can take place with maximum efficiency (Sayal et al., 2025).

Some examples of AI-based production optimization applications include:

- Dynamic scheduling that automatically adjusts the production time and sequence.
- Resource allocation based on historical performance and current workloads.
- Adjustment of machine configuration without manual intervention.

On the other hand, in the context of collaborative robotics (cobots), AI allows for safe and productive interactions between humans and machines. Cobots can learn from human interactions, recognize safe zones, and adjust rhythms and workloads based on the needs of the operator (Abdullah et al., 2025). This is the essence of Industry 5.0: synergy between technology and humans, not just substitution.

Strategic advantages of deploying AI-based cobots include:

- Improved safety and ergonomics of work.
- High adaptability to changing production needs.
- Reduced worker training time for repetitive or technical tasks.

With such a comprehensive role, AI not only makes factories smarter, but also more humane and resilent in the face of global dynamics.

Table 1. Functions and Benefits of AI in Smart Manufacturing

AI Functions	**Real Implementation**	**Key Benefits**
Predictive Maintenance	Early detection of engine malfunctions through sensor data	Reduce downtime, optimize maintenance schedules
Quality Control	Automatic inspection with computer vision	Improve quality consistency, speed up inspections
Production Optimization	Real-time production adjustments	Capacity efficiency, minimize waste
Human-Robot Collaboration	Adaptive interaction of cobots with humans	Improved safety, productivity, and ergonomics
Decision Automation	Automated production schedule preparation	Responsive to demand and supply chain

INTERNET OF THINGS AS AN INTELLIGENT FACTORY NERVOUS SYSTEM

The Strategic Role of IoT in the Context of Industry 5.0

In the Industry 5.0 landscape, the Internet of Things (IoT) is emerging as a key infrastructure that enables the transformation of manufacturing into a responsive, connected, and data-driven ecosystem. IoT is not only a connecting technology between machines and digital networks, but also the foundation for contextual and intelligent production. In smart manufacturing, IoT acts as a central nervous system that continuously streams data from various physical entities to advanced decision-making systems, such as Artificial Intelligence (AI) and manufacturing execution systems (MES) (Das et al., 2025).

Functionally, IoT connects machines, sensors, software, and humans into a single platform that allows real-time detection of environmental conditions, machine operational status, material position, and other production variables. This connectivity is critical to improving process efficiency, accelerating responses to disruptions, and enabling end-to-end visibility across the value chain. The application of IoT not only increases the speed of information flow, but also enables more autonomous, flexible, and adaptive production processes to changes in demand or external disruptions (Alzubaidi et al., 2025).

With the increasing complexity of the production process, the existence of IoT is the main driver of the realization of the concept *of zero-latency manufacturing*, where all crucial information can be collected, processed, and acted upon in a very short time. In this context, IoT is not only a technological instrument, but also a strategic *enabler* in realizing sustainable and customer-oriented manufacturing (Hassan et al., 2025).

Implementation of IoT in Production, Maintenance, and Logistics

IoT in manufacturing can be implemented at various levels, from machine monitoring, quality control, energy management, to logistics asset tracking. On the production line, IoT sensors embedded in the equipment are able to detect variables such as temperature, pressure, vibration, speed, or wear level of components continuously. This information enables predictive decision-making, prevents unexpected breakdowns, and increases the operating life of the appliance.

In addition, IoT supports intelligent inventory and logistics management. Automated scanning systems such as RFID and barcodes integrated with location sensors (GPS) allow for real-time tracking of the position and status of goods. This has a direct impact on improving stock accuracy, material distribution efficiency, and reducing *stockout* and *overstock* (Sayal et al., 2025).

In the context of quality control, IoT sensors can automatically measure product parameters such as dimensions, weight, color, or surface. When combined with AI systems, the inspection process becomes much faster, more accurate, and free from human subjectivity (Arnob et al., 2025). IoT also plays an important role in energy management by providing detailed data on electricity consumption per machine or production zone, allowing for optimization of energy load and reduction of operational costs (Alzubaidi et al., 2025).

Examples of real implementation:

- General Electric uses IoT sensors in industrial turbine management systems to reduce engine failures.
- Amazon optimizes logistics and warehousing with IoT-based robotic and real-time monitoring systems.
- Toyota integrates IoT with AI to accelerate defect detection on vehicle assembly lines.

Challenges, Solutions, and Future Directions of IoT in Manufacturing

Although promising, the application of IoT in the manufacturing industry is inseparable from technical, organizational, and security challenges. One of the main challenges is the interoperability of devices and systems, given the large number of vendors and different communication protocol standards. Without an open architecture approach and clear integration standards, IoT systems are vulnerable to data fragmentation and inefficiencies (Aamer et al., 2025).

Another issue is data security and privacy, especially since IoT sensors transmit sensitive data continuously over an open network. Vulnerability to cyberattacks, device *spoofing*, or data interception can cause production disruptions to the leakage of strategic company information. Therefore, it is necessary to strengthen the system through end-to-end encryption, device authentication, as well as the implementation of *firewalls* and intrusion detection systems (Abdullah et al., 2025; Arnob et al., 2025).

To address these challenges, approaches such as:

- Edge computing for local data processing and latency reduction,
- AIoT (Artificial Intelligence of Things) for real-time contextual analysis,
- and Multivendor compatible Industrial IoT (IIoT) Platforms.

Going forward, the evolution of IoT will be driven by technologies such as 6G, Low-Power Wide-Area Network (LPWAN), and digital twins, which will strengthen simulation and adaptive response capabilities in production systems. In addition, the trend of using *cloud-hybrid* based IoT and integration with blockchain for *operational data auditability* is becoming increasingly relevant in sectors that require high transparency (Hassan et al., 2025).

BLOCKCHAIN FOR TRUST, TRANSPARENCY, AND TRACEABILITY

The Strategic Role of Blockchain in the Era of Distributed Manufacturing

Blockchain is here as a technological solution that brings transparency, integrity, and security in an increasingly complex and distributed digital manufacturing environment. In the era of Industry 5.0, manufacturing is no longer local or linear, but involves a global process that is digitally connected and includes many parties, from raw material suppliers, factories, distributors, to end consumers. Products are no longer made in one fixed location, but rather through a series of stages spread across countries, time zones, and regulations. In this context, the need for a reliable and transparent record-keeping system is increasingly crucial, especially to ensure the authenticity of data, avoid falsification, and strengthen trust between stakeholders.

Working Principles of Blockchain and Leverage on Traceability

Blockchain technology allows the recording of every activity or transaction permanently and *immutably* through a distributed ledger. Each log of data is equipped with a timestamp, the identity of the perpetrator, and a cryptographic link to the previous block, forming a chain of data that cannot be forged. This makes Blockchain very suitable to support *traceability*, which is the ability to track the origin and journey of a product with high accuracy. In the manufacturing industry, this can include tracking raw materials from their source, production process track record, quality inspection, to final delivery to consumers.

Blockchain for Supply Chain Resilience and Product Recall

In the manufacturing sector, especially in the food and beverage industry, the accuracy and traceability of data have direct implications for consumer safety and brand reputation. Blockchain allows the complete recording of the origin of raw materials starting from the initial farmer or producer, distribution processes such as transportation and storage, to product processing and packaging. This approach makes the entire product lifecycle traceable in real-time and verified for authenticity. In emergency situations such as product *recalls*, Blockchain systems help companies respond quickly, identify affected batches, and act appropriately without disrupting other parties (Majumdar and Awasthi, 2025). By eliminating data manipulation, Blockchain also helps prevent product counterfeiting and increases customer trust.

Smart Contracts as Automation of Interaction Between Entities

One of the superior features of Blockchain is smart *contracts*, which are code-based digital contracts that can be executed automatically when certain conditions are met. *Smart contracts* offer reduced reliance on manual processes and improve collaboration efficiency in blockchain-based systems, especially when combined with IoT and AI (Ji et al., 2024). In complex manufacturing ecosystems, smart contracts serve as a transaction automation tool such as supplier payments, shipment validation, or the assessment of new suppliers based on quality parameters. With *if-then* logic, smart contracts process all transactions without manual intervention, avoiding bureaucratic delays, and reducing the risk of fraud or collusion. This creates a faster, more efficient, and openly auditable supply chain ecosystem.

Global Supply Chain Visibility and Decentralization of Trust

Blockchain enables comprehensive supply chain visibility, answering the long-standing challenge of information fragmentation. With decentralized logging and consensus validation, all parties in the supply chain from suppliers to distributors can access up-to-date data without having to trust each other completely. Figure 2 show the Global Supply Chain Visibility with Blockchain Technology.

Figure 2. Global Supply Chain Visibility with Blockchain Technology

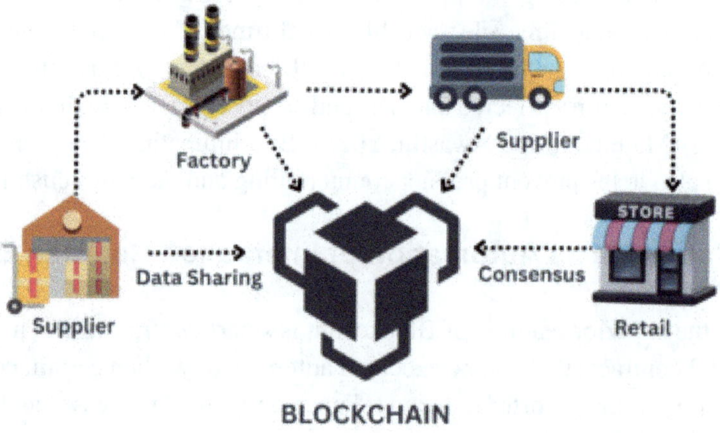

Figure 2 shows how Blockchain technology is the main foundation in creating global supply chain visibility. In this model, various entities such as Suppliers, Factories, and Retailers are connected through Data Sharing and Consensus mechanisms. Every movement of goods and transaction is recorded in a decentralized network to ensure that the information received by all parties is accurate, transparent, and cannot be manipulated.

Data such as delivery location, storage conditions (temperature, humidity), and payment status can be shared securely and encrypted. This enables more open and transparent collaboration between stakeholders. Through the implementation of a distributed ledger, Blockchain supports comprehensive traceability from raw materials to final product distribution.

Real Benefits in a Highly Regulated Industry

Highly regulated manufacturing sectors such as pharmaceuticals, defense, and high-tech electronics benefit greatly from Blockchain integration. The use of blockchain in critical ecosystems such as pharmaceuticals, defense, and electronics brings digital reliability that was previously difficult to achieve through conventional systems (Majumdar and Awasthi, 2025). In pharmaceuticals, each batch of drugs can be traced from factory to pharmacy, ensuring patient safety and avoiding counterfeiting. In defense, the authenticity of components is essential for national security. While in the electronics industry, Blockchain guarantees that every microcomponent comes from an official source and is free from counterfeits. Thus, Blockchain is not just a tool, but a digital trust infrastructure in today's manufacturing.

THE INTEGRATION FRAMEWORK AI, IOT, AND BLOCKCHAIN

The integration *of Artificial Intelligence* (AI), *Internet of Things* (IoT), and *Blockchain* has become a transformational framework in building smart manufacturing systems that are adaptive, accurate, and trustworthy. Each technology brings its own advantages: IoT serves as a neural system that streams real-time data from the physical environment, AI acts as a brain that processes and infers that information for intelligent decision-making, while Blockchain acts as a digital trust backbone that guarantees the integrity, security, and traceability of the entire process. When combined, the three not only strengthen the system individually, but create synergies that transform the manufacturing operational paradigm to be autonomous, responsive, and transparent.

AI, IoT, and Blockchain Integration Framework Architecture

The integration architecture between *Artificial Intelligence* (AI), *Internet of Things* (IoT), and *Blockchain* in smart manufacturing forms a layered system that complements and reinforces each other. In general, the system consists of three main layers: perception and action (IoT), processing and analytics (AI), and distribution and security (Blockchain). These three layers form the backbone of an adaptive, autonomous, and trusted intelligent manufacturing ecosystem.

The IoT layer serves as a digital perception system consisting of sensors, actuators, and other connected devices. IoT sensors are embedded in production machines, assembly lines, warehouses, and even in the products themselves. They collect real-time data such as temperature, pressure, engine vibration, position of goods, production speed, humidity, and energy consumption. Actuators work to provide a response or action based on the signal received, such as adjusting the temperature, stopping the production process when an anomaly occurs, or changing an automated logistics line.

The AI layer is the brain of the system. By leveraging machine learning, deep learning, or reinforcement learning algorithms, AI analyzes data from the IoT layer to recognize patterns, predict failures, optimize production, or recommend corrective actions. For example, AI can rearrange production schedules based on current market demand or estimate when a machine needs to be repaired before it is completely broken (Ji et al., 2024).

Blockchain Layer The Blockchain layer is responsible for maintaining the integrity, transparency, and security of all data and processes that occur. Every resulting AI analysis and operational track record will be recorded in the Blockchain network permanently. This ensures that each activity is traceable, non-manipulative, and securely shared with interested internal and external parties. With this architecture, manufacturing systems are not only intelligent, but also transparent and trusted across the board (Majumdar and Awasthi, 2025).

Integration Workflows in Smart Manufacturing

In a smart manufacturing system that integrates IoT, AI, and Blockchain, the entire process runs in a workflow that is cyclical, adaptive, and interdependent. Each technology plays a key role in this cycle to create a smart, responsive, and reliable production ecosystem. Figure 3 Show the Smart Manufacturing Workflow.

Figure 3. Smart Manufacturing Workflow

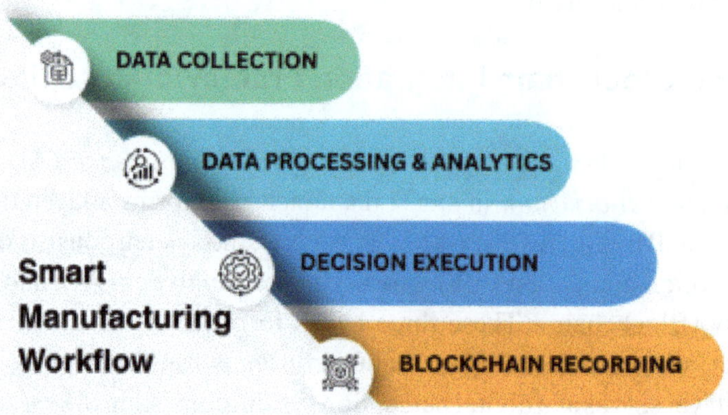

The first stage is Data Collection, where IoT sensors scattered across various production points act as the main monitoring tool. These sensors collect real-time data from production machines, assembly lines, internal logistics, even from the surrounding environment such as temperature, humidity, or energy consumption. This data is very diverse and continues to flow endlessly, forming the information foundation of the entire system.

After that, after that, the collected data will enter the Data Processing & Analytics stage. This is where AI takes over. Using machine learning or deep learning algorithms, AI classifies data, detects anomalies, predicts possible machine failures (predictive maintenance), or calculates projected market demand based on previous trends. These analytical results allow the system to understand operational conditions more deeply and contextually (Ji et al., 2024).

The next stage is Decision Execution, where decisions are made automatically based on the results of AI analysis. The system can immediately make adjustments to the production line, schedule maintenance, or provide early warning to the operator if a potential problem is detected. This creates a system that is not only reactive, but also proactive.

Lastly is Blockchain Recording. All important decisions, predictive analytics, as well as relevant operational data are recorded into the Blockchain system. This record ensures that all information is transparent, immutable, and can be audited at any time. This provides a high level of trust for both internal parties and external partners (Majumdar and Awasthi, 2025).

With this cycle, smart manufacturing can run sustainably, efficiently, and reliably amidst modern industrial dynamics.

Strategic Advantages of Integrated Framework

With the integration of digitally connected manufacturing systems, cybersecurity risks have increased dramatically. This is where the role of Blockchain becomes crucial as a record system that cannot be modified unilaterally. Each node in the network keeps a copy of the data, and any transactions or changes must be validated through consensus. This prevents data manipulation by irresponsible parties. By transparently recording activity logs from machines, users, and AI systems, Blockchain strengthens the security of the supply chain against internal and external cyber threats. As outlined by (Ji et al., 2024)The application of blockchain reduces the risk of critical data leakage and improves the cyber resilience of distributed production systems.

One of the main advantages is operational autonomy. With the support of AI capable of analyzing real-time data from IoT, production systems can make decisions automatically without waiting for human intervention. For example, machines can stop processes if they detect anomalies, or reset production schedules based on demand spikes. This speeds up response and reduces reliance on manual supervision.

Furthermore, this integration strengthens the resilience of the system. AI is able to predict potential machine failures or disruptions in the supply chain based on continuous IoT sensor data. Thus, disruptions can be identified early and responded to adaptively, minimizing downtime, production losses, and operational risks.

When it comes to end-to-end transparency, Blockchain plays a crucial role. All activities, from data collection, analytical processes, to final decisions, can be permanently recorded and decentralized in the Blockchain network. This allows for accurate and reliable digital audits, both internally and by external partners such as regulators or customers.

Lastly, in terms of data security, Blockchain guarantees that information cannot be manipulated or accessed by unauthorized parties. With network encryption and consensus mechanisms, sensitive data such as analytical results, production status, or supplier information can be protected to the maximum.

With all these advantages, the AI, IoT, and Blockchain integration framework becomes a strategic foundation for manufacturing that is not only smart, but also resilient, transparent, and future-proof.

To clarify the transformation from the Industry 4.0 approach towards an AI-IoT-Digital Twin-based intelligent framework, the following table presents a comparison of the key characteristics of the two approaches. This aims to enable even non-technical audiences to understand the fundamental strategic and technological differences.

Table 2. Comparison of Traditional Industry 4.0 vs AI-IoT-Digital Twin Framework

Aspects	Traditional Industry 4.0	Framework AI-IoT-Digital Twin
Focus	Automation and cyber-physical systems	Human augmentation & adaptive intelligence
Architecture	Fragmented (Silos)	Layered modular system
Decision Making	Rule-based and manual control	Real-time analytics and AI-driven predictions
Transparency	Limited and internal	Blockchain-based permanent data trail
System Durability	Reactive to interference	Predictive and adaptive to change
Data Security	Centralistic and prone to manipulation	Decentralized and non-modifiable
Product Customization	Uniform mass production	Personalized mass production

Implementation Challenges and Recommendations

While the integration of AI, IoT, and Blockchain in manufacturing systems offers a variety of strategic advantages, the implementation process is not easy. There are a number of technical, resource, and managerial challenges that need to be overcome in order for this transformation to run effectively and sustainably.

Here are some of the main challenges faced in the implementation of this technology integration:

1. The first challenge is the complexity of integrating heterogeneous systems. Every manufacturing company usually has a variety of different information systems and hardware, ranging from ERP, SCADA, to legacy production systems. Connecting such legacy systems with new technologies such as AI, IoT sensors, and Blockchain networks requires flexible and compatible architectures, as well as careful integration planning.
2. Second, there is an urgent need for universal communication standards. Many IoT devices from different vendors use non-uniform protocols, making it dif-

ficult to exchange data seamlessly. Without good interoperability, automation and analytics processes will be hampered or result in inconsistent data.

3. The third challenge is the high initial cost of implementation. From investments in sensor devices, network infrastructure, data storage, HR training, to AI model development and Blockchain integration, all of which require large capital in the early stages. This is often an obstacle for medium or small-scale companies.
4. Fourth, is the lack of human resources with multidisciplinary expertise. It requires talent who is able to understand AI, IoT, cybersecurity, and Blockchain principles at the same time, which is currently quite rare in many developing countries. According to (Ji *et al.*, 2024) affirms that the convergence of AI, IoT, and Blockchain is driving the creation of greener and more transparent industrial systems.

To overcome this, some strategic recommendations include:

- Adopt a middleware platform to make integration between systems more modular and efficient.
- Organizing cross-division training to improve the competence of internal human resources.
- Start from a small-scale pilot project to test and mitigate risk.
- Using a private Blockchain, which is more energy-efficient and better suited for closed manufacturing environments.

With the right steps, these challenges can be turned into opportunities for long-term industrial transformation.

USE CASE

The integration between Artificial Intelligence (AI), Internet of Things (IoT), and Blockchain is no longer just a theoretical concept in the modern manufacturing world. Its implementation has yielded tangible results that significantly change various aspects of operations, from the production line to the final distribution. The synergy of these three technologies creates a manufacturing system that is not only efficient, but also transparent, adaptive, and consumer-centric (Rafiq et al., 2025).

IoT enables real-time data collection from machines, work environments, and supply chains. AI processes this data to detect anomalies, predict maintenance, and optimize production. The blockchain then guarantees the security and legitimacy of the entire process, by recording each step permanently and immutably. The result is a system that is able to make automated and reliable decisions in a short period of time.

The concrete implementation of this integration has been implemented in various business sectors ranging from food and beverage, automotive, pharmaceutical, to electronics. The four key cases that will be discussed in this chapter show that AI, IoT, and Blockchain not only improve efficiency and accuracy, but also strengthen customer trust and ensure supply chains run ethically and transparently (Alazzam et al., 2023).

Predictive Maintenance

Predictive Maintenance is one of the earliest and most widespread forms of integration between Artificial Intelligence (AI), Internet of Things (IoT), and Blockchain in the manufacturing industry. The goal is to minimize unplanned downtime and extend the operational life of machines through a data-driven approach and intelligent prediction.

In this system, IoT sensors embedded in production machines continuously collect data such as temperature, vibration, pressure, humidity, energy consumption, and operational frequency. This real-time data provides a comprehensive picture of the condition of the machine without having to stop the production process. The data is then analyzed by AI algorithms, especially machine learning, to identify patterns that have the potential to be indicators of damage. AI can study the normal behavior of machines and detect anomalies that may not be visible to humans.

When a pattern that leads to a machine failure is detected, the AI system automatically provides an early warning to the technician or maintenance manager. This allows the company to perform maintenance in a timely manner before major damage occurs that can lead to financial losses and operational disruptions.

The entire process, from data collection, AI analysis results, to maintenance actions taken, is recorded in the Blockchain. This recording ensures the integrity and traceability of the data. With a distributed ledger system that cannot be modified, management can audit maintenance history at any time for the purposes of quality assurance, internal audits, reporting to regulators, or even proving in the case of warranty claims.

A real example of this application can be seen at Siemens. The company uses IoT and AI technology to monitor the condition of industrial gas turbines in real-time. As a result, Siemens has managed to reduce downtime by up to 30% and extend the life of the equipment through more accurate and efficient maintenance.

Quality Assurance

Modern Quality Assurance (QA) has shifted from manual inspection to automated systems based on AI and computer vision. High-resolution cameras connected to

IoT send product images to AI models to detect defects such as cracks, missizing, or color differences in real-time (Charfare et al., 2024).

The blockchain then records the results of QA to ensure that each unit of the product has a quality record that cannot be manipulated. This is especially important in the food, pharmaceutical, and electronics industries, where trust and regulation are very high. If any component fails inspection, the system can automatically isolate it and trigger a waste or recycling flow.

Real-life example: Foxconn uses a vision-based AI inspection system (AI Nx-VAE) to improve defect detection accuracy from about 95% to 99%, alongside a 50% reduction in manual inspection efforts. Reportedly, inspection accuracy has reached over 99.9%, approaching virtually zero-defect levels, with all results securely recorded, consistent with the implementation of blockchain-based traceability systems (Shahbazi & Byun, 2021).

Supply Chain Visibility

Global supply chains often experience challenges such as shipping delays, loss of goods, or unclear origins. The combination of IoT, AI, and Blockchain brings end-to-end visibility in real-time.

- IoT is used to track logistics locations and conditions (temperature, humidity, GPS position).
- AI AI analyzes data to predict potential delays or supply disruptions based on weather, traffic, or port policies (Yamoah, Mensah and Frimpong, 2025).
- Blockchain records every move and transaction, guaranteeing the authenticity and security of products from the starting point to the end consumer (Tahsin et al., 2025).

Real-life example: IBM and Maersk developed a blockchain platform called *TradeLens*, which monitors container shipments from port of origin to destination in real-time, leverages AI to detect potential logistical bottlenecks, and creates transparent and efficient shipping flows (Ahmed & Rios, 2022).

Mass Customization

Today's consumers demand products that are tailored to their preferences, but at a price and speed of mass production. This is known as mass customization. The integration of AI, IoT, and Blockchain makes this possible.

- Digital interfaces (such as web applications or in-store kiosks) are used to capture customer preferences: color, size, product features, etc.
- The AI then calculates the optimal combination of design and production lines based on consumer data, raw material stocks, and production capacity.
- IoT allows production lines to adapt in real-time to such unique configurations.
- Blockchain stores all transactions and design specifications as evidence and documentation, while ensuring the security of customer data (Khan et al., 2025).

Real Example: Nike developed AI-based shoe configuration technology that connects to automated production systems for personalization and efficiency. Customers can customize their shoe design (color, size, features) with accurate recommendations via AI/AR (e.g. *Nike Fit* app), which is then automatically produced. Customer designs and metadata can be stored as digital assets such as NFT linked-to-physical products, supporting product traceability and authentication (Periyasamy & Periyasami, 2023).

CONSUMER-CENTRIC OUTCOMES

Technology is just a tool, the end goal is human beings as end users. In the context of Industry 5.0, digital transformation driven by AI, IoT, and Blockchain is not only for the internal efficiency of manufacturing, but also to provide direct added value to consumers. The integration of these technologies creates a faster, safer, and more personalized production ecosystem all centered on customer needs and expectations (Khan et al., 2025).

By prioritizing the consumer experience, smart manufacturing enables companies to respond to the challenges of the new era: from the need for transparency, speed, quality, to personal preference. The following are the key outcomes of the consumer-centric manufacturing approach:

Personalized Product Offerings

Modern consumers are no longer satisfied with generic products. They want items that reflect their personal identity, lifestyle, or values. Through the integration of AI, IoT, and Blockchain:

- AI analyzes consumer behavior data, market trends, and customer feedback to design the most relevant products.

- IoT enables flexible production and real-time reconfiguration to meet unique specifications.
- Blockchain securely stores consumer preferences, supporting the processing of custom orders in a transparent and verifiable manner (Verma, 2025).

Example: Modular furniture manufacturers such as “Tylko” allow customers to design their own cabinets or shelves through a digital interface. AI adapts the design to the structure of the house, IoT enables automated production, and Blockchain ensures specifications are permanently stored as proof of design rights.

Faster Time-to-Market

In today's competitive landscape, time is of the essence. With integrated technology:

- AI accelerates the design and decision-making process.
- IoT supports communication and production execution without lag.
- Blockchain minimizes administrative delays with smart contracts and automatic document recording (Majumdar and Awasthi, 2025).

The result is faster product launch times, which provide customers with a real-time experience. They don't have to wait months for the latest innovations, the product arrives faster in their hands.

Case Study: Tesla is accelerating the production process of electric cars with the integration of AI-based predictive systems and blockchain-based supply chain tracking, thereby speeding up the cycle from design to delivery (Yamoah, Mensah and Frimpong, 2025).

Higher Product Quality and Reliability

Consumers not only want fast and personalized products, but also high quality and durable. An AI-based automated inspection system connected to IoT sensors is capable of detecting microdefects before the product leaves the factory.

In addition, Blockchain provides quality assurance through digital certifications that cannot be manipulated, increasing consumer trust in brands (Islam et al., 2025).

Example: In the healthcare industry, startups such as “Chronicled” use AI to ensure the quality of drugs during the production and distribution process, with IoT for temperature monitoring, as well as Blockchain for validity tracking down to the patient's hands (Das et al., 2025).

Transparent and Ethical Supply Chains

Today's consumers care about how products are made, not just the end result. They want to know: Are the raw materials ethical? Are employees covered? Is the environment harmed?

- Blockchain provides a transparent data chain from upstream to downstream (Admoko et al., 2024).
- IoT collects environmental and logistics data in real-time.
- AI analyzes the entire chain to identify potential violations or non-conformities (Tahsin et al., 2025).

Example: Clothing brand Patagonia provides a digital system that allows customers to trace the origin of their clothing materials to cotton farmers or textile workers, using Blockchain and IoT technology.

CHALLENGES AND CONSIDERATIONS

Although the integration of Artificial Intelligence (AI), Internet of Things (IoT), and Blockchain in smart manufacturing promises a great revolution in efficiency, quality, and customer experience, its implementation is not immune to complex challenges and considerations, both from the technical, economic, and ethical sides. Transformation towards an AI-IoT-Blockchain-based industry is not only about adopting technology, but about transforming the entire industrial ecosystem, from production processes, human resources, regulations, to organizational culture (Chen et al., 2024).

Some of the key challenges that the industry must face in implementing an AI-IoT-Blockchain-based ecosystem include:

- System Interoperability

Many manufacturing companies still use different legacy systems, making it difficult to integrate new technologies. Combining IoT devices from various vendors, inserting AI models in existing systems, and adapting decentralized Blockchain technology with centralized IT infrastructure creates complex challenges. Without a standardized framework, data integration becomes vulnerable to leakage or duplication (Alkhodair and Alkhudhayr, 2025).

- Data Security and Privacy

IoT generates massive amounts of data, which is then utilized by AI and recorded by Blockchain. However, maintaining the confidentiality of sensitive information such as customer data, machine activity, or supply chains in an open network is a serious challenge (Sekti, 2025). Attacks on the network or manipulation of AI data can cause financial losses to a company's reputation.

- High Initial Investment Costs

Implementing IoT sensor networks, training AI, and building Blockchain systems requires large funds. Costs for infrastructure, training, system integration, and technology consulting can be a barrier, especially for small and medium-sized businesses without gradual funding support.

- Shortage of Skilled Experts

Human resources with multidisciplinary skills such as programming, data science, cybersecurity, and manufacturing understanding are needed. However, most of the manufacturing workforce is still familiar with traditional systems. Without a comprehensive reskilling and upskilling program, technology adoption will stall (Soegoto et al., 2025).

- Cross-Border Regulation and Compliance

Differences in regulations in different countries, especially related to data protection and the legality of digital transactions, can complicate implementation. A concrete example is the incompatibility of the use of Blockhain with GDPR regulations in Europe. Companies need to ensure that their system is legal and efficient.

For instance, the GDPR (EU), CCPA (California, USA), and PIPL (China) each impose different requirements regarding data ownership, user consent, and data deletion, which could conflict with the immutable nature of blockchain-based records.

a. GDPR: Right to rectification and erasure (Articles 16 & 17) clash with blockchain's immutability, which complicates compliance in public ledger systems. Solutions like off-chain storage or append-only records are explored in recent studies (Zafar, 2025).
b. CCPA: Blockchain's permanent retention of user data may conflict with rights granted to California residents, such as deletion upon request, especially if immutable records include personal data (Liyanaarachchi et al., 2024).
c. While specific Scopus-indexed studies on PIPL (China's law) in blockchain manufacturing contexts are sparse, the PIPL was enacted in August 2021 and

mandates explicit user consent, data localization, and deletion rights, raising similar conflicts with permanent ledger systems

In addition to technical challenges, there are several strategic considerations that must also be considered for the transformation to be effective and sustainable:

- Organizational Cultural Resistance

Digitalization is not only about technology, but also changes in the way we work. If top management supports the transformation, but operational workers resist it for fear of losing their jobs or discomfort with the new system, then internal resistance will arise. A comprehensive *change management* strategy is very important (Akram et al., 2022).

- Trust and Collaboration Between Partners

Although Blockchain is referred to as a "trustless" technology, in reality its implementation still requires transparent human collaboration. *Smart contracts* and AI models are only as effective as data and commitment of the parties. If biased data or parameters are not mutually agreed, the results can be inaccurate (Kraus and Kraus, 2025).

FUTURE OUTLOOK

The future of smart manufacturing will be greatly influenced by the continued evolution of Artificial Intelligence (AI), Internet of Things (IoT), and Blockchain, as the industry grows to become more resilient, adaptive, and ethical. These three technologies will be the backbone of industrial transformation towards the Industry 5.0 era, where collaboration between humans and machines becomes more prominent than just automation (Alkhodair and Alkhudhayr, 2025). In this section, we will explore the key trends and possible breakthroughs that will shape the digital manufacturing landscape in the future.

Federated Learning and Decentralized AI

Federated learning will be a key approach to AI training in a global manufacturing environment without sacrificing data privacy. This technology allows training of AI models locally in individual factories, without the need to send raw data to the center (Alzubaidi et al., 2025). This approach maintains compliance with data regulations and reduces the risk of sensitive information leakage. This model allows for learning-based insight sharing, without sharing actual data, creating new synergies within a decentralized industrial ecosystem (Essaid and Ju, 2025).

In addition, distributed AI strengthens data security by decentralizing processing sources and lowering latency in system response, making it suitable for application in adaptive decision-making in factory environments (Sayal et al., 2025)

6G and Ultra-High-Speed IoT

If 5G has already accelerated IoT connectivity in the industry, then 6G will bring the next significant leap. With near-zero latency and ultra-wide bandwidth, 6G enables real-time transmission of high-resolution video, complex sensor signals, and machine-to-machine communication at scale (Chen et al., 2024). It will support augmented intelligence instantly on the production line, as well as enable haptic interaction between humans and machines in remote factories.

The IoT of the future will be more than just a monitoring tool, it will act as a cybernetic system capable of learning the habits of operators, recognizing the context of the environment, and adjusting responses automatically (Das et al., 2025). Thus, smart factories will transform into autonomous systems that are able to adapt to market demand, raw material conditions, and even weather predictably.

Quantum Resistant Blockchain and Generative Smart Contracts

While blockchain already guarantees integrity and transparency, new challenges arise from the potential threat of quantum computing to conventional cryptography. Therefore, going forward we will see the adoption of quantum-resistant blockchains, which are designed with post-quantum cryptographic algorithms to ensure long-term data security.

In addition, there will be a generative smart contract, which is a digital contract that can dynamically adjust based on changing conditions. Generative contracts can adjust conditions automatically, such as changing the logistics schedule when there is a delay in delivery without the need for manual intervention (Rafiq et al., 2025). For example, logistics contracts between factories can modify agreements automatically in the event of supply disruptions, without human intervention. This will be particularly useful in managing complex and frequently changing global supply chains.

Ethical Framework and Responsible AI

One of the key pillars in the future of this technology integration is the development of a responsible AI ethics and policy framework. Ethics and responsibility are major concerns in the development of future AI. Intelligent systems must be designed to be fair, transparent, and auditable by humans (Olawale, Olawumi and Oladapo, 2025). In the context of manufacturing, AI not only makes technical decisions, but also impacts human work, safety, and operational fairness. Therefore, companies must develop AI that is unbiased, auditable, and upholds the principles of transparency.

Explainable AI (XAI) technology will become standard in helping users understand the reasoning behind algorithmic decisions, thereby increasing accountability and trust (Rafiq et al., 2025). Fairness audits on AI models will be part of the industry's compliance with the principles of fairness and nondiscrimination but can still be understood and supervised by humans.

CONCLUSION

The integration of Artificial Intelligence (AI), Internet of Things (IoT), and Blockchain in smart manufacturing is more than just a technological convergence, it is the foundation of a new industrial paradigm that aligns with the principles of Industry 5.0, emphasizing both technological advancement and human-centric values.

This chapter has examined how AI functions as the cognitive core for predictive analytics and autonomous decision-making, how IoT acts as a sensory and control network that captures real-time operational data, and how Blockchain secures the integrity, transparency, and traceability of manufacturing processes. Together, these technologies create a synergistic framework that enables smart factories to be not only more efficient internally, but also more transparent, personalized, and responsive to consumers.

Integrated manufacturing systems powered by these technologies offer significant advantages: from dynamic product customization and predictive maintenance to end-to-end supply chain visibility. As a result, they enhance customer trust, reduce waste, and boost overall value delivery.

However, realizing this future demands more than technical readiness. To truly advance toward Industry 5.0, manufacturers and technology stakeholders must take deliberate strategic steps:

1. Pilot Testing the Integrated Framework Before full-scale deployment, companies should conduct pilot implementations of the AI-IoT-Blockchain architecture

in controlled environments. This allows for early identification of integration challenges, performance benchmarks, and customization needs across diverse industrial contexts.

2. Adoption of Open Standards and Interoperability Protocols Ensuring smooth communication between legacy systems and emerging technologies requires the adoption of open, non-proprietary standards. This step is crucial for avoiding vendor lock-in and enabling broader cross-platform integration.
3. Human-Centered Co-Design Processes To ensure that these technologies augment rather than replace the human workforce, it is essential to involve operators, engineers, and end-users in the system design process. Through participatory design methods, organizations can build ergonomic, inclusive, and ethically aligned smart manufacturing environments.

Looking forward, the future of smart manufacturing will likely incorporate decentralized AI models, ultra-fast IoT networks powered by 6G, and Blockchain systems resilient to quantum threats. The goal is not merely to build more advanced factories, but to shape a responsible industrial ecosystem that harmonizes intelligence, transparency, and humanity.

In conclusion, AI, IoT, and Blockchain are not auxiliary tools but transformative enablers. Organizations that proactively embrace this triadic integration, while also addressing ethical, social, and technical concerns, will be best positioned to lead in the next era of industrial innovation.

REFERENCES

Aamer, A., Zadeh, A., Mali, P., & Bolick, C. (2025). Emerging technologies and principle-based project management: A systematic literature review and research agenda. *Management Review Quarterly*, *75*(2), 1761–1811. DOI: 10.1007/s11301-024-00419-y

Abdullah, M., Mengash, H. A., Maray, M., Alrslani, F. A. F., Alkhudhayr, H., Alghanmi, N. A., Subahi, A., & Majdoubi, J. (2025). Federated learning with Blockchain on Denial-of-Service attacks detection and classification of edge IIoT networks using Deep Transfer Learning model. *Computers & Electrical Engineering*, *124*, 110319. Advance online publication. DOI: 10.1016/j.compeleceng.2025.110319

Admoko, D. A., Darmawan, B., Ana, A., & Dwiyanto, V. (2024). A Cluster-Based Bibliometric Analysis of the Emerging Technological Landscape in Logistics using Vosviewer. *Journal of Advanced Research in Applied Sciences and Engineering Technology*, *42*(2), 234–249. DOI: 10.37934/araset.42.2.234249

Ahmed, W. A. H., & Rios, A. (2022). *Chapter 18 - Digitalization of the international shipping and maritime logistics industry: a case study of TradeLens* (B. L. MacCarthy & D. B. T.-T. D. S. C. Ivanov (eds.); pp. 309–323). Elsevier. 10.1016/B978-0-323-91614-1.00018-6

Akram, S. V., Malik, P. K., Singh, R., Gehlot, A., Juyal, A., Ghafoor, K. Z., & Shrestha, S. (2022). Implementation of Digitalized Technologies for Fashion Industry 4.0: Opportunities and Challenges. *Scientific Programming*, *2022*, 1–17. Advance online publication. DOI: 10.1155/2022/7523246

Alkhodair, M., & Alkhudhayr, H. (2025). Harnessing Industry 4.0 for SMEs: Advancing Smart Manufacturing and Logistics for Sustainable Supply Chains. *Sustainability (Basel)*, *17*(3), 813. Advance online publication. DOI: 10.3390/su17030813

Alzubaidi, L., Jebur, S. A., Jaber, T. A., Mohammed, M. A., Alwzwazy, H. A., Saihood, A., Gammulle, H., Santamaria, J., Duan, Y., Fookes, C., Jurdak, R., & Gu, Y. (2025). ATD Learning: A secure, smart, and decentralised learning method for big data environments. *Information Fusion*, *118*, 102953. Advance online publication. DOI: 10.1016/j.inffus.2025.102953

Arnob, A. K. B., Chowdhury, R. R., Chaiti, N. A., Saha, S., & Roy, A. (2025). A comprehensive systematic review of intrusion detection systems: Emerging techniques, challenges, and future research directions. *Journal of Edge Computing*, *4*(1), 73–104. DOI: 10.55056/jec.885

Charfare, R. H., Desai, A. U., Keni, N. N., Nambiar, A. S., & Cherian, M. M. (2024). IoT-AI in Healthcare: A Comprehensive Survey of Current Applications and Innovations. *International Journal of Robotics and Control Systems*, *4*(3), 1446–1472. DOI: 10.31763/ijrcs.v4i3.1526

Chen, Y., Lu, Y., Bulysheva, L., & Kataev, M. Y. (2024). Applications of Blockchain in Industry 4.0: A Review. *Information Systems Frontiers*, *26*(5), 1715–1729. DOI: 10.1007/s10796-022-10248-7

Das, P., Kumar, N., Jain, C., & Singh, M. (2025). Intelligent IoT-enabled healthcare solutions implementing federated meta-learning with blockchain. *Journal of Industrial Information Integration*, *45*, 100797. Advance online publication. DOI: 10.1016/j.jii.2025.100797

Essaid, M., & Ju, H. (2025). Blockchain Solutions for Enhancing Security and Privacy in Industrial IoT. *Applied Sciences (Basel, Switzerland)*, *15*(12), 6835. Advance online publication. DOI: 10.3390/app15126835

Hassan, A. H., Ahmed, E. M., Hussien, J. M., Sulaiman, R. B., Abdulhak, M., & Kahtan, H. (2025). A cyber physical sustainable smart city framework toward society 5.0: Explainable AI for enhanced SDGs monitoring. *Research in Globalization*, *10*, 100275. Advance online publication. DOI: 10.1016/j.resglo.2025.100275

Islam, R., Bose, R., Roy, S., Khan, A. A., Sutradhar, S., Das, S., Ali, F., & AlZubi, A. A. (2025). Decentralized trust framework for smart cities: A blockchain-enabled cybersecurity and data integrity model. *Scientific Reports*, *15*(1), 23454. Advance online publication. DOI: 10.1038/s41598-025-06405-y

Jap, K. P. (2024). Driving Competitive Edge in Sarawak's Manufacturing Industry: Leveraging Supply Chain Management, Smart Integration, and Circular Economy Practices. *Recoletos Multidisciplinary Research Journal*, *12*(2), 103–118. DOI: 10.32871/rmrj2412.02.08

Ji, B., Zhang, J., Wang, Y., Liu, J., & Wang, W. (2024). Achievable Rate Maximization for IRS-Assisted System with Relay Cooperation of IoT Network. *IEEE Transactions on Consumer Electronics*, *70*(1), 1020–1028. DOI: 10.1109/TCE.2023.3319491

Khan, A. A., Yang, J., Awan, S. A., Baqasah, A. M., Alroobaea, R., Chen, Y.-L., Ku, C. S., & Por, L. Y. (2025). Artificial Intelligence, Internet of Things, and Blockchain Empowering Future Vehicular Developments: A Comprehensive Multi-Hierarchical Lifecycle Review. *Human-Centric Computing and Information Sciences*, *15*, 1–19. DOI: 10.22967/HCIS.2025.15.013

Kraus, K., & Kraus, N. (2025). INSTITUTIONALIZATION OF THE METAVERSE BASED ON THE DEVELOPMENT OF THE EXABYTE ECONOMY AND GIG ECONOMY. *Journal of Vasyl Stefanyk Precarpathian National University*, *12*(2), 6–13. DOI: 10.15330/jpnu.12.2.6-13

Liyanaarachchi, G., Viglia, G., & Kurtaliqi, F. (2024). Addressing challenges of digital transformation with modified blockchain. *Technological Forecasting and Social Change*, *201*, 123254. 10.1016/j.techfore.2024.123254. DOI: 10.1016/j.techfore.2024.123254

Majumdar, S., & Awasthi, A. (2025). From Vulnerability to Resilience: Securing Public Safety GPS and Location Services with Smart Radio, Blockchain, and AI-Driven Adaptability. *Electronics (Basel)*, *14*(6), 1207. Advance online publication. DOI: 10.3390/electronics14061207

Obaidat, M. A., Rawashdeh, M., Alja'afreh, M., Abouali, M., Thakur, K., & Karime, A. (2024). Exploring IoT and Blockchain: A Comprehensive Survey on Security, Integration Strategies, Applications and Future Research Directions. *Big Data and Cognitive Computing*, *8*(12), 174. Advance online publication. DOI: 10.3390/bdcc8120174

Olawale, R. A., Olawumi, M. A., & Oladapo, B. I. (2025). Sustainable farming with machine learning solutions for minimizing food waste. *Journal of Stored Products Research*, *112*, 102611. Advance online publication. DOI: 10.1016/j.jspr.2025.102611

Periyasamy, A. P., & Periyasami, S. (2023). Rise of digital fashion and metaverse: Influence on sustainability. *Digital Economy and Sustainable Development*, *1*(1), 1–26. DOI: 10.1007/s44265-023-00016-z

Rafiq, J. E., Namir, A., Zakrani, A., Amraouy, M., & Bennane, A. (2025). A SYSTEMATIC MAPPING STUDY OF THE EVOLUTION OF EDUCATIONAL PRACTICES USING DISRUPTIVE DIGITAL TECHNOLOGY. *The Journal of Educators Online*, *22*(1). Advance online publication. DOI: 10.9743/JEO.2025.22.1.19

Sayal, A., Johri, A., Chaithra, N., Alhumoudi, H., & Alatawi, Z. (2025). Optimizing audit processes through open innovation: Leveraging emerging technologies for enhanced accuracy and efficiency. *Journal of Open Innovation*, *11*(3), 100573. Advance online publication. DOI: 10.1016/j.joitmc.2025.100573

Sekti, B. A. (2025a). Adversarial machine learning in industrial cybersecurity: Challenges and solutions. In *AI-Enhanced Cybersecurity for Industrial Automation* (pp. 363–386). DOI: 10.4018/979-8-3373-3241-3.ch018

Sekti, B. A. (2025b). Machine learning and artificial intelligence (AI) in manufacturing. In *Integrating Digital Innovation and Integrated Frameworks in Manufacturing* (pp. 255–292). DOI: 10.4018/979-8-3373-1082-4.ch011

Sekti, B. A. (2025c). Machine Learning vs. AI: Key Concepts. In *Implementing Enterprise Cybersecurity With AI* (pp. 1–27). DOI: 10.4018/979-8-3373-2252-0.ch001

Shahbazi, Z., & Byun, Y. C. (2021). Smart manufacturing real-time analysis based on blockchain and machine learning approaches. *Applied Sciences (Basel, Switzerland), 11*(8), 3535. Advance online publication. DOI: 10.3390/app11083535

Soegoto, E. S., Meliala, B. N., Luckyardi, S., & Kurniawan, B. (2025). COMPUTER SCIENCE RESEARCH IN INDONESIA TO CREATE SUSTAINABLE INFRASTRUCTURE FOR UNITED NATIONS SUSTAINABLE DEVELOPMENT GOALS. *Journal of Engineering Science and Technology, 20*(3), 670–685.

Tahsin, R., Rantu, S. B. A., Rahman, M., Salman, S., & Karim, M. R. (2025). Towards the adoption of AI, IoT, and Blockchain technologies in Bangladesh's maritime industry: Challenges and insights. *Results in Engineering, 25*, 103825. Advance online publication. DOI: 10.1016/j.rineng.2024.103825

Verma, R. (2025). The Confluence of Cryptography, Blockchain and Artificial Intelligence. In *The Confluence of Cryptography*. Blockchain and Artificial Intelligence., DOI: 10.1201/9781032711515

Yamoah, L. E., Mensah, R. O., & Frimpong, A. (2025). The benefits, challenges and implications for integrating emerging technologies in risk evaluation procedures for supply chains in transportation logistics. *Discover Sustainability, 6*(1), 476. Advance online publication. DOI: 10.1007/s43621-025-01295-6

Zafar, A. (2025). Reconciling blockchain technology and data protection laws: Regulatory challenges, technical solutions, and practical pathways. *Journal of Cybersecurity, 11*(1), tyaf002. Advance online publication. DOI: 10.1093/cybsec/tyaf002

Chapter 8

AI in Wildlife Conservation

Muhamad Ilham Suparno
http://orcid.org/0009-0006-3572-3163
Universitas Esa Unggul, Indonesia

Yohanes Bowo Widodo
http://orcid.org/0000-0001-6135-3350
Universitas Mohammad Husni Thamrin Jakarta, Indonesia

Jusung Moon
http://orcid.org/0009-0004-2513-9364
CCRI, Asia University, Taiwan

Sourasis Chattopadhyay
http://orcid.org/0009-0000-7435-6550
Kalinga Institute of Industrial Technology, India

ABSTRACT

Artificial Intelligence (AI) is transforming wildlife conservation by enabling faster, more accurate, and scalable approaches to species monitoring, habitat mapping, and behavioral analysis. Through computer vision, AI can automatically detect and classify animals in millions of camera trap images, while acoustic models identify species through their vocalizations in complex environments. Satellite and drone imagery integrated with AI supports habitat assessment and anti-poaching surveillance. Digital twin ecosystems offer dynamic simulations for predicting environmental changes and guiding proactive interventions. Despite challenges such as limited datasets, interpretability issues, and ethical concerns, AI is becoming an

DOI: 10.4018/979-8-2600-0013-7.ch008

essential tool in conservation science. When deployed transparently and inclusively, AI enhances human capacity to respond effectively to the biodiversity crisis and supports long-term ecological stewardship.

1. INTRODUCTION

Biodiversity is facing an unprecedented decline. The World Wildlife Fund (WWF) has reported that wildlife populations have plummeted by an average of 69% since 1970, driven by habitat loss, poaching, climate change, and pollution. To reverse this alarming trend, conservation efforts must evolve from traditional methods into data-driven, scalable, and predictive systems. Artificial Intelligence (AI), defined as a set of technologies that enable machines to sense, comprehend, learn, and act autonomously or semi-autonomously, is increasingly at the heart of this transformation (Rahaman et al., 2025). A lightweight artificial intelligence (AI) model that is particularly appropriate for use for the classification of African ungulate in areas with typically lower resources where wildlife is found (Petso et al., 2025).

Over the past five years, Artificial Intelligence (AI) has emerged as a transformative force in biodiversity monitoring and wildlife management. From classifying millions of camera trap images to interpreting acoustic recordings of elusive species and predicting migration routes using spatiotemporal models, AI now supports real-time decision-making across vast geographic scales. The integration of AI with Internet of Things (IoT) sensors, drones, satellite imagery, and even digital twins is fostering the creation of intelligent ecological systems capable of sensing and responding dynamically to environmental changes and emerging threats (Rohhila et al., 2025). These technologies collectively enable conservationists to monitor complex ecosystems more efficiently, enhancing both accuracy and responsiveness in environmental management. The healthcare ecosystem is migrating from legacy systems to the Internet of Things (IoT), and resulting in digital-based care (Al-saggaf et al., 2023).

A major breakthrough has been the use of computer vision in processing camera trap images, which often number in the thousands per week in protected areas. Manual classification is slow and resource-intensive, but AI models—particularly Convolutional Neural Networks (CNNs)—have achieved over 90% accuracy across multiple ecosystems and species. Similarly, bioacoustic monitoring has become a key frontier in AI-driven conservation. Deep learning models such as Recurrent Neural Networks (RNNs) and spectrogram-based CNNs can detect and classify calls of birds, amphibians, and marine mammals from massive audio datasets. Systems like BirdNET, trained on over 1,000 bird species, have proven reliable in real-world environments. Beyond detection, AI also supports prediction through machine learning algorithms such as Random Forests and Gradient Boosting, which are used in species distribution modeling (SDM) to forecast habitat changes under climate stress (Gaurav et al., 2026). These predictive insights are helping policymakers anticipate biodiversity shifts and design future protected areas. Protected areas face the growing challenge of balancing biodiversity conservation with the pressures of nature-based tourism. Geospatial explicit frameworks that integrating social big data analytics and species distribution modeling (SDM) can assess the ecological pressures caused by tourism (Liu & Liu, 2025).

One of the most promising frontiers is the integration of AI with digital twin ecosystems—virtual replicas of real-world environments that simulate ecological interactions and responses to land-use changes, fires, or climate pressures. By combining live sensor data with adaptive AI models, digital twins can dynamically update predictions and guide conservation policies more effectively. Similarly, AI is revolutionizing anti-poaching operations by analyzing spatial and temporal patterns of illegal activity, generating optimized patrol routes, and detecting anomalies in real time (Sharma et al., 2024). However, the widespread adoption of AI in conservation brings several challenges. Data bias remains a critical issue, as many AI models are trained on datasets that underrepresent tropical and arid regions or rare species. The opaque nature of deep learning models also raises interpretability concerns, driving the development of explainable AI (XAI) techniques to make conservation decisions more transparent and accountable (Mubarakali & AlJarullah, 2025).

Ethical implications are equally significant. Deploying drones, cameras, or acoustic sensors in indigenous or remote communities raises privacy and consent concerns that demand culturally sensitive approaches. AI in conservation must avoid technological colonialism and prioritize community participation. Moreover, capacity gaps persist in biodiversity-rich regions of the Global South, where limited infrastructure and technical expertise hinder AI deployment. Addressing these disparities requires open-access tools, cross-institutional partnerships, and inclusive training initiatives. Despite these challenges, the potential of AI to transform conservation is unparalleled. As computational power becomes more affordable and cloud-based models more accessible, future conservation efforts may feature fully autonomous observatories, intelligent wildlife corridors, and interactive digital twin reserves. Ultimately, AI offers not only analytical precision but also new opportunities for public engagement through virtual and augmented reality experiences, fostering global empathy and action for biodiversity (AlZu'bi et al., 2019).

2. AI TECHNOLOGIES IN WILDLIFE CONSERVATION

2.1 Computer Vision and Camera Traps

Camera traps have long been essential tools for ecological monitoring and wildlife research. These motion-activated cameras enable non-intrusive observation of species in their natural habitats, providing valuable insights into animal presence, abundance, and behavior. However, the manual processing of millions of images generated by these devices is labor-intensive and susceptible to human error. In recent years, advances in computer vision and deep learning have made it possible to automate this process, significantly increasing efficiency, scalability, and accuracy. Computer vision, a subfield of artificial intelligence (AI), uses algorithms particularly convolutional neural networks (CNNs) to analyze and interpret visual data. These models can be trained to recognize species, detect individuals, count population sizes, and classify behaviors. Once trained, these systems can rapidly process thousands of images, significantly reducing the burden on ecologists and improving consistency in classification (Jo et al., 2022).

One of the most widely adopted tools in this domain is Microsoft's MegaDetector, an open-source object detection model designed for camera trap imagery. It categorizes images into broad classes animal, human, vehicle, or empty and is often used as a preprocessing step before species identification. MegaDetector has been integrated into large-scale conservation efforts such as Snapshot Serengeti, which monitors mammal populations across the Tanzanian plains. By filtering out non-target images, MegaDetector allows researchers to focus on relevant wildlife content, improving both processing speed and accuracy. Another notable system is Wildbook, which employs computer vision to identify individual animals based on unique natural patterns, such as zebra stripes, whale shark spots, or elephant ear shapes. This functionality allows researchers to monitor individual life histories, assess survival rates, and estimate population sizes without physical tagging. Tracking animal behavior in a grouped situation is important for precision farming, which is a challenge in diverse and crowded environments (Parmiggiani et al., 2023).

More advanced AI applications also involve behavioral recognition. Using time-lapse imagery and video data, models can classify actions such as foraging, grooming, or territorial displays. These data contribute to behavioral ecology studies, particularly when observing elusive or nocturnal species. Camera trap networks can also function under nighttime or low-light conditions using infrared or thermal imaging. AI models trained on such datasets can distinguish heat signatures and motion patterns in the absence of visual cues, enabling 24/7 monitoring. Recent developments include smart camera traps that feature embedded AI chips capable of on-site inference. These devices can detect species, filter empty frames, and transmit only meaningful data, thus reducing storage and energy consumption. This edge-computing approach is particularly useful in remote conservation areas with limited connectivity (Saini et al., 2023).

2.2 Acoustic Monitoring

Acoustic monitoring is a powerful method for studying wildlife, especially species that are cryptic, nocturnal, or inhabit inaccessible environments. Many animals produce vocalizations that are unique to species, individuals, or behaviors. By recording and analyzing these sounds, researchers can detect species presence, estimate population sizes, and monitor behavior without visual contact. The rapid growth of bioacoustics has been facilitated by AI techniques capable of parsing massive audio datasets. Recurrent neural networks (RNNs) and CNNs are particularly effective for analyzing spectrograms visual representations of sound frequencies over time. These models can identify call patterns, distinguish between overlapping vocalizations, and classify sounds even in noisy environments.

One of the most impactful projects in this area is the Elephant Listening Project, which uses autonomous acoustic sensors to detect forest elephant calls in Central African rainforests. These sensors collect low-frequency rumbles that are processed by AI models to monitor elephant movements, social behavior, and responses to poaching threats. Additionally, these systems can detect gunshots and chainsaw sounds, serving as early-warning systems for illegal activities. Another important application is bird song analysis, which is commonly used in avian diversity studies. In the Amazon rainforest, AI has been used to monitor frogs and birds based on their acoustic signatures. Deep learning models capable of distinguishing among dozens of frog species based on call characteristics, even in acoustically dense environments (Rahaman, Chattopadhyay, et al., 2022). This method provides a non-invasive alternative to visual surveys and can be scaled over vast areas.

AI-powered acoustic systems are also used to evaluate habitat quality. Soundscape ecology examines patterns in biotic, geophonic, and anthropogenic sounds to assess ecosystem health. For instance, reductions in vocal activity may signal ecological degradation, while increases in anthropogenic noise may indicate encroachment or fragmentation. Challenges persist in this field, particularly regarding ambient noise, overlapping species calls, and variations in terrain that affect sound propagation. However, recent models incorporating transfer learning and noise augmentation techniques are improving the robustness and generalizability of acoustic classifiers.

In underwater environments, AI has enabled real-time detection of whale and dolphin vocalizations, helping conservationists monitor migration routes, calving grounds, and the impact of shipping noise on marine megafauna. CNN-RNN hybrids could detect endangered whale calls in the Pacific, contributing to shipping lane adjustments and noise mitigation policies. Moreover, acoustic data offers continuous monitoring. While visual surveys are limited by daylight and weather, acoustic recorders can operate 24/7 for months, providing time-series data that is invaluable for detecting long-term changes in population dynamics or behavioral shifts.

2.3 Satellite and Drone Imaging

Remote sensing via satellites and drones has opened new frontiers in wildlife monitoring by providing synoptic and high-resolution views of landscapes, habitats, and even species. These tools complement on-ground observations by capturing data at scales and resolutions otherwise unattainable. Satellites such as Landsat 8, Sentinel 2, and PlanetScope provide multispectral imagery that, when analyzed with AI, can reveal vegetation indices, water bodies, land-use change, and habitat fragmentation. Deep learning models, particularly U-Net architectures, are used for semantic segmentation, allowing precise classification of land cover types and monitoring of deforestation or wetland degradation. AI has also enabled species-level monitoring via satellite. For example, CNNs have been trained to detect large animals such as elephants or whales from high-resolution satellite images. This approach allows researchers to conduct broad-scale censuses without disturbing animals or relying on costly aerial surveys.

Drone-based imaging adds even greater flexibility. Drones equipped with RGB, thermal, LiDAR, or hyperspectral sensors can collect data at customizable altitudes and angles. This enables detailed assessments of canopy structure, microhabitats, and animal distribution at local scales. AI models like YOLO (You Only Look Once) and Mask R-CNN are applied to drone footage for real-time species detection and tracking. A notable implementation is in Kenya and South Africa, where AI-powered UAV patrols assist in anti-poaching operations. These drones fly over protected areas at night using thermal cameras to detect poachers. AI models process the data in real-time, distinguishing humans from wildlife and triggering alerts for rapid ranger response.

Furthermore, drone swarms equipped with AI coordination protocols are being tested to patrol large conservation landscapes. These systems communicate in real time to avoid overlaps, adjust flight paths based on animal movement, and share data for centralized analysis. This approach maximizes coverage while reducing the risk of missing critical events. Another promising application is the integration of AI with drone-based LiDAR for 3D habitat reconstruction. This technique provides detailed structural data about forest canopies, tree height, and understory complexity factors essential for modeling species-habitat relationships. Satellite and drone imagery, when combined with historical datasets and ecological models, also support predictive analytics. For instance, AI models can forecast habitat suitability under various climate scenarios, aiding long-term conservation planning and the identification of climate refugia.

However, these technologies come with their own set of limitations. High-resolution satellite imagery is costly and may be restricted by cloud cover. Drone deployment requires permits, trained operators, and weather-dependent scheduling. Additionally, AI models require substantial computing power and reliable training data to function effectively across varied terrains and biomes. Table 1 shows the Comparison of AI Techniques Across Modalities.

Table 1. Comparison of AI Techniques Across Modalities

AI Technique	Sensor/Input	Application	Accuracy (%)	Source
CNN	Camera Trap Images	Species detection, behavior recognition	92–97	Martínez Balvanera & Mac Aodha (2025)
RNN + CNN	Spectrogram (Acoustic Data)	Bird/frog call detection	89–94	Jensen et al. (2022)
YOLOv5	Thermal Drone Footage	Poacher and wildlife tracking	90–95	Dhamotharan et al. (2025)
U-Net + RF	Satellite Imagery	Habitat segmentation, deforestation detection	85–93	Zhang et al. (2023)

3. DIGITAL TWINS IN ECOLOGY AND BIODIVERSITY

3.1 Concept of Ecological Digital Twins

Digital twins (DTs) are advanced virtual replicas of real-world systems that can be updated in real time through continuous input from physical data sources. In ecology, Ecological Digital Twins (EDTs) refer to dynamic, interactive virtual ecosystems that simulate species populations, their behaviors, and interactions with biotic and abiotic components of their habitats. These models are not just passive representations but evolve based on incoming environmental data and can be used for decision-making in conservation and ecological forecasting. Integrating real-time data with machine learning through digital twin frameworks could offer promising directions for climate-resilient agriculture and space-based plant growth systems (Liang et al., 2025).

Simulating Animal Populations and Migration in Virtual Ecosystems

One of the most promising applications of EDTs is the simulation of animal population dynamics and migration within lifelike digital environments. These simulations use complex models based on population ecology, ethology, and biogeography. A notable implementation is the Cranes Radar project, which developed a digital twin for the Eurasian crane (Grus grus) to track and predict its migratory routes across Europe. Integrating satellite telemetry data, weather patterns, and habitat variables, this DT provided valuable insights into how migration patterns respond to environmental disturbances such as habitat fragmentation or climate anomalies.

The TwinEco framework is a unified platform where animal migration, predation, breeding behavior, and mortality can be dynamically modeled. It captures key ecological phenomena such as carrying capacity, predator-prey relationships, stochastic events, and interspecies interactions in a synchronized manner. With artificial intelligence-driven prediction layers, TwinEco adapts its simulations to real-world anomalies like unexpected droughts or disease outbreaks, allowing researchers to visualize and test future ecological states. As virtual copies of real-world phenomena, digital twins are rapidly gaining popularity in industry, academia and policy. Their main strength is informing decision makers in an operational environment by giving detailed up-to-date information about the systems represented in the digital twins, such as industrial production systems or weather forecasts (De Koning, 2025; Safiyev & Shikhaliyeva, 2025).

These models are especially beneficial for endangered species. By simulating different conservation interventions (e.g., introducing corridors, habitat restoration), researchers can identify which strategies yield optimal survival rates under varying environmental conditions. For instance, the response of caribou populations in Northern Europe to expanding logging roads and climate-driven permafrost loss was analyzed using a virtual boreal ecosystem model.

Predicting Species Response to Climate Scenarios or Deforestation

Digital twins in biodiversity modeling are instrumental in predicting species' responses to anthropogenic impacts such as deforestation, land-use change, and climate variability. By leveraging EDTs, conservationists can simulate various "what-if" scenarios and assess species resilience or extinction probability under future climate projections like those derived from CMIP6 datasets. The Scandinavian Virtual Forest initiative, for instance, modeled climate-induced phenological shifts among migratory birds and boreal mammals. It found that some species were unable to synchronize their breeding with the availability of food resources, potentially leading to reproductive failures and population declines. In these simulations, tree cover loss and warming temperatures directly altered species distribution models (SDMs), helping researchers identify climate refugia and prioritize conservation zones. Intelligent transportation systems (ITS) have been attracting the attention of industry and academia alike for addressing issues raised by the 2030 agenda for sustainable development goals (SDG) (Martinez et al., 2025).

Moreover, EDTs assist in forecasting the introduction and spread of invasive species in disturbed habitats. Simulating the removal of canopy trees in temperate forests, DTs revealed a significant increase in the establishment likelihood of Impatiens glandulifera and other aggressive non-natives. Such predictive models can inform early detection systems and control strategies. In summary, EDTs enable predictive, systems level insights into ecosystem behavior and biodiversity risks, equipping researchers and policymakers with tools for anticipatory and adaptive conservation strategies. Table 2 shows the Comparison of Key Ecological Digital Twin Platforms.

Table 2. Comparison of Key Ecological Digital Twin Platforms

Digital Twin Platform	Geographic Focus	Target Species/ System	Technologies Used	Real-time Integration	Key Applications
Cranes Radar	Europe (Germany)	*Grus grus* (Common Crane)	GPS telemetry, AI migration modeling	Yes	Migration prediction, conservation planning
TwinEco	Global (multi-site)	Multi-species ecosystems	AI modeling, ecological simulators	Yes	Biodiversity resilience testing, policy modeling
Virtual Forest	Scandinavia	Boreal mammals and flora	Remote sensing, forestry data, IoT sensors	Yes	Forest management, rewilding simulations
Poyang Lake EDT	China	Wetland ecosystems	3D landscape reconstruction, drone data	Partial	Water-level modeling, wetland species dynamics
Biodiversity DT (RDA)	Pan-European	Biodiversity indicators	FAIR data, semantic web integration	Not Yet	Monitoring ecosystem health, reporting to EU

3.2 Integration with IoT and Edge Devices

Modern EDTs achieve their full potential when integrated with Internet of Things (IoT) and edge computing technologies, creating a live link between physical and virtual ecosystems. Real-time data streaming from ecological sensors can continuously calibrate and enrich digital models, allowing dynamic simulations and rapid response planning (Ahmed et al., 2022). Figure 1 shows the Conceptual Diagram of an Ecological Digital Twin Ecosystem.

Figure 1. Conceptual Diagram of an Ecological Digital Twin Ecosystem

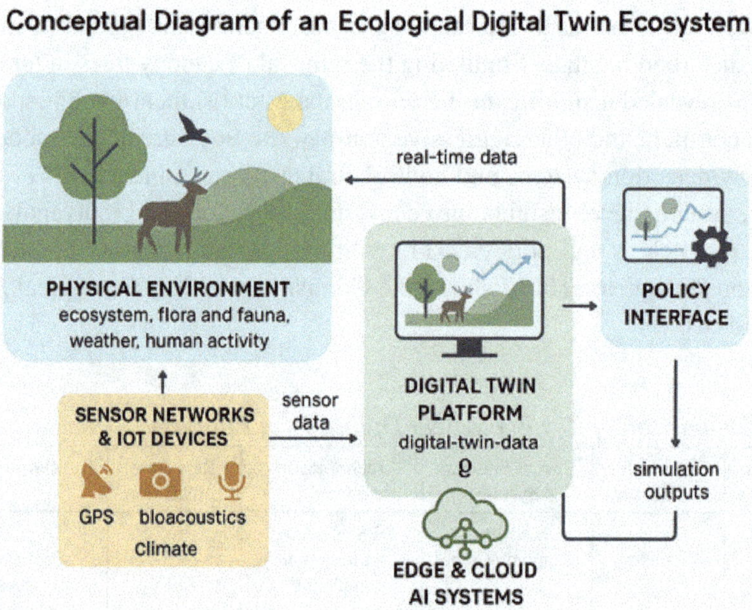

Remote Sensors Transmitting Data to the Twin in Real-Time

Sensors placed across terrestrial and aquatic ecosystems are now capable of tracking a wide range of parameters such as animal movement (via GPS collars), temperature and humidity (via microclimate loggers), acoustic signals (via bio-acoustic recorders), and phenological events (via automated cameras). These data streams are fed into digital twins to update their state and maintain high fidelity. In Germany, a network of autonomous environmental sensors was deployed across forest reserves to gather data on insect biomass, bird activity, plant flowering, and other biological indicators. This real-time data integration allowed the EDT to simulate forest succession processes, identify early signs of ecosystem stress, and recommend mitigation steps. Edge computing plays a critical role by allowing initial processing to occur near the sensor sites, which is particularly important for remote areas with limited bandwidth. For example, video feeds can be pre-processed for animal detection before being transmitted to the central EDT server, reducing both latency and data load.

Such architectures not only enable real-time ecological forecasting but also support field-level alert systems for poaching, species migration disruptions, or fire ignition thus closing the feedback loop between virtual simulation and physical action.

Enabling Dynamic Policy Simulations (e.g., Fencing, Fire Outbreaks)

Digital twins can simulate the impacts of proposed environmental policies in a virtual environment, allowing policy-makers to test hypotheses before enacting changes on the ground. For example, EDTs can model the ecological consequences of installing fences to restrict animal movement (e.g., in agricultural conflict zones) and estimate how such interventions alter migration patterns, gene flow, or predator-prey dynamics. One case from Northern Europe modeled various fire management strategies (e.g., controlled burns, firebreak zoning) and their impact on ecosystem regeneration, biodiversity retention, and carbon emissions. These simulations helped optimize fire management to maintain biodiversity while minimizing risk.

Another example from Finland involved simulating selective logging policies in boreal forests using an EDT model. By varying logging intensities and harvest rotations, researchers could estimate the trade-offs between timber yield and biodiversity, helping balance economic and ecological goals. Digital twins are also being applied to simulate invasive species control programs, restoration planning, and urban green infrastructure deployment. Their ability to incorporate temporal dynamics, spatial heterogeneity, and feedback loops makes them uniquely powerful in scenario testing and ecosystem management planning.

Case: "Virtual Forest" Digital Twin Models in Scandinavia

The Virtual Forest initiative stands out as a large-scale implementation of an ecological digital twin. Developed by a Nordic research consortium involving Norway, Sweden, and Finland, it integrates satellite remote sensing, ground-based sensors, and ecological modeling into a continuously updating forest ecosystem simulation platform. The model includes parameters such as soil carbon, biomass accumulation, understorey dynamics, tree species turnover, and animal habitat availability. Real-time monitoring informs how disturbances (e.g., logging, storms, bark beetle outbreaks) influence ecosystem composition and function. The Virtual Forest has been particularly instrumental in simulating the effect of EU biodiversity policies and climate targets on ecosystem structure and service delivery.

For instance, by simulating "business-as-usual" forestry versus rewilding strategies, researchers found that protecting only 20% of core habitats could result in up to 60% higher biodiversity index in key faunal groups over a 25-year horizon. These findings influence regional land-use planning and contribute to global biodiversity assessments. The project also fosters public engagement and education. Using immersive 3D visualization, Virtual Forests allow policymakers, citizens, and students to experience simulated ecosystem responses to human actions, thereby strengthening environmental awareness and stewardship.

4. USE CASES AND APPLICATIONS

4.1 Anti-Poaching Systems

Technological advances in artificial intelligence (AI), edge computing, and remote sensing are revolutionizing anti-poaching strategies in wildlife conservation. Traditional patrol-based approaches are increasingly being supplemented and in some areas replaced by predictive analytics and autonomous surveillance systems capable of real-time monitoring and threat detection (Sekti, 2025b)(Sekti, 2025a).

Predictive Analytics to Locate High-Risk Zones

The backbone of modern anti-poaching systems is predictive analytics, which involves analyzing historical poaching data, geographic information, and environmental conditions to identify potential future incidents. AI models such as random forests and deep learning architectures are trained on spatial and temporal patterns of poaching to generate risk maps.

A method that integrates satellite imagery and convolutional neural networks (CNNs) to detect areas vulnerable to poaching in real time. By identifying recurring spatial patterns such as proximity to roads or water sources, the system can guide ranger patrols more effectively and prioritize areas where intervention is most likely to prevent wildlife crimes. This proactive approach represents a shift from reactive enforcement to anticipatory conservation, enabling limited field resources to be deployed with greater efficiency and effectiveness.

Drone Patrols With Real-Time AI Threat Detection

Unmanned aerial vehicles (UAVs), commonly known as drones, are increasingly used for aerial surveillance of protected areas. When equipped with AI, these drones can automatically identify potential poaching threats such as human intrusions, animal carcasses, or environmental anomalies like fires or gunshots. A drone-based AI surveillance system capable of classifying targets from aerial imagery using deep learning algorithms. This system identifies humans, vehicles, and even weapons with high precision, especially in remote or difficult-to-access areas. The AI processes visual and thermal imagery onboard, which reduces the dependency on external cloud servers and ensures faster responses.

Furthermore, such drones have proven valuable during nighttime operations. Infrared sensors combined with machine learning models help detect unauthorized human presence or injured animals in darkness, which would otherwise go unnoticed by ground patrols.

Case: PAWS System (Protection Assistant for Wildlife Security)

The Protection Assistant for Wildlife Security (PAWS) system is a state-of-the-art application of game theory and machine learning in anti-poaching strategy. Developed collaboratively by computer scientists and conservationists, PAWS is designed to model the behavior of poachers and optimize ranger patrol paths accordingly. The use of Stackelberg security games to simulate the interaction between park rangers and poachers. In this framework, poachers are considered rational agents who adapt their behavior based on patrol patterns (Rahaman, Wisnujati, et al., 2022). PAWS leverages this model to recommend patrol strategies that maximize the likelihood of poacher deterrence and capture. Deployed in multiple countries such as Uganda and Cambodia, PAWS has demonstrated measurable improvements in anti-poaching outcomes, including reductions in snare density and improved ranger efficiency. Its integration with local data and adaptability to regional contexts makes it a versatile tool for conservation authorities. Table 3 shows the Comparison of Key Anti-Poaching Technologies. Figure 2 shows the Corridor Optimization Workflow Using Multi-Criteria GIS and Machine Learning.

Table 3. Comparison of Key Anti-Poaching Technologies

Technology	Functionality	AI Component	Real-Time Capable	Reference
PAWS System	Predictive patrol optimization	Game-theory + ML	No (planning stage)	Fang et al. (2021)
Edge-AI Drones	Thermal imaging, anomaly detection	Deep Learning (CNN)	Yes	Aliane (2025)
Spatial Risk Mapping	Hotspot detection using past incidents	Random Forest, CNN	Batch training	Xu et al. (2020)
Acoustic Sensors	Gunshot & chainsaw detection	Signal Classification	Yes	[Emerging prototypes]

Figure 2. Corridor Optimization Workflow Using Multi-Criteria GIS and Machine Learning

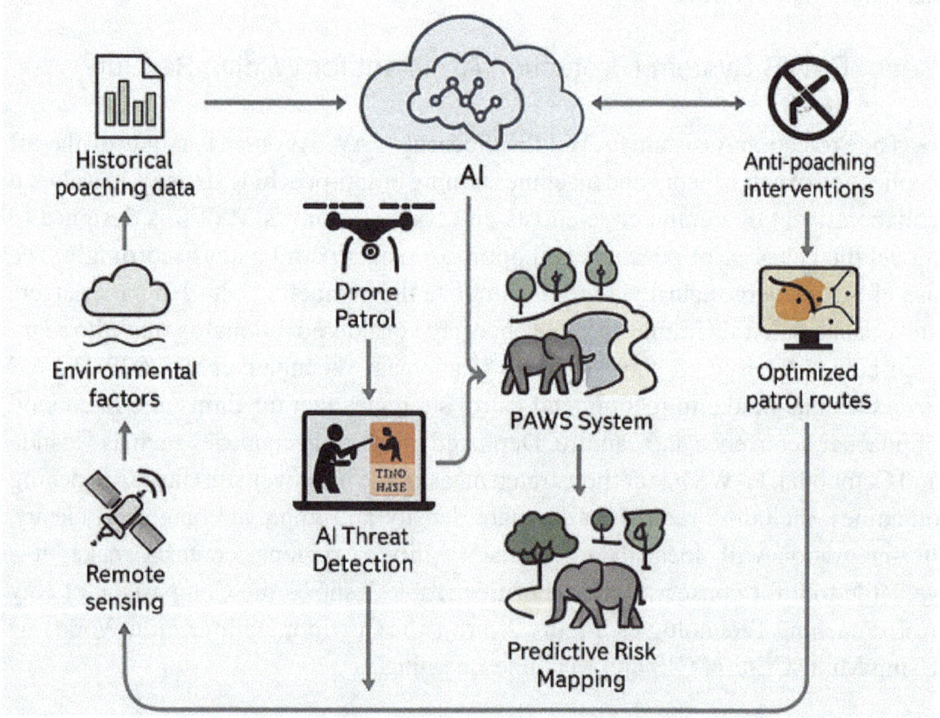

4.2 Conservation Planning

Conservation planning has matured from being static and map-based to dynamic and data-driven. With the rise of computational ecology and the integration of optimization models, stakeholders can now evaluate trade-offs between ecological, economic, and social objectives in real time.

Prioritizing Habitats and Corridors Using Optimization Models

Habitat loss and fragmentation are among the principal threats to biodiversity worldwide. To combat this, conservationists employ advanced optimization techniques to identify critical habitats and design ecological corridors that connect fragmented landscapes. A hybrid modeling approach in Kunming, China, integrating ecological network models and spatial prioritization tools. Their research identified avian corridors in an urbanizing region by coupling multi-scenario simulations and resistance surface modeling. The findings informed urban planning policies by identifying habitat patches that function as stepping stones for bird movement across the city.

Similarly, in farmers' preferences for integrating wildlife corridors into agricultural landscapes. Their optimization framework accounted for both ecological connectivity and farmer land-use preferences, illustrating that landscape-scale conservation is feasible even in intensively used rural areas when socio-economic constraints are integrated. A graph-based ecological connectivity optimization tool (GECOT) to maintain biodiversity in regions with complex urban-rural interfaces. Their model used graph theory to rank habitat patches by centrality and resistance, then optimized corridor placement to maximize species flow across a fragmented matrix. Such approaches are increasingly supported by AI algorithms capable of handling high-dimensional data, uncertainty, and multiple conflicting objectives, providing more realistic conservation solutions that go beyond traditional binary land classification.

Stakeholder-in-the-Loop Simulations With Virtual Stakeholders

Effective conservation planning must incorporate human behavior and decision-making. Stakeholder-in-the-loop modeling integrates virtual representations of stakeholders such as farmers, developers, or indigenous communities into the conservation planning process, allowing planners to simulate and adapt to diverse perspectives. Participatory modeling can be embedded into corridor planning by allowing landowners to evaluate scenarios in real time. Using interactive simulation platforms, stakeholders could input their land-use constraints or preferences and receive feedback on how different conservation layouts affect both biodiversity and economic returns.

Such participatory models can be connected to conservation optimization tools like MARXAN or Zonation, allowing simulations to adapt to stakeholder input dynamically. This enhances not only the ecological quality of conservation outcomes but also their social acceptance and long-term viability. The importance of including stakeholder simulations in tropical forest restoration projects. Their agent-based model showed that excluding local communities from the planning phase often led to project failure due to land-use conflicts, whereas simulations that involved community agents led to more equitable and sustainable outcomes.

4.3 Citizen Science Platforms

Citizen science represents one of the most inclusive forms of data generation in biodiversity research. Through mobile applications, web portals, and image annotation platforms, non-experts can contribute to large-scale data collection and processing, enhancing the reach and scale of scientific research. Crowdsourced Wildlife Labeling (Zooniverse). Platforms like Zooniverse have transformed the way ecological data is processed. Projects such as Snapshot Serengeti or Penguin Watch allow volunteers to identify species in millions of camera trap images. These labels are aggregated using statistical methods to ensure accuracy, and the results are then fed into AI models for automated image classification.

Crowdsourced image labels from Zooniverse achieved over 95% agreement with expert labels. The volume and speed of citizen input far exceeded what could be achieved through expert only labeling, allowing researchers to keep pace with the explosive growth of image data from field sensors. Moreover, the labeled datasets generated by volunteers now serve as training data for supervised learning models in wildlife recognition. These AI systems can be retrained periodically as new species or conditions are introduced into the dataset.

AI Platforms Trained Using Non-Expert Input

The integration of non-expert data into AI model training workflows is a significant advancement in the field of conservation technology. While citizen-labeled data may be noisier than expert labels, new training techniques such as semi-supervised learning and ensemble modeling have improved their utility. A hybrid training strategy where deep learning models are initially trained on high-confidence, expert labeled data. In a second stage, the models are fine-tuned using large volumes of citizen-labeled data. This approach increases model robustness and generalization while maintaining high precision (Beltrán, 2025; Blanco-Aza et al., 2025).

The Wildbook AI project is another example of leveraging public input for model training. Citizens upload images of animals like whale sharks or zebras, which are then analyzed using computer vision algorithms to track individual animals over time. This has greatly expanded the geographic and taxonomic scope of animal tracking programs. The rise of mobile applications like iNaturalist has also allowed real-time biodiversity reporting from virtually any location on Earth. These apps use AI to suggest species identifications, which users can confirm or correct, creating a feedback loop that continually improves model performance. Table 4 shiws the Key Citizen Science Platforms Supporting AI-based Biodiversity Monitoring.

Table 4. Key Citizen Science Platforms Supporting AI-based Biodiversity Monitoring

Platform	Data Type	Public Role	AI Use Case	Scale
Zooniverse	Camera trap images	Species identification	Image classification (CNNs)	100M+ labels
Wildbook AI	Animal photos	Submit photos, IDs	Individual recognition	30+ species tracked
iNaturalist	Mobile app sightings	Species tagging	Geolocation and ML tagging	Global, 100M records
Pl@ntNet	Plant images	Plant species IDs	Image recognition, crowd model	20,000+ species

5. CHALLENGES AND LIMITATIONS

Digital technologies such as AI, IoT, and digital twins have shown tremendous promise in biodiversity monitoring and conservation. However, several key limitations constrain their performance and scalability. These challenges include data-related biases, ethical issues around surveillance and consent, and technical barriers associated with deployment in remote and ecologically sensitive areas.

5.1 Data Bias and Generalization Issues

One of the most significant challenges in ecological AI systems is the problem of generalization, which refers to the inability of models trained in one geographical or ecological context to perform effectively in others. Many high-performing AI models are developed using datasets from well-studied regions such as North America, Europe, or African savannahs. When these models are applied to underrepresented areas such as Southeast Asia, the Congo Basin, or the Amazon, their accuracy often declines sharply. This limitation is largely due to the scarcity of labeled data from tropical rainforests, mountainous terrains, or marine environments. Rare and endangered species, which are the most in need of monitoring, frequently lack sufficient records to train machine learning algorithms. For example, available camera trap images or acoustic data for species like the Javan rhinoceros or the vaquita porpoise are too limited to produce robust detection models (Mohammad et al., 2025; Sharafat et al., 2025; V. et al., 2025).

Sampling bias further compounds this issue by affecting spatial data quality. Sensors and camera traps are commonly placed near accessible areas such as roads or research stations, leaving remote habitats underrepresented. This imbalance reduces model robustness and risks distorting conservation priorities by emphasizing well-studied areas over ecologically critical but less accessible regions. Machine learning models are also prone to errors when datasets are dominated by common species, resulting in overfitting toward abundant animals such as deer or common birds, while neglecting rare or cryptic species. Although recent methods such as data augmentation and synthetic image generation have improved model diversity, accurate ground-truth data remain essential. In marine ecosystems, the scarcity of annotated underwater imagery and audio recordings limits the performance of AI systems, making biodiversity assessments disproportionately biased toward terrestrial and near-shore environments.

5.2 Ethical and Social Implications

The growing use of digital surveillance technologies in conservation has introduced complex ethical and social challenges, particularly regarding privacy, consent, data ownership, and historical power imbalances with Indigenous and local communities. The deployment of drones, camera traps, and satellite tracking in Indigenous territories is often carried out without proper consultation or informed consent. For example, forest monitoring programs in Nepal raised concerns among local residents who feared criminalization and loss of control over ancestral lands. Such practices risk reproducing colonial patterns of exclusion under the pretext of environmental protection. In some areas, UAV surveillance has triggered historical trauma and deepened mistrust between conservation authorities and Indigenous groups. The absence of transparent communication about data collection and control often leads to community resistance or vandalism of equipment. Even passive monitoring tools, such as acoustic sensors, may unintentionally capture private human conversations, raising concerns about privacy violations in communal or sacred spaces where customary governance systems are already in place (Camilleri, 2024; Lim, 2024).

Data ownership and control represent another major ethical concern in the digital conservation landscape. In many community-based projects, ecological data are extracted locally but stored, analyzed, and commercialized by institutions in the Global North, creating exploitative knowledge hierarchies. Ethical frameworks such as the CARE Principles for Indigenous Data Governance, which emphasize collective benefit, authority to control, responsibility, and ethics, have been proposed to counterbalance the more technocratic FAIR data principles. However, implementation remains inconsistent, especially in projects led by private entities or international NGOs. Additionally, many digital conservation platforms lack multilingual accessibility and culturally relevant visualization, limiting Indigenous participation in data interpretation and decision-making. The use of opaque AI models further compounds these issues, as black-box algorithms often influence land-use decisions and resource restrictions without community oversight. These challenges highlight the need for transparent, inclusive, and rights-based governance structures in the application of AI and digital technologies for conservation.

5.3 Technical Barriers

The deployment of AI and sensor technologies in remote ecosystems faces significant operational and engineering challenges, including power constraints, harsh environmental conditions, and limitations in computing capability. Most AI-driven devices rely on batteries or solar panels, which are difficult to maintain in dense forests or regions with limited sunlight. Drone batteries drain rapidly in humid environments, and camera traps often fail due to condensation, fungal growth, or interference from wildlife. AI inference tasks such as real-time image or acoustic analysis require substantial computational resources that are often unavailable in wilderness settings lacking internet or stable power infrastructure. Edge-AI solutions must therefore operate efficiently on low-power, low-memory chips. Designing such systems for long-duration monitoring remains a major technical frontier. Field studies in the Amazon and other tropical regions have reported frequent sensor failures caused by moisture ingress, magnetic disruption, and physical damage by animals. Moreover, retrieving stored data from remote areas often requires manual collection, adding logistical and financial burdens to conservation efforts.

Data labeling also presents a critical bottleneck for scaling ecological AI. Complex habitats such as rainforests, coral reefs, and deep-sea environments host immense biodiversity but lack comprehensive, well-labeled datasets. Training AI systems to identify species from acoustic or visual data often demands weeks of expert annotation and still produces high error rates due to environmental noise and visual ambiguity. In marine contexts, low visibility and poor lighting further degrade imagery, complicating manual annotation. The absence of standardized taxonomies, inconsistent metadata, and limited open-access datasets hinder collaborative model development and algorithmic refinement across regions. Environmental harshness compounds these issues, as extreme heat, saltwater corrosion, dense vegetation, or animal interference frequently damage equipment. Devices such as GPS collars and camera traps can also affect animal behavior or welfare, while satellite-based systems, though less intrusive, are costly and often lack the resolution needed for fine-scale behavioral studies. These persistent barriers highlight the need for more resilient hardware, automated data processing methods, and standardized data-sharing frameworks to advance ecological AI in challenging field conditions. Figure 3 shows the Challenges and Limitations of AI in Wildlife Conservation.

Figure 3. Challenges and Limitations of AI in Wildlife Conservation

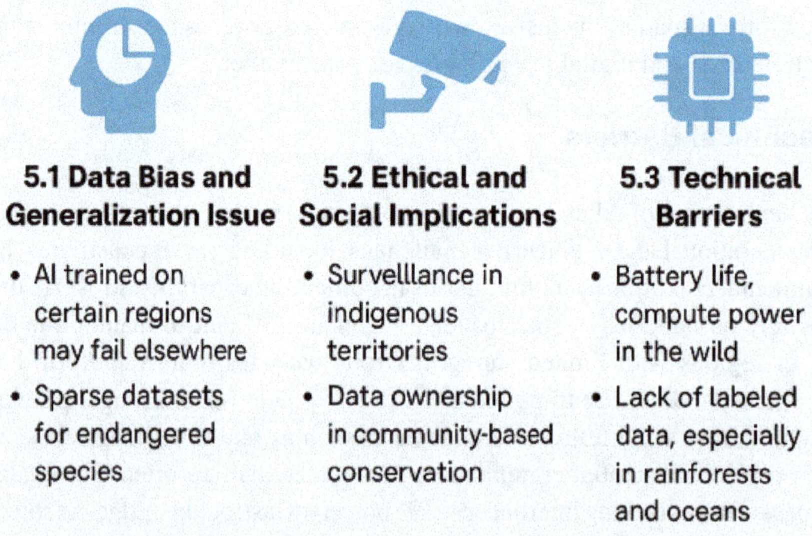

6. THE ROLE OF AI AND METAVERSE IN PUBLIC ENGAGEMENT

Artificial Intelligence (AI) and the Metaverse are transforming how people engage with biodiversity, conservation, and climate education. These technologies create immersive, interactive, and data-driven experiences that make complex ecological processes easier to understand and emotionally compelling. By integrating 3D simulations, virtual ecosystems, and AI-driven interactivity, learners can explore species behavior and environmental feedback loops without direct access to remote or fragile habitats. This approach expands accessibility and deepens public connection to nature through experiential learning.

6.1 Immersive Simulations for Education and Advocacy

Immersive learning environments in the Metaverse allow users to engage through multiple senses such as sight, sound, and touch, enhancing comprehension and emotional engagement. Virtual coral reef simulations, for instance, help users witness the effects of bleaching events, building empathy for marine conservation. AI contributes by personalizing these experiences through natural language processing and reinforcement learning that adjust content complexity, generate tailored narratives, and provide real-time feedback. Studies have shown that students using immersive biodiversity platforms demonstrate higher retention and empathy than those using traditional materials, particularly among learners with limited exposure to nature.

Virtual field trips guided by AI avatars are increasingly used as alternatives to physical excursions, providing educational access in areas where travel is limited. Similarly, advocacy organizations use immersive storytelling to support policy awareness and donor engagement. Projects such as the Amazon Rainforest Virtual Reality experience allow stakeholders to explore deforestation hotspots, observe habitat loss, and understand the human dimensions of environmental change. These experiences strengthen empathy, raise awareness, and have been shown to increase support for conservation initiatives.

6.2 Virtual Safaris and Digital Reconstructions of Extinct Ecosystems

Virtual safaris represent an innovative form of ecotourism and environmental education that allows global audiences to experience natural habitats in real time. By combining live wildlife feeds, GPS tracking, and AI-based species recognition, platforms like Wildverse and WildEarth deliver dynamic, educational safaris from anywhere in the world. These experiences democratize access to wildlife observation while reducing ecological footprints and minimizing the risks associated with traditional tourism in fragile or politically unstable regions. AI-generated commentary enhances user understanding by identifying species behavior and suggesting contextual ecological information.

Beyond live experiences, AI also powers digital reconstructions of extinct or endangered ecosystems, offering both historical and predictive insights. Using fossil records, climate models, and habitat simulations, AI algorithms recreate plausible environments such as the Pleistocene tundra or pre-industrial Amazon. These reconstructions help scientists and policymakers visualize baseline conditions for restoration and assess long-term ecological change. In museums and classrooms, interactive displays of extinct habitats promote environmental literacy and encourage reflection on biodiversity loss and recovery. Integrating such tools into education and cultural institutions builds awareness and appreciation of nature's historical and future resilience.

6.3 Gamified Biodiversity Awareness in Schools and Museums

Gamification has emerged as an effective approach to improving biodiversity literacy, particularly among younger audiences. Educational games enhanced with AI offer adaptive difficulty, instant feedback, and personalized progress tracking, making learning interactive and rewarding. Titles such as EcoAgents, MyBiome, and Extinction Crisis VR place players in roles such as ecologists or park rangers, challenging them to manage ecosystems, protect wildlife, and balance conservation with economic pressures. These simulations cultivate ecological reasoning, systems thinking, and empathy for real-world environmental challenges. Museums have adopted similar techniques through AR-based games where visitors can scan fossils, navigate rainforest mazes, or collect digital badges while engaging with biodiversity exhibits.

Gamified platforms are also being linked to citizen science initiatives where players contribute real-world biodiversity data through gameplay. For example, in Species Hunters, users submit wildlife photos that are validated by AI and integrated into research databases. This fusion of gaming and science transforms entertainment into meaningful conservation action. Furthermore, integrating local languages and traditional ecological knowledge into these experiences ensures inclusivity and cultural relevance. National education systems in countries such as India, Brazil, and South Africa have begun adopting AI-powered biodiversity learning apps aligned with the Sustainable Development Goals (SDGs), showing promising results in raising environmental awareness at the school level.

6.4 Challenges and Limitations

Despite their transformative potential, the use of AI and the Metaverse in biodiversity engagement presents several challenges. Limited access to high-speed internet, VR equipment, and digital infrastructure in rural or low-income regions perpetuates a digital divide that restricts inclusivity. Cultural bias in simulation design can reduce local relevance, while excessive gamification risks trivializing serious environmental issues. Additionally, AI-generated content can oversimplify ecological uncertainty and omit socio-political context, leading to misconceptions if not properly curated or explained.

To address these issues, developers and educators must embrace participatory and interdisciplinary collaboration. Platforms should be co-designed with ecologists, educators, artists, and community representatives to ensure cultural sensitivity, scientific integrity, and accessibility. Sustainable deployment will also require integrating open-source tools, affordable hardware options, and localized content development. By combining technological innovation with inclusive design, AI and the Metaverse can evolve into ethical and effective mediums for environmental education and advocacy.

7. FUTURE DIRECTIONS

Emerging technologies in artificial intelligence (AI), distributed computing, and immersive visualization are rapidly transforming how biodiversity is monitored, protected, and incorporated into decision-making. In the coming decade, ecological AI is expected to evolve through several frontier innovations, including privacy-preserving federated learning systems, autonomous AI agents for ecological patrols, digital twin marketplaces for climate solutions, and immersive policymaker interfaces that connect AR/VR with dynamic environmental models. These advancements promise not only to enhance precision and scalability in conservation but also to redefine the collaboration between humans and intelligent systems.

7.1 Federated Learning for Wildlife AI Across Regions Without Sharing Raw Data

Federated learning (FL) enables machine learning models to be collaboratively trained across multiple decentralized servers without transferring raw data to a central location. This approach is particularly valuable in ecological research, where data privacy, sovereignty, or logistical constraints make centralized data collection impractical. Through FL, national parks, universities, and community conservancies can jointly train AI models for species recognition, poaching risk prediction, or animal migration analysis while keeping sensitive images, audio, or GPS data stored locally. This enhances both privacy and model robustness across diverse habitats and environmental conditions.

For example, African countries tracking elephant migrations through GPS collars can co-develop predictive models without exchanging sensitive location data, preserving wildlife security while improving generalization across ecosystems. FL also mitigates the issue of rare species data imbalance by allowing regional contributions to inform collective learning. However, technical challenges such as communication latency, seasonal model drift, and limited computational capacity on edge devices persist. Emerging innovations such as asynchronous model updates and lightweight architectures are improving FL efficiency, positioning it as a cornerstone of collaborative, privacy-conscious conservation AI (Rahaman et al., 2024).

7.2 Autonomous AI Agents for Ecological Patrols

The deployment of autonomous AI agents—drones, terrestrial robots, and satellites equipped with real-time decision-making capabilities—is revolutionizing digital conservation. Unlike manually operated sensors, these agents can independently observe, navigate, and respond to ecological events. Multi-agent systems (MAS) are increasingly used in diverse ecosystems such as rainforests, savannas, and wetlands, where aerial drones monitor vegetation health, ground robots detect illegal activities, and static sensors collect environmental metrics. Each agent contributes local intelligence to a shared environmental objective, creating adaptive and scalable monitoring networks.

Notable examples include the PatrolBot initiative in Southeast Asia, where solar-powered ground robots equipped with AI vision autonomously patrol national parks and report poaching or habitat degradation. Reinforcement learning algorithms train these agents to optimize patrol routes based on dynamic threat data. Similar technologies are being applied in marine environments through underwater vehicles that detect coral bleaching or illegal trawling, and in wildfire monitoring using AI-enabled surveillance drones. Key challenges involve improving power autonomy, terrain adaptability, and ethical governance, particularly in landscapes inhabited by Indigenous communities..

7.3 Digital Twin Marketplaces for Climate Resilience Models

Digital twins, or virtual replicas of ecological and climate systems, are emerging as critical tools for simulating environmental change and guiding policy interventions. In the near future, these models will be accessible through digital twin marketplaces that function like app stores, where users can license, integrate, and customize ecosystem simulations. Such marketplaces will allow governments, NGOs, and researchers to deploy environmental models—ranging from flood response to carbon sequestration—through standardized and interoperable frameworks supported by FAIR and W3C protocols. These systems will enable data from satellites, sensors, and community observations to converge into dynamic, multi-scalar simulations.

For instance, a coastal municipality in Indonesia could subscribe to a mangrove resilience twin to test various adaptation scenarios, such as replanting or seawall construction, and evaluate their ecological and social trade-offs. Citizen scientists may also contribute local data, democratizing access to advanced modeling tools. However, issues related to intellectual property, model validation, and potential misuse for "greenwashing" remain significant concerns. The long-term success of these marketplaces will depend on open standards, transparent verification processes, and inclusive participation that ensures both scientific rigor and social equity..

7.4 AR/VR + Digital Twins for Policymaker Interaction With Biodiversity Models

Immersive technologies such as augmented reality (AR) and virtual reality (VR) are transforming how policymakers and stakeholders engage with biodiversity data. When integrated with ecological digital twins, these interfaces allow users to visualize and manipulate complex models in intuitive 3D environments. For example, planners in Borneo have used immersive rooms to simulate the impact of proposed roads on orangutan populations and test restoration strategies in real time. Each habitat, species, and infrastructure element is rendered with behavioral logic, enabling decision-makers to experiment with conservation corridors, fire regulations, or land-use changes while observing potential outcomes immediately.

These tools foster transparency, inclusivity, and participatory governance by allowing Indigenous and rural communities to engage meaningfully in conservation planning, even when they lack access to technical modeling tools. Future policymaking interfaces may feature collaborative VR spaces where ministries co-develop biodiversity strategies, immersive dashboards for tracking Sustainable Development Goal (SDG) targets, and AI-generated narratives that translate model results into accessible language. While challenges such as hardware costs, cross-disciplinary design needs, and policy uptake persist, immersive modeling environments hold great promise for bridging the gap between ecological science and decision-making.

8. CONCLUSION

The convergence of Artificial Intelligence (AI), digital twins, and immersive technologies is reshaping the future of biodiversity conservation. These tools are no longer experimental but are becoming central to how we observe, analyze, and protect ecosystems. AI enhances ecological intelligence by enabling real-time species detection, predictive habitat modeling, and autonomous surveillance through drones and IoT sensors. Digital twins extend these capabilities by creating dynamic virtual ecosystems that simulate environmental changes and inform evidence-based decisions. Meanwhile, immersive technologies such as AR and VR are transforming conservation communication and education, bringing abstract ecological processes to life and fostering public empathy for nature. Together, these technologies form a powerful triad that links data-driven insight, interactive decision-making, and global collaboration.

Despite this technological promise, several ethical, technical, and institutional challenges remain. AI systems still face limitations in data quality, generalizability, and explainability, while digital twins and autonomous agents raise concerns about privacy, surveillance, and equity. Federated learning and explainable AI (XAI) offer potential solutions by promoting transparency, distributed collaboration, and local data sovereignty. However, success will depend on inclusive governance frameworks that respect Indigenous data rights, ensure equitable access to technology, and integrate local ecological knowledge. Conservation technologies must therefore evolve not only in sophistication but also in accountability and cultural sensitivity.

Looking ahead, the fusion of AI and immersive technologies holds great potential to scale and democratize conservation efforts. As computational resources become more accessible and digital infrastructures more interconnected, the future may bring fully autonomous ecological observatories, interactive policymaking interfaces, and global networks of federated ecological AI. Yet technology alone is not the solution; it is a catalyst. The true challenge lies in aligning innovation with ethics, inclusivity, and ecological justice. In this new era of digital conservation, progress will be measured not only by data precision or model accuracy but by our collective ability to use intelligence, both human and artificial, to sustain life on Earth.

REFERENCES

Ahmed, M. A., Gallardo, J. L., Zuniga, M. D., Pedraza, M. A., Carvajal, G., Jara, N., & Carvajal, R. (2022). LoRa Based IoT Platform for Remote Monitoring of Large-Scale Agriculture Farms in Chile. *Sensors (Basel), 22*(8), 2824. Advance online publication. DOI: 10.3390/s22082824 PMID: 35458808

Al-saggaf, A. A., Sheltami, T., Alkhzaimi, H., & Ahmed, G. (2023). Lightweight Two-Factor-Based User Authentication Protocol for IoT-Enabled Healthcare Ecosystem in Quantum Computing. *Arabian Journal for Science and Engineering, 48*(2), 2347–2357. Advance online publication. DOI: 10.1007/s13369-022-07235-0 PMID: 36164325

AlZu'bi, S., Hawashin, B., Mujahed, M., Jararweh, Y., & Gupta, B. B. (2019). An efficient employment of internet of multimedia things in smart and future agriculture. *Multimedia Tools and Applications, 78*(20), 29581–29605. DOI: 10.1007/s11042-019-7367-0

Beltrán, M. (2025). AI algorithms under scrutiny: GDPR, DSA, AI Act and CRA as pillars for algorithmic security and privacy in the European Union. *Computers & Security, 158*, 104628. Advance online publication. DOI: 10.1016/j.cose.2025.104628

Blanco-Aza, D., Robles-Gómez, A., Pastor-Vargas, R., Tobarra, L., Vidal-Balboa, P., & Méndez-Suárez, M. (2025). Comprehensive AI-driven privacy risk assessment in mobile apps and social networks. *Cluster Computing, 28*(14), 914. Advance online publication. DOI: 10.1007/s10586-025-05624-2

Camilleri, M. A. (2024). Artificial intelligence governance: Ethical considerations and implications for social responsibility. *Expert Systems: International Journal of Knowledge Engineering and Neural Networks, 41*(7), e13406. Advance online publication. DOI: 10.1111/exsy.13406

De Koning, K. (2025). The crane radar: Development and deployment of an operational eco-digital twin. *Ecological Informatics, 85*, 102938. Advance online publication. DOI: 10.1016/j.ecoinf.2024.102938

Gaurav, A., Pan, V. S. H., Arya, V., Raman, R., Gupta, B. B., & Chui, K. T. (2026). AI-driven lightweight CNN model for sustainable vegetable classification in smart food systems. *Green Technologies and Sustainability, 4*(1), 100257. Advance online publication. DOI: 10.1016/j.grets.2025.100257

Jo, K., Chang, D. J., Min, J. W., Yoo, Y.-S., Lyu, B., Kwon, J. W., & Baek, J. (2022). Author Correction: Long-term prediction models for vision-threatening diabetic retinopathy using medical features from data warehouse. In *Scientific Reports* (Vol. 12, Issue 1). Springer Science and Business Media LLC. DOI: 10.1038/s41598-022-18012-2

Liang, S., Duc Long, N. V., Parvin, M. I., Escribà-Gelonch, M., Lantin, S., & Hessel, V. (2025). Digital twin for lettuce growth in six climate zones ('Climate 2050'). *Computers and Electronics in Agriculture*, *238*, 110880. Advance online publication. DOI: 10.1016/j.compag.2025.110880

Lim, T. (2024). Environmental, social, and governance (ESG) and artificial intelligence in finance: State-of-the-art and research takeaways. *Artificial Intelligence Review*, *57*(4), 76. Advance online publication. DOI: 10.1007/s10462-024-10708-3

Liu, C.-L., & Liu, W.-Y. (2025). Assessing tourism pressure on wildlife in a protected area: A social big data approach using photo-sharing data and species distribution modeling. *Ecological Informatics*, *92*, 103441. Advance online publication. DOI: 10.1016/j.ecoinf.2025.103441

Martinez, V. M. G., Campelo, D. R., & Ribeiro, M. R. N. (2025). Sustainable Intelligent Transportation Systems via Digital Twins: A Contextualized Survey. *IEEE Open Journal of Intelligent Transportation Systems*, *6*, 363–392. DOI: 10.1109/OJITS.2025.3553696

Mohammad, A. A. S., Mohammad, S. I. S., Al Oraini, B., Vasudevan, A., Hindieh, A., Altarawneh, A., Alshurideh, M. T., & Ali, I. (2025). Strategies for applying interpretable and explainable AI in real world IoT applications. *Discover Internet of Things*, *5*(1), 71. Advance online publication. DOI: 10.1007/s43926-025-00155-z

Mubarakali, A., & AlJarullah, A. (2025). IoT and XAI-driven data aggregation framework for intelligent decision-making in smart healthcare systems. *Sustainable Computing : Informatics and Systems*, *48*, 101179. Advance online publication. DOI: 10.1016/j.suscom.2025.101179

Parmiggiani, A., Liu, D., Psota, E., Fitzgerald, R., & Norton, T. (2023). Don't get lost in the crowd: Graph convolutional network for online animal tracking in dense groups. *Computers and Electronics in Agriculture*, *212*, 108038. Advance online publication. DOI: 10.1016/j.compag.2023.108038

Petso, T., Jamisola, R. S.Jr, Alibhai, S., Namoshe, M., Mmereki, W., & Jewell, Z. (2025). An investigation of lightweight AI models to classify African ungulate species from tracks. *Ecological Informatics*, *92*, 103393. Advance online publication. DOI: 10.1016/j.ecoinf.2025.103393

Rahaman, M., Chattopadhyay, S., & Anwar, N. (2022). *A Case Study: Physical Layer Security Analysis for Internet of Vehicle (IoV)*. 283–291.

Rahaman, M., Lin, C. Y., Rachmat, I., Bansal, R., & Prayitno. (2024). Secure Health Features: Implementing Hyperledger Fabric in Blockchain-Driven Healthcare Management Systems. In *Digital Forensics and Cyber Crime Investigation*. CRC Press.

Rahaman, M., Putra, K. T., Irawan, B., & Biyanto, T. R. (2025). Industrial Evolution: The Integration of AI in Robotics and Drone Systems. In *AI Developments for Industrial Robotics and Intelligent Drones* (pp. 85–114). IGI Global Scientific Publishing. DOI: 10.4018/979-8-3693-2707-4.ch005

Rahaman, M., Wisnujati, A., Widodo, A. M., Haque, A., Sakar, R., & Chen, H. C. (2022). *Privacy Preservation Agri-Food SCM Operation Based on Online/Offline RFID Using Block Chain*. 413–426. DOI: 10.2991/978-94-6463-084-8_34

Rohhila, S., Singh, K. N., Singh, A. K., & Gupta, B. B. (2025). DeepKey-TPE: Using Deep Learning to Generate Key for Image Security With Continued Usability Through Thumbnail-Preserving Encryption. *IEEE Transactions on Consumer Electronics*, *71*(4), 1–1. DOI: 10.1109/TCE.2025.3605213

Safiyev, E. S., & Shikhaliyeva, S. Y. (2025). ANALYSIS OF ECOLOGY AND EFFICIENCY OF OVERHEAD POWER LINES OF ULTRA-HIGH VOLTAGE. *International Journal on Technical and Physical Problems of Engineering*, *17*(62), 91–100.

Saini, D. K. J. B., Mishra, A., Siddharth, D., Joshi, P., Bansal, R., Bansal, S., & Chui, K. T. (2023). Development of Enhanced Chimp Optimization Algorithm (OFCOA) in Cognitive Radio Networks for Energy Management and Resource Allocation. [IJSSCI]. *International Journal of Software Science and Computational Intelligence*, *15*(1), 1–20. DOI: 10.4018/IJSSCI.335898

Sekti, B. A. (2025a). IT Service Information Security Management. In *Cases on Information Systems Service Management* (pp. 61–93). DOI: 10.4018/979-8-3373-2352-7.ch003

Sekti, B. A. (2025b). Machine learning and artificial intelligence (AI) in manufacturing. In *Integrating Digital Innovation and Integrated Frameworks in Manufacturing* (pp. 255–292). DOI: 10.4018/979-8-3373-1082-4.ch011

Sharafat, S., Kabya, N. D., Emu, R. I., Ahmed, M. U., Onik, J. C., Islam, M. A., & Khan, R. (2025). An IoT-enabled AI system for real-time crop prediction using soil and weather data in precision agriculture. *Smart Agricultural Technology*, *12*, 101263. Advance online publication. DOI: 10.1016/j.atech.2025.101263

Sharma, A., Singh, S. K., Kumar, S., Thakur, R., Gupta, B. B., & Arya, V. (2024). IoT-enabled smart farming with Industry 5.0. *Journal of High Speed Networks, 30*(3), 477–496. DOI: 10.3233/JHS-230258

V., J. M. N., Flórez, S. L., Corchado, J. M., & De la Prieta, F. (2025). Edge AIoT-based agricultural recommendation platform to improve humus productivity in vermicomposting processes. *Pervasive and Mobile Computing, 112*. DOI: 10.1016/j.pmcj.2025.102080

Chapter 9
Designing the Future:
Human-Centric Innovation for a Compassionate Digital World

Pravin Kumar
http://orcid.org/0009-0008-9393-7324
Brainware University, India

ABSTRACT

This chapter examines how human-centric innovation can be a part of solving the ethical, emotional, and social dilemma of digital change. Based on the human-cantered design, self-determination theory, and service-dominant logic, it discusses how empathy, the concept of psychological safety, and co-creation can be implemented as part of innovation approaches to allow employee engagement and consumer trust. The research employs a qualitative method approach to interviewing and analyzing documents in the form of semi-structured interviews, and determining the major practices that can align the technology with human values. The results suggest the importance of the responsible use of emerging technologies, inclusive leadership, and ethical frameworks in long-term resilience in organizations. The outcome of the study is that humanistic innovation is not discretionary but a requirement in digitally embraced, sustainable, and socially accountable change.

INTRODUCTION

It is the 21st century, which is reflective of a digital revolution that has never been witnessed in the world before, that has changed the way organizations and consumers behave in a manner never before seen. Artificial intelligence (AI), the Internet of Things, and blockchain are all topics that have progressed on the spectrum of automation, connectivity, and decentralization as a result of new technologies emerging.

DOI: 10.4018/979-8-2600-0013-7.ch009

These have given the businesses the capabilities of streamlining business operations, making better decisions, and making products more productive. It has, however, been observed that, by and large, the ultimate perfection of such innovations has been achieved at the expense of the human experience. Given that the organizations are keen to implement these tools, there is an enhanced understanding gaining ground that the digital change should be more open, compassionate, and ethically tenable.

Such developments have seen the emergence of the term "human-centric innovation," which has gained fame. The tactics of this method transform the individuals, workers, customers, and stakeholders into the center of the innovation process. It encourages the creation of technologies and processes that are able to multiply the abilities of human beings, ideally, the prosperity, encourage well-being, and allow for healthy and sustainable development. Unlike only technology-related innovations, human-centered innovation is concerned with the concept of cooperation with individuals, with their experience, and with their emotional intelligence as the most important element of any meaningful progress. It is not merely that adoption of the new tools would go well, but they must be employed in a manner that supplements the values of human beings and the needs of society.

To this end, in January 2023, the World Economic Forum published the Future of Jobs Report (2023), indicating that over 80 percent of the global leaders have recognized the significance of human-centric innovation as one of the primary dimensions of ensuring sustainable growth and the general well-being of the smaller humans in the workforce. This is where the currently emerging requirement for introducing empathy, moral values, and inclusivity to the digital transformation emerges.

The need to be more human-centric can be justified on the premise that the world is evolving towards Industry 5.0 and the Experience Economy. Compared to Industry 4.0, which is essentially an efficiency-driven paradigm, the strategy of Industry 5.0 involves augmenting human intelligence with machine intelligence. It is more about customization, innovation, and co-creation in the technology ecosystems. Similarly, the Experience Economy brings out the point that customers no longer desire objects or services; instead, they desire memorable, captivating, and emotionally enthralling encounters. In this case, the business must generate value brought about by the supply of goods and services, as well as foster beliefs of trust, loyalty, and meaning, which is achieved through the establishment of human contact with an element of genuineness.

Although prior studies have addressed the technological change to Industry 5.0 and the experiential demands of the customers in detail, there exists a significant study gap in the area of integration of internal (staff-centered) and external (customer-centered) innovation activities. This gap is bridged by this chapter through the incorporation of current industry evidence, including the WEF Future of Jobs Report (2023), indicating that employee engagement in an organization is rated 20-30 ints higher, and consumer trust indicators are 12-18% higher by organizational future worker approaches founded on human-centric innovation models. It accomplishes this by showing how empathetic, ethical, and co-creative organizational efforts may be used as a dual-value method to enhance employee empowerment and consumer confidence, both at the same time, and this is something not focused on in earlier models.

The chapter also advances the literature by filling a major gap, which is the gap between employee-based and consumer-based models of innovation. As other literature considers these areas independently, this study introduces a combination of human-centric innovation strategies that integrate internal and external value creation. This contribution contributes to the existing body of knowledge by giving it a unified approach to integrating organizational culture, user empathy, and technological ethics.

Research Question

The key question in this chapter is as follows: How can organizations bring together internal (employee-centered) and external (consumer-centered) innovation processes into a cohesive human-centric system in order to reinforce trust, well-being, and long-term value creation?

Hypothesis (Exploratory Proposition)

People-focused innovation that is backed by leadership empathy, ethical technology application, and participatory design promotes employee empowerment and consumer trust better than the conventional model of efficiency-oriented digital innovation.

Scholarly Contribution

The study makes a contribution to the literature by (1) filling the gaps in employee-centric and consumer-centric innovation, (2) offering a single model of dual-value human-centric innovation, and (3) offering qualitative data, which is presented by companies worldwide and proves how empathy, ethics, and co-creation lead to tangible results.

During the shifts of economies and business, it is becoming obvious that the driver of sustainable competitive advantage is less, now, that of technological innovations and more about throughput innovations that augment, rather than impair, the human condition. This has triggered a move away from the current technology-centric paradigm of innovations defined by speed, automation, and efficiency to innovations that are rooted in empathy, empowerment, and moral and ethical responsibility.

Innovation as a socially conscious practice will evaluate its own innovation practices and requirements, and merely being an innovator and an open and responsive one is no longer sufficient.

The other facet of this shift entails the elements of empathy, ethics, well-being, and sustainability in the innovation process. Designers, engineers, and strategists may understand what the users desire and feel through empathy, thus coming up with more effective and meaningful solutions efficiently. Moral innovation, or rather, means that new technology cannot be used up or even exacerbate inequality. Well-being is concerned with all aspects of the success, emotional, intellectual, and physical well-being of people who are affected by innovation, and sustainability ensures that economic development is achieved without compromising the environment and social prospects of the future. All these comprise what would make one a success in innovating in a world of digitalization.

Further, there is an obvious sense of urgency to bring on an integrated innovation framework, taking into account the perspectives of the consumers and the employees in parallel. In most organizations, innovation work is secluded, focusing on either the efficiency of employees in using the internal software or the consumer in marketing and product development activities. However, this division fails to describe the interrelatedness between the workplace and the marketplace ventures too well. Highly motivated, valued, and ethically supported employees will tend to produce good customer experiences. Conversely, consumers are also demanding more transparency and responsible and socially responsible conduct from the purchasing companies. Therefore, the ability to align internal innovation with external expectations is critical to business endurance over the long term.

The chapter's addition to literature is expressed by outlining how bridging the gap between internal and external innovation within a humanistic approach contributes not only to organizational efficiency but also strengthens the trust among society. It is qualitative evidence that demonstrates how empathetic leadership, ethical design, and inclusive culture are also the working levers to transform the inner world by the production of value towards the outside world.

The side story on human-centered innovation is raising the question for companies of what comes after production and profitability. Introduction of human-based concepts into the core strategies will also make the organizations more competitive and ensure significant, multifaceted, and sustainable changes. Based on the way companies are instilling human-centric innovation in various sectors, the chapter addresses the theories, action plans, and real-life practices of a smarter, kinder, fairer, and more human innovation.

Statement of the Problem

Numerous organizations still exist in a paradigm that values speed, scale, and cost efficiency instead of looking after their people, notwithstanding the never-before-seen investments in advanced technologies. The people the digital tools are supposed to empower end up marginalized using the same tools that promise empowerment. The heart of this paradox is three interrelated issues.

To begin with, an efficiency logic continues to prevail in innovation agendas to the detriment of the human experience. Automation dashboards that can track the throughput are uncommon for tracking whether employees feel motivated or whether customers feel truly understood. According to your source text, companies are keen on digitizing and fail to focus on the human experience, hence measuring and prioritizing optimization over empathy, inclusion, and trust.

Human experience in the digital adoption seems to have fallen through the organizational cracks, with one of the findings in the PwC Global Workforce Survey (2022) showing that only 31 percent of organizations measure employee engagement or motivation and productivity.

Technology acts as a drag instead of an opportunity when it increases productivity by limiting personnel choices in directions or markets, instead of decreasing the stress due to increased productivity.

Second, organizations usually isolate employees and consumers as silos instead of looking at these two dimensions as the two sides of the same value creation system. Inward-facing digital projects, which include robotic process automation, AI dashboards, and self-service HR portals, are designed to increase the efficiency of the staff, whereas outward-facing projects would include chatbots, recommendation engines, and immersive stores, whose purpose is to maximize loyalty and revenues. But the two agendas rarely meet, and there arises a vacuum whereby employee insight can add value to customer innovation, and vice versa.

According to Gartner's 2023 Digital Workplace Trends, which is shown through the digital customer experience index (customer satisfaction indicator), in the case of enterprise organizations that pass through such silos and use integrative strategies of innovation, a 23 percent increase in the customer satisfaction indicator and an 18 percent increase in the internal effectiveness indicator are realized.

This disintegration does not allow companies to realize that happy, empowered employees can often be the epicenter of a memorable customer experience.

Third, the speed of AI, IoT, and data analytics implementation has surpassed the creation of adequate ethical protection measures, leading to feelings of disconnection and sometimes even backlash in the populace. Such activities of biased algorithms, non-transparent data manipulation, and deskilling workflows are a loss of trust when users perceive that they are being observed more than nurtured. According to the attached document, in the absence of clear ethical values, technology may exploit weaknesses or increase inequality, destroying the very social license on which digital business models rest.

The absence of an integrative innovation system that appreciates and promotes human flourishing across all factions of the stakeholders is also present. The existing models lie in the aspects of technical feasibility and viability on the market, but they do not address the issues of psychological safety, cultural diversity, and the impact of development on society in the long term. This research problem discloses how companies can re-course their digital transformation strategies to attain the stability of efficiency, empathy, employee and consumer visions, protective strategies, and inclusive behaviors that capitalize on human flourishing.

Objectives

The general purpose of this chapter is to explore why human-focused innovation can be a revolutionary policy to reorganize relations, even at the workplace, as well as the state of customer participation in a more digitized world. With the emergence of new technologies, such as artificial intelligence (AI), the Internet of Things (IoT), and blockchain, which are shaking up the business environment more and more, it is important not to forget that all these novelties should not contradict human values, emotional stability, and ethical behavior. With regard to this, the research will seek to address the question of how organizations can transform into more accommodating models of systems that are more empathetic and sustainable based on technology.

The main objectives include examining how human-centric innovation can transform the employee-consumer relationship. The study aims to determine how the design of innovation based on human needs and motivators can positively contribute to trust, collaboration, and value creation over a long period across the boundaries of organizations.

The second major goal in this study is to study the impact of ethical and compassionate use of digital technologies on both organizational culture and consumer perception. This involves exploring how technologies can be applied with responsibility to businesses without the sacrifice of privacy, autonomy, and well-being, while retaining competitive challenges.

Furthermore, the chapter will make comparisons and contrasts between the real-life examples of human-centric innovation in various industries, including manufacturing, healthcare, retail, and education, among other industries. Such case studies provide a feasible insight as to how theory can be implemented and what the success with the incorporation of empathy and ethics into digital strategies may entail.

The top initiatives include the Responsible AI initiatives by Microsoft, the Sustainable Living Plan of Unilever, and the AI-powered upskilling platforms by TCS, which may be read as exemplars of how to include ethical innovation practices.

Finally, the study aims to investigate how leadership, organizational culture, and values can assist in the digital transformation that has to be not only effective but also humane and equal.

Theoretical Framework

In this part, the three fundamental theories where the knowledge of human-centric innovation is coined will be addressed, and they include Human-Centered Design (HCD), Self-Determination Theory (SDT), and Service-Dominant Logic (SDL). The three frameworks present a unique outlook in ensuring that there is alignment between innovation and the human values, inspirations, and experiences.

Human-Centered Design (HCD): Human-centered design includes the aspects of empathy and co-creation and the incorporation of iteration into the innovation process. During the HCD process, designers would desire in-depth information about the users in terms of how they feel, what they do, and what they accompany. Another way through which HCD ensures that the solutions are not manipulative, irrelevant, and inconsequential is by ensuring that they involve the users in the design process in an active and iterative way.

Self-Determination Theory (SDT): SDT is a theory in the psychology of human action, motivation, and well-being that asserts that the most optimal procedure is by meeting the three universal and basic psychological needs that form autonomy (the urge to experience control), competence (the urge to feel effective), and relatedness (the urge to feel connected to others). The results of intrinsic motivation, engagement, and performance are environments that accommodate such needs.

Service-Dominant Logic (SDL): SDL is the thinking that refutes the conventional beliefs about the product having its value; however, it is in search of alternative thinking that value can be co-created in the server-user interface. The shift in this kind of thinking is based upon the fact that value creation shifts away to intangible elements like services, experiences, and relationships as the existing core instead of tangible products.

All these three theories collaborate to create a commonalities platform through which it is possible to plan and implement the human-oriented innovation. As an example, the focus of HCD on empathy allows it to identify and satisfy the psychological needs identified in SDT, e.g., creating tools or systems that give their users more control over decision-making processes or developing feedback practices that make users feel more competent. Likewise, SDL complements SDT and HCD in interpreting the innovation process as a co-creative service exchange with users, not as passive beneficiaries but as active contributors, and once again validates the psychological need for relatedness and engagement.

Therefore, the combination of the theories applied leads to the creation of an overall innovation strategy that is not only technically successful but also emotionally and socially appealing.

HCD, SDT, and SDL interaction constitute a logical human-centered system. HCD defines the principles of empathy-driven design, SDT describes the intrinsic motivation needs that such designs should be fulfilling, and SDL places the employees and the consumers in the role of co-creators of value. With this integration, employee autonomy and competence (SDT) have been institutionalized into the co-creation process (SDL), enabled by the use of empathetic design practices (HCD). This theoretical syncretism is the basis upon which human-centric innovation can be understood as a single construct.

Even though the roots of HCD, SDT, and SDL are rooted in disparate disciplinary heritages, they overlap substantively in a human-centric innovation environment. HCD offers the methodological basis of empathetic co-creation, SDT offers the motivational processes, such as autonomy, competence, and relatedness, through which user and employee interaction is organized, and SDL redefines innovation as a process of relational value co-creation instead of a product-oriented exchange. Such frameworks together will provide a consistent reasoning: empathy-based design (HCD) will lead to solutions that fulfill intrinsic psychological needs (SDT), which will further facilitate more profound service co-creation and trust (SDL). This threefold combination eliminates familiar strains in digital novelty through matching electronic possibility to human drive and service-generated worth creation.

Conceptual Framework

The theoretical framework of the research is created on the basis of the synergetic interaction of leadership, organizational culture, employee experience, and consumer trust in the wider environment of human-based innovation. It states that to be truly life-altering and long-term, innovation should focus on the human interactions that connect technological progress with moral commitment and emotionality (Brynjolfsson & McAfee, 2017).

At the heart of this framework is an understanding that leadership and culture serve as very important enablers of human-centric innovation. Leaders prescribe the vision and tone in which organizations engage in their digital transformation, and their adherence to being empathetic, inclusive, and sustainable has a direct effect on internal culture (Edmondson & Lei, 2014). The work culture that embraces psychological safety, good communication, and a sense of purpose allows employees to become self-empowered and contribute to the innovation efforts in meaningful ways. Such a positive environment, in turn, improves the experience of employees by establishing motivation, creativity, and the feeling of belonging, which are the driving forces of engagement and performance (Deci et al., 2017).

The good staff experience created by the human-focused culture and leadership entails an increase in the most honest and stable relations with the consumer. Valued, morally empowered employees are prepared to offer understanding, responsive, and individualized services (Pine & Gilmore, 2021). Such levels of relational depth make consumers more trusting, which is becoming more crucial since the digital surveillance and data breaches concept and the artificial intelligence-dominated decision process (Bozic & Kuppelwieser, 2019). Having developed trust, it becomes a long-term contributor to brand loyalty and customer co-creation, which returns again to the innovation cycle (Kuppelwieser & Finsterwalder, 2016).

The framework focuses on humanistic innovation with the convergence of technology, morality, and compassion. It perceives AI and IoT as means of elevating human potential, yet it needs an ethical application (Autor, 2019). Accessibility and inclusivity are ensured by empathy and fairness, and accountability through ethics (Khurana et al., 2019). Such a strategy will allow making technology more social, thus resulting in improved workplace relationships, relationships with customers, and society (Kankanhalli et al., 2015).

Figure 1 is a visual representation of the way leadership and culture establish the parameters of the positive working experience of the employees. In their turn, empowered employees provide the trust on the part of consumers and, in this way, underpin the feedback-based sustainable cycles of innovation that remain humanistic.

Figure 1. Flow of Human-Centric Innovation through Organizational Dynamics

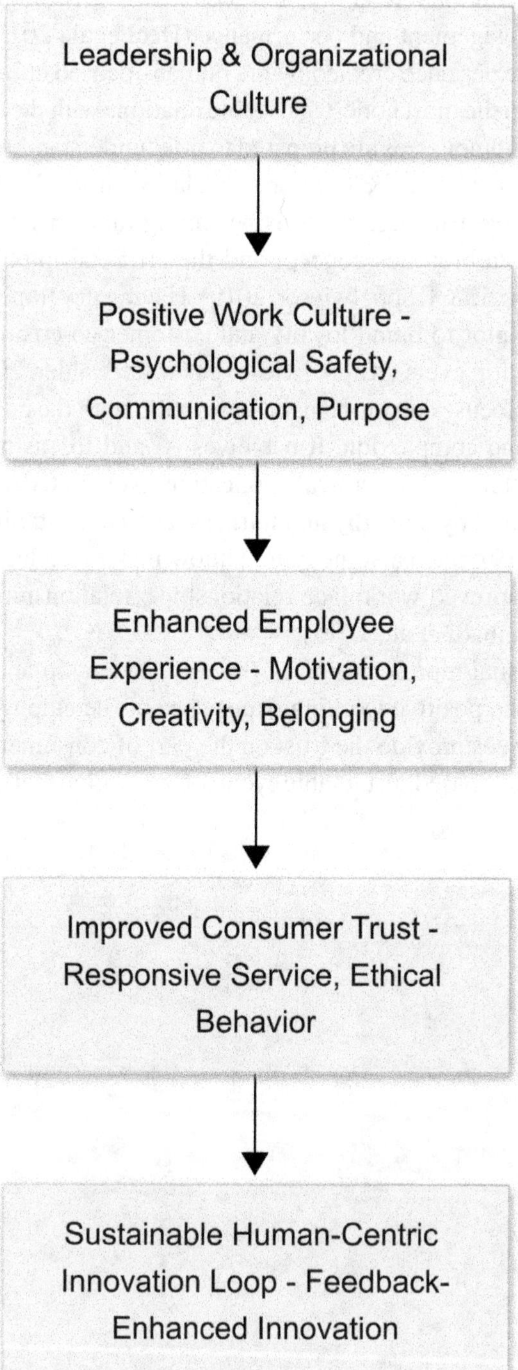

Source: Author's illustration

Figure 2. Human-Centric Innovation Framework

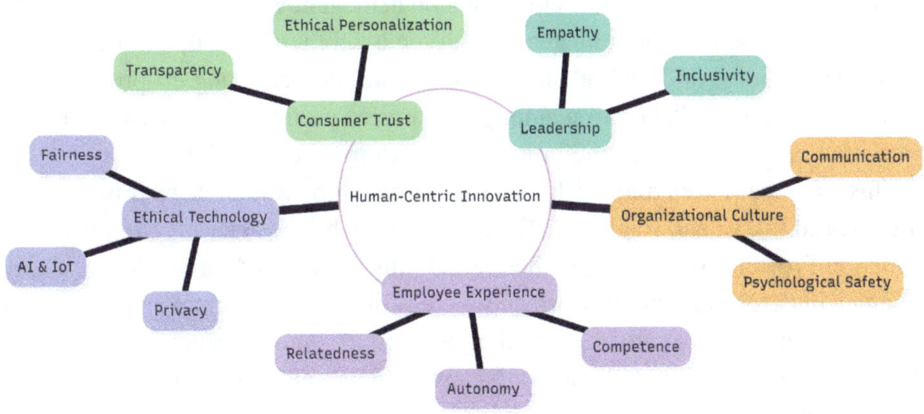

Source: Author's illustration

The mind map is a brief visual depiction of the Human-Centric Innovation Framework, showing the influence of leadership and organizational culture on employee experience, thus making consumer trust stronger. It also signifies the use of ethical and compassionate technology as one of the pillars. The picture reveals the interdependent flow of these components, thus helping the audience to grasp the idea of human-centered principles being the basis for purposeful and lasting novation.

LITERATURE REVIEW

Evolution of Innovation: From Techno-Centric to Human-Centric

Often understood as a technical invention and economic efficiency, innovation has experienced a massive paradigm shift in the last few decades (Mazzucato, 2018). The earlier forms of innovation emphasis were on speed, cost savings, and process improvements, adding more attention to the mechanical and systemic features of change. Such techno-focused strategies tended to promote technological dominance against human experience and resulted in a heavy productivity increase but also generated a gap between innovation and human values (Nambisan et al., 2019).

However, the paradigm began to change in recent years to a more inclusive, empathetic, and people-oriented perspective. The trend is driven by the shortcomings of automation-first strategies and the unanticipated impacts of the digital transformation, leading to the concept of human-centric innovation (Parviainen et al., 2017). Unlike simply intensifying the machines, the new framework strives to increase capabilities, well-being, and inclusion in the innovation process for people.

New technologies should have a human focus on their ethical, emotional, and social implications, and individuals should move into becoming co-producers of value, encouraging collaboration amongst interested parties and a balance between innovation and societal accountability (Ramaswamy & Ozcan, 2018).

This has been strengthened by recent scholarship. Research by Fischer and Amabile (2022), Li and Raghav (2023), and a study by the Harvard Digital Transformation Project (2024) point to the idea of human-centered innovation as a way of enhancing cross-functional work and increasing the rate of innovation adoption by 30-40 percent in digitally advanced organizations. Another study conducted by MIT Sloan (2023) additionally offers that emotional intelligence and ethical design are currently primary forces behind digital trust.

Employee-Centric Innovation and Digital Transformation

According to recent research (e.g., Deloitte, 2023; McKinsey, 2023), employees are considered active innovation partners, and participatory digitalization can raise adoption rates by 2535 percent within an organization. Innovation, in this regard, should be humanistic to foster participatory digitalization that enables autonomy, creativity, and emotional interactions in the workplace (Kolbjørnsrud et al., 2017).

Organizations nowadays are appreciating the role of employee well-being, inclusiveness, and skill acquisition in promoting innovation. The technologies used in the digital transformation of organizations affected by the pandemic and focused on employee-centric approaches include AI, IoT, collaborative platforms, and more, but are designed to enhance human capabilities rather than to substitute human beings (Ritter & Pedersen, 2020). To give an example, more customized means of upskilling individuals about their career goals could be made available via AI-based learning systems, and IoT devices could support making workplaces healthier, safer, and more responsive (Davenport & Kalakota, 2019).

76% of the workforce would like to work at organizations that embrace ethical innovation and ESG, such as emotional well-being, and organizations that made investments in these processes also experienced a 30 percent increase in retention.

Participatory innovation among the employees within an organization leads to a high state of change adoption and cultural convergence. The participatory innovation process works since it is empowering teams, technology modifications are planned according to the needs of the operational process, and workers feel better connected to the cause. Digital policies that are ethical enhance the power of trust and raise the degree of resistance to change (Dwivedi et al., 2021). Leaders adopt the concept of human dignity and inclusion, forming innovation-ready cultures.

Consumer Engagement, Trust, and Experience Personalization

On the consumer side, the innovation on the consumer side has also been on an experiential front instead of looking at the functionality level. As the experience economy emerges, it is not enough for a consumer to purchase a product or service anymore; he/she want something more: to be engaged with the product or service and feel that it is personalized and authentic (Lemon & Verhoef, 2016). This transformation needs businesses to redesign new ways of providing customer journeys and new ways of value measurement.

Human-centric innovation begins with the consumer at the center of digital strategy but uses technology to personalize the experience, earn trust, and automate the delivery of services (Loureiro, 2023). AI and big data give businesses the ability to mine consumer behavior and tastes down to the finest levels in order to perform hyper-personalized marketing, dynamic price tagging, and offer personalized products across applications (Libai et al., 2020). But this amount of personalization should be handled with caution. Trust need not take long to wear thin when the consumer only feels surveyed as opposed to understood.

As the Tech Vision 2023 report by Accenture warns, with no ethical check box, the sources of over-personalization will result in lost consumer trust since 57 percent of consumers are quitting brands that have invasive approaches to data.

To establish trust in the digital world, one must have transparency, ethical principles, and areas of human interaction. The algorithms of personalization should be clear, explanatory, and privacy-concerned (Pappas et al., 2017). Ethical innovation will demand a decent price, reach, and variety of user experience. Consumers will be better informed about the companies that use sustainable business and ethical value chains (Liu et al., 2015).

Gaps in Integrating Digital Technologies with Ethics and Well-Being

Most organizations continue to find it difficult to incorporate ethical considerations together with human welfare in their innovation practices, even after embracing the use of digital tools and services. Technology has changed so fast that regulations or moral standards to control its use have found it hard to keep up intact, where unwanted effects include algorithmic bias, unemployment, emotional burnout, and violations of privacy.

Intent and implementation still exist as a difference in applying ethics to technologies and their design and deployment. Business organizations can foster ethical values within their mission statements, but do not apply such values in their AI systems, data governance, or employee performance metrics. Also, well-being programs tend to be viewed as standalone HR solutions instead of being part and parcel of an innovation approach.

It is an ethical problem that there does not exist a coherent and powerful framework that takes ethics and well-being as core drivers of new value creation. This includes communication with economic agents, continuous ethical reasoning within the process of design and development of new designs and products, and enhancing cross-disciplinary dialogue among technologists, ethicists, designers, researchers, and end users. Ethical impact assessments and other tools can also point out the gaps and connect to them.

Connection With UN SDGs: Decent Work and Responsible Production

Some of the Sustainable Development Goals that are developed by the United Nations and aligned with human-centered innovation are SDG 8: Decent Work and Economic Growth and SDG 12: Responsible Consumption and Production. These goals concentrate on the applicability of decent work, fair and good development, sustainable development, and ethical supply chains, which are important constituents of the idea of humanistic designing and ethical technology execution.

SDG 8 entails the issue of achieving sustained, inclusive, and sustainable economic growth, full employment, and decent work for all. Human-centric innovation helps to achieve this by creating in the workplace environments that are based on psychological safety, learning, diversity development, and well-being. Digital enabling technologies can contribute to reducing job requirements, enabling gig working conditions and remote work environments when used with human principles, and supporting the creation of a personal career to strengthen it.

SDG 12 on solving sustainable consumption and production patterns is connected with the issue of innovation, as it proposes that organizations have to restructure the product life cycle, the use of resources, and how people interact. The supply chains can be made more transparent with the help of such technologies as IoT and blockchain, whereas AI can also be used to streamline the production process to reduce waste. However, transformative innovation embraces deep-rooted sustainability as well, in which efficiency and commercial profitability are no longer the success metrics but rather value achievement and environmental management.

Implementing these SDG principles in their agendas of innovation, organizations gain not only the future-proofing of their organizational strategies but also the foundation of responsible players within society. The humane approach to innovation can serve as a strong vehicle to change the sustainability and equity that must be viewed through economic productivity, but also social and environmental considerations.

METHODOLOGY

The current research study espouses a qualitative exploratory research design to examine the issue of human-centric innovation and its application in the different sectors and regions within the organization. Since the objective of the study is to obtain an insight into detailed, situation-specific, and subjective experiences, in particular concerning employee motivation, consumer trust, organizational values, and ethical digital practice, the qualitative approach would be best suited. In contrast to quantitative approaches, which usually limit phenomena to defined variables, qualitative inquiry embraces depth, richness, and discovery and thus is particularly suited to the study of the subtle interrelationship between technology, ethics, and the human experience.

The nature of human-based innovation in the era of the Internet can be characterized as both evolving and under-theorized, thus fitting the qualitative design that is employed here and is exploratory by its nature. Although technological transformation is a popular research area, the incorporation of human values into innovation strategies, such as empathy, well-being, and sustainability, is relatively new. The proposed study, hence, aims at creating knowledge and conceptual understanding using the first example of narratives and company records.

Data Collection Methods

Two types of complementary sources of data, namely (1) semi-structured interviews and (2) document analysis, are employed to give a comprehensive picture of human-centric innovation when it has been in practice.

The chief technique of data reception is a semi-structured interview. Such interviews are carried out among a well-considered sample of professionals working at the front line of innovation, human resource development, ethical implementation of technologies, and digital change. The audience is composed of innovation leaders, HR professionals, marketing managers, technology architects, and digital strategists. Semi-structured interviews will facilitate flexibility and at the same time structure the study, with the help of which the researcher will be able to dig deeper and ask more questions about the personal opinions, nut-making, and organizational issues.

The interview questions will aim at addressing a large pool of themes, which may touch on the role of leadership in influencing the innovation culture, employee contribution in the design of the technology, ethical issues in the implementation of digitization, customer interaction styles, and the way an organization can align with human values. The interviewing process includes virtual interviews in various time zones with permission to record and transcribe to ensure accuracy and analysis.

Documents are used to collect contextual data as well as to verify the results of interviews. The organizational policies of each of the firms involved, the innovation policies, the CSR (Corporate Social Responsibility) reports, the annual reports, and the sustainability disclosures are examined. The documents provide insight and details of formal commitment, strategic priorities, and reported outcomes concerning human-centered innovation, ethics, and digital transformation. This document analysis will not only complement the qualitative dataset, but it will also complement the triangulation process, which will make the findings more reliable.

Sampling Strategy

The chapter will use purposive sampling to include the likes of global, multi-sectoral organizations with innovative practices and ethical leadership. The sample represents the large-named companies that effectively use the concepts of empathy, diversity, sustainability, and digital innovation in their business models and have received public recognition for these aspects in their business models: Microsoft, Unilever, and Tata Consultancy (TCS). All these firms remain in the Just Capital Responsible Company Index (2023) and the Forbes Ethical Tech List, contributing to their reputation as humanistic leaders.

These companies are found in different sectors such as technology, consumer goods, consulting, and manufacturing, and also in both developed economies and emerging economies. Such diversity helps in making sure that the study covers as many practices, challenges, and contextual differences as possible. It is not a statistical generalization but an analytical one when findings on deep cases should contribute to theories and managerial knowledge.

The participants will be chosen based on their familiarity and participation in the decision-making processes that involve innovation, technological uptake, and stakeholder interest. The invitations via professional networks and industry forums are made, and the final participant pool is represented well in terms of industry, geography, and functional expertise.

Justification for Qualitative Design

The qualitative approach is heavily supported by the fact that the research questions are human-centric.

Numerical indicators cannot just define empathy, ethics, and user experience-based innovation. It requires contextual sensitivity, interpretive richness, and sensitivity to multi-layered stories that are full of values. This method of qualitative research examines humanity-oriented innovation by incorporating subjective knowledge, which in this case is the feeling of empowerment and reliability. It is capable of providing a multi-faceted model of comprehending how firms can convert the abstract ideas of values, including empathy and ethics, into action to supplement the literature and sustainable innovation strategies.

DATA ANALYSIS

In this part, the authors validate practical outcomes of the research, and it depends on the semi-structured interviews and the analysis of the documents of the selected companies, including Microsoft, Unilever, and Tata Consultancy Services (TCS). A thematic analysis developed the tool of defining and understanding the topicalities, patterns, and outliers in the testimonies of technologically strategic individuals, human resources experts, and innovational leaders. The concept of innovation through tools can be realized in the real business context (through human beings) and comprehended by the use of the four major themes, namely, ethical innovation, psychological safety, trust, and purpose, and by analyzing the idea of technology as a driving force.

Thematic Analysis Procedure

The thematic analysis was based on the 6 steps proposed by Braun and Clarke (2006). To begin with, all the interview transcripts were transcribed manually and read with repetitions to familiarize oneself. Second, two independent coders created the open codes through an inductive method. Third, similar codes were clustered together collaboratively through a combination of the constant comparison technique by the coders into preliminary themes. Fourth, themes were checked against the raw data to align with the themes and provide their traceability. Fifth, the refined themes were identified and labelled depending on common patterns across firms. Eventually, the data saturation was accomplished at the 14th interview, where no new themes were found. To a great extent, the agreement between the coders was very good, and any differences of opinion that arose were resolved by discussion until consensus was achieved.

Ethical Innovation as a Strategic Imperative

There was a theme running through all the interviews involving the need for ethics as a tool of innovation strategies. Leaders were keen to point out that technology cannot develop within an ethical vacuum. Instead, designing innovation should occur on frames that embrace equity, inclusiveness, and openness. The activists at Microsoft and Unilever highlighted that their companies introduced their digital ethics committees, audited their algorithms, and published their data transparency reports to assist in reducing implicit or unconscious bias and pursue corporate responsibility.

A digital ethics officer of Microsoft noted, *"Ethics is not a brake on innovation; it's the steering wheel. Without it, we might go fast, but in the wrong direction."*

Ethical innovation has been considered as a means of building trust in those concerned about surveillance and privacy of the data, and the loss of a job through automation has been addressed. Ethics became one of the main pillars of the innovation strategy of companies such as Unilever and TCS, which use ethical sourcing and digital traceability in the supply chain and product development.

One interviewee mentioned that ethics in innovation is no longer a choice, and users will demand to understand how their data is secured on the other side before they will place their trust in the digital service.

One respondent stressed the importance of users not feeling that clarity is demonstrated in the way their data is managed, with no level of personalization creating trust.

Analyzing the ethical initiatives of Microsoft and Unilever, it is possible to draw a comparative analysis of their programs presented in Table 1 and explain how these companies implement fairness, transparency, and accountability within their innovation ecosystems. This table demonstrates that human-centered innovation is not some abstract, hypothetical concept but the practice that industry giants seek to engage in in order to win trust and maintain responsible technology.

To exemplify this, it can be mentioned that Unilever experienced an increase of 12 percent in consumer trust indicators, and Microsoft experienced an increase of 15 percent in ethical consideration compliances on the incorporation of these ethical innovation frameworks (Internal ESG Reports, 2023).

Table 1. Ethical Innovation Practices by Leading Companies

Company	Ethical Innovation Practice	Purpose
Microsoft	Creation of digital ethics boards	To guide responsible tech development
Microsoft	Conducting algorithmic reviews	To detect and mitigate bias in AI systems
Microsoft	Publishing data transparency reports	To ensure accountability and user trust
Unilever	Implementation of a digital ethics framework	To support fairness and inclusivity in innovation
Unilever	Integration of ethical sourcing in supply chain design	To promote responsible consumption and production
Unilever	Deployment of digital traceability in products	To increase consumer trust and transparency

Case Study Spotlight: Microsoft's Human-Centric Innovation Approach

Microsoft is an interesting case study of how human-centered conceptualization of innovation can be introduced into a large and high-tech company. To make the process of ethical control institutionalized, the company formed a responsible AI office and an AI, Ethics, and Effects in Engineering and Research (AETHER) Committee. With these governing bodies, algorithms can be audited, bias assessed, and the relevant development and implementation of AI technologies in all products can be directed.

In addition to the benefits in terms of ethics, Microsoft pursues psychological safety through a culture of growth mindset, which promotes experimentation and failure learning. It uses its digital sandboxes to allow employees to co-create tools without hierarchy and possession of the creative process. Moreover, the hybrid work system concept that is currently being developed at Microsoft is the direct result of employee feedback because it becomes clear that the focus on innovation is also directly correlated with workforce needs.

At the consumer level, Microsoft has introduced transparency in the use of data by implementing privacy dashboards that give consumers visibility with the ability to control their data usage. This is all in a greater attempt by the firm to instill trust, transparency, and purpose-driven innovation in a digital-first world.

According to research done, following the program of the co-creative design process, the satisfaction levels of employees increase by 28 percent, and a 17 percent increase in the combined score on consumer trust in services that employ transparent AI practices takes place within teams. The results suggest that combining empathy, ethics, and empowerment into what innovation could comprise may be an important factor and can generate tangible organizational and market-level value.

The Unilever Sustainable Living Lab demonstrates how human-centric innovation embraces sustainability, ethics, and consumer empowerment by providing consumers with the means of tracing the origin of products consumed with the help of digital transparency dashboard applications. Within this program, consumer trust rose by 12 percent in 2021-23 (Unilever ESG Report, 2023).

Psychological Safety and Empowered Work Environments

The problem of workplace innovation in terms of psychological safety was referred to extensively. The interviewees emphasized multiple times that employees would not be invited to active participation in the innovation process unless they are safe, heard, and respected. Psychological safety has been determined as one of the preconditions of co-creation.

The innovation president has said that in case we fear being able to communicate, we would not be able to co-create solutions.

According to another interviewee, they feel psychologically safe when leaders promote experimentation with no punishment, and employees are not afraid to present something bold and creative.

Technological innovation that is humanistic thrives in organizational cultures where mistakes are not punished, innovation is conducted through experiments, and the walls of hierarchies are mellowed. As an example, Microsoft has created so-called "digital sandboxes" in which cross-functional groups can create prototypes without official supervision. This is a positive effect in the creation process because, as well as making it more rapid, it induces a sense of belonging and creativity among the workers.

Another interviewee stated, *"When leaders normalize learning from mistakes, employees feel emotionally secure to experiment."*

Also, organizations have been investing in excellent internal communication networks, which allow feedback and favor inclusivity. Initiatives to target mental well-being and indicators of employee experience are being monitored in innovative companies along with more classical KPIs.

Trust, Purpose, and Customer Loyalty

On the side of the consumer, trust and purpose became the new themes that came up as drivers of both digital engagement and brand commitment. Marketing and strategy interviewees explained that the modern-day consumer marketplace is no longer satisfied by the ease of use of transactional transactions but more by the attachment and veracity of brand ethics.

One of the Unilever marketing leaders expounded, *"Consumers today want to know that their data is not just protected but respected. Our value proposition now includes digital trust as a core promise."*

This trend has made businesses develop technologies that are not only friendly to use but also emotionally intelligent. To give an illustration, one of these companies applies AI to create ethical nudges, as opposed to unethical marketing strategies. A different retail firm has also introduced IoT-enhanced packaging to allow customers to find the source of products and, in doing so, enhance the sustainability pledges of the brand.

One participant said, "When the purpose of a company is in line with the expectations of society, consumers are more emotionally attached and ready to use the digital services offered by a particular brand.

A technology strategist observed that purpose-driven innovation helps consumers to believe that the brand is not only intelligent but also human.

There is a growing convergence of consumer loyalty strategies and ethical/social responsibilities. Since becoming digital leaders, the transparency of data use has been added to their value proposition to position ethical behavior as a competitive edge. To develop relational value, high-trust organizations vigorously teach the customer and provide cycle feedback.

Technology as a Tool to Enhance, Not Replace, Human Potential

Another common understanding among interviewees was that technology has the potential to enhance, as opposed to limit, the human capacity. Automation, AI, and collaborative robots (cobots) in particular were framed many times as an augmentation strategy.

According to one of the TCS product managers, *"We don't deploy AI to replace our people; we use it to elevate them. It's about enabling creativity, not eliminating roles."*

In manufacturing, cobots were termed as game-changers, able to perform some of the redundant or dangerous jobs, as human workers still focused on quality and delivering innovation. This type of duality enhances work fulfillment and efficiency.

As an example, TCS uses learning platforms powered by AI that assess employee profiles and tailor their development. Such systems promote independence, learning efficiency, and ethical data use as they are conveyed straightforwardly.

These kinds of technologies imply a break with the old paradigms of automation as a means of promoting efficiencies and facilitating an augmented approach that treats individuals with respect and dignity. A free flow of information and ethics around data would bring about trust in the computerized systems, thereby leading to increased stakeholder participation.

Real-World Outcomes: Satisfaction, Retention, and Loyalty

The results of human-focused innovation have become concrete in the organizations under research. Attributable values cited by respondents in regard to the design ethics and empathetic measures were those of higher employee satisfaction and staff retention, besides customer loyalty.

One of the indicators within a case of Unilever showed lower attrition in work units where workers collaboratively built digital tools. In line with this, Microsoft has indicated an increase in the engagement ratings in the teams using hybrid work simulations through participatory workshops.

On their part, consumers had higher retention rates and net promoter scores when the brands were involved in transparency, personalization, and sustainability. These results were supplemented by internal files, which demonstrated that companies are starting to communicate underlying human effects of innovation in their ESG disclosures, a movement towards whole-person, people-centric performance indicators.

DISCUSSION

The empirical evidence of this chapter indicates that human-centric innovation is no longer a vision, a desire, or an initiative, but a strategy in the fast-paced digital ecosystem (Nambisan et al., 2019). Based on a review of semi-structured interviews and document studies of various globally reputed companies like Microsoft, Unilever, and Tata Consultancy Services (TCS), the study reaffirms that companies that base their innovation on empathy, inclusion, and ethics are perfectly placed to command trust, improve employee and customer satisfaction, and achieve sustainable business (Bozic & Kuppelwieser, 2019).

Alignment With and Extension of Theoretical Frameworks

The results support and enliven the three theoretical perspectives applied to this research: Human-Centered Design (HCD), Self-Determination Theory (SDT), and Service-Dominant Logic (SDL), all of which were justified by various practices in the real world.

The participatory strategies of HCD-based organizations were observed in the studied organizations. The HCD emphasis on empathy and co-creation applies, to mention but a few, to digital sandboxes of Microsoft and design sprints accomplished by employees thereof. These zones allow these workers to brainstorm and play with ideas, which can be tested and retested. These practices demonstrate that the application of HCD is not only related to the design of products and services but may also affect organizational structure and the culture of innovation (Kankanhalli et al., 2015).

The research also confirms the applicability of Self-Determination Theory (SDT), especially on the aspect of highlighting psychological needs (autonomy, competence, and relatedness) as the main elements of engagement and motivation (Deci et al., 2017). The use of upskilling tools by TCS that interface with AI, allowing the learning path to be aligned to the individual needs of the employees, can also directly complement autonomy and competence (Brynjolfsson & McAfee, 2017). Likewise, channels that permit peer feedback and sharing of knowledge promote relatedness and shared development (Edmondson & Lei, 2014). The anticorrelation between well-being programs and innovation practices that has been witnessed in several companies conforms to how the realization of these psychological needs helps minimize attrition and increases job satisfaction.

Service-Dominant Logic (SDL) seeks co-founding value development by using a feedback loop, ethical personalization, and the creation of a collective brand. It emphasizes the aspect of services and interaction in the creation of value (Kuppelwieser & Finsterwalder, 2016). Relational exchange is manifested in the interest shown in the use of user feedback in personalization algorithms and data privacy policy (Ramaswamy & Ozcan, 2018). These theories are connected and may be used to determine certain actions and outcomes that will encourage a human-centered paradigm.

Human-Centric Innovation as a Business Imperative

The evidence in the industry has been able to support the finding that human-oriented innovation leads to sustainable competitive advantage. According to McKinsey (2023) reports, 20-30 percent of employees in organizations that apply human-centric innovation models have a higher retention rate and 12-18 percent more consumer trust than those that use the traditional efficiency-based digital strategies.

Interviewed leaders explained how the human-centric principles have become embedded in strategic planning and the development of leaders. Ethical innovation is no longer considered as one of the constituents of the CSR department but as part of the corporate governance and brand integrity (Khurana et al., 2019). Such a transition is indicative of a heightened realization that value creation over the long term is impossible without the detachment of the stakeholder trust and appeal.

Those companies that are not able to reconcile with human-centric innovation are under the threat of reputation, talent loss, and client loss (Frey & Osborne, 2017). On the other hand, the ones focusing on psychological safety, transparency, and ethical design are experiencing real-life paybacks, such as increased employee enthusiasm, consumer retention, and agility to change (Liu et al., 2015).

Emotional Engagement, Inclusive Leadership, and Digital Ethics

Another strong point of this piece of research is that it sheds light on the emotional and moral aspects of innovation.

The firms that have an emotional connection to the innovation process record an average of more than 35 percent compared to an engineered buy-in of the innovation process, and the stakeholder trust gains increase by 21 percent.

Emotional mobilization in the workforce, as well as among its consumers, came up as a strong generator of organizational strength and innovativeness (Pappas et al., 2017). When the employees felt listened to, secure, and empowered, they were more inclined to bring in innovative ideas and also engage in the change initiatives. Similarly, the long-term loyalty also showed a better response to consumers who were made to feel that a brand was authentic and ethically acceptable (Lemon & Verhoef, 2016).

The research study introduces the centrality of inclusive leadership in the facilitation of such emotional bonds. Being more empathetic, transparent, and participatory, managers who helped develop a trusting and collaborative context of innovations were more likely to stay focused (Kolbjørnsrud et al., 2017). It needs to be mentioned that such a leadership style is also supportive of diversity, equity, and inclusion; tolerates varying views; and eliminates obstacles to collaboration.

Ethics are required in the digital world and help businesses gain compliance with the regulations and build brand equity (Parviainen et al., 2017). Data governance under data-monitored ecosystems increases the trust of stakeholders offered by responsible data use and opportunities to opt out, as well as transparency reports (Grover et al., 2019). It portrays the addition of another innovation logic that involves emotional intelligence and digital responsibility.

Emotional engagement was proposed as a formidable intermediary between human-centered innovation and long-term relationships with stakeholders (Loureiro, 2023). This emotional level is especially applicable within the framework of the Experience Economy, as the consumers and employees tend to be not only functionally utility enabled but also meaningfully and affectively engaged with technology and organizations (Pine & Gilmore, 2021). The results apply to and inform the theory of self-determination (SDT) as it can show that emotional engagement is both an outcome and a predictor of satisfaction of basic psychological needs: autonomy (user control over and ability to customize the experience), competence (a sense of conflicted effectiveness and maintenance in interactions), and relatedness (a sense of emotional connection to a brand or platform). Incorporating these needs, the organizations not only encourage the adoption of innovation but also achieve trust, emotional connection, and long-lasting loyalty, all of which are crucial markers in the Industry 5.0 settings.

These are the findings that are closer to Self-Determination Theory (SDT), which states that people become emotionally engaged when they feel autonomy, competence, and relatedness. Human-centric innovation supports these requirements by instilling a sense of ownership in employees, mastery of skills, and relational trust between and amongst customers.

Relevance to Industry 5.0 and the Experience Economy

The need to convert to the Experience Economy and Industry 5.0 becomes all the more real with the findings (Autor, 2019). Industry 5.0 focuses on the interaction of human beings and machines as it promotes individuality, innovativeness, and national well-being. The research proves that the companies are already putting into practice these principles by incorporating the use of cobots, AI-strengthened learning facilities, and crowdsourcing innovation plans (Davenport & Kalakota, 2019).

Likewise, the underlying strategies of the Experience Economy that relate to the development of memorable and meaningful interactions resonate well with the consumer-side conclusions (Libai et al., 2020). The businesses that personalize the encounters to user taste, support privacy, and serve a reason are not pitching the services alone; they are co-designing the experiences. These strategies appeal to the contemporary consumer taste, where emotional satisfaction and a morally compelling brand experience are sought.

Considered collectively, it is implied by these results that the concept of human-centered innovation is not merely consistent with these forward-looking paradigms; it is a part and parcel of their effectiveness (Dwivedi et al., 2021).

Comparative Analysis With Past Research and Models

The more comprehensive and humane model presented in this chapter, in comparison to other preceding innovation models based on a focus on lean production, process optimization, or eliminating disruptive technologies, represents one alternative to the current trend. Though the older models were cost-driven and focused on efficiency and speed on a scale, their emphasis has been more on social impacts, ignored as well as human dignity. Conversely, the contemporary set of results denotes that emotional security, morality, and user empowerment are not trade-offs but innovators.

The work is also based on and continues previous research on the need to develop more participatory and ethical processes of digital transformation. It provides empirical support for theoretical arguments regarding the nature of the superiority of the inclusive design and safety of the psychological sense, as well as the inconsistencies in the implementation of these notions into the functioning of multiple areas.

Further, introducing HCD, SDT, and SDL in analysis and interpretation provides an inclusive model that can be used in future research on innovation. It shows that design, motivation, and value creation theories not only harmonize well together, but they also complement one another, even when going into practice with realistically grounded innovation problems.

IMPLICATIONS

The implications of this research are extensive, not only in the academic theory but also in daily management and real-life innovation strategy. By comparing and contrasting how the companies in various industries are injecting empathy, ethics, and technology into their innovation efforts, the research not only contributes to the scholarly discussion but also allows business executives, policymakers, and technology designers to act as well. The above implications indicate that human-centric innovation is a powerful force that can change not only internal organizational processes but also external market relations.

Theoretical Implications

This research makes an important addition to the theoretical work on innovation because it confirms the combination of Human-Centered Design (HCD), Self-Determination Theory (SDT), and Service-Dominant Logic (SDL) into a single conceptual framework. Conventionally, these theories are viewed as disciplinary or dissociative. Nonetheless, the study proves that they can become multidimensional and dynamic together to state a human-centric understanding of innovation.

The SDT fit and the HCD principles of empathy and participatory design are displayed to complement each other; the SDL broadens the picture once again by positing both employees and consumers as co-producers of value. The results provide a picture that such theories do not work independently, but rather, they are integrated into the real world, enabling the design of innovation processes around user experience, ethical engagement, and cross-input.

Furthermore, this incorporation enhances the academic explanation of co-created value as it applies to each relationship between employees and consumers. Empirical evidence, as set out in the study, shows that value creation today is not limited to a product or service itself; it is also based on the way people experience innovation processes. What makes the outcome of innovation more sustainable, inclusive, and powerful is the engagement of the employees in the design of the tools they utilize and the involvement of the consumers in the design of brand interactions.

The study also expands these constructs into untouched areas like ethical deployment of AI, psychological safety in the workplace, and value-driven customer design. It encourages future researchers to examine additional connections between motivation, design, and service logic within a digital transformation.

Managerial Implications

In terms of management, the chapter provides a definite way to construct action plans to create technologically advanced yet human-centered innovation strategies. It is no longer a question of whether empathy and ethics are relevant to businesses; leaders have to make them important components of business strategic competence that are integrated into all strata of organizational decision-making.

The ability to lead based on empathy, ethical reasoning, and inclusion-based communication is one of the major implications. Now, innovation leadership cannot occur without the capacity to listen well to employees and consumers, the people who buy products, to interpret the emotional and moral cues that they send, and to create cultures of psychological safety. Managers should move the management of work towards the provision of an innovative environment that is grounded on trust and collaboration, where experimentation is seen as a means of learning and failure as a way of learning.

The study is concerned with the importance of innovation policies that lead to dignity, inclusion, and well-being. Technologies should also capitalize on the skills of individuals, such as open data apps and explainable AI. Managers should use innovation KPIs to be correlated with human-centered KPIs, such as disability measures like employee engagement and trust ratings, as these indices reveal that they consider people over results.

Practical Implications

Practically, this study offers a set of **concrete guidelines and principles** that organizations can adopt to operationalize human-centric innovation:

- **Responsible Use of AI, IoT, and Personalization Technologies**

To use AI and IoT, organizations should not view them as substitutes for human input; instead, organizations can use the technology to assist in learning, personalization, and workplace enhancement. Their implementation should be guided by ethical models that will help them improve the human experience and not destroy it. Open consent systems, transparency dashboards, and human supervision are the main characteristics of responsible use of technology.

- **Consumer-Centered Service Design Models**

Service design approaches in use by companies should integrate customers into the design of their online experiences. These involve the production of service flows jointly, the customization of interfaces, and instilling empathy in the touchpoints throughout the consumer journey. Support in this engagement process can be provided with the use of such tools as empathy mapping, journey mapping, and user feedback loops.

- **Embedding Values and Purpose into Innovation Practices**

The businesses should make sure that their innovation pipelines not only run over technological feasibility but also in a way that they correspond to organizational values and social purpose. Ethical charters and purpose-driven structures should drive innovation labs, product teams, and units of digital transformation. This practice facilitates brand differentiation and trust among the stakeholders.

The study focuses on the need for organizations to adopt human-centric practices in their organizations by way of adopting policies, training programs, and performance incentives. The fact that innovation should coincide with the UN Sustainable Development Goals (SDGs) and enhance ethical growth can enable even businesses to work in an economy that prizes purpose, impact, and authenticity.

RECOMMENDATIONS

Based on the results and implications of this research, several applicable recommendations can be presented to assist the work of organizations, policymakers, and practitioners who need to promote the work in the field of human-centric innovation. These recommendations are centered on integrating moral integrity, compassion, creation-with, and inclusion in the implementation and development of innovation strategies. They deal with the systemic transformation in finding a balance between technological progress, human flourishing, and sustainable development.

Invest in Ethical Innovation Ecosystems

Companies should transform the way they implement technology and should consider building comprehensive ethical systems of innovation in a manner that is not piecemeal. These ecosystems are to be preconditioned on strong bases of undoubted ethical norms that put technology application and human values on the same level, manifesting justice, accountability, and transparency. This means overcoming compliance and seeking an attempt to be proactive and highlight and restrain ethical threats that accompany artificial intelligence (AI), automation, and data-driven systems.

To ensure the regulation of innovation, organizations ought to integrate structures such as digital ethics committees, interdisciplinary review committees, and stakeholder advisory committees. It is also important to include ethics in the continuous lifecycle of innovation, which can include ideation, implementation, and post-implementation processes. Its continuous communication regarding its openness with civil society, academia, and regulatory agencies can also boost the level of trust and create a new wave of responsible innovation.

Involve Employees and Consumers in Co-Design Processes

Authentically human-centric innovation must come with the co-creation of space with those who get the biggest effect of it: workers and end-users. The companies in question should be enthusiastic about involving passive end-users as the end receivers and working with them to design, test, and further improve technologies, services, and processes.

Employees can gain knowledge through the participatory innovation method that is experienced through platforms like design thinking workshops, digital sandboxing, and innovation sprints, and in the process, deliberate on operational inefficiencies on top ideas that are led by the front lines. Such an inclusive strategy will not only give more relevant solutions but also enhance the motivation, commitment, and ownership of the employees. The employees will be ready to use and popularize innovations in which they were involved.

Firms ought to integrate consumer experience labs, feedback, and journey mapping sessions to capture in real life the needs, emotions, and aspirations that encourage individualization, brand loyalty, and value co-creation. The reviews and requirements of users should be accommodated through the digital interface to engage in a continuous relationship, thus fostering innovation and partnership with stakeholders.

Prioritize Digital Literacy and Well-Being Programs

With the increased digitalization of work and life, organizations also have a role to play in ensuring digital literacy and the well-being of the individuals they represent. One of them is the arming of employees and consumers with the knowledge, the skills, and the resilience capabilities of engaging with the innovation and reaping its positive benefits.

The employees should be provided with steady upskilling assignments, individualized learning routes, and coaching programs allowing them to flourish in the digitalized settings. Programs also need to encompass more than technical skills and must also include critical thinking, ethical reasoning, and the ability to develop emotionally ready skills.

Organizations should embrace digital well-being through their oversaturation monitoring, encouraging healthy screen use, and implementing a flexible working schedule. Sustainable innovation takes much interest in work-life balance, psychological safety, and mental health promotion. Communities can be educated through digital literacy programs on how to use privacy and interactivity in digital environments.

Encourage Multi-Stakeholder Collaborations for Inclusive Innovation

Digital transformation possesses ethical, social, and technological problems that cannot be addressed in one organization. In this light, companies should be at the forefront of promoting multi-stakeholder arrangements that lead to aligning many voices and knowledge in coming up with end-accessible innovation systems.

They should include government connections, non-governmental organizations, universities, startups, and those minority populations who are deprived. These collaborations can find areas of blindness, get the silenced voices heard, and open innovation to all. It is also possible to collaboratively dive into experimental fields, like AI ethics, sustainability, and future-of-work projects, and not needlessly reinvent the wheel.

Industry consortia and innovation clusters are particularly well-suited to assume the role with the creation of open-source tools, ethical standards, and cross-sector guidelines that can be developed to benefit the economy at large. Lessons, errors, and experiences: such collaborative platforms result in communal learning and an institutional memory as a means of ensuring that potentially hazardous errors are not duplicated.

Organizations can optimize innovation and grow in a more scalable manner and attain equity when managing diversity, equity, and inclusion. Human-oriented innovation is a strategic, structural, and cultural operating transformation. Sustainability in the digital age is provided through investment in ethical ecosystems, co-design, digital well-being, and inclusive partnerships.

LIMITATIONS OF THE STUDY

The present study is based on a qualitative exploratory design, which constrained the generalizability of the results. While interviews and document analysis offer useful information, the number of cases is very limited, so different industries or regions may not be represented. In addition, some of the qualitative responses might be the personal views of the people or the organization's side of the story, which cannot possible to confirmed. Further research may consider these constraints by having larger data sets, cross-industrial comparisons, or using a mixed-method design to extend and deepen the generalizability of the results.

FUTURE RESEARCH DIRECTIONS

Although this research is informative about the strategic, emotional, and ethical perspectives of human-centric innovation, it also identifies various areas of future research. The significance of this has been highlighted by these opportunities that gave importance to the continued scholarly exploration in an attempt to create greater, more generalizable, and action-oriented knowledge in various situations.

To begin with, a quantitative study is urgently required to verify and confirm the relationships postulated in this qualitative study. The measurement of variables like employee engagement, psychological safety, rates of innovation adoption, or consumer loyalty in a broader sample can be based on the use of surveys, longitudinal tracking, or experimental approaches in future research. Such a quantitative base would not only increase the external validity of the existing findings but also enable institutions to benchmark practices related to human-centric innovation based on standard measures. To give one example, theoretical and statistical research could be conducted on the connection between inclusive leadership and retention rates or the rates of ethical use of AI and customer confidence in this service.

Second, the researchers of the future have to strive to include greater cultural and geographic diversity. The current research has mainly targeted global companies as well as those operating in the advanced and emerging economies, but a void still exists in the way human-centric innovation perception and practice are perceived and applied in location-based companies, start-up organizations, or public service in any region. Cultural comparisons provided by comparative research between cultures, including the difference that occurs between collectivist and individualist societies, may help to illuminate the influence of cultural norms on empathy-related leadership, consumer-related expectations, and digital ethics.

Third, the longitudinal study must be conducted to assess the future dynamics of human-inclined innovation on organizational performance. Even though we have seen overnight shifts in staff satisfaction and consumer engagement, it is interesting to examine how innovations are beginning to exert an influence on the long-term outcomes, such as brand value, employee retention, innovation ROI, and social contribution. These tests would be useful to sort out the issue of whether human-based strategies produce any sustained competitive advantage and business resilience in turbulent conditions.

Lastly, the integration of digital ethics frameworks and governance models should be the highlighted aspect of future research. Although the issue of ethical intent is largely recognized, practical application is still haphazardly done. How organizations can institutionally make ethical decisions, do algorithmic audits, make data transparent, and manage dilemmas between personalization and privacy needs to be studied. The study might fill in the gaps to develop a uniform framework of governance that can enable the large-scale and responsible innovation process.

CONCLUSION

The increasing sophistication of the digital age necessitates a paradigm shift in the conceptualization, development, and implementation of innovation. This chapter has examined why the new age demands a human-centric approach to innovation, which is an innovative shift that envisioned empathy, ethics, and inclusion as the focal point of technology and organizational change. At the stage where efficiency and profitability simply are not the only ways of prioritizing, in the age of a flurry of rapid changes in the fields of artificial intelligence, IoT, and data analysis, another trend is emerging to the fore: the prioritization of E toward the reduction of the gulf in privilege. In turn, the notion of innovation has to change so that the complex needs of people can be taken into consideration and relationships of trust and well-being can be developed in the long term.

The results of this study support the idea that empathy can hardly be considered a soft skill that can be relegated to the periphery, but rather a strategic tool of productive innovation. Institutions that can immerse themselves in the emotional truth of employees and consumers stand a better chance of bringing about a solution that sticks, persists, and becomes scalable. Ethical responsibility is also a business requirement as opposed to a regulatory add-on. Practicing ethical measures on the digital platform is something that must be taken into account by companies, drilling down to the principles of fair play, openness, and responsibility. Diversity enhances innovation further through increasing perspectives, participation, and the creation of products and services that capture the diversity of human experience.

The fundamental difference between these priorities is that the focus of innovation is ultimately on purpose, speed of operations, empowerment, and societal relevance, as opposed to technology-driven innovation that seeks to achieve speed in operations. This chapter proves that such a change is morally correct as well as a winning business tactic. Companies that base their innovation strategy on the human values of autonomy, trust, and well-being attain improved working engagement, consumer loyalty, and organizational resilience.

Businesses that incorporate human values in their digital design always achieve better performance compared to their competitors. With +20% in employee retention, +15% in customer loyalty, as the McKinsey Global Report (2023), Global report claims.

In this respect, people-oriented innovation does not manifest itself as a luxury or specialty philosophy but as a sustainable and competitive necessity.

The paradigm shift will also represent general international changes like Industry 5.0 and the Experience Economy. Industry 5.0 is focused on human/intelligent technology collaboration and is meant to foster innovation aimed at growing creativity and individual satisfaction. In the meantime, the experience economy demands that companies create effective and memorable experiences. Human-centered innovation is the convergence of these changes and a pathway forward by which companies that want to succeed in the coming world will increasingly evaluate technologies according to the quality of human results they make possible.

The study featured in this chapter suggests shifting the focus of innovation not to short-term efficiencies but to more long-term, meaningful effects. This incorporates the idea of inclusive leadership, ethical digital infrastructures, and ingraining co-creation into internal and external innovation processes. Organizations need to broaden the parameters of success to encompass the psychological security of the employees, the dignity of the consumers, and the sustainability of the society in which they live.

In this study, the authors stress that ethical models, governance structures, and emotional intelligence should be a part of innovation design. The vision plans should be transparent, interactive, and spacious to increase the empowerment of human beings against the balancing of digital abilities and human dignity. Empathic leadership, human-centered designs, and ethical governance are key components of the sustainability of value and a future that is not only intelligent but also human.

The research concludes to suggest that the human-centricity approach should be the strategic asset of innovation in every sphere of life in order to ensure that technological development of the future will not contradict human welfare and social evolution.

REFERENCES

Autor, D. H. (2019, May). Work of the Past, Work of the Future. In *AEA Papers and Proceedings* (Vol. 109, pp. 1-32). 2014 Broadway, Suite 305, Nashville, TN 37203: American Economic Association.

Bozic, B., & Kuppelwieser, V. G. (2019). Customer trust recovery: An alternative explanation. *Journal of Retailing and Consumer Services, 49*, 208–218. DOI: 10.1016/j.jretconser.2019.04.002

Braun, V., & Clarke, V. (2006). Using thematic analysis in psychology. *Qualitative Research in Psychology, 3*(2), 77–101. DOI: 10.1191/1478088706qp063oa

Brynjolfsson, E., & Mcafee, A. N. D. R. E. W. (2017). The business of artificial intelligence. *Harvard Business Review, 7*(1), 1–2.

Davenport, T., & Kalakota, R. (2019). The potential for artificial intelligence in healthcare. *Future Healthcare Journal, 6*(2), 94–98. DOI: 10.7861/futurehosp.6-2-94

Deci, E. L., Olafsen, A. H., & Ryan, R. M. (2017). Self-determination theory in work organizations: The state of a science. *Annual Review of Organizational Psychology and Organizational Behavior, 4*(1), 19–43. DOI: 10.1146/annurev-orgpsych-032516-113108

Dwivedi, Y. K., Hughes, L., Ismagilova, E., Aarts, G., Coombs, C., Crick, T., Duan, Y., Dwivedi, R., Edwards, J., Eirug, A., Galanos, V., Ilavarasan, P. V., Janssen, M., Jones, P., Kar, A. K., Kizgin, H., Kronemann, B., Lal, B., Lucini, B., & Williams, M. D. (2021). Artificial Intelligence (AI): Multidisciplinary perspectives on emerging challenges, opportunities, and agenda for research, practice and policy. *International Journal of Information Management, 57*, 101994. DOI: 10.1016/j.ijinfomgt.2019.08.002

Edmondson, A. C., & Lei, Z. (2014). Psychological safety: The history, renaissance, and future of an interpersonal construct. *Annual Review of Organizational Psychology and Organizational Behavior, 1*(1), 23–43. DOI: 10.1146/annurev-orgpsych-031413-091305

Frey, C. B., & Osborne, M. A. (2017). The future of employment: How susceptible are jobs to computerisation? *Technological Forecasting and Social Change, 114*, 254–280. DOI: 10.1016/j.techfore.2016.08.019

Grover, P., Kar, A. K., & Janssen, M. (2019). Diffusion of blockchain technology: Insights from academic literature and social media analytics. *Journal of Enterprise Information Management, 32*(5), 735–757. DOI: 10.1108/JEIM-06-2018-0132

Kankanhalli, A., Ye, H., & Teo, H. H. (2015). Comparing potential and actual innovators. *Management Information Systems Quarterly*, *39*(3), 667–682. DOI: 10.25300/MISQ/2015/39.3.07

Khurana, S., Haleem, A., & Mannan, B. (2019). Determinants for integration of sustainability with innovation for Indian manufacturing enterprises: Empirical evidence in MSMEs. *Journal of Cleaner Production*, *229*, 374–386. DOI: 10.1016/j.jclepro.2019.04.022

Kolbjørnsrud, V., Amico, R., & Thomas, R. J. (2017). Partnering with AI: How organizations can win over skeptical managers. *Strategy and Leadership*, *45*(1), 37–43. DOI: 10.1108/SL-12-2016-0085

Kuppelwieser, V. G., & Finsterwalder, J. (2016). Transformative service research and service dominant logic: Quo Vaditis? *Journal of Retailing and Consumer Services*, *28*, 91–98. DOI: 10.1016/j.jretconser.2015.08.011

Lemon, K. N., & Verhoef, P. C. (2016). Understanding customer experience throughout the customer journey. *Journal of Marketing*, *80*(6), 69–96. DOI: 10.1509/jm.15.0420

Libai, B., Bart, Y., Gensler, S., Hofacker, C. F., Kaplan, A., Kötterheinrich, K., & Kroll, E. B. (2020). Brave new world? On AI and the management of customer relationships. *Journal of Interactive Marketing*, *51*(1), 44–56. DOI: 10.1016/j.intmar.2020.04.002

Liu, Y., Eisingerich, A. B., Auh, S., Merlo, O., & Chun, H. E. H. (2015). Service firm performance transparency: How, when, and why does it pay off? *Journal of Service Research*, *18*(4), 451–467. DOI: 10.1177/1094670515584331

Loureiro, S. M. C. (2023). Overview of the brand journey and opportunities for future studies. *Italian Journal of Marketing*, *2023*(2), 179–206. DOI: 10.1007/s43039-023-00069-0

Mazzucato, M. (2018). Mission-oriented innovation policies: Challenges and opportunities. *Industrial and Corporate Change*, *27*(5), 803–815. DOI: 10.1093/icc/dty034

Nambisan, S., Wright, M., & Feldman, M. (2019). The digital transformation of innovation and entrepreneurship: Progress, challenges and key themes. *Research Policy*, *48*(8), 103773. DOI: 10.1016/j.respol.2019.03.018

Pappas, I. O., Kourouthanassis, P. E., Giannakos, M. N., & Chrissikopoulos, V. (2017). Sense and sensibility in personalized e-commerce: How emotions rebalance the purchase intentions of persuaded customers. *Psychology and Marketing*, *34*(10), 972–986. DOI: 10.1002/mar.21036

Parviainen, P., Tihinen, M., Kääriäinen, J., & Teppola, S. (2017). Tackling the digitalization challenge: how to benefit from digitalization in practice. *International journal of information systems and project management, 5*(1), 63-77.

Pine, B. J., & Gilmore, J. H. (2021). *The Experience Economy: Competing for customer time, attention, and money*. No Title.

Ramaswamy, V., & Ozcan, K. (2018). What is co-creation? An interactional creation framework and its implications for value creation. *Journal of Business Research, 84*, 196–205. DOI: 10.1016/j.jbusres.2017.11.027

Ritter, T., & Pedersen, C. L. (2020). Analyzing the impact of the coronavirus crisis on business models. *Industrial Marketing Management, 88*, 214–224. DOI: 10.1016/j.indmarman.2020.05.014

Compilation of References

Aamer, A., Zadeh, A., Mali, P., & Bolick, C. (2025). Emerging technologies and principle-based project management: A systematic literature review and research agenda. *Management Review Quarterly*, *75*(2), 1761–1811. DOI: 10.1007/s11301-024-00419-y

Ab Rahim, H., Ibrahim, S., Kamaruddin, S. B. A., Ghani, N. A. M., & Musirin, I. (2020). Exploration on digital marketing as business strategy model among Malaysian entrepreneurs via neurocomputing. *IAES International Journal of Artificial Intelligence*, *9*(1), 18. DOI: 10.11591/ijai.v9.i1.pp18-24

Abdelqawy, D., El-Korany, A., Kamel, A., & Makady, S. (2022). Hub-OS: An interoperable IoT computing platform for resources utilization with real-time support. *Journal of King Saud University. Computer and Information Sciences*, *34*(4), 1498–1510. https://doi.org/https://doi.org/10.1016/j.jksuci.2022.02.011. DOI: 10.1016/j.jksuci.2022.02.011

Abdel-rahman, H. (2024). Actual Economy: Local Solutions for Global Challenges—2024 BUILDING EFFECTIVE PARTNERSHIPS BETWEEN NON-GOVERNMENTAL ORGANIZATIONS (NGOS). *AND BUSINESSES FOR ENVIRONMENTAL CONSERVATION Actual Economy: Local Solutions for Global Challenges*, *2024*(2019), 290–293.

Abdullah, M., Mengash, H. A., Maray, M., Alrslani, F. A. F., Alkhudhayr, H., Alghanmi, N. A., Subahi, A., & Majdoubi, J. (2025). Federated learning with Blockchain on Denial-of-Service attacks detection and classification of edge IIoT networks using Deep Transfer Learning model. *Computers & Electrical Engineering*, *124*, 110319. Advance online publication. DOI: 10.1016/j.compeleceng.2025.110319

Abrantes Baracho, R. M., Magalhães Vidigal, M. J., da Silva Santiago, L. G., Porto, M. F., & Pereira Moreira, L. H. (2025). Virtual Reality and Building Information Modeling in Architecture. *Procedia Computer Science*, *256*, 673–680. DOI: 10.1016/j.procs.2025.02.166

Abro, G.-E.-M., Zahid, F., Azhar Ali, S. S., & Aromoye, I. A. (2025). Exploring the Potential Benefits and Overcoming the Constraints of Virtual and Augmented Reality in Operator Training. *Transportation Research Procedia*, *84*, 625–632. DOI: 10.1016/j.trpro.2025.03.117

Abughalia, A., & Stechert, C. (2025). Immersive Onboarding: Designing a Training Framework for Effective Virtual Reality Integration in Product Development. *Procedia CIRP*, *136*, 432–437. DOI: 10.1016/j.procir.2025.08.075

Adel, A. (2022). Future of industry 5.0 in society: Human-centric solutions, challenges and prospective research areas. *Journal of Cloud Computing (Heidelberg, Germany)*, *11*(1), 40. https://journalofcloudcomputing.springeropen.com/counter/pdf/10.1186/s13677-022-00314-5. DOI: 10.1186/s13677-022-00314-5 PMID: 36101900

Admoko, D. A., Darmawan, B., Ana, A., & Dwiyanto, V. (2024). A Cluster-Based Bibliometric Analysis of the Emerging Technological Landscape in Logistics using Vosviewer. *Journal of Advanced Research in Applied Sciences and Engineering Technology*, *42*(2), 234–249. DOI: 10.37934/araset.42.2.234249

Aheleroff, S., Xu, X., Zhong, R. Y., & Lu, Y. (2021). Digital Twin as a Service (DTaaS) in Industry 4.0: An Architecture Reference Model. *Advanced Engineering Informatics*, *47*, 101225. DOI: 10.1016/j.aei.2020.101225

Ahmad, Z., Jaffri, Z., Chen, M., & Bao, S. (2025). Understanding GANs: Fundamentals, variants, training challenges, applications, and open problems. *Multimedia Tools and Applications*, *84*(12), 10347–10423. DOI: 10.1007/s11042-024-19361-y

Ahmed, W. A. H., & Rios, A. (2022). *Chapter 18 - Digitalization of the international shipping and maritime logistics industry: a case study of TradeLens* (B. L. MacCarthy & D. B. T.-T. D. S. C. Ivanov (eds.); pp. 309–323). Elsevier. 10.1016/B978-0-323-91614-1.00018-6

Ahmed, B. S., Azzalin, T., Kassler, A., Thore, A., & Lindbäck, H. (2025). Smart manufacturing: MLOps-enabled event-driven architecture for enhanced control in steel production. *Journal of Systems and Software*, *230*, 112542. DOI: 10.1016/j.jss.2025.112542

Ahmed, M. A., Gallardo, J. L., Zuniga, M. D., Pedraza, M. A., Carvajal, G., Jara, N., & Carvajal, R. (2022). LoRa Based IoT Platform for Remote Monitoring of Large-Scale Agriculture Farms in Chile. *Sensors (Basel)*, *22*(8), 2824. Advance online publication. DOI: 10.3390/s22082824 PMID: 35458808

Ahmed, S., Alshater, M. M., El Ammari, A., & Hammami, H. (2022). Artificial intelligence and machine learning in finance: A bibliometric review. *Research in International Business and Finance*, *61*, 101646. https://doi.org/https://doi.org/10.1016/j.ribaf.2022.101646. DOI: 10.1016/j.ribaf.2022.101646

Akash, T. R., Sany, N. J., Akter, L., & Sarna, S. A. (2025). Privacy—Preserving Technique in cybersecurity: Balancing Data Protection and User Rights. *Journal of Computer Science and Technology Studies*, *7*(4), 248–263. DOI: 10.32996/jcsts.2025.7.3.90

Akram, S. V., Malik, P. K., Singh, R., Gehlot, A., Juyal, A., Ghafoor, K. Z., & Shrestha, S. (2022). Implementation of Digitalized Technologies for Fashion Industry 4.0: Opportunities and Challenges. *Scientific Programming*, *2022*, 1–17. Advance online publication. DOI: 10.1155/2022/7523246

Alaca, Y., & Çelik, Y. (2023). Cyber attack detection with QR code images using lightweight deep learning models. *Computers & Security*, *126*, 103065. https://doi.org/https://doi.org/10.1016/j.cose.2022.103065. DOI: 10.1016/j.cose.2022.103065

Alex, L., Mai, R., & Rauschnabel, P. A. (2026). Similar but different: The differential implications of augmented and virtual reality experiences for raising engagement towards climate change actions. *Computers in Human Behavior*, *174*, 108798. DOI: 10.1016/j.chb.2025.108798

Alfeo, A. L., Cimino, M. G. C. A., & Vaglini, G. (2022). Degradation stage classification via interpretable feature learning. *Journal of Manufacturing Systems*, *62*, 972–983. DOI: 10.1016/j.jmsy.2021.05.003

Alhakamy, A. (2024). Extended Reality (XR) Toward Building Immersive Solutions: The Key to Unlocking Industry 4.0. *ACM Computing Surveys*, *56*(9), 1–38. DOI: 10.1145/3652595

AL-Hawamleh, A. M. (2024). Securing the future: Framework fundamentals for cyber resilience in advancing organizations. *Journal of System and Management Sciences*, *14*(10), 130–150.

Alkhodair, M., & Alkhudhayr, H. (2025). Harnessing Industry 4.0 for SMEs: Advancing Smart Manufacturing and Logistics for Sustainable Supply Chains. *Sustainability (Basel)*, *17*(3), 813. Advance online publication. DOI: 10.3390/su17030813

Almeida, L. G. G., de Vasconcelos, N. V., Winkler, I., & Catapan, M. F. (2023). Innovating Industrial Training with Immersive Metaverses: A Method for Developing Cross-Platform Virtual Reality Environments. *Applied Sciences (Basel, Switzerland)*, *13*(15), 8915. Advance online publication. DOI: 10.3390/app13158915

Al-saggaf, A. A., Sheltami, T., Alkhzaimi, H., & Ahmed, G. (2023). Lightweight Two-Factor-Based User Authentication Protocol for IoT-Enabled Healthcare Ecosystem in Quantum Computing. *Arabian Journal for Science and Engineering*, *48*(2), 2347–2357. Advance online publication. DOI: 10.1007/s13369-022-07235-0 PMID: 36164325

AlZu'bi, S., Hawashin, B., Mujahed, M., Jararweh, Y., & Gupta, B. B. (2019). An efficient employment of internet of multimedia things in smart and future agriculture. *Multimedia Tools and Applications*, *78*(20), 29581–29605. DOI: 10.1007/s11042-019-7367-0

Alzubaidi, L., Jebur, S. A., Jaber, T. A., Mohammed, M. A., Alwzwazy, H. A., Saihood, A., Gammulle, H., Santamaria, J., Duan, Y., Fookes, C., Jurdak, R., & Gu, Y. (2025). ATD Learning: A secure, smart, and decentralised learning method for big data environments. *Information Fusion*, *118*, 102953. Advance online publication. DOI: 10.1016/j.inffus.2025.102953

Amaizu, G. C., Njoku, J. N., Lee, J. M., & Kim, D. S. (2024). Metaverse in advanced manufacturing: Background, applications, limitations, open issues & future directions. *ICT Express*, *10*(2), 233–255. DOI: 10.1016/j.icte.2024.02.010

Anadkat, D. & Amit Sata. (2023a). Indian Design on Movable Bottom Pouring Resistance Melting Furnace With Process Monitoring Attachment (Patent 351953–001). Indian Design.

Anadkat, D. & Amit Sata. (2023b). Indian Design on Vertical Centrifugal Casting setup for holding moulds with different aspect ratio (Patent 351952–001). Indian Design.

Anadkat, D., & Sata, A. (2022). Internet of Things Enabled Vertical Centrifugal Casting (An Implementation). National Conference Cum Industry Meet on Foundry 4.0, 35–39.

Anadkat, D., Dave, A., Sata, A., Shukla, M., & Jarboui, S. (2024). Digital twinning of vertical centrifugal casting. *Concurrent Engineering, Research and Applications*, *32*(1–4), 78–89. DOI: 10.1177/1063293X241296463

Anadkat, D., Sata, A., Shukla, M., Jarboui, S., & Mobarsa, D. (2025). Designing an immersive interactive environment for IIoT-enhanced vertical centrifugal casting. *Frontiers in Education*, *9*, 1507851. Advance online publication. DOI: 10.3389/feduc.2024.1507851

Arnob, A. K. B., Chowdhury, R. R., Chaiti, N. A., Saha, S., & Roy, A. (2025). A comprehensive systematic review of intrusion detection systems: Emerging techniques, challenges, and future research directions. *Journal of Edge Computing*, *4*(1), 73–104. DOI: 10.55056/jec.885

Asad, M., & Otoum, S. (2024). Federated Learning for Personalized User Experiences in the Metaverse. *2024 2nd International Conference on Intelligent Metaverse Technologies & Applications (iMETA)*, 050–055. DOI: 10.1109/iMETA62882.2024.10807979

Assad, F., Konstantinov, S., Patsavellas, J., & Salonitis, K. (2024). A framework for enabling metaverse for sustainable manufacturing. *Procedia CIRP*, *128*, 108–113. DOI: 10.1016/j.procir.2024.06.010

Augustine, P. (2020). The industry use cases for the Digital Twin idea. In *Advances in Computers* (Vol. 117, Issue 1, pp. 79–105). DOI: 10.1016/bs.adcom.2019.10.008

Autor, D. H. (2019, May). Work of the Past, Work of the Future. In *AEA Papers and Proceedings* (Vol. 109, pp. 1-32). 2014 Broadway, Suite 305, Nashville, TN 37203: American Economic Association.

Ayinaddis, S. G. (2025). Artificial intelligence adoption dynamics and knowledge in SMEs and large firms: A systematic review and bibliometric analysis. *Journal of Innovation & Knowledge*, *10*(3), 100682. DOI: 10.1016/j.jik.2025.100682

Aziz, S., Jung, D. W., & Zaman, U. K. uz, & Aqeel, A. Bin. (2023). Digital Twins in Smart Manufacturing. Handbook of Manufacturing Systems and Design, 53–68. DOI: 10.1201/9781003327523-6

Balogh, M., Földvári, A., & Varga, P. (2023). Digital Twins in Industry 5.0: Challenges in Modeling and Communication. *NOMS 2023-2023 IEEE/IFIP Network Operations and Management Symposium*, 1–6. DOI: 10.1109/NOMS56928.2023.10154424

Bankins, S., Formosa, P., Montefiore, T., Richards, D., Cenacchi, F., & McEwan, M. (2025). Virtual reality and work: Ethical and inclusion implications of facial representation in VR. *The Journal of Strategic Information Systems*, *34*(4), 101937. DOI: 10.1016/j.jsis.2025.101937

Baporikar, N., & Shikokola, S. (2020). Information technology adoption dynamics for SMEs in the manufacturing sector of Namibia. [IJICTRAME]. *International Journal of ICT Research in Africa and the Middle East*, *9*(2), 60–77. DOI: 10.4018/IJICTRAME.2020070104

Bellalouna, F. (2020). Industrial Use Cases for Augmented Reality Application. 2020 11th IEEE International Conference on Cognitive Infocommunications (CogInfoCom), 11–18. DOI: 10.1109/CogInfoCom50765.2020.9237882

Bellalouna, F. (2021). The Augmented Reality Technology as Enabler for the Digitization of Industrial Business Processes: Case Studies. *Procedia CIRP*, *98*, 400–405. DOI: 10.1016/j.procir.2021.01.124

Beltrán, M. (2025). AI algorithms under scrutiny: GDPR, DSA, AI Act and CRA as pillars for algorithmic security and privacy in the European Union. *Computers & Security*, *158*, 104628. Advance online publication. DOI: 10.1016/j.cose.2025.104628

Benjamens, S., Dhunnoo, P., & Meskó, B. (2020). The state of artificial intelligence-based FDA-approved medical devices and algorithms: An online database. *NPJ Digital Medicine*, *3*(1), 118. DOI: 10.1038/s41746-020-00324-0 PMID: 32984550

Bhoraniya, D., Kanzaria, P., Anadkat, D., & Sata, A. (2018). Development of Vertical Centrifugal Casting (VCC) *Experimental Setup. National Conference on Excellence in Design, Manufacturing and Automation.*

Biswas, M., Akhund, T. M. N. U., Ferdous, M. J., Kar, S., Anis, A., & Shanto, S. A. (2021, July). Biot: Blockchain based smart agriculture with internet of thing. In *2021 fifth world conference on smart trends in systems security and sustainability (WorldS4)* (pp. 75-80). IEEE. DOI: 10.1109/WorldS451998.2021.9513998

Blanco-Aza, D., Robles-Gómez, A., Pastor-Vargas, R., Tobarra, L., Vidal-Balboa, P., & Méndez-Suárez, M. (2025). Comprehensive AI-driven privacy risk assessment in mobile apps and social networks. *Cluster Computing*, *28*(14), 914. Advance online publication. DOI: 10.1007/s10586-025-05624-2

Boopathy, P., Deepa, N., Maddikunta, P. K. R., Victor, N., Gadekallu, T. R., Yenduri, G., Wang, W., Pham, Q. V., Huynh-The, T., & Liyanage, M. (2025). The Metaverse for Industry 5.0 in NextG Communications: Potential Applications and Future Challenges. *IEEE Open Journal of the Computer Society*, *6*, 4–24. DOI: 10.1109/OJCS.2024.3497335

Boschert, S., & Rosen, R. (2016). Digital Twin—The Simulation Aspect. Mechatronic Futures, 59–74. DOI: 10.1007/978-3-319-32156-1_5

Bozic, B., & Kuppelwieser, V. G. (2019). Customer trust recovery: An alternative explanation. *Journal of Retailing and Consumer Services*, *49*, 208–218. DOI: 10.1016/j.jretconser.2019.04.002

Braun, V., & Clarke, V. (2006). Using thematic analysis in psychology. *Qualitative Research in Psychology*, *3*(2), 77–101. DOI: 10.1191/1478088706qp063oa

Breque, M., De Nul, L., & Petridis, A. (2021). Industry 5.0: towards a sustainable, human-centric and resilient European industry. *Luxembourg, LU: European Commission, Directorate-General for Research and Innovation, 46*. Available: https://op.europa.eu/en/publication-detail/-/publication/468a892a-5097-11eb-b59f-01aa75ed71a1

Brynjolfsson, E., & Mcafee, A. N. D. R. E. W. (2017). The business of artificial intelligence. *Harvard Business Review*, *7*(1), 1–2.

Bujari, A., Calvio, A., Garbugli, A., & Bellavista, P. (2023). A Layered Architecture Enabling Metaverse Applications in Smart Manufacturing Environments.

Camilleri, M. A. (2024). Artificial intelligence governance: Ethical considerations and implications for social responsibility. *Expert Systems: International Journal of Knowledge Engineering and Neural Networks*, *41*(7), e13406. Advance online publication. DOI: 10.1111/exsy.13406

Cao, K., Hu, S., Shi, Y., Colombo, A. W., Karnouskos, S., & Li, X. (2021). A Survey on Edge and Edge-Cloud Computing Assisted Cyber-Physical Systems. *IEEE Transactions on Industrial Informatics*, *17*(11), 7806–7819. DOI: 10.1109/TII.2021.3073066

Cao, X. (2025). Research on the Interactive Design of Artificial Intelligence in Augmented Reality and Virtual Reality. *Journal of Cases on Information Technology*, *27*(1), 1–22. Advance online publication. DOI: 10.4018/JCIT.392403

Charfare, R. H., Desai, A. U., Keni, N. N., Nambiar, A. S., & Cherian, M. M. (2024). IoT-AI in Healthcare: A Comprehensive Survey of Current Applications and Innovations. *International Journal of Robotics and Control Systems*, *4*(3), 1446–1472. DOI: 10.31763/ijrcs.v4i3.1526

Charmet, F., Tanuwidjaja, H. C., Ayoubi, S., Gimenez, P. F., Han, Y., Jmila, H., Blanc, G., Takahashi, T., & Zhang, Z. (2022). Explainable artificial intelligence for cybersecurity: A literature survey. *Annales Des Telecommunications. Annales des Télécommunications*, *77*(11–12), 789–812. DOI: 10.1007/s12243-022-00926-7

Chatterjee, S., Rana, N. P., Dwivedi, Y. K., & Baabdullah, A. M. (2021). Understanding AI adoption in manufacturing and production firms using an integrated TAM-TOE model. *Technological Forecasting and Social Change*, *170*, 120880. DOI: 10.1016/j.techfore.2021.120880

Chen, Y., Lu, Y., Bulysheva, L., & Kataev, M. Y. (2024). Applications of Blockchain in Industry 4.0: A Review. *Information Systems Frontiers*, *26*(5), 1715–1729. DOI: 10.1007/s10796-022-10248-7

Chinta, S. (2024). Edge AI for Real-Time Decision Making in IOT Networks. *International Journal of Innovative Research in Computer and Communication Engineering, 12*(09), 11293–11309. DOI: 10.15680/IJIRCCE.2024.1209044

Choi, S., Jung, K., & Do Noh, S. (2015). Virtual reality applications in manufacturing industries: Past research, present findings, and future directions. *Concurrent Engineering, Research and Applications, 23*(1), 40–63. DOI: 10.1177/1063293X14568814

Chui, K. T., Upadhyay, U., Kumar, A., Sharma, G., Saini, A. K., Arya, V., & Gaurav, A. (2023). Mitigating Risks in the Cloud-Based Metaverse Access Control Strategies and Techniques. *International Journal of Cloud Applications and Computing, 14*(1), 1–30. DOI: 10.4018/IJCAC.313572

Coelho, P., Bessa, C., Landeck, J., & Silva, C. (2023). Industry 5.0: The Arising of a Concept. *Procedia Computer Science, 217*, 1137–1144. DOI: 10.1016/j.procs.2022.12.312

Correia, J. B., Abel, M., & Becker, K. (2023). Data management in digital twins: A systematic literature review. *Knowledge and Information Systems, 65*(8), 3165–3196. DOI: 10.1007/s10115-023-01870-1

Costin, H., & Eslava, A. (2022). Emerging technology trends in hospitality and tourism. *University of South Florida (USF) M3 Publishing, 17*(9781732127593), 11. https://www.doi.org/10.5038/9781732127593

Cunningham, J. (2025). Painting in gray: The legal and ethical ambiguities of AI-generated art. *Journal of Information. Communication and Ethics in Society, 23*(3), 384–391. DOI: 10.1108/JICES-01-2025-0011

Das, P., Kumar, N., Jain, C., & Singh, M. (2025). Intelligent IoT-enabled healthcare solutions implementing federated meta-learning with blockchain. *Journal of Industrial Information Integration, 45*, 100797. Advance online publication. DOI: 10.1016/j.jii.2025.100797

Davenport, T., & Kalakota, R. (2019). The potential for artificial intelligence in healthcare. *Future Healthcare Journal, 6*(2), 94–98. DOI: 10.7861/futurehosp.6-2-94

De Koning, K. (2025). The crane radar: Development and deployment of an operational eco-digital twin. *Ecological Informatics, 85*, 102938. Advance online publication. DOI: 10.1016/j.ecoinf.2024.102938

Deci, E. L., Olafsen, A. H., & Ryan, R. M. (2017). Self-determination theory in work organizations: The state of a science. *Annual Review of Organizational Psychology and Organizational Behavior, 4*(1), 19–43. DOI: 10.1146/annurev-orgpsych-032516-113108 della Volpe, M., Castro Peña, M. Y., Jaramillo-Gutiérrez, A., & Morris Molina, L. H. (2023). A Scientometric Overview of Industry 5.0: The Research Developments in the European Union. *Digitalization, Sustainable Development, and Industry, 5*(0), 249–265. DOI: 10.1108/978-1-83753-190-520231013

Dinçer, S. G., & Dilek, H. Y. (2025). 3D printing and virtual reality in the study of muqarnas: A comparative approach. *Ain Shams Engineering Journal, 16*(12), 103742. DOI: 10.1016/j.asej.2025.103742

Ding, W., Li, J., Qin, R., Kozma, R., & Wang, F.-Y. (2023). A New Architecture and Mechanism for Decentralized Science MetaMarkets. *IEEE Transactions on Systems, Man, and Cybernetics. Systems, 53*(9), 5321–5330. DOI: 10.1109/TSMC.2023.3266223

Dwivedi, Y. K., Hughes, L., Baabdullah, A. M., Ribeiro-Navarrete, S., Giannakis, M., Al-Debei, M. M., Dennehy, D., Metri, B., Buhalis, D., Cheung, C. M. K., Conboy, K., Doyle, R., Dubey, R., Dutot, V., Felix, R., Goyal, D. P., Gustafsson, A., Hinsch, C., Jebabli, I., & Wamba, S. F. (2022). Metaverse beyond the hype: Multidisciplinary perspectives on emerging challenges, opportunities, and agenda for research, practice and policy. *International Journal of Information Management, 66*, 102542. Advance online publication. DOI: 10.1016/j.ijinfomgt.2022.102542

Dwivedi, Y. K., Hughes, L., Ismagilova, E., Aarts, G., Coombs, C., Crick, T., Duan, Y., Dwivedi, R., Edwards, J., Eirug, A., Galanos, V., Ilavarasan, P. V., Janssen, M., Jones, P., Kar, A. K., Kizgin, H., Kronemann, B., Lal, B., Lucini, B., & Williams, M. D. (2021). Artificial Intelligence (AI): Multidisciplinary perspectives on emerging challenges, opportunities, and agenda for research, practice and policy. *International Journal of Information Management, 57*, 101994. https://doi.org/https://doi.org/10.1016/j.ijinfomgt.2019.08.002. DOI: 10.1016/j.ijinfomgt.2019.08.002

Edmondson, A. C., & Lei, Z. (2014). Psychological safety: The history, renaissance, and future of an interpersonal construct. *Annual Review of Organizational Psychology and Organizational Behavior, 1*(1), 23–43. DOI: 10.1146/annurev-orgpsych-031413-091305

Egbengwu, V., Garn, W., & Turner, C. J. (2025). Metaverse for Manufacturing: Leveraging Extended Reality Technology for Human-Centric Production Systems. *Sustainability (Basel), 17*(1), 280. Advance online publication. DOI: 10.3390/su17010280

El-Hajj, M. (2025). Cybersecurity and Privacy Challenges in Extended Reality: Threats, Solutions, and Risk Mitigation Strategies. *Virtual Worlds, 4*(1), 1–30. DOI: 10.3390/virtualworlds4010001

Eneyew, D. D., Capretz, M. A. M., & Bitsuamlak, G. T. (2022). Toward Smart-Building Digital Twins: BIM and IoT Data Integration. *IEEE Access : Practical Innovations, Open Solutions*, *10*, 130487–130506. DOI: 10.1109/ACCESS.2022.3229370

Essaid, M., & Ju, H. (2025). Blockchain Solutions for Enhancing Security and Privacy in Industrial IoT. *Applied Sciences (Basel, Switzerland)*, *15*(12), 6835. Advance online publication. DOI: 10.3390/app15126835

Fan, Z., Diao, X., Zhang, Y., Liu, M., Chen, F., Huang, Z., & Yan, H. (2019). Analysis of residual stress in electrical penetration assembly based on a Fiber Bragg grating sensor. *Sensors (Basel)*, *19*(1), 18. DOI: 10.3390/s19010018 PMID: 30577580

Feijóo, C., Kwon, Y., Bauer, J. M., Bohlin, E., Howell, B., Jain, R., & Xia, J. (2020). Harnessing artificial intelligence (AI) to increase wellbeing for all: The case for a new technology diplomacy. *Telecommunications Policy*, *44*(6), 101988. DOI: 10.1016/j.telpol.2020.101988 PMID: 32377031

Fei, N., Lu, Z., Gao, Y., Yang, G., Huo, Y., Wen, J., Lu, H., Song, R., Gao, X., Xiang, T., Sun, H., & Wen, J.-R. (2022). Towards artificial general intelligence via a multimodal foundation model. *Nature Communications*, *13*(1), 3094. DOI: 10.1038/s41467-022-30761-2 PMID: 35655064

Feng, J., & Zhao, J. (2023). Resource allocation for augmented reality empowered vehicular edge metaverse. *IEEE Transactions on Communications*.

Fernández-Caramés, T. M., & Fraga-Lamas, P. (2024). Forging the Industrial Metaverse for Industry 5.0: Where Extended Reality, IIoT, Opportunistic Edge Computing, and Digital Twins Meet. *IEEE Access : Practical Innovations, Open Solutions*, *12*, 95778–95819. DOI: 10.1109/ACCESS.2024.3422109

Frey, C. B., & Osborne, M. A. (2017). The future of employment: How susceptible are jobs to computerisation? *Technological Forecasting and Social Change*, *114*, 254–280. DOI: 10.1016/j.techfore.2016.08.019

Gaurav, A., Pan, V. S. H., Arya, V., Raman, R., Gupta, B. B., & Chui, K. T. (2026). AI-driven lightweight CNN model for sustainable vegetable classification in smart food systems. *Green Technologies and Sustainability*, *4*(1), 100257. Advance online publication. DOI: 10.1016/j.grets.2025.100257

Ghirmai, S., Mebrahtom, D., Aloqaily, M., Guizani, M., & Debbah, M. (2022). Self-Sovereign Identity for Trust and Interoperability in the Metaverse. Proceedings - 2022 IEEE SmartWorld, Ubiquitous Intelligence and Computing, Autonomous and Trusted Vehicles, Scalable Computing and Communications, Digital Twin, Privacy Computing, Metaverse, SmartWorld/UIC/ATC/ScalCom/DigitalTwin/PriComp/Metaverse 2022, 2468–2475. DOI: 10.1109/SmartWorld-UIC-ATC-ScalCom-DigitalTwin-PriComp-Metaverse56740.2022.00345

Gilchrist, A. (2016). *Industry 4.0*. Apress., DOI: 10.1007/978-1-4842-2047-4

Grieves, M., & Vickers, J. (2016). Digital twin: Mitigating unpredictable, undesirable emergent behavior in complex systems. In *Transdisciplinary Perspectives on Complex Systems: New Findings and Approaches* (pp. 85–113). Springer International Publishing. DOI: 10.1007/978-3-319-38756-7_4

Grieves, M., & Hua, E. Y. (2024). *Digital Twins, Simulation, and the Metaverse* (Grieves, M., & Hua, E. Y., Eds.). Springer Nature Switzerland., DOI: 10.1007/978-3-031-69107-2

Grover, P., Kar, A. K., & Janssen, M. (2019). Diffusion of blockchain technology: Insights from academic literature and social media analytics. *Journal of Enterprise Information Management*, *32*(5), 735–757. DOI: 10.1108/JEIM-06-2018-0132

Guo, J., Leng, J., Zhao, J. L., Zhou, X., Yuan, Y., Lu, Y., Mourtzis, D., Qi, Q., Huang, S., Song, X., Liu, Q., & Wang, L. (2024). Industrial metaverse towards Industry 5.0: Connotation, architecture, enablers, and challenges. *Journal of Manufacturing Systems*, *76*, 25–42. DOI: 10.1016/j.jmsy.2024.07.007

Gupta, B. B., Gaurav, A., Albeshri, A. A., & Alsalman, D. (2023). New paradigms of sustainable entrepreneurship in metaverse: A micro-level perspective. *The International Entrepreneurship and Management Journal*, *19*(3), 1449–1465. DOI: 10.1007/s11365-023-00875-0

Gupta, B. B., Gaurav, A., & Arya, V. (2024). Fuzzy logic and biometric-based lightweight cryptographic authentication for metaverse security. *Applied Soft Computing*, *164*, 111973. DOI: 10.1016/j.asoc.2024.111973

Gupta, B. B., Gaurav, A., Arya, V., & Alhalabi, W. (2024). Data science in sustainable entrepreneurship: A multidisciplinary field of applications. *Technological Forecasting and Social Change*, *209*, 123798. DOI: 10.1016/j.techfore.2024.123798

Gupta, B. B., Gaurav, A., Arya, V., & Alhalabi, W. (2024). The evolution of intellectual property rights in metaverse based Industry 4.0 paradigms. *The International Entrepreneurship and Management Journal, 20*(2), 1111–1126. DOI: 10.1007/s11365-023-00940-8

Gupta, B. B., Gaurav, A., & Kumar Panigrahi, P. (2023). Analysis of security and privacy issues of information management of big data in B2B based healthcare systems. *Journal of Business Research, 162*, 113859. DOI: 10.1016/j.jbusres.2023.113859

Gupta, B. B., & Panigrahi, P. K. (2022). Analysis of the Role of Global Information Management in Advanced Decision Support Systems (DSS) for Sustainable Development. [JGIM]. *Journal of Global Information Management, 31*(2), 1–13. DOI: 10.4018/JGIM.320185

Habib, M. I., Muke, P. Z., & Machado, J. M. (2025). IoT-integrated smart toilet design for enhancing safety, precaution, and energy efficiency. *Journal of Building Pathology and Rehabilitation, 10*(2), 109. Advance online publication. DOI: 10.1007/s41024-025-00618-4

Hailu, T., Mackay, L., Gajic, M., & Ferreira, J. A. (2016). From voltage stiff to voltage weak DC distribution grid: Opportunities and challenges. *2016 IEEE 2nd Annual Southern Power Electronics Conference, SPEC 2016*, 1–6. DOI: 10.1109/SPEC.2016.7846172

Halamová, J., Ottingerová, L., Haladova, Z. B., & Greenberg, L. S. (2025). Unfinished business in virtual reality: Development and preliminary evaluation of an empty chair intervention grounded in emotion-focused therapy. *Internet Interventions : the Application of Information Technology in Mental and Behavioural Health, 42*, 100885. DOI: 10.1016/j.invent.2025.100885 PMID: 41210519

Hamash, M., Tiernan, P., & Young, G. (2025). Virtual reality in post-primary education research trends from 2013 to 2024: A systematic-narrative review. *Computers & Education: X Reality, 7*, 100123. DOI: 10.1016/j.cexr.2025.100123

Hamid, I., & Rahman, M. M. H. (2025). AI, machine learning and deep learning in cyber risk management. *Discover Sustainability, 6*(1), 389. Advance online publication. DOI: 10.1007/s43621-025-01012-3

Hassan, A. H., Ahmed, E. M., Hussien, J. M., Sulaiman, R. B., Abdulhak, M., & Kahtan, H. (2025). A cyber physical sustainable smart city framework toward society 5.0: Explainable AI for enhanced SDGs monitoring. *Research in Globalization, 10*, 100275. Advance online publication. DOI: 10.1016/j.resglo.2025.100275

Hassan, N., Yau, K.-L. A., & Wu, C. (2019). Edge Computing in 5G: A Review. *IEEE Access : Practical Innovations, Open Solutions*, *7*, 127276–127289. DOI: 10.1109/ACCESS.2019.2938534

Hermann, M., Pentek, T., & Otto, B. (2016, January). Design Principles for Industrie 4.0 Scenarios. 2016 49th Hawaii International Conference on System (HICSS).

He, Y., Guo, J., & Zheng, X. (2018). From Surveillance to Digital Twin: Challenges and Recent Advances of Signal Processing for Industrial Internet of Things. *IEEE Signal Processing Magazine*, *35*(5), 120–129. DOI: 10.1109/MSP.2018.2842228

Hill, G. N., & Whitty, M. A. (2021). Embedding metadata in images at time of capture using physical Quick Response (QR) codes. *Information Processing & Management*, *58*(3), 102504. https://doi.org/https://doi.org/10.1016/j.ipm.2021.102504. DOI: 10.1016/j.ipm.2021.102504

Hosseini, S., Abbasi, A., Magalhaes, L. G., Fonseca, J. C., da Costa, N. M. C., Moreira, A. H. J., & Borges, J. (2024). Immersive Interaction in Digital Factory: Metaverse in Manufacturing. *Procedia Computer Science*, *232*, 2310–2320. DOI: 10.1016/j.procs.2024.02.050

Huang, Y., Li, Y., & Cai, Z. (2023). Security and Privacy in Metaverse: A Comprehensive Survey. *Big Data Mining and Analytics*, *6*(2), 234–247. DOI: 10.26599/BDMA.2022.9020047

Huang, Z., Wei, S., Chen, Z., & Wang, L. (2023). Iterative Contraction Stability Control Strategy for Planar Prismatic-Rotational Underactuated Robot. *IEEE Access : Practical Innovations, Open Solutions*, *11*, 55947–55953. DOI: 10.1109/ACCESS.2023.3281556

Hutson, J., Banerjee, G., Kshetri, N., Odenwald, K., & Ratican, J. (2023). Architecting the Metaverse: Blockchain and the Financial and Legal Regulatory Challenges of Virtual Real Estate. *Journal of Intelligent Learning Systems and Applications*, *15*(01), 1–23. DOI: 10.4236/jilsa.2023.151001

Hwang, G. J., & Chien, S. Y. (2022). Definition, roles, and potential research issues of the metaverse in education: An artificial intelligence perspective. *Computers and Education: Artificial Intelligence*, *3*, 100082. Advance online publication. DOI: 10.1016/j.caeai.2022.100082

Irshad, R. R., Hussain, S., Hussain, I., Ahmad, I., Yousif, A., Alwayle, I. M., Alattab, A. A., Alalayah, K. M., Breslin, J. G., Badr, M. M., & Rodrigues, J. J. P. C. (2023). An Intelligent Buffalo-Based Secure Edge-Enabled Computing Platform for Heterogeneous IoT Network in Smart Cities. *IEEE Access : Practical Innovations, Open Solutions*, *11*, 69282–69294. DOI: 10.1109/ACCESS.2023.3288815

Islam, R., Bose, R., Roy, S., Khan, A. A., Sutradhar, S., Das, S., Ali, F., & AlZubi, A. A. (2025). Decentralized trust framework for smart cities: A blockchain-enabled cybersecurity and data integrity model. *Scientific Reports*, *15*(1), 23454. Advance online publication. DOI: 10.1038/s41598-025-06405-y

Ivanov, D., & Dolgui, A. (2020). Viability of intertwined supply networks: Extending the supply chain resilience angles towards survivability. A position paper motivated by COVID-19 outbreak. *International Journal of Production Research*, *58*(10), 2904–2915. DOI: 10.1080/00207543.2020.1750727

Iyelolu, T. V., Agu, E. E., Idemudia, C., & Ijomah, T. I. (2024). Driving SME innovation with AI solutions: overcoming adoption barriers and future growth opportunities. *International Journal of Science and Technology Research Archive*, *7*(1), 036-054. .DOI: 10.53771/ijstra.2024.7.1.0055

Jap, K. P. (2024). Driving Competitive Edge in Sarawak's Manufacturing Industry: Leveraging Supply Chain Management, Smart Integration, and Circular Economy Practices. *Recoletos Multidisciplinary Research Journal*, *12*(2), 103–118. DOI: 10.32871/rmrj2412.02.08

Ji, B., Zhang, J., Wang, Y., Liu, J., & Wang, W. (2024). Achievable Rate Maximization for IRS-Assisted System with Relay Cooperation of IoT Network. *IEEE Transactions on Consumer Electronics*, *70*(1), 1020–1028. DOI: 10.1109/TCE.2023.3319491

Jim, J. R., Hosain, M. T., Mridha, M. F., Kabir, M. M., & Shin, J. (2023). Toward Trustworthy Metaverse: Advancements and Challenges. *IEEE Access : Practical Innovations, Open Solutions*, *11*(September), 118318–118347. DOI: 10.1109/ACCESS.2023.3326258

Jo, K., Chang, D. J., Min, J. W., Yoo, Y.-S., Lyu, B., Kwon, J. W., & Baek, J. (2022). Author Correction: Long-term prediction models for vision-threatening diabetic retinopathy using medical features from data warehouse. In *Scientific Reports* (Vol. 12, Issue 1). Springer Science and Business Media LLC. DOI: 10.1038/s41598-022-18012-2

Jose Diaz Rivera, J., Muhammad, A., & Song, W. C. (2024). Securing Digital Identity in the Zero Trust Architecture: A Blockchain Approach to Privacy-Focused Multi-Factor Authentication. *IEEE Open Journal of the Communications Society*, *5*(March), 2792–2814. DOI: 10.1109/OJCOMS.2024.3391728

Jover, V., & Sempere, S. (2025). Creating Digital Twins to Celebrate Commemorative Events in the Metaverse. *Computers*, *14*(7), 273. DOI: 10.3390/computers14070273

Jung, D., Tran Tuan, V., Quoc Tran, D., Park, M., & Park, S. (2020). Conceptual Framework of an Intelligent Decision Support System for Smart City Disaster Management. *Applied Sciences (Basel, Switzerland)*, *10*(2), 666. DOI: 10.3390/app10020666

Jung, S. H., & Jeon, I. (2022). A study on the components of the Metaverse ecosystem. *Journal of Digital Convergence*, *20*(2), 163–174. DOI: 10.14400/JDC.2014.12.2.163

Kakkar, P., Mittal, S., Ulaganathan, S., Kannadasan, T., & Kanuparthi, S. L. (2025). Advancing the Metaverse: The Convergence of Digital Twins, AI, and Emerging Technologies. *2025 International Conference on Advanced Computing Technologies (ICoACT)*, 01–06. DOI: 10.1109/ICoACT63339.2025.11004721

Kankanhalli, A., Ye, H., & Teo, H. H. (2015). Comparing potential and actual innovators. *Management Information Systems Quarterly*, *39*(3), 667–682. DOI: 10.25300/MISQ/2015/39.3.07

Kar, A. K., Mikalef, P., Nishant, R., Luo, X., & Gupta, M. (2025). Metaverse opportunities and challenges: A research agenda and editorial on the special issue on the evolution of Metaverse platforms (part 2). *Decision Support Systems*, *194*, 114456. Advance online publication. DOI: 10.1016/j.dss.2025.114456

Kareem, A. N., Chyad, M. A., Salman Al-Gburib, Z. D., Ibrahim, H. H., & Sharaf, H. K. (2024). Exploring the Industrial Metaverse: Empowering Meta-Operators with Industry 5.0 Principles and XR Technologies. JOIV : International Journal on Informatics Visualization, 8(3–2), 1735. DOI: 10.62527/joiv.8.3-2.1534

Kasanga, G. (2020). *Passenger and luggage tracking system using sensor networks for public transport* (Doctoral dissertation, The University of Zambia). Available: https://dspace.unza.zm/handle/123456789/7180

Kazim, E., & Soares Koshiyama, A. (2020). Human Centric AI: A Comment on the IEEE's Ethically Aligned Design. SSRN *Electronic Journal*. DOI: 10.2139/ssrn.3575140

Khan, A. A., Yang, J., Awan, S. A., Baqasah, A. M., Alroobaea, R., Chen, Y.-L., Ku, C. S., & Por, L. Y. (2025). Artificial Intelligence, Internet of Things, and Blockchain Empowering Future Vehicular Developments: A Comprehensive Multi-Hierarchical Lifecycle Review. *Human-Centric Computing and Information Sciences*, *15*, 1–19. DOI: 10.22967/HCIS.2025.15.013

Khatib, D. M. El, Al Falasi, F., Anani, H. Al, & Shurrab, W. (2023). The Effect of Virtual Reality and Augmented Reality on Managing Projects. 2023 International Conference on Business Analytics for Technology and Security (ICBATS), 1–10. DOI: 10.1109/ICBATS57792.2023.10111112

Khurana, S., Haleem, A., & Mannan, B. (2019). Determinants for integration of sustainability with innovation for Indian manufacturing enterprises: Empirical evidence in MSMEs. *Journal of Cleaner Production*, *229*, 374–386. DOI: 10.1016/j.jclepro.2019.04.022

Kim, J. G. (2021). A study on metaverse culture contents matching platform. *International Journal of Advanced Culture Technology*, *9*(3), 232–237.

Kolbjørnsrud, V., Amico, R., & Thomas, R. J. (2017). Partnering with AI: How organizations can win over skeptical managers. *Strategy and Leadership*, *45*(1), 37–43. DOI: 10.1108/SL-12-2016-0085

Kour, R., Karim, R., Venkatesh, S. N., & Kumar, U. (2025). Metaverse in industrial contexts—A comprehensive review. *Frontiers in Virtual Reality*, *6*(January), 1–19. DOI: 10.3389/frvir.2025.1488926

Kourtesis, P. (2024). A Comprehensive Review of Multimodal XR Applications, Risks, and Ethical Challenges in the Metaverse. *Multimodal Technologies and Interaction*, *8*(11), 1–43. DOI: 10.3390/mti8110098

Kraus, K., & Kraus, N. (2025). INSTITUTIONALIZATION OF THE METAVERSE BASED ON THE DEVELOPMENT OF THE EXABYTE ECONOMY AND GIG ECONOMY. *Journal of Vasyl Stefanyk Precarpathian National University*, *12*(2), 6–13. DOI: 10.15330/jpnu.12.2.6-13

Kritzinger, W., Karner, M., Traar, G., Henjes, J., & Sihn, W. (2018). Digital Twin in manufacturing: A categorical literature review and classification. *IFAC-PapersOnLine*, *51*(11), 1016–1022. DOI: 10.1016/j.ifacol.2018.08.474

Kulkov, I., Berggren, B., Hellström, M., & Wikström, K. (2021). Navigating uncharted waters: Designing business models for virtual and augmented reality companies in the medical industry. *Journal of Engineering and Technology Management*, *59*, 101614. DOI: 10.1016/j.jengtecman.2021.101614

Kumar, A., Shankar, A., Behl, A., Gupta, B. B., & Mavuri, S. (2023). Lights, Camera, Metaverse!: Eliciting Intention to Use Industrial Metaverse, Organizational Agility, and Firm Performance. [JGIM]. *Journal of Global Information Management, 31*(8), 1–20. DOI: 10.4018/JGIM.333169

Kumar, H., Rauschnabel, P. A., Agarwal, M. N., Singh, R. K., & Srivastava, R. (2024). Towards a theoretical framework for augmented reality marketing: A means-end chain perspective on retailing. *Information & Management, 61*(2), 103910. DOI: 10.1016/j.im.2023.103910

Kuo, H. A., Hong, T. Y., & Chien, C. F. (2025). A deep reinforcement learning based digital twin framework for resilient production planning under demand uncertainty and an empirical study in semiconductor wafer fabrication. *Computers & Industrial Engineering, 208*, 111389. DOI: 10.1016/j.cie.2025.111389

Kuppelwieser, V. G., & Finsterwalder, J. (2016). Transformative service research and service dominant logic: Quo Vaditis? *Journal of Retailing and Consumer Services, 28*, 91–98. DOI: 10.1016/j.jretconser.2015.08.011

Kurniawan, A. W. (2025). Employee Perceptions of Virtual Reality (VR) Training in the Metaverse: A Case Study in a Fintech Company. [JUMPER]. *Journal Management & Economics Review, 2*(6), 2025.

Langås, E. F., Zafar, M. H., & Sanfilippo, F. (2025). Exploring the synergy of human-robot teaming, digital twins, and machine learning in Industry 5.0: A step towards sustainable manufacturing. *Journal of Intelligent Manufacturing*. Advance online publication. DOI: 10.1007/s10845-025-02580-x

Le Dinh, T., Vu, M. C., & Tran, G. T. (2025). Artificial Intelligence in SMEs: Enhancing Business Functions Through Technologies and Applications. *Information (Basel), 16*(5), 415. DOI: 10.3390/info16050415

Lee, L.-H., Braud, T., Zhou, P. Y., Wang, L., Xu, D., Lin, Z., Kumar, A., Bermejo, C., & Hui, P. (2024). All One Needs to Know about Metaverse: A Complete Survey on Technological Singularity, Virtual Ecosystem, and Research Agenda. Foundations and Trends® in Human-Computer Interaction, 18(2–3), 100–337. DOI: 10.1561/1100000095

Lee, J., Bagheri, B., & Kao, H. A. (2015). A Cyber-Physical Systems architecture for Industry 4.0-based manufacturing systems. *Manufacturing Letters, 3*, 18–23. DOI: 10.1016/j.mfglet.2014.12.001

Lee, J., & Kundu, P. (2022). Integrated cyber-physical systems and industrial metaverse for remote manufacturing. *Manufacturing Letters*, *34*, 12–15. DOI: 10.1016/j.mfglet.2022.08.012

Lemon, K. N., & Verhoef, P. C. (2016). Understanding customer experience throughout the customer journey. *Journal of Marketing*, *80*(6), 69–96. DOI: 10.1509/jm.15.0420

Leutheuser, V., Müller, J. M., & Voigt, K. I. (2025). The Industrial Metaverse: Towards a Research Agenda of its Sustainability Implications. *Procedia Computer Science*, *253*, 505–514. DOI: 10.1016/j.procs.2025.01.112

Leveraging, AI and Machine Learning for Enhanced Data Analytics and Visualization in Database Management With Digital Twins. (2025). *Journal of Database Management361*DOI: 10.4018/JDM.388135

Liang, S., Duc Long, N. V., Parvin, M. I., Escribà-Gelonch, M., Lantin, S., & Hessel, V. (2025). Digital twin for lettuce growth in six climate zones ('Climate 2050'). *Computers and Electronics in Agriculture*, *238*, 110880. Advance online publication. DOI: 10.1016/j.compag.2025.110880

Libai, B., Bart, Y., Gensler, S., Hofacker, C. F., Kaplan, A., Kötterheinrich, K., & Kroll, E. B. (2020). Brave new world? On AI and the management of customer relationships. *Journal of Interactive Marketing*, *51*(1), 44–56. DOI: 10.1016/j.intmar.2020.04.002

Li, K., Cui, Y., Li, W., Lv, T., Yuan, X., Li, S., Ni, W., Simsek, M., & Dressler, F. (2023). When Internet of Things Meets Metaverse: Convergence of Physical and Cyber Worlds. *IEEE Internet of Things Journal*, *10*(5), 4148–4173. DOI: 10.1109/JIOT.2022.3232845

Li, K., Zhang, Y., Huang, Y., Tian, Z., & Sang, Z. (2023). Framework and capability of industrial IoT infrastructure for smart manufacturing. *Standards*, *3*(1), 1–18. DOI: 10.3390/standards3010001

Li, L., Lei, B., & Mao, C. (2022). Digital twin in smart manufacturing. *Journal of Industrial Information Integration*, *26*, 100289. Advance online publication. DOI: 10.1016/j.jii.2021.100289

Lim, T. (2024). Environmental, social, and governance (ESG) and artificial intelligence in finance: State-of-the-art and research takeaways. *Artificial Intelligence Review*, *57*(4), 76. Advance online publication. DOI: 10.1007/s10462-024-10708-3

Li, S., Xie, H. L., Zheng, P., & Wang, L. (2024). Industrial Metaverse: A proactive human-robot collaboration perspective. *Journal of Manufacturing Systems*, *76*, 314–319. Advance online publication. DOI: 10.1016/j.jmsy.2024.08.003

Li, S., Yang, Y., Han, C., Sun, Y., Attar, R. W., & Gupta, B. B. (2025). Addressing consumer needs: Effects of firms remediation strategies on satisfaction and brand usage intent in AI-powered voice assistant service failures. *International Journal of Information Management*, *85*, 102951. DOI: 10.1016/j.ijinfomgt.2025.102951

Liu, X., Liu, H., Kong, Q., & Zhang, N. (2024). Policy Research in the Metaverse Technologies Enabled Publishing Industry in China (2016–2023). 255–271. DOI: 10.1007/978-3-031-59988-0_15

Liu, C.-L., & Liu, W.-Y. (2025). Assessing tourism pressure on wildlife in a protected area: A social big data approach using photo-sharing data and species distribution modeling. *Ecological Informatics*, *92*, 103441. Advance online publication. DOI: 10.1016/j.ecoinf.2025.103441

Liu, Y., Eisingerich, A. B., Auh, S., Merlo, O., & Chun, H. E. H. (2015). Service firm performance transparency: How, when, and why does it pay off? *Journal of Service Research*, *18*(4), 451–467. DOI: 10.1177/1094670515584331

Liyanaarachchi, G., Kurtaliqi, F., Viglia, G., & Frau, M. (2026). The virtue-value spectrum: Managing ethical and pragmatic tensions in virtual reality retail for consumer wellbeing. *Journal of Business Research*, *203*, 115810. DOI: 10.1016/j.jbusres.2025.115810

Liyanaarachchi, G., Viglia, G., & Kurtaliqi, F. (2024). Addressing challenges of digital transformation with modified blockchain. *Technological Forecasting and Social Change*, *201*, 123254. 10.1016/j.techfore.2024.123254. DOI: 10.1016/j.techfore.2024.123254

Loureiro, S. M. C. (2023). Overview of the brand journey and opportunities for future studies. *Italian Journal of Marketing*, *2023*(2), 179–206. DOI: 10.1007/s43039-023-00069-0

Lowry, P. B., Boh, W. F., Petter, S., & Leimeister, J. M. (2025). Long Live the Metaverse: Identifying the Potential for Market Disruption and Future Research. *Journal of Management Information Systems*, *42*(1), 3–38. DOI: 10.1080/07421222.2025.2455770

Lv, Z., Shang, W.-L., & Guizani, M. (2022). Impact of Digital Twins and Metaverse on Cities: History, Current Situation, and Application Perspectives. *Applied Sciences (Basel, Switzerland)*, *12*(24), 12820. Advance online publication. DOI: 10.3390/app122412820

Lyu, Z., & Fridenfalk, M. (2024). Digital twins for building industrial metaverse. *Journal of Advanced Research*, *66*, 31–38. DOI: 10.1016/j.jare.2023.11.019 PMID: 38008176

Majumdar, S., & Awasthi, A. (2025). From Vulnerability to Resilience: Securing Public Safety GPS and Location Services with Smart Radio, Blockchain, and AI-Driven Adaptability. *Electronics (Basel)*, *14*(6), 1207. Advance online publication. DOI: 10.3390/electronics14061207

Martinez, V. M. G., Campelo, D. R., & Ribeiro, M. R. N. (2025). Sustainable Intelligent Transportation Systems via Digital Twins: A Contextualized Survey. *IEEE Open Journal of Intelligent Transportation Systems*, *6*, 363–392. DOI: 10.1109/OJITS.2025.3553696

Masood, T., & Egger, J. (2021). Augmented Reality: Focusing on Photonics in Industry 4.0. *IEEE Journal of Selected Topics in Quantum Electronics*, *27*(6), 1–11. DOI: 10.1109/JSTQE.2021.3093721

Masubuchi, Y., Hiraki, T., Hiroi, Y., Ibara, M., Matsutani, K., Zaizen, M., & Morita, J. (2025). Development of Digital Twin Environment through Integration of Commercial Metaverse Platform and IoT Sensors of Smart Building. 2025 IEEE Conference on Virtual Reality and 3D User Interfaces Abstracts and Workshops (VRW), 852–855. DOI: 10.1109/VRW66409.2025.00173

Mazzucato, M. (2018). Mission-oriented innovation policies: Challenges and opportunities. *Industrial and Corporate Change*, *27*(5), 803–815. DOI: 10.1093/icc/dty034

Menon, S., & Jain, K. (2021). Blockchain technology for transparency in agri-food supply chain: Use cases, limitations, and future directions. *IEEE Transactions on Engineering Management*, *71*, 106–120. DOI: 10.1109/TEM.2021.3110903

Mirza, T., Tuli, N., & Mantri, A. (2022). Virtual Reality, Augmented Reality, and Mixed Reality Applications: Present Scenario. 2022 2nd International Conference on Advance Computing and Innovative Technologies in Engineering (ICACITE), 1405–1412. DOI: 10.1109/ICACITE53722.2022.9823482

Mmaduekwe, U. (2024). Bias and Fairness Issues in Artificial Intelligence-driven Cybersecurity. *Current Journal of Applied Science and Technology*, *43*(6), 109–119. DOI: 10.9734/cjast/2024/v43i64391

Mohammad, A. A. S., Mohammad, S. I. S., Al Oraini, B., Vasudevan, A., Hindieh, A., Altarawneh, A., Alshurideh, M. T., & Ali, I. (2025). Strategies for applying interpretable and explainable AI in real world IoT applications. *Discover Internet of Things*, *5*(1), 71. Advance online publication. DOI: 10.1007/s43926-025-00155-z

Mosharraf, M. (2025). Data governance in metaverse: Addressing security threats and countermeasures across the data lifecycle. *Technology in Society*, *82*, 102910. Advance online publication. DOI: 10.1016/j.techsoc.2025.102910

Moslehpour, M., Dwikesumasari, P. R., Pappachan, P., Lin, P.-K., Sakina, N., & Rahaman, M. (2024). Incorporating Web Semantics, the Technology Acceptance Model, and the Theory of Planned Behavior for Analyzing User Intentions on Dating Apps. [IJSWIS]. *International Journal on Semantic Web and Information Systems*, *20*(1), 1–20. DOI: 10.4018/IJSWIS.356388

Mubarakali, A., & AlJarullah, A. (2025). IoT and XAI-driven data aggregation framework for intelligent decision-making in smart healthcare systems. *Sustainable Computing : Informatics and Systems*, *48*, 101179. Advance online publication. DOI: 10.1016/j.suscom.2025.101179

Mushtaq, M., Jha, R. K., Sabraj, M. C., & Jain, S. (2024). Attack Modeling and Security Analysis Using Machine Learning Algorithms Enabled with Augmented Reality and Virtual Reality. *International Journal of Computer Network and Information Security*, *16*(4), 118–129. DOI: 10.5815/ijcnis.2024.04.08

Mystakidis, S. (2022). Metaverse. *Encyclopedia*, *2*(1), 486–497. DOI: 10.3390/encyclopedia2010031

Nambisan, S., Wright, M., & Feldman, M. (2019). The digital transformation of innovation and entrepreneurship: Progress, challenges and key themes. *Research Policy*, *48*(8), 103773. DOI: 10.1016/j.respol.2019.03.018

Nasri, M. (2025). Towards Intelligent VR Training: A Physiological Adaptation Framework for Cognitive Load and Stress Detection. 419–423. DOI: 10.1145/3699682.3727575

Negri, E., Fumagalli, L., & Macchi, M. (2017). A Review of the Roles of Digital Twin in CPS-based Production Systems. *Procedia Manufacturing*, *11*, 939–948. DOI: 10.1016/j.promfg.2017.07.198

Nepal, R., Pavlovich, R. J., & Guilherme, C. E. (2023). VirtualWorx™: Transforming Maintenance Concepts through Augmented Reality Collaboration Capabilities. *2023 Annual Reliability and Maintainability Symposium (RAMS)*, 1–5. DOI: 10.1109/RAMS51473.2023.10088179

Ng Corrales, L., Lambán, M. P., Hernandez Korner, M. E., & Royo, J. (2020). Overall Equipment Effectiveness: Systematic Literature Review and Overview of Different Approaches. *Applied Sciences (Basel, Switzerland)*, *10*(18), 6469. DOI: 10.3390/app10186469

Ngo, T. T. A., Tran, T. T., An, G. K., & Nguyen, P. T. (2025). Investigating the influence of augmented reality marketing application on consumer purchase intentions: A study in the E-commerce sector. *Computers in Human Behavior Reports, 18*, 100648. DOI: 10.1016/j.chbr.2025.100648

Nleya, S. M., & Velempini, M. (2024). Industrial Metaverse: A Comprehensive Review, Environmental Impact, and Challenges. *Applied Sciences (Basel, Switzerland), 14*(13), 5736. DOI: 10.3390/app14135736

Nwasra, N., Omar, K., & Qaisar, Z. H. (2025). The Role of AI in Predictive UX Shaping the Future of Metaverse Interactions. *2025 1st International Conference on Computational Intelligence Approaches and Applications (ICCIAA)*, 1–8. DOI: 10.1109/ICCIAA65327.2025.11013689

Obaidat, M. A., Rawashdeh, M., Alja'afreh, M., Abouali, M., Thakur, K., & Karime, A. (2024). Exploring IoT and Blockchain: A Comprehensive Survey on Security, Integration Strategies, Applications and Future Research Directions. *Big Data and Cognitive Computing, 8*(12), 174. Advance online publication. DOI: 10.3390/bdcc8120174

Olawale, R. A., Olawumi, M. A., & Oladapo, B. I. (2025). Sustainable farming with machine learning solutions for minimizing food waste. *Journal of Stored Products Research, 112*, 102611. Advance online publication. DOI: 10.1016/j.jspr.2025.102611

Omoniwa, B., Hussain, R., Javed, M. A., Bouk, S. H., & Malik, S. A. (2019). Fog/edge computing-based IoT (FECIoT): Architecture, applications, and research issues. *IEEE Internet of Things Journal, 6*(3), 4118–4149. DOI: 10.1109/JIOT.2018.2875544

Otoum, Y., Gottimukkala, N., Kumar, N., & Nayak, A. (2024). Machine Learning in Metaverse Security: Current Solutions and Future Challenges. *ACM Computing Surveys, 56*(8), 1–36. DOI: 10.1145/3654663

Owusu-Antwi, K., & Amenuvor, F. E. (2023). Understanding the Metaverse: A Review of Virtual Worlds and Augmented Reality Environments. *Current Journal of Applied Science and Technology, 42*(23), 42–48. DOI: 10.9734/cjast/2023/v42i234172

ÖZKAL. İ., & BAŞÇİFTÇİ, F. (2024). *Deep Learning in the Metaverse: A Systematic Literature Review and Future Perspectives*. DOI: 10.2139/ssrn.5022041

Panda, D. K., Panigrahi, P. K., Attar, R. W., & Gupta, B. B. (2024). Open Source Adoption for Digital Transformation and Data Management During the COVID-19 Crisis. [JDM]. *Journal of Database Management, 35*(1), 1–26. DOI: 10.4018/JDM.360708

Pang, J., Zheng, P., Fan, J., & Liu, T. (2025). Towards cognition-augmented human-centric assembly: A visual computation perspective. *Robotics and Computer-integrated Manufacturing*, *91*, 102852. DOI: 10.1016/j.rcim.2024.102852

Pappachan, P. Sreerakuvandana, & Rahaman, M. (2024). Conceptualising the Role of Intellectual Property and Ethical Behaviour in Artificial Intelligence. In Handbook of Research on AI and ML for Intelligent Machines and Systems (pp. 1–26). IGI Global. DOI: 10.4018/978-1-6684-9999-3.ch001

Pappachan, P., Rahaman, M., Cages, N., & Gupta, B. B. (2025). Case Studies of Cyber Incidents in Space Missions. In *Advanced Cyber Defense for Space Missions and Operations: Concepts and Applications* (pp. 383–400). IGI Global Scientific Publishing. DOI: 10.4018/979-8-3693-7939-4.ch016

Pappachan, P., Rahaman, M., Sreerakuvandana, S., Bansal, S., & Arya, V. (2024). Beyond Current Cryptography: Exploring New Frontiers. In *Innovations in Modern Cryptography* (pp. 1–30). IGI Global Scientific Publishing. DOI: 10.4018/979-8-3693-5330-1.ch001

Pappas, I. O., Kourouthanassis, P. E., Giannakos, M. N., & Chrissikopoulos, V. (2017). Sense and sensibility in personalized e-commerce: How emotions rebalance the purchase intentions of persuaded customers. *Psychology and Marketing*, *34*(10), 972–986. DOI: 10.1002/mar.21036

Parmiggiani, A., Liu, D., Psota, E., Fitzgerald, R., & Norton, T. (2023). Don't get lost in the crowd: Graph convolutional network for online animal tracking in dense groups. *Computers and Electronics in Agriculture*, *212*, 108038. Advance online publication. DOI: 10.1016/j.compag.2023.108038

Parviainen, P., Tihinen, M., Kääriäinen, J., & Teppola, S. (2017). Tackling the digitalization challenge: how to benefit from digitalization in practice. *International journal of information systems and project management, 5*(1), 63-77.

Peng, D., Yang, X., Tang, W., & Fan, L. (2020). A Dual-NIC Mutual Backup Solution of Access Point Handoff in SDN-based Mobile Networks. 2020 IEEE 6th International Conference on Computer and Communications (ICCC), 542–547. DOI: 10.1109/ICCC51575.2020.9345033

Pereira, A. C., Alves, A. C., & Arezes, P. (2023). Augmented Reality in a Lean Workplace at Smart Factories: A Case Study. *Applied Sciences (Basel, Switzerland)*, *13*(16), 9120. Advance online publication. DOI: 10.3390/app13169120

Peretz-Andersson, E., Tabares, S., Mikalef, P., & Parida, V. (2024). Artificial intelligence implementation in manufacturing SMEs: A resource orchestration approach. *International Journal of Information Management, 77*, 102781. DOI: 10.1016/j.ijinfomgt.2024.102781

Periyasamy, A. P., & Periyasami, S. (2023). Rise of digital fashion and metaverse: Influence on sustainability. *Digital Economy and Sustainable Development, 1*(1), 1–26. DOI: 10.1007/s44265-023-00016-z

Petso, T., Jamisola, R. S.Jr, Alibhai, S., Namoshe, M., Mmereki, W., & Jewell, Z. (2025). An investigation of lightweight AI models to classify African ungulate species from tracks. *Ecological Informatics, 92*, 103393. Advance online publication. DOI: 10.1016/j.ecoinf.2025.103393

Phattanaviroj, T., Moslehpour, M., Pappachan, P., Cajes, N. C., Gupta, B. B., & Rahaman, M. (2026). A novel predictive framework for green transportation and EV policy towards sustainable mobility and emission reduction. *Green Technologies and Sustainability, 4*(1), 100260. DOI: 10.1016/j.grets.2025.100260

Pine, B. J., & Gilmore, J. H. (2021). *The Experience Economy: Competing for customer time, attention, and money*. No Title.

Pitzalis, R. F., Giordano, A., Di Spigno, A., Cowell, A., Niculita, O., & Berselli, G. (2025). Application of augmented reality-based digital twin approaches: A case study to industrial equipment. *International Journal of Advanced Manufacturing Technology, 138*(7), 3747–3763. DOI: 10.1007/s00170-025-15755-w

Politi, T., Denazis, S., Koufopavlou, O., Antonopoulos, C., Faliagka, E., Prevedourou, D., Kostis, N., Tranoris, C., Voros, N., Christophorou, C., Ioannou, I., Vassiliou, V., Ioannou, I., & Nikiforidis, M. (2025). *Exploiting Digital Twins and Metaverse Technologies for the Digital Transformation of City Transportation*., DOI: 10.1007/978-3-031-82818-8_63

Proietti, S., & Magnani, R. (2025). Assessing AI Adoption and Digitalization in SMEs: A Framework for Implementation. *arXiv preprint arXiv:2501.08184*. /arxiv.2501.08184.DOI: 10.32388/0N53P4

Rafiq, J. E., Namir, A., Zakrani, A., Amraouy, M., & Bennane, A. (2025). A SYSTEMATIC MAPPING STUDY OF THE EVOLUTION OF EDUCATIONAL PRACTICES USING DISRUPTIVE DIGITAL TECHNOLOGY. *The Journal of Educators Online, 22*(1). Advance online publication. DOI: 10.9743/JEO.2025.22.1.19

Rahaman, M., Chappu, B., Jana, S., Haque, A., Firmansyah, G., & Chattopadhyay, S. (2025). Security Benefits in Small Medium Business Enterprise Through Cloud Adoption. In N. Nedjah, G. Martinez Perez, & B. B. Gupta (Eds.), *International Conference on Smart Systems and Advanced Computing (SysCom 2022)* (pp. 168–180). Springer Nature Switzerland. DOI: 10.1007/978-3-031-40905-9_18

Rahaman, M., Chattopadhyay, S., & Anwar, N. (2022). *A Case Study: Physical Layer Security Analysis for Internet of Vehicle (IoV)*. 283–291.

Rahaman, M., Lin, C. Y., Rachmat, I., Bansal, R., & Prayitno. (2024). Secure Health Features: Implementing Hyperledger Fabric in Blockchain-Driven Healthcare Management Systems. In *Digital Forensics and Cyber Crime Investigation*. CRC Press.

Rahaman, M., Putra, K. T., Irawan, B., & Biyanto, T. R. (2025). Industrial Evolution: The Integration of AI in Robotics and Drone Systems. In AI Developments for Industrial Robotics and Intelligent Drones (pp. 85–114). IGI Global Scientific Publishing. DOI: 10.4018/979-8-3693-2707-4.ch005

Rahaman, M., Wisnujati, A., Widodo, A. M., Haque, A., Sakar, R., & Chen, H. C. (2022). Privacy Preservation Agri-Food SCM Operation Based on Online/Offline RFID Using Block Chain. 413–426. DOI: 10.2991/978-94-6463-084-8_34

Rahaman, M., Bakkireddygari, S. S., Chattopadhyay, S., Gomez, A. L., Arya, V., & Bansal, S. (2024). Infrastructure and Network Security. In *Metaverse Security Paradigms* (pp. 108–144). IGI Global Scientific Publishing., DOI: 10.4018/979-8-3693-3824-7.ch005

Rahaman, M., Cajes, N., Gupta, B. B., Chui, K. T., & Nedjah, N. (2025). Defending against smishing attacks: State-of-the-art techniques, challenges, limitations, and future directions. *Computer Networks*, *273*, 111758. DOI: 10.1016/j.comnet.2025.111758

Rahaman, M., Cajes, N., Gupta, B. B., Nedjah, N., & Chui, K. T. (2025). Real-Time Machine Learning Techniques in Robotics for Detecting Phishing Attacks. *2025 IEEE International Conference on Real-Time Computing and Robotics (RCAR)*, 1124–1129. DOI: 10.1109/RCAR65431.2025.11139819

Rahaman, M., Pappachan, P., Batul, I., Widodo, A. M., & Gupta, B. B. (2025). Communication Modalities and Tools. In *Unveiling Social Dynamics and Community Interaction in the Metaverse* (pp. 39–64). IGI Global Scientific Publishing. DOI: 10.4018/979-8-3693-8628-6.ch003

Rajamurugu, N., & Karthik, M. K. (2022). Introduction, History, and Concept of Digital Twin. In *Digital Twin Technology* (pp. 19–32). Wiley., DOI: 10.1002/9781119842316.ch2

Raj, N., Menon, H. P., Satheesh, A., & Naveen, P., N. A., & R, V. K. (2025). Architectural Visualization using Augmented Reality. *2025 International Conference on Intelligent and Innovative Technologies in Computing, Electrical and Electronics (IITCEE)*, 1–6. DOI: 10.1109/IITCEE64140.2025.10915400

Rajput, D., Singh, S. K., Kumar, S., Vashisht, H., Chui, K. T., & Gupta, B. B. (2024). SentinelMet: Enhancing Metaverse Security through Deep Learning Techniques in 6G. *2024 IEEE International Conference on Advanced Networks and Telecommunications Systems (ANTS)*, 1–6. DOI: 10.1109/ANTS63515.2024.10898831

Raman, R., Kautish, P., Siddiqui, A., Siddiqui, M., & Nedungadi, P. (2025). The role of metaverse technologies in energy systems towards sustainable development goals. *Energy Reports*, *13*, 4459–4476. DOI: 10.1016/j.egyr.2025.04.012

Ramaswamy, V., & Ozcan, K. (2018). What is co-creation? An interactional creation framework and its implications for value creation. *Journal of Business Research*, *84*, 196–205. DOI: 10.1016/j.jbusres.2017.11.027

Reiners, D., Davahli, M. R., Karwowski, W., & Cruz-Neira, C. (2021). The Combination of Artificial Intelligence and Extended Reality: A Systematic Review. *Frontiers in Virtual Reality*, *2*, 721933. Advance online publication. DOI: 10.3389/frvir.2021.721933

Ritter, T., & Pedersen, C. L. (2020). Analyzing the impact of the coronavirus crisis on business models. *Industrial Marketing Management*, *88*, 214–224. DOI: 10.1016/j.indmarman.2020.05.014

Rohhila, S., Singh, K. N., Singh, A. K., & Gupta, B. B. (2025). DeepKey-TPE: Using Deep Learning to Generate Key for Image Security With Continued Usability Through Thumbnail-Preserving Encryption. *IEEE Transactions on Consumer Electronics*, *71*(4), 1–1. DOI: 10.1109/TCE.2025.3605213

Saemann, A., de Wilde, D., Guzman, R., Soleman, J., & Greuter, L. (2025). Augmented and Virtual Reality in Open Neurovascular Surgery: A Systematic Review of the Literature. *World Neurosurgery*, *124632*. Advance online publication. DOI: 10.1016/j.wneu.2025.124632 PMID: 41205868

Safiyev, E. S., & Shikhaliyeva, S. Y. (2025). ANALYSIS OF ECOLOGY AND EFFICIENCY OF OVERHEAD POWER LINES OF ULTRA-HIGH VOLTAGE. *International Journal on Technical and Physical Problems of Engineering*, *17*(62), 91–100.

Saini, M., Kumar, S., Singh, S. K., Bansal, A., Han, C., Gupta, B. B., & Psannis, K. (2025). Transforming User Experience in the Metaverse Through Emotional Intelligence and Affective Computing. In Unveiling Social Dynamics and Community Interaction in the Metaverse (pp. 303–332). IGI Global Scientific Publishing. DOI: 10.4018/979-8-3693-8628-6.ch015

Saini, D. K. J. B., Mishra, A., Siddharth, D., Joshi, P., Bansal, R., Bansal, S., & Chui, K. T. (2023). Development of Enhanced Chimp Optimization Algorithm (OFCOA) in Cognitive Radio Networks for Energy Management and Resource Allocation. [IJSSCI]. *International Journal of Software Science and Computational Intelligence*, *15*(1), 1–20. DOI: 10.4018/IJSSCI.335898

Sajwan, V., Gandhi, A. B., Kumar Chopra, N., Praveen, S., Thapliyal, M., Jaleel, U., Pandey, S. D., Kumar, R., & Negi, D. (2024). Technological Transformations: A Comprehensive Review of AI, IoT, VR, AR, and Emerging Technologies in Diverse Industries. *2024 International Conference on Advances in Computing, Communication and Materials (ICACCM)*, 1–5. DOI: 10.1109/ICACCM61117.2024.11059157

Sarhan, A., Leray, M., Creusier, T., & Gao, J. (2024). Augmented Reality Knowledge Management for Industrial Transformation and Innovation. *Procedia CIRP*, *128*, 19–24. DOI: 10.1016/j.procir.2024.06.004

Saurabh, K., Upadhyay, P., & Rani, N. (2024). Unified Metaverse Architecture Powered by Blockchain Decentralized Autonomous Organizations (DAO). 421–427. DOI: 10.1007/978-3-031-50188-3_37

Sayal, A., Johri, A., Chaithra, N., Alhumoudi, H., & Alatawi, Z. (2025). Optimizing audit processes through open innovation: Leveraging emerging technologies for enhanced accuracy and efficiency. *Journal of Open Innovation*, *11*(3), 100573. Advance online publication. DOI: 10.1016/j.joitmc.2025.100573

Schmidt, S., Köysürenbars, I., & Steinicke, F. (2024). Frankenstein's Monster in the Metaverse: User Interaction With Customized Virtual Agents. *IEEE Transactions on Visualization and Computer Graphics*, *30*(11), 7162–7171. DOI: 10.1109/TVCG.2024.3456205 PMID: 39255104

Schwaeke, J., Peters, A., Kanbach, D. K., Kraus, S., & Jones, P. (2025). The new normal: The status quo of AI adoption in SMEs. *Journal of Small Business Management*, *63*(3), 1297–1331. DOI: 10.1080/00472778.2024.2379999

Sekti, B. A. (2025a). Adversarial machine learning in industrial cybersecurity: Challenges and solutions. In *AI-Enhanced Cybersecurity for Industrial Automation* (pp. 363–386). DOI: 10.4018/979-8-3373-3241-3.ch018

Sekti, B. A. (2025a). Information Security Awareness. In User-Centric Cybersecurity Implications for Sustainable Digital Transformation (pp. 111–145). DOI: 10.4018/979-8-3373-3171-3.ch004

Sekti, B. A. (2025b). IT Service Information Security Management. In Cases on Information Systems Service Management (pp. 61–93). DOI: 10.4018/979-8-3373-2352-7.ch003

Sekti, B. A. (2025c). Machine Learning vs. AI: Key Concepts. In *Implementing Enterprise Cybersecurity With AI* (pp. 1–27). DOI: 10.4018/979-8-3373-2252-0.ch001

Sekti, B. A. (2026b). *Machine Learning and Artificial Intelligence (AI) in Manufacturing*. 255–257. DOI: 10.4018/979-8-3373-1082-4.ch011

Sekti, B. A. (2026). AI Technology Management Concepts and Strategies. In Lai, P. (Ed.), *AI Technology Management and Value Creation* (pp. 1–32). IGI Global Scientific Publishing., DOI: 10.4018/979-8-3373-2497-5.ch001

Sekti, B. A. (2026a). Cybersecurity Challenges in Smart City Development. *Cybersecurity Challenges in Smart City Development, 75–77*, 75–102. Advance online publication. DOI: 10.4018/979-8-3373-3326-7.ch003

Shahbazi, Z., & Byun, Y. C. (2021). Smart manufacturing real-time analysis based on blockchain and machine learning approaches. *Applied Sciences (Basel, Switzerland), 11*(8), 3535. Advance online publication. DOI: 10.3390/app11083535

Shahriar, S., Allana, S., Hazratifard, S. M., & Dara, R. (2023). A Survey of Privacy Risks and Mitigation Strategies in the Artificial Intelligence Life Cycle. *IEEE Access : Practical Innovations, Open Solutions, 11*, 61829–61854. DOI: 10.1109/ACCESS.2023.3287195

Shaikh, F. K., Karim, S., Zeadally, S., & Nebhen, J. (2022). Recent trends in internet-of-things-enabled sensor technologies for smart agriculture. *IEEE Internet of Things Journal, 9*(23), 23583–23598. DOI: 10.1109/JIOT.2022.3210154

Sharafat, S., Kabya, N. D., Emu, R. I., Ahmed, M. U., Onik, J. C., Islam, M. A., & Khan, R. (2025). An IoT-enabled AI system for real-time crop prediction using soil and weather data in precision agriculture. *Smart Agricultural Technology, 12*, 101263. Advance online publication. DOI: 10.1016/j.atech.2025.101263

Sharma, A., Kumar, S., Singh, S. K., Jawla, S., Arya, V., & Chui, K. T. (2025). Virtual Identity and Self-Expression in the Metaverse. In Unveiling Social Dynamics and Community Interaction in the Metaverse (pp. 93–110). IGI Global Scientific Publishing. DOI: 10.4018/979-8-3693-8628-6.ch005

Sharma, A., Singh, S. K., Kumar, S., Thakur, R., Gupta, B. B., & Arya, V. (2024). IoT-enabled smart farming with Industry 5.0. *Journal of High Speed Networks*, *30*(3), 477–496. DOI: 10.3233/JHS-230258

Shelke, Y., & Chakraborty, C. (2021). Augmented Reality and Virtual Reality Transforming Spinal Imaging Landscape: A Feasibility Study. *IEEE Computer Graphics and Applications*, *41*(3), 124–138. DOI: 10.1109/MCG.2020.3000359 PMID: 32746083

Sherdil, K., & Madhavji, N. H. (1996). Human-oriented improvement in the software process. 144–166. DOI: 10.1007/BFb0017741

Silva, R., Pereira, I., Nicola, S., Madureira, A., Bettencourt, N., Reis, J. L., Santos, J. P., & de Oliveira, D. A. (2024). Navigating the Future of Enterprises: Insights into Digital Transformation, Virtual Reality, and the Metaverse. 2024 IEEE 22nd Mediterranean Electrotechnical Conference (MELECON), 1146–1151. DOI: 10.1109/MELECON56669.2024.10608539

Singh, J., Kumar, S., Singh, S. K., Singh, D., Singh, A., Arya, V., & Ratnaparkhi, A. (2025). Virtual Economies and Social Structures in the Metaverse. In Unveiling Social Dynamics and Community Interaction in the Metaverse (pp. 111–138). IGI Global Scientific Publishing. DOI: 10.4018/979-8-3693-8628-6.ch006

Singh, M., Singh, S. K., Kumar, S., Madan, U., & Maan, T. (2023). Sustainable Framework for Metaverse Security and Privacy: Opportunities and Challenges (pp. 329–340). DOI: 10.1007/978-3-031-22018-0_30

Singh, S. K., Gupta, S., Kumar, S., Gupta, B. B., Alhalabi, W., Arya, V., & Zhang, J. (2024). A novel Cumulative Indicator score using Indicator averaging for optimizing local business websites of enterprise systems. *Enterprise Information Systems*, *18*(2), 2301658. DOI: 10.1080/17517575.2023.2301658

Singh, T., Gupta, S., Satakshi, , & Kumar, M. (2022). Performance Analysis and Deployment of Partitioning Strategies in Apache Spark. *Procedia Computer Science*, *218*, 594–603. DOI: 10.1016/j.procs.2023.01.041

Soegoto, E. S., Meliala, B. N., Luckyardi, S., & Kurniawan, B. (2025). COMPUTER SCIENCE RESEARCH IN INDONESIA TO CREATE SUSTAINABLE INFRASTRUCTURE FOR UNITED NATIONS SUSTAINABLE DEVELOPMENT GOALS. *Journal of Engineering Science and Technology*, *20*(3), 670–685.

Soni, S., Yadav, U., & Soni, A. (2022). Virtual Reality & Augmented Reality: A way to Digital Transformation of Customer Engagement. *2022 International Conference on Machine Learning, Big Data, Cloud and Parallel Computing (COM-IT-CON)*, 1, 573–577. DOI: 10.1109/COM-IT-CON54601.2022.9850954

Srivastava, G., Jhaveri, R. H., Bhattacharya, S., Pandya, S., Rajeswari, Maddikunta, P. K. R., Yenduri, G., Hall, J. G., Alazab, M., & Gadekallu, T. R. (2022). *XAI for Cybersecurity: State of the Art, Challenges, Open Issues and Future Directions.*

Strazzeri, I., Notebaert, A., Barros, C., Quinten, J., & Demarbaix, A. (2024). Virtual Reality Integration for Enhanced Engineering Education and Experimentation: A Focus on Active Thermography. *Computers*, *13*(8), 199. Advance online publication. DOI: 10.3390/computers13080199

Sumon, R. I., Uddin, S. M. I., Akter, S., Mozumder, M. A. I., Khan, M. O., & Kim, H. C. (2024). Natural Language Processing Influence on Digital Socialization and Linguistic Interactions in the Integration of the Metaverse in Regular Social Life. *Electronics (Basel)*, *13*(7), 1331. DOI: 10.3390/electronics13071331

Sun, J. (2025). The integration of virtual reality and augmented reality technology in immersive media art. *Systems and Soft Computing*, *7*, 200377. DOI: 10.1016/j.sasc.2025.200377

Swarnakar, S., Banerjee, C., Basu, J., & Saha, D. (2023). A Multi-Agent-Based VM Migration for Dynamic Load Balancing in Cloud Computing Cloud Environment. [IJCAC]. *International Journal of Cloud Applications and Computing*, *13*(1), 1–14. DOI: 10.4018/IJCAC.320479

Tahsin, R., Rantu, S. B. A., Rahman, M., Salman, S., & Karim, M. R. (2025). Towards the adoption of AI, IoT, and Blockchain technologies in Bangladesh's maritime industry: Challenges and insights. *Results in Engineering*, *25*, 103825. Advance online publication. DOI: 10.1016/j.rineng.2024.103825

Taj, I., & Zaman, N. (2022). Towards Industrial Revolution 5.0 and Explainable Artificial Intelligence: Challenges and Opportunities. *International Journal of Computing and Digital Systems*, *12*(1), 285–310. DOI: 10.12785/ijcds/120124

Tamim, Z. H., Akter, B., Rahman, M., Kaiser, M. S., Rahman, M. A., Ogliari, E., & Tanasiev, V. (2025). Exploring equitable opportunities and cultural preservation in smart tourism through sustainable and accessible Virtual Reality. *Sustainable Cities and Society: Advances*, *1*(1), 100007. DOI: 10.1016/j.scsadv.2025.100007

Tang, F., Chen, X., Zhao, M., & Kato, N. (2023). The Roadmap of Communication and Networking in 6G for the Metaverse. *IEEE Wireless Communications*, *30*(4), 72–81. DOI: 10.1109/MWC.019.2100721

Tang, H., Cheng, M., Bhatti, U. A., Xu, B., Zhou, N., Guo, R., & Wei, B. (2025). Digital twin-driven reinforcement learning-based operational management for customized manufacturing. *Engineering Applications of Artificial Intelligence*, *159*, 111754. DOI: 10.1016/j.engappai.2025.111754

Tang, Y., You, J., & Chen, L. (2025). Exploring user perception in mobile shopping: A comparison between augmented reality and virtual reality. *Design and Artificial Intelligence*, *100039*(3), 100039. Advance online publication. DOI: 10.1016/j.daai.2025.100039

Tao, F., Qi, Q., Liu, A., & Kusiak, A. (2018). Data-driven smart manufacturing. *Journal of Manufacturing Systems*, *48*, 157–169. DOI: 10.1016/j.jmsy.2018.01.006

Tao, F., Zhang, H., Liu, A., & Nee, A. Y. C. (2019). Digital Twin in Industry: State-of-the-Art. *IEEE Transactions on Industrial Informatics*, *15*(4), 2405–2415. DOI: 10.1109/TII.2018.2873186

Truong, T.-C., & Diep, Q. B. (2023). Technological Spotlights of Digital Transformation in Tertiary Education. *IEEE Access : Practical Innovations, Open Solutions*, *11*, 40954–40966. DOI: 10.1109/ACCESS.2023.3270340

Tukur, M., Schneider, J., Househ, M., Dokoro, A. H., Ismail, U. I., Dawaki, M., & Agus, M. (2024). The Metaverse digital environments: A scoping review of the techniques, technologies, and applications. *Journal of King Saud University. Computer and Information Sciences*, *36*(2), 101967. Advance online publication. DOI: 10.1016/j.jksuci.2024.101967

Ud Din, I., & Almogren, A. (2023). Exploring the psychological effects of Metaverse on mental health and well-being. *Information Technology & Tourism*, *25*(3), 367–389. DOI: 10.1007/s40558-023-00259-8

V., J. M. N., Flórez, S. L., Corchado, J. M., & De la Prieta, F. (2025). Edge AIoT-based agricultural recommendation platform to improve humus productivity in vermicomposting processes. *Pervasive and Mobile Computing*, *112*. DOI: 10.1016/j.pmcj.2025.102080

Varghese, D. J. (2024). Metaverse Liability and the Future of Tort Law. *Available at SSRN* 5043578.

Verma, R. (2025). The Confluence of Cryptography, Blockchain and Artificial Intelligence. In *The Confluence of Cryptography*. Blockchain and Artificial Intelligence., DOI: 10.1201/9781032711515

Vincenza Ciasullo, M., Troisi, O., & Cosimato, S. (2018). How Digital Platforms Can Trigger Cultural Value Co-Creation?—A Proposed Model. *Journal of Service Science and Management*, *11*(02), 161–181. DOI: 10.4236/jssm.2018.112013

Walentek, D., & Ziora, L. (2023). A systematic review on the use of augmented reality in management and business. *Procedia Computer Science*, *225*, 861–871. DOI: 10.1016/j.procs.2023.10.073

Wang, C., Garro, V., Sundstedt, V., Hu, Y., & Goswami, P. (2025). Immersive analytics meets artificial intelligence: A systematic review. *Computational Visual Media*, *•••*, 1–34. DOI: 10.26599/CVM.2025.9450452

Wang, H., Ning, H., Lin, Y., Wang, W., Dhelim, S., Farha, F., Ding, J., & Daneshmand, M. (2023). A Survey on the Metaverse: The State-of-the-Art, Technologies, Applications, and Challenges. *IEEE Internet of Things Journal*, *10*(16), 14671–14688. DOI: 10.1109/JIOT.2023.3278329

Wang, X., Li, J., Ning, Z., Song, Q., Guo, L., Guo, S., & Obaidat, M. S. (2023). Wireless Powered Mobile Edge Computing Networks: A Survey. *ACM Computing Surveys*, *55*(13s), 1–37. Advance online publication. DOI: 10.1145/3579992

Wang, Z., Tao, Z., Lan, Y., Chen, Y., Xie, Q., Li, Q., Lu, C., & Zhang, W. (2023). Different mechanisms mediating cybervictimization and internalizing/externalizing problems: The moderating role of emotion regulation strategies. *Computers in Human Behavior*, *144*, 107748. https://doi.org/https://doi.org/10.1016/j.chb.2023.107748. DOI: 10.1016/j.chb.2023.107748

Wu, J.-F., Zhang, Z., Wu, Y., & Tang, X.-J. (2025). The effectiveness of immersive media in promoting consumer Products: Augmented vs. Virtual reality. *Journal of Retailing and Consumer Services*, *86*, 104323. DOI: 10.1016/j.jretconser.2025.104323

Yamoah, L. E., Mensah, R. O., & Frimpong, A. (2025). The benefits, challenges and implications for integrating emerging technologies in risk evaluation procedures for supply chains in transportation logistics. *Discover Sustainability*, *6*(1), 476. Advance online publication. DOI: 10.1007/s43621-025-01295-6

Yang, B. (2023). Virtual Reality and Augmented Reality for Immersive Learning: A Framework of Education Environment Design. [iJET]. *International Journal of Emerging Technologies in Learning, 18*(20), 23–36. DOI: 10.3991/ijet.v18i20.44209

Yang, Y., Zhou, J., & Yang, Z. (2025). *Integrated Sensing*. Computing, and Semantic Communication with Fluid Antenna for Metaverse.

Yan, R., Peng, L., Bin, G., Wang, S., & Cheng, Y. (2017). Residual Recurrent Neural Network with Sparse Training for Offline Arabic Handwriting Recognition. *Proceedings of the International Conference on Document Analysis and Recognition, ICDAR, 1*, 1031–1037. DOI: 10.1109/ICDAR.2017.171

Ye, X., Yang, J., & Huang, X. (2025). Transforming communication skills in music education: A cross-cultural study of virtual reality training in the 21st century. *Acta Psychologica, 261*, 105800. DOI: 10.1016/j.actpsy.2025.105800 PMID: 41138599

Yigit, Y., Maglaras, L. A., Buchanan, W. J., Canberk, B., Shin, H., & Duong, T. Q. (2024). AI-Enhanced Digital Twin Framework for Cyber-Resilient 6G Internet of Vehicles Networks. *IEEE Internet of Things Journal, 11*(22), 36168–36181. DOI: 10.1109/JIOT.2024.3455089

Zafar, A. (2025). Reconciling blockchain technology and data protection laws: Regulatory challenges, technical solutions, and practical pathways. *Journal of Cybersecurity, 11*(1), tyaf002. Advance online publication. DOI: 10.1093/cybsec/tyaf002

Zhong, R. Y., Xu, X., Klotz, E., & Newman, S. T. (2017). Intelligent Manufacturing in the Context of Industry 4.0: A Review. *Engineering (Beijing), 3*(5), 616–630. DOI: 10.1016/J.ENG.2017.05.015

Zhou, K., Liu, T., & Zhou, L. (2015). Industry 4.0: Towards future industrial opportunities and challenges. 2015 12th International Conference on Fuzzy Systems and Knowledge Discovery (FSKD), 2147–2152. DOI: 10.1109/FSKD.2015.7382284

Zhou, F., Zhang, N., Li, X., Han, C., & Gupta, B. B. (2025). Managing inter-organizational dependencies operation for discovering digital business model innovation in corporate innovation ecosystem. *Operations Management Research : Advancing Practice Through Research, 18*(2), 574–590. DOI: 10.1007/s12063-024-00501-4

Živičnjak, M., Rogić, K., & Bajor, I. (2025). Augmented reality technologies application in the warehouse system. *Transportation Research Procedia, 83*, 35–42. DOI: 10.1016/j.trpro.2025.02.007

About the Contributors

Brij B. Gupta received the PhD degree from Indian Institute of Technology (IIT) Roorkee, India (One of the oldest technical institutes in Asia). In more than 19 years of his professional experience, he published over 500 papers in journals/ conferences including 40 books and 10 Patents with over 30000 citations. He has received numerous national and international awards including 2022 Best researcher award from Asia University, Taiwan (2022), Canadian Commonwealth Scholarship (2009), Govt. of Canada, Visvesvaraya Faculty Research Fellowship Award (2017), MeitY, Govt of India, IEEE GCCE outstanding and WIE best paper awards and Best Faculty Award (2018 & 2019), NIT KKR, India respectively. Prof Gupta is also serving as Distinguished Research Scientist with LoginRadius Inc., USA which is one of leading cybersecurity companies in the world, especially in the field of customer identity and access management (CIAM). He has been recognized as a Clarivate Web of Science Highly Cited Researcher in Computer Science (top 0.1% researchers globally) consecutively in 2022 and 2023 and has been included in Stanford University's ranking of the world's top 2% scientists consecutively in 2020, 2021, 2022, and 2023. He is also a visiting/adjunct professor with several universities (i.e. Temple University, Macquarie University, Yamaguchi University, University of Murcia, Deakin University, Staffordshire University, Swinburne University of Technology, etc) worldwide. He is also an IEEE Senior Member (2017) and also selected as 2021 Distinguished Lecturer in IEEE CTSoc. Dr Gupta is also serving as Member-in-Large, Board of Governors, IEEE Consumer Technology Society (2022-2024). Prof. Gupta is also leading IJSWIS, IJSSCI and IJCAC, IGI Global, as Editor-in-Chief. Moreover, he is also serving as lead-editor of Book Series with CRC, World Scientific and IET press. He also served as TPC members and organized/special session chairs in ICCE 2021, GCCE 2014-2021 and TPC Chair in 2018 INFOCOM:CCSNA Workshop, Publicity Co-chair in 2020 ICCCN, etc. Dr Gupta is also serving/served as Associate/Guest Editor of IEEE TII, IEEE TITS, IoT, IEEE Big Data, ASOC, FGCS, etc. At present, Prof. Gupta is working as Director,

International Center for AI and Cyber Security Research and Innovations, and Distinguished Professor with the Department of Computer Science and Information Engineering (CSIE), Asia University, Taiwan. His research interests include cyber security, cloud computing, artificial intelligence, intrusion detection, blockchain technologies, cyber physical systems, social media and networking.

Yuk Ming Tang is currently the Senior Lecturer in the Department of Industrial and Systems Engineering at The Hong Kong Polytechnic University. He is the Lab-in-charge of the Integrated Product Design Laboratory, Deputy Lab-in-charge of Ng Tat Lun Digital Factory, a key and initiating member of the Joint Research Centre for Immersive Learning and Educational Technology (CILME), and Co-PI of the Non-PAIR Research Centre for Assistive Technology. Additionally, Dr. Tang is the President of the Institute of Industrial and Systems Engineers (IISE) - Hong Kong and a Member of The Hong Kong Institution of Engineers (MHKIE). His achievements have been highly recognized, as evidenced by his receipt of the Faculty Award for Outstanding Achievement in Teaching (Individual), Faculty Merit Award in Teaching (Individual) and Service (Team), Distinguished Educator Award, Best Researcher Award, among others. Additionally, he has been nominated for the UGC Teaching Award in the General Faculty Members category. Dr. Tang's research interests include Artificial Intelligence (AI), Virtual Reality (VR), Internet of Things, Digital Twin, blockchain, sustainable technology in Industry 4.0, and healthcare applications. In the span of three years, Dr. Tang has published over 80 internationally referred journal articles, 10 book chapters, edited 4 books, and received 2 patents. His publications are mainly published in top-ranked journals such as Computers & Education (C&E), Expert Systems with Applications (ESWA), Information Sciences, Engineering Applications of Artificial Intelligence, and others. He serves as an editor in several renowned journals, including Internet of Things and Journal of Industrial Information Integration. He was a speaker at the Hospital Authority Convention and was interviewed in the episodes of "香港故事_創科夢工場:活在元宇宙" and "Innovation GPS" (創科導航), television programs on local channels RTHK and TVB, respectively.

***

Vinsens Aji Pamungkas is an emerging researcher affiliated with the Department of Computer Science, Esa Unggul University. His academic interests include Artificial Intelligence, Business Information Systems, Human-Technology Interaction, Social Networking, and Risk Management. Despite being an undergraduate student, he has actively engaged in collaborative research, academic writing, and scientific discussions in technology-related disciplines. He is passionate about bridging the gap between digital innovation and human behavior in organizational and societal contexts. His goal is to contribute to impactful, interdisciplinary knowledge through research and academic publishing.

Lailita Ayuningtias is an emerging researcher with a strong passion for Artificial Intelligence (AI), immersive technologies, and their real-world applications. Her research interests span intelligent systems, human-computer interaction, and the integration of emerging technologies such as augmented/virtual reality (AR/VR) and AI in business transformation. She is particularly focused on how intelligent technologies can drive innovation, enhance user experience, and shape the future of Industry 5.0. Lailita is committed to interdisciplinary collaboration and advancing ethical, impactful, and inclusive technological solutions.

Sourasis Chattopadhyay is a Research Associate at KIIT University and former Research Assistant at Asia University, Taiwan. He holds a master's degree in computer science and information from Asia University and a bachelor's in electrical engineering from KIIT University. His interdisciplinary work spans operations research, data analytics, and optimization, with a focus on mathematical modelling for real-world problem-solving. Sourasis has co-authored peer-reviewed papers on supply chain optimization, ethical AI, and smart systems, and has collaborated with researchers from institutions including KTH, UC Berkeley, and Asia University. His current interests lie in algorithmic optimization, IoT-based infrastructure, and AIintegrated decision-making

Pravin Kumar is an experienced academic with over a decade of teaching Marketing Management and related subjects at reputed institutions across India. He currently serves as Assistant Professor at Brainware University, Kolkata, and has previously taught at different Management Institutions. He holds a Ph.D. in Management from T.M. Bhagalpur University, focusing on visual merchandising on consumer behavior in branded apparel. He also holds an MBA in Marketing and an M.A. in English, reflecting his interdisciplinary background. Dr. Kumar has published widely in Scopus, UGC-CARE, and peer-reviewed journals on topics including consumer behavior, brand personality, and AI in sales. He has presented at numerous national and international seminars and FDPs on subjects like cross-cultural marketing and leadership. His industry experience in the automobile and pharmaceutical sectors adds practical value to his teaching. Known for his engaging teaching style and commitment to Universal Design for Learning.

Ryan Putra Laksana is a lecturer at the Faculty of Computer Science, Universitas Esa Unggul, Indonesia. He has extensive experience in teaching and research related to Information Technology, with a particular focus on the Internet of Things (IoT), project management, and other IT-related subjects. His academic interests include the development of intelligent systems, the integration of IoT in modern infrastructures, and the application of agile methodologies in IT project management. Ryan actively engages in research and collaborative projects aimed at advancing digital innovation and technology adoption in education and industry. His dedication to fostering technological literacy and developing practical IT solutions reflects his commitment to bridging the gap between academic research and real-world implementation.

Mohammad Norman Gaza Laksono is a quantum physics researcher with a strong background in condensed matter physics and computational quantum mechanics. He earned his physics degree from Universitas Indonesia and master study at Uppsala University, Sweden. He has conducted extensive research on nodal-line semimetals at the Quantum Lab of Universitas Indonesia and has served as a research assistant at the National Research and Innovation Agency (BRIN). His work focuses on quantum computing, semimetals, and nuclear and particle physics, contributing to advancements in theoretical and applied quantum research. With experience in both experimental and computational approaches, he continues to explore quantum materials and their potential applications in next-generation technologies.

Amit Sata is an alumina of Indian Institute of Technology Bombay where he has earned his postgraduation as well as PhD, and has more than 20 years of experience at academic as well as industrial level. Dr Sata is currently a professor in Department of Mechanical Engineering. He is also heading Innovation & Entrepreneurship Cell at Marwadi University. He has his startup Udhyog 4.0 that mainly focused on transformation of existing manufacturing enterprises into SMART manufacturing enterprises through indigenous hardware and software at affordable cost. Dr Sata has also received seed fund of 20 lacs from Government for that. Dr Sata has filed more than 125 IPRs including patent, design as well as copyrights, and 80% of them are already been granted. He is also guiding several research scholars, and post-graduate as well as undergraduate students. His area of research focused on extending applications of disruptive technologies including AI, Data Analytics, Metaverse to the domain of manufacturing engineering. He has published more than 100 research papers at national as well as international level, and won several best paper awards. Dr Sata has also received grant of 36 lacs for research project SMART Foundry 2020 from Department of Science and Technology – Government of India, and received grant of 1 crore from Centre for Entrepreneurship Development Cell – Gandhinagar to develop skill enhancement centre, MUJCAL – Association for Foundry Technology. He is also coordinator of Entrepreneurship Capacity Building

Cell (ECBC) supported by Savli Incubation Centre, and IDEA lab supported by AICTE. Dr Sata is also part of several international as well as national level committees for development of Indian and international standards in the domain of Artificial Intelligence, Digital Twin, IoT, etc. He is also an active counsel member of the Indian Institute of Foundrymen (IIF) and Confederation of Indian Industry (CII). Dr Sata has also provided several industrial consultancy to regional industries. Dr Sata is awarded with Best Innovator Award for the year of 2021 and 2023 by Marwadi University. He also awarded with Chandran Menon Award for Applied Research and Innovative Technology by Indian Institute of Foundrymen (IIF) -India for the year of 2022. Dr Sata is committed for development of indigenous innovations especially in the domain of high valued products that will help in reducing imports of India.

Binastya Anggara Sekti has been a lecturer at the Faculty of Computer Science, Esa Unggul University, Jakarta, since 2016. He is actively involved in the Artificial Intelligence and Information Security Study Group. He holds a Bachelor's degree in Informatics Engineering from the Bandung Institute of Technology and a Master's degree in Information Systems Management from Trisakti University, Jakarta. Prior to entering academia, he accumulated over 25 years of professional experience as an IT practitioner in various companies across Jakarta. His work focused on developing data centers for internet service providers and delivering IT solutions for the manufacturing and oil & gas sectors. His research interests include artificial intelligence, cybersecurity, and the development of IT infrastructure.

Mohan Singh received the Graduateship degree in electronics and Telecommunication engineering from IETE, New Delhi, India, in 2007, the M.B.A. degree from PTU Punjab, in 2010, the M. Tech. degree from JIIT Noida, Uttar Pradesh, India, in 2012 and the Ph.D. degree from JIIT Noida, India, in 2022. From 2003 to 2008, he is having industrial experience as a technical trainer. From 2009 to 2025, he was an Assistant Professor with Uttar Pradesh Technical University, Lucknow, India. He is having more than 17 years of research and teaching experience around the country. He is currently an Assistant Professor at G.L.B.I.T.M., Greater Noida, India. His research interest includes signal processing and satellite image processing using machine learning.

Seema Singh received the B. Sc. Degree with Zoology, Biology, and Chemistry from Agra University, Uttar Pradesh, India, in 1997, the M. Sc. degree from D.S. College Aligarh, Uttar Pradesh, India, in 1999. She is having more than 18 years of research and teaching experience around the country. And currently doing M. Ed. From C.C.S. University Meerut, India.

Kapil Dev Tyagi received the B.E. degree in electronics and communication engineering from Rajasthan University, Jaipur, India, in 2003, the M. Tech. degree from IIT Delhi, New Delhi, India, in 2010, and the Ph.D. degree from CARE, IIT Delhi, in 2016. From 2003 to 2007, he was a Lecturer with Uttar Pradesh Technical University, Lucknow, India. From 2007 to 2008, he was a Scientist-C with Indian Space Research Organization, Bengaluru, India. Since August 2016 he has done 8 consultancy projects for CARE, IIT Delhi. He is currently an Associate Professor at Jaypee University, Noida, India.

Vaibhav Bhushan Tyagi has completed his B. Tech in 2007 from UPTU Lucknow, M. Tech from IIT Roorkee in 2011, and Ph.D. in 2015. He is having more than 15 years of research and teaching experience around the globe. Presently he is working as Associate Professor (ECE) and Dean FICT at ISBAT University, Kampala, Uganda. He has worked in several administrative and academic positions in India, Ethiopia, and Uganda. His research interest includes Sensor applications in signal processing, signal modeling, artificial intelligence, and deep learning.

Defia Ulandari is an information technology professional with interests in information systems and digital solution development. Her work focuses on designing and applying technology-driven solutions to enhance process efficiency, support data-informed decision-making, and facilitate digital transformation across organizational and societal contexts.

Index

A

Acoustic Monitoring 271
AI 1, 2, 3, 4, 5, 6, 7, 11, 12, 13, 14, 15, 16, 17, 20, 21, 22, 23, 24, 25, 26, 27, 28, 29, 30, 32, 33, 34, 36, 37, 39, 40, 41, 42, 43, 44, 46, 47, 48, 49, 50, 51, 52, 53, 54, 56, 57, 58, 59, 60, 61, 62, 63, 64, 65, 66, 67, 68, 69, 70, 71, 72, 73, 74, 75, 76, 78, 79, 80, 82, 86, 102, 103, 104, 110, 111, 112, 113, 114, 115, 116, 117, 121, 124, 127, 128, 129, 130, 132, 133, 135, 136, 137, 139, 140, 141, 142, 143, 144, 147, 149, 150, 151, 152, 153, 154, 155, 157, 158, 159, 162, 163, 180, 183, 184, 186, 188, 190, 191, 192, 193, 194, 195, 197, 198, 199, 200, 206, 216, 220, 223, 230, 231, 233, 234, 235, 236, 237, 238, 239, 240, 241, 242, 243, 245, 247, 248, 249, 250, 251, 252, 253, 254, 255, 256, 257, 258, 259, 260, 261, 263, 264, 265, 267, 268, 269, 270, 271, 272, 273, 275, 278, 279, 280, 281, 282, 283, 284, 285, 286, 287, 288, 289, 290, 291, 292, 293, 294, 295, 297, 301, 302, 303, 305, 308, 309, 310, 314, 315, 316, 317, 318, 321, 322, 323, 325, 326, 327, 330, 331
Artificial Intelligence 2, 3, 5, 7, 11, 15, 16, 17, 33, 36, 37, 39, 40, 41, 42, 44, 47, 54, 56, 58, 60, 62, 64, 68, 69, 71, 74, 75, 78, 80, 81, 82, 83, 84, 86, 99, 101, 102, 106, 110, 111, 116, 122, 125, 127, 129, 131, 132, 152, 158, 159, 160, 161, 162, 163, 180, 183, 185, 186, 188, 190, 191, 193, 195, 200, 227, 233, 234, 238, 242, 243, 247, 251, 252, 256, 258, 260, 263, 265, 267, 268, 270, 274, 278, 286, 289, 291, 293, 294, 295, 297, 302, 305, 325, 328, 330
Augmented Reality 1, 3, 5, 23, 48, 61, 66, 83, 84, 87, 98, 100, 114, 120, 122, 123, 124, 125, 127, 128, 129, 130, 132, 134, 135, 136, 137, 138, 139, 140, 141, 142, 143, 144, 146, 147, 148, 149, 152, 155, 156, 157, 158, 159, 160, 162, 173, 187, 193, 205, 237, 269, 291
Automation 1, 3, 4, 6, 7, 12, 16, 17, 20, 23, 24, 40, 42, 75, 76, 102, 121, 165, 190, 191, 192, 193, 220, 226, 234, 235, 236, 238, 241, 245, 250, 251, 258, 264, 297, 299, 301, 307, 314, 317, 325

B

Biodiversity Monitoring 268, 283
Blockchain 1, 3, 5, 17, 20, 23, 24, 30, 36, 37, 46, 47, 48, 49, 52, 53, 81, 83, 86, 95, 97, 104, 116, 119, 120, 121, 136, 150, 152, 153, 154, 155, 157, 161, 162, 163, 164, 166, 177, 178, 179, 183, 184, 185, 197, 198, 200, 205, 220, 221, 230, 233, 234, 235, 236, 237, 238, 244, 245, 246, 247, 248, 249, 250, 251, 252, 253, 254, 255, 256, 257, 258, 259, 260, 261, 262, 263, 264, 265, 295, 297, 302, 310, 330
Blockchain Technology 37, 48, 53, 244, 245, 246, 256, 265, 330
Business Transformation 83, 120, 127, 128, 129, 143, 149

C

Camera Traps 270, 284, 285, 286
Computer Vision 39, 42, 44, 45, 59, 63, 99, 130, 240, 241, 252, 267, 268, 270, 283
Consumer Engagement 64, 65, 309, 327

D

Data Privacy 8, 13, 15, 16, 26, 27, 29, 70, 72, 74, 86, 117, 119, 149, 152, 161, 258, 289, 319
Decentralized Finance 161, 163, 164
Deep Learning 39, 41, 44, 45, 57, 79, 81,

186, 199, 229, 235, 238, 239, 247, 248, 268, 269, 270, 271, 272, 278, 279, 280, 282, 295
Digital Experience 174, 210
Digital Identity 119, 121, 136, 142, 155, 157, 162, 166, 169, 221, 222
Digital Twins 2, 28, 39, 40, 41, 42, 43, 44, 45, 46, 47, 48, 49, 50, 51, 52, 53, 54, 55, 56, 57, 58, 59, 60, 61, 62, 66, 67, 68, 69, 70, 71, 72, 73, 74, 75, 76, 77, 78, 79, 80, 81, 83, 95, 97, 102, 103, 104, 116, 117, 121, 155, 190, 191, 192, 193, 194, 195, 196, 197, 198, 199, 200, 206, 208, 211, 221, 222, 224, 225, 227, 229, 244, 268, 269, 273, 274, 276, 277, 283, 290, 291, 292, 294
Digitization 88, 122, 234, 311

E

Emerging Technologies 1, 16, 17, 18, 23, 24, 25, 26, 27, 29, 30, 32, 34, 79, 111, 159, 160, 261, 262, 264, 265, 289, 297
Employee Engagement 297, 298, 301, 323, 327
etc 11, 12, 22, 26, 194, 201, 205, 206, 254
Ethical Design 173, 174, 175, 185, 300, 308, 319
Ethical Innovation 303, 308, 309, 313, 314, 319, 324
Experience Economy 298, 309, 320, 321, 329, 332

H

Human-AI Collaboration 3, 5, 6, 21, 22, 25, 48
Human-Centered Design 3, 303, 318, 322

I

Immersive Technologies 62, 83, 84, 86, 87, 88, 90, 91, 93, 94, 98, 101, 102, 103, 107, 108, 109, 116, 119, 120, 121, 128, 132, 133, 135, 143, 145, 146, 149, 152, 155, 185, 193, 220, 237, 291, 292
Inclusive Leadership 297, 319, 320, 327, 329
Industry 1, 2, 3, 4, 5, 6, 7, 8, 9, 10, 11, 12, 16, 20, 21, 23, 25, 26, 27, 28, 29, 30, 32, 33, 34, 36, 39, 40, 41, 42, 43, 44, 47, 49, 50, 54, 55, 56, 59, 60, 61, 62, 68, 71, 72, 74, 75, 77, 79, 84, 86, 87, 88, 91, 94, 98, 99, 102, 103, 104, 109, 110, 114, 115, 118, 123, 127, 139, 149, 157, 187, 190, 191, 192, 193, 194, 196, 198, 200, 206, 208, 210, 211, 213, 216, 219, 222, 223, 224, 225, 226, 227, 228, 229, 231, 233, 234, 238, 241, 242, 243, 244, 246, 250, 252, 254, 255, 256, 258, 259, 260, 262, 263, 265, 274, 275, 296, 298, 312, 314, 319, 320, 321, 326, 329
Industry 5.0 1, 2, 3, 4, 5, 6, 7, 8, 9, 10, 11, 12, 16, 20, 21, 23, 25, 27, 30, 32, 33, 34, 36, 39, 40, 41, 42, 43, 44, 47, 49, 50, 54, 55, 56, 60, 61, 62, 68, 71, 72, 75, 77, 79, 86, 102, 196, 226, 227, 228, 233, 234, 238, 241, 242, 244, 254, 258, 260, 296, 298, 320, 321, 329

M

Machine Learning 39, 40, 41, 42, 44, 45, 46, 47, 57, 63, 64, 79, 80, 81, 82, 112, 158, 160, 180, 186, 188, 194, 220, 223, 235, 236, 238, 239, 247, 248, 252, 264, 265, 269, 273, 279, 284, 289, 295
Manufacturing Process 59, 205, 219
Mass Customization 68, 234, 239, 253
Metal Casting 189, 194, 196, 200, 205, 206, 207, 208, 210, 213, 214, 219, 220, 222, 223
Metaverse 39, 40, 41, 42, 43, 44, 45, 46, 47, 48, 49, 51, 52, 53, 54, 60, 61, 62, 63, 64, 65, 66, 67, 68, 69, 70, 71, 72, 73, 74, 75, 76, 77, 79, 80, 81, 82, 83, 86, 95, 104, 116, 117, 118, 119, 122, 124, 153, 154, 155, 156, 157, 158, 160, 161, 162, 163, 164, 165, 166, 167, 168, 169, 170, 171, 172, 173, 174, 175, 176, 177, 178, 179, 180, 181, 182, 183, 184, 185, 186, 187,

188, 189, 190, 191, 192, 193, 194, 195, 196, 197, 198, 199, 200, 201, 205, 206, 207, 208, 209, 210, 211, 214, 215, 216, 217, 218, 219, 220, 221, 222, 223, 225, 226, 227, 228, 229, 230, 231, 264, 286, 287, 288, 289
Metaverse Economy 86, 116, 117, 118, 155, 161, 162, 164

P

Play-to-Earn 162, 170, 171, 185
Predictive Maintenance 15, 16, 23, 24, 39, 42, 44, 46, 47, 53, 54, 56, 70, 95, 102, 103, 116, 190, 195, 216, 234, 240, 241, 248, 252, 260

R

Real-Time Monitoring 2, 45, 50, 54, 55, 58, 59, 195, 216, 217, 219, 235, 243, 277, 278
Resilience 7, 8, 10, 59, 67, 93, 96, 98, 127, 135, 137, 140, 143, 154, 186, 220, 227, 234, 244, 249, 264, 274, 275, 288, 290, 297, 325, 327, 328

S

Small Business 1, 3, 5, 7, 11, 12, 13, 15, 16, 17, 18, 20, 23, 25, 26, 27, 30, 33, 34, 37
Smart Contracts 46, 48, 52, 118, 119, 153, 161, 162, 163, 164, 165, 177, 178, 185, 235, 245, 255, 258, 259
Smart Manufacturing 37, 39, 47, 54, 59, 76, 77, 104, 191, 210, 213, 214, 216, 220, 225, 226, 228, 230, 234, 235, 236, 237, 238, 241, 242, 247, 248, 249, 254, 256, 258, 260, 261, 262, 265
Supply Chain Transparency 104
Surveillance Capitalism 162, 167, 168, 179
Sustainability 7, 8, 9, 12, 24, 30, 31, 34, 36, 40, 67, 76, 79, 86, 103, 124, 139, 155, 162, 165, 172, 198, 199, 226, 228, 234, 237, 262, 264, 265, 293, 300, 310, 311, 312, 315, 316, 318, 326, 329, 331

U

UAV Surveillance 284
User Autonomy 161, 168, 173, 174, 185

V

Virtual Assets 45, 83, 95, 162, 165, 185, 195
Virtual Reality 1, 3, 5, 20, 23, 48, 61, 64, 81, 83, 84, 87, 98, 100, 111, 117, 118, 120, 122, 123, 124, 125, 127, 128, 129, 130, 132, 134, 135, 136, 137, 138, 139, 140, 141, 142, 143, 144, 145, 147, 148, 149, 152, 155, 157, 158, 159, 160, 161, 162, 173, 185, 190, 193, 196, 205, 223, 225, 226, 229, 230, 237, 287, 291

W

Wildlife Conservation 267, 270, 278, 286